Library Service for Genealogists

GALE GENEALOGY AND LOCAL HISTORY SERIES

Series Editor: J. Carlyle Parker, Head of Public Services and Assistant Library Director, California State College, Stanislaus; and Founder and Librarian Volunteer, Modesto California Branch Genealogical Library of the Genealogical Department of the Church of Jesus Christ of Latter-day Saints, Salt Lake City, Utah

Also in this series:

BLACK GENESIS—*Edited by James M. Rose and Alice Eichholz*

BLACK ROOTS IN SOUTHEASTERN CONNECTICUT, 1650-1900—*Edited by Barbara W. Brown and James M. Rose*

CITY, COUNTY, TOWN, AND TOWNSHIP INDEX TO THE 1850 FEDERAL CENSUS SCHEDULES—*Edited by J. Carlyle Parker*

CONNECTICUT RESEARCHER'S HANDBOOK—*Edited by Thomas Kemp**

FREE BLACK HEADS OF HOUSEHOLDS IN THE NEW YORK STATE FEDERAL CENSUS, 1790-1830—*Edited by Alice Eichholz and James M. Rose*

GENEALOGICAL HISTORICAL GUIDE TO LATIN AMERICA—*Edited by Lyman De Platt*

GENEALOGICAL RESEARCH FOR CZECH AND SLOVAK AMERICANS—*Edited by Olga K. Miller*

AN INDEX TO GENEALOGICAL PERIODICAL LITERATURE, 1960-1977—*Edited by Kip Sperry*

AN INDEX TO THE BIOGRAPHEES IN 19TH-CENTURY CALIFORNIA COUNTY HISTORIES—*Edited by J. Carlyle Parker*

MONTANA'S GENEALOGICAL RECORDS—*Edited by Dennis L. Richards**

A PERSONAL NAME INDEX TO ORTON'S "RECORDS OF CALIFORNIA MEN IN THE WAR OF THE REBELLION, 1861 TO 1867"—*Edited by J. Carlyle Parker*

PERSONAL NAME INDEX TO THE 1856 CITY DIRECTORIES OF CALIFORNIA—*Edited by Nathan C. Parker*

PERSONAL NAME INDEX TO THE 1856 CITY DIRECTORIES OF IOWA—*Edited by Elsie L. Sopp*

A SURVEY OF AMERICAN GENEALOGICAL PERIODICALS AND PERIODICAL INDEXES—*Edited by Kip Sperry*

*in preparation

General Editor: Paul Wasserman, Professor and former Dean, School of Library and Information Services, University of Maryland

Managing Editor: Denise Allard Adzigian, Gale Research Company

Library Service for Genealogists

Volume 15 in the Gale Genealogy and Local History Series

J. Carlyle Parker

Head of Public Services and Assistant Library Director
California State College, Stanislaus
and
Founder and Librarian Volunteer
Modesto California Branch Genealogical Library of the
Genealogical Department of the Church of Jesus Christ of
Latter-day Saints
Salt Lake City, Utah

Gale Research Company
Book Tower, Detroit, Michigan 48226

Library of Congress Cataloging in Publication Data

Parker, J   Carlyle.
    Library service for genealogists.

    (Gale genealogy and local history series ; v. 15)
    Includes index.
    1. United States—Genealogy—Bibliography.
2. Genealogy—Bibliography. 3. United States—
History, Local—Bibliography. 4. Libraries—Special
collections—Genealogy. 5. Libraries—Special
collections—Local history. I. Title.
Z5313.U5P37 [CS9]   016.929'1   80-26032
ISBN 0-8103-1489-4

To
Janet

VITA

J. Carlyle Parker is head of public services and assistant library director at California State College, Stanislaus. He also founded and is the volunteer librarian of the Modesto California Branch Genealogical Library of the Genealogical Department of the Church of Jesus Christ of Latter-day Saints, Salt Lake City. He holds a B.A. in history from Brigham Young University and an M.L.S. from the University of California, Berkeley.

Parker has authored numerous articles and reviews for library and genealogical journals, and compiled and edited several bibliographies, indexes, and union catalogs. He also has conducted oral history interviews and is an instructor and lecturer on genealogical, historical, and oral history research.

CONTENTS

Contents

Contents

Contents

Contents

PREFACE

For several years it has been my pleasure to be of service to genealogists and local historians, both young and old, assisting them in locating and obtaining research materials. This service as a librarian began with some very simple inquiries from genealogists and local historians—inquiries such as how to determine what materials had been published, how to locate them, how to obtain them, and, in some cases, how to use them. These inquiries at first fell only on sympathetic ears, but as they continued to be asked I realized the seriousness of the problem and became intrigued by the challenge of possibly finding the solution.

Years of study and research have evolved the solutions that are contained in this volume. Many of them are simple and would appear to be obvious, while other solutions are complicated and involved. Nevertheless, all are essential, have been tested and have proven useful in varying degrees.

When Dr. Paul Wasserman invited me to edit a series of books for the Gale Research Company in 1974, I never dreamed that it would take so long to complete this volume of the Gale Genealogy and Local History Series. In 1975 I was also invited by Harry Rowe, member of the Editorial Committee of the Public Libraries Division of the American Library Association, to prepare a guide for the Public Library Division on the development and administration of genealogical collections. I met with the committee at their June 1975 meeting in San Francisco and explained to them that I had a contract to publish such a book with Gale Research Company. The committee agreed that they would be happy to see Gale publish such a work and encouraged me to finish it. Three indexes and several other distractions later, here it is.

I am grateful to Beatrice Anderson, Virginia Ocken, and other genealogists and local historians of central California who prodded me on with their many questions. Acknowledgment is given to the many authors for their works that have aided me in my research and evaluation of sources. Many research specialists of the Genealogical Department of the Church of Jesus Christ of Latter-day Saints and the Family and Local History Studies faculty of Brigham Young University have been extremely helpful in their reassurances that I have been pursuing some useful solutions to the problems of genealogical and local history research.

Preface

Janet, my wife, and my children Denise, Nathan, and Bret, have not only been patient and understanding, but have assisted me. Janet has read, corrected, reread, and suggested numerous improvements in the text. In a letter dated 16 February 1977, to our daughter at college, she wrote the following line concerning her workaholic spouse: "He has the 'umph' to move a mountain of sand with a teaspoon." I'm sincerely grateful to her that in the final stages of this work she picked up another teaspoon and joined me in throwing sand by proofreading, typing, and encouraging me to level the mountain.

Gratitude is expressed to the unseen multitude of librarians and library staff members who have assisted me in the search for books, including interlibrary loans, making photoduplicated copies of periodical articles, and helping to select, catalog, index, and prepare bibliographies helpful to genealogists. Particular thanks is given to Jane Johnson, head of the interlibrary loan office of the Library, California State College, Stanislaus, for the hundreds of interlibrary loan transactions processed by her and her excellent assistants, Marilyn Weed, Janet Sivori, and Diane Hoffman.

Most of the work was done through the facilities of the Library, California State College, Stanislaus, and the Modesto California Branch Genealogical Library. Other libraries and archives used include the Genealogical Department Library of the Church of Jesus Christ of Latter-day Saints in Salt Lake City, Utah, and its branch libraries in Los Angeles, Oakland, Ogden, Reno, Sacramento, Stockton, and Vancouver, British Columbia; the Library of Congress; the Library of the National Society of the Daughters of the American Revolution; the Brigham Young University Library; the San Francisco Public Library; the National Archives, and its branch in San Bruno, California; the California State Library and its Sutro Branch in San Francisco; the Stanislaus County Free Public Library; the Stockton-San Joaquin Public Library; the Multnomah County Library in Portland, Oregon; the Library of the Genealogical Forum of Portland, Oregon; the University of California Library at Berkeley; and the University of British Columbia. Many thanks to all their staffs.

Mrs. Bert Harter, secretary of the American Society of Genealogists, was helpful in providing a list of recent Jacobus Award winners. The Board for Certification of Genealogists provided and permitted me to include their statement entitled, "Heraldry for United States Citizens." Their assistance is appreciated.

INTRODUCTION

Many books have been intentionally excluded from this bibliography, particularly some general how-to-do-it books. There is a proliferation of how-to-do-it books that are quite unnecessary. The author has considered and/or reviewed almost all books that have been reported in book trade catalogs and blurbs and/or reviewed in various archival, genealogical, historical, and library journals. Many of the titles cited helped to identify additional sources to review, discard, or add to the bibliographies that appear in this volume.

Most entries include the OCLC number (e.g., 315166); the Library of Congress card order number (e.g., 74-187078); the Dewey decimal classification number (e.g., 016.929/1); and the Library of Congress classification number (e.g., Z5319.U53). Some Superintendent of Documents classification numbers (e.g., I19.16:567) have also been included, as well as numbers for the Library of American Civilization (e.g., LAC 16943). These numbers are included to assist librarians in locating copies. Since many of them are reference materials, they may be hard to obtain on interlibrary loan.

Some entries for reprints contain additional OCLC numbers, Library of Congress card order numbers, and bibliographic data for more than one publisher. This information is included in order to alert librarians that more than one reprint is available. Reprint prices for some books vary considerably and some savings can be made by comparing prices.

As a general rule, throughout this book the Genealogical Department of the Church of Jesus Christ of Latter-day Saints will be referred to as the Genealogical Department or GD. Its older and more popular names, the Genealogical Society of the Church of Jesus Christ of Latter-day Saints or the Genealogical Society of Utah, will be used only in older bibliographic entries and works that have continued to use "Society" instead of "Department." They are one and the same organization and library, although any of the names may be used. This editor prefers "Department." Many of the Department's microfilm numbers are also included for works on microfilm (e.g., GD 857,129).

LIST OF ABBREVIATIONS

DAR	National Society, Daughters of the American Revolution, Genealogical Library, Washington, D.C.
GD	Genealogical Department of the Church of Jesus Christ of Latter-day Saints, Salt Lake City, Utah
LAC	LIBRARY OF AMERICAN CIVILIZATION
LC	Library of Congress, Washington, D.C.
NA	National Archives, Washington, D.C.

Chapter 1

ADMINISTRATION

This chapter is addressed specifically to library administrators, but it is not exclusively for them. Many of the items covered are discussed in detail in other chapters but only mentioned here briefly for administrators' benefit because they will probably not read the entire book. However, some ideas expressed in this chapter are not expressed elsewhere. Therefore, the chapter is recommended reading for all librarians.

SUPPLIES

Genealogists like lots of forms to assist them in the organization of their research. It is very helpful to genealogists if a library can provide a few forms for sale. If this is not possible, librarians should at least know where they are locally available or provide catalogs from which they can be ordered.

STAFFING

If it is at all possible, even in the smallest library, at least one of the librarians should be encouraged to develop some skill in assisting genealogists. She or he should be encouraged to study and attend useful seminars, workshops, or courses in genealogical research. Such a person need not be a history major, just an interested, intelligent, eager-to-serve, pleasant, and teachable librarian. Middle-sized and larger libraries may find it necessary to dedicate a large percentage of one or more staff member's time to the service of genealogists. If this is necessary, staffing will have to be built into the budget planning and allocations.

It is also very helpful for the interested librarians to do their own genealogical research, as it gives them increased insight into the requirements of genealogical research, empathy for genealogists and a better knowledge of at least some areas of genealogical research techniques. If a professional librarian cannot be encouraged to learn genealogical research skills and a paraprofessional is available who is already doing genealogical research, it may be necessary to turn to that person for assistance instead of a librarian, until some interested librarian can be added to the staff.

CIRCULATION

Every effort should be made to make the genealogical collections of all libraries into a cooperative network, system, or area-circulating collection. Local history materials that are not available in duplicate, gazetteers, bibliographies, and indexes may have to be exceptions. Some types of special services, such as photoduplicating of needed pages or entries and telephone reference assistance, should be provided in order to permit patrons who are unable to travel to have access to noncirculating materials.

The only way to provide adequate service for genealogists is for all libraries in the nation to fully cooperate in interlibrary loan programs and, when possible, to prepare union catalogs. Microfilm copies of the shelf lists of both circulating and noncirculating genealogical collections, similar to the one now available for the Sutro Library in San Francisco, should be made, distributed or marketed, and periodically updated.

BUDGET

Budget allocations for collection development depend on the size of the library and the decisions of how much of a genealogical collection will be developed. Extra allocations may be necessary over a few years to build a balanced collection. Continued support is, of course, necessary.

Budgets should include allocations for the microfilming or duplicating of local history materials in order to make these fine collections available for genealogists on interlibrary loans. Budgets may also need to include funding for increased interlibrary loan activities that would provide the small libraries that are usually on the receiving end of interlibrary loans to give a little more in return by sharing their local history materials that relate to genealogical research. Microfilm and microfiche equipment may need to be purchased in order for all branches to have access to them. This does not mean that all branches should be equipped with readers, but readers should be provided branch patrons as microform materials are borrowed on interlibrary loan. Large readers could be moved around a system's branches for patrons as needed, or portable microfilm and microfiche readers could be delivered by the headquarters library with the microform materials as it is delivered through interlibrary loan van services. Microform readers are necessary as both the National Archives of the United States and the Public Archives of Canada provide microfilm copies of census schedules on interlibrary loan to any library in the United States. Newspapers are also available in microform, and many more materials will be made available in the future in both microfilm and microfiche.

Funding should also be provided for librarians to attend genealogical seminars in order to learn basic genealogical research skills in general, as well as specific resources of the states and countries that patrons are pursuing. This funding may require some travel funds as well as per diem, registration fees, and release time.

FACILITIES

Normally the genealogical collection should not require any special space allocations. However, if it is combined with a local history collection that may have some special quarters or security, space may become a problem requiring extra funding. In many collections genealogical materials should simply be integrated into the general collection, requiring a few extra shelves. Larger collections are best shelved in areas readily accessible to as many tables as patronage may require and where reshelving can be done either from the tables where books were used or a very close-by reshelving area.

SERVICES

Besides providing adequate funding, staffing, and facilities, library administrators must also assure that genealogists are adequately served. The rights of genealogists to the use of libraries should not be denied or abridged in any way. Referrals to other libraries, archives, and government agencies should be done with a knowledge of their services and/or their holdings and with no appearance or intent of "passing the buck."

When the occasion arises library administrators should make it clearly known to genealogists that their interests are supported by the library as far as the library can afford to do so, and that any denial of services or abridgment of their rights to library use should be brought to his or her attention. The library staff should also be advised of the library administration's support of adequate library service for genealogists.

VOLUNTEERS

If there is any place where volunteers can be used very successfully in libraries it is in connection with the genealogical collection. Many librarians have found local genealogical volunteers an excellent asset. They are particularly helpful in libraries where there is no librarian with genealogical expertise. In such cases adequate advertising of the hours of their availability is essential.

Local genealogical societies or the Church of Jesus Christ of Latter-day Saints are possible sources to be solicited for volunteers. However, reliance on volunteers should not be used as an excuse for the librarians to ignore and neglect learning how to assist genealogists and develop a basic sound reference collection of genealogical research materials.

COLLECTION DEVELOPMENT

Throughout this book there are suggestions concerning collection development that relate to most chapters and the resources covered therein. The following chapter also covers the subject and lists basic sources needed for all libraries, including branches, basic genealogical reference materials for medium-sized libraries, and how to handle gifts. The cost of the basic list for all libraries is currently $45.73 and the medium-sized libraries collection, $319.98. Larger libraries should cooperate in their acquisitions of genealogical materials beyond these basic materials and in the preparation of a union catalog or mini-union catalog of the cooperating libraries' holdings.

Chapter 2

COLLECTION DEVELOPMENT

There should be no question as to whether or not even the smallest public library will develop a genealogical collection. The question rather should be how much of a genealogical collection will be developed. Genealogical collections for the small public library need not be large. However, smaller libraries must have access to larger collections with additional advanced and more expensive genealogical resources.

All public library genealogical collections need some basic genealogical reference materials. Large libraries should expand their reference collections to assist in the research of the greatest number of their patrons' national, ethnic, religious, or state origins. The use of many of these reference materials for genealogical research is explained in this work. There are other sources mentioned that supplement these basic works, and, many, of course, unmentioned here, some of which are found in P. William Filby's AMERICAN & BRITISH GENEALOGY & HERALDRY (1975) and GENEALOGICAL AND LOCAL HISTORY BOOKS IN PRINT (1975-77). Beyond the acquisition of these basic reference materials, collection development becomes development of a research collection. Only the very large libraries are, or will be, able to provide the funds, space, and staff for such collections. Research collections should be sent gifts of research titles not needed in smaller libraries, that could be of assistance to others through interlibrary loan.

If a true spirit of cooperation in the expansion and development of the interlibrary loan circulation of local history collections were fostered by all libraries of the nation, there would be less demand on the large research genealogical collections. The majority of the research needs of every genealogist are centered in a community, town, city, or county. All of these jurisdictions have library service of some kind and should have a library that is collecting local history materials for the jurisdiction that it serves. If each of these libraries would collect, or acquire in microform, in multiple copies, the abstracts of its area's vital records, cemetery records, probates, copies of its land records, and census schedules and circulate them on interlibrary loan, the majority of the genealogical research needs could be taken care of by the small- and medium-sized libraries. Such a concept of library service could also eliminate the need for union lists of genealogical materials. Genealogists could assume and trust that

Collection Development

the library serving the community of their ancestors would try its best to collect the records and history of their ancestor. Genealogists could then borrow the necessary materials on interlibrary loan, preferably in microform, or be able to purchase a copy of the microform, if desired.

Throughout this book, with the exception of this chapter, the prices of books have been excluded. Prices change so often, it is nearly impossible to keep up with them. Nevertheless, they have been included here to illustrate how inexpensively basic genealogical collections can be developed in small- and middle-sized libraries.

A BASIC COLLECTION FOR ALL LIBRARIES

All libraries and library branches should have these materials:

"Application for Search of Census Records," Form BC-600.

>Write for free forms from the U.S. Bureau of the Census, Pittsburg, Kansas 66762.

Colket, Meredith Bright, and Bridgers, Frank E. GUIDE TO GENEALOGICAL RECORDS IN THE NATIONAL ARCHIVES. National Archives Publication no. 64-8. 1964. Washington, D.C.: National Archives and Records Service, General Service, General Services Administration, 1979. $2.50.

>For sale by the Superintendent of Documents, GS4.6/2:G28.

Consumer Guide. TRACING YOUR ROOTS. New York: Bell Publishing Co., 1977. $3.98.

Everton, George B., ed. THE HANDY BOOK FOR GENEALOGISTS. 6th ed., rev. and enl. Logan, Utah: Everton Publishers, 1971. $10.25.

GENEALOGICAL HELPER. $14.50 per year. Logan, Utah: Everton Publishers, September 1947--. Bimonthly.

Greenwood, Val D. THE RESEARCHER'S GUIDE TO AMERICAN GENEALOGY. Baltimore: Genealogical Pub. Co., 1973. $12.50.

"List of Genealogists Accredited by the Genealogical Department."

>Free. Write to the Genealogical Department, 50 East North Temple Street, Salt Lake City, Utah 84150.

"List of Persons Certified." $2.00

>Board of Certification of Genealogists, 1307 New Hampshire Avenue, N.W., Washington, D.C. 20036.

"Order and Billing for Copies of Veteran's Records," GS Form 6751.

    Write for free forms from Military Service Records (NNCC), National Archives (GSA), Washington, D.C. 20408.

U.S. National Archives and Records Service. FEDERAL POPULATION CEN-SUSES 1790-1890: A CATALOG OF MICROFILM COPIES OF THE SCHEDULES. Pub. 71-3. Washington, D.C.: 1979. GS4.2P81/2 790-890.

    Write the National Archives, Washington, D.C. 20408. Free.

_____. GENEALOGICAL RECORDS IN THE NATIONAL ARCHIVES. Rev. General Services Administration General Information Leaflet, no. 5. Washington, D.C.: 1977. GS4.2:G28.

    Write the National Archives, Washington, D.C. 20408. Free.

_____. MILITARY SERVICE RECORDS IN THE NATIONAL ARCHIVES OF THE UNITED STATES. General Services Administration General Information Leaflet, no. 7. Washington, D.C.: 1977. 35¢. GS4.22:7.

    Free copy available from the National Archives, Washington, D.C. 20408.

_____. 1900 FEDERAL POPULATION CENSUS. Washington, D.C.: 1979.

    Write the National Archives, Washington, D.C. 20408. Free.

_____. REVOLUTIONARY WAR PENSION AND BOUNTY-LAND-WARRANT APPLICATION FILES. National Archives Microfilm Publications Pamphlet Describing M804. Washington, D.C.: 1974.

    Write the National Archives, Washington, D.C. 20408. Free.

U.S. Public Health Service. WHERE TO WRITE FOR BIRTH AND DEATH RECORDS, U.S. AND OUTLYING AREAS. Rev. DHEW Pub. no. HRA 78-1142. Washington, D.C.: Superintendent of Documents, 1978. HE20.6202:B53.

    Free copy available from the Division of Vital Statistics, Public Health Service, National Center for Health Statistics, DHEW, Hyattsville, Md. 20782.

_____. WHERE TO WRITE FOR BIRTH AND DEATH RECORDS, U.S. CITIZENS WHO WERE BORN OR DIED OUTSIDE OF THE U.S. AND BIRTH CERTIFICA-TIONS FOR ALIEN CHILDREN ADOPTED BY U.S. CITIZENS. DHEW Pub. no. HRA 77-1143. Washington, D.C.: 1977. HE20.6202:B53/2.

    Write the Division of Vital Statistics, Public Health Service, National Center for Health Statistics, DHEW, Hyattsville, Md. 20782. Free.

_____. WHERE TO WRITE FOR DIVORCE RECORDS, U.S. AND OUTLYING AREAS. Rev. DHEW Pub. no. HRA 78-1145. Washington, D.C.: Superintendent of Documents, 1978. HE 20.6202:D64.

> Free copy available from the Division of Vital Statistics, Public Health Service, National Center for Health Statistics, DHEW, Hyattsville, Md. 20782.

_____. WHERE TO WRITE FOR MARRIAGE RECORDS, U.S. AND OUTLYING AREAS. Rev. DHEW Pub. no. HRA 78-1144. Washington, D.C.: Superintendent of Documents, 1978. HE20.6202:M34.

> Free copy available from the Division of Vital Statistics, Public Health Service, National Center for Health Statistics, DHEW, Hyattsville, Md. 20782.

Total cost of this collection: $45.73. (All prices listed are subject to change.)

ADDITIONAL TITLES FOR MEDIUM-SIZED LIBRARIES

AMERICAN LIBRARY DIRECTORY. 32d ed. New York: Bowker, 1979. $49.95.

Cache Genealogical Library. Logan, Utah. HANDBOOK FOR GENEALOGICAL CORRESPONDENCE. Rev. ed. Logan, Utah: Everton Publishers, 1974. $8.50.

Doane, Gilbert Harry, and Bell, James B. SEARCHING FOR YOUR ANCESTORS: THE HOW AND WHY OF GENEALOGY. 5th rev. ed. Minneapolis: University of Minnesota Press, 1980. $10.95.

Filby, P. William, comp. AMERICAN & BRITISH GENEALOGY AND HERALDRY: A SELECTED LIST OF BOOKS. 2d ed. Chicago: American Library Association, 1975. $25.00.

GENEALOGICAL AND LOCAL HISTORY BOOKS IN PRINT. 2 vols. Springfield, Va.: Netti Schreiner-Yantis, 6818 Lois Drive, 22150. 1975-77. Vol. 1, $4.00. Vol. 2, $5.95.

> Volume 1 entitled, GENEALOGICAL BOOKS IN PRINT.

GENEALOGICAL RESEARCH: METHODS AND SOURCES. 2 vols. Edited by Milton Rubincam, Jean Stephenson, and Kenn Stryker-Rodda. Washington, D.C.: American Society of Genealogists, 1966, 1971. $6.50 each.

Peterson, Clarence Stewart. CONSOLIDATED BIBLIOGRAPHY OF COUNTY HISTORIES IN FIFTY STATES IN 1961, CONSOLIDATED 1935-1961. 2d ed. Baltimore: Genealogical Pub. Co., 1973. $10.00.

Stemmons, John D. THE U.S. CENSUS COMPENDIUM: A DIRECTORY OF CENSUS RECORDS, TAX LISTS, POLL LISTS, PETITIONS, DIRECTORIES, ETC. WHICH CAN BE USED AS A CENSUS. Logan, Utah: Everton Publishers, 1973. $9.50.

Stemmons, John D., and Stemmons, E. Diane. THE CEMETERY RECORD COM-PENDIUM: COMPRISING A DIRECTORY OF CEMETERY RECORDS AND WHERE THEY MAY BE LOCATED. Logan, Utah: Everton Publishers, 1979. $14.95.

_____. THE VITAL RECORD COMPENDIUM. Logan, Utah: Everton Pub-lishers, 1979. $19.95.

Thomson, Sarah K. INTERLIBRARY LOAN POLICIES DIRECTORY. Chicago: American Library Association, 1975. $7.95.

U.S. Library of Congress. GENEALOGIES IN THE LIBRARY OF CONGRESS: A BIBLIOGRAPHY. 3 vols. Edited by Marion J. Kaminkow. Magna Carta Book Co., 1972-77. $148.50. Vol. 3 supplement only, 1977, $23.50.

U.S. Library of Congress. Catalog Publication Division. NATIONAL UNION CATALOG REGISTER OF ADDITIONAL LOCATIONS. Cumulative Microform Edition. Washington, D.C.: Library of Congress, 1976. Microfiche $35.00.

U.S. National Bureau of Standards. CODES FOR NAMED POPULATED PLACES AND RELATED ENTITIES OF THE STATES OF THE UNITED STATES. Federal Information Processing Standards Publication, no. 55. Springfield, Va.: Na-tional Technical Information Service, 1978. C13.52:55. Paper and Microfiche $15.00 (N.T.I.S., Springfield, Va. 22161).

> Needed only by libraries that do not have Rand McNally's COMMERCIAL ATLAS AND MARKETING GUIDE, 1936-- .

Vallentine, John F. LOCALITY FINDING AIDS FOR U.S. SURNAMES. 2d ed. Logan, Utah: Everton Publishers, 1977. $3.95.

Xerox University Microfilms. GENEALOGIES AND FAMILY HISTORIES: A CATALOG OF OUT-OF-PRINT TITLES. Ann Arbor, Mich.: 1973. Out-of-print. New ed. in progress.

Total cost of collection for medium-sized libraries:	$382.15
Four titles are not exclusively genealogical materials and will assist other patrons:	-107.90
Total genealogical materials:	$274.25
Total cost of basic collection for all libraries and library branches:	45.73
Grand total for medium-sized libraries:	$319.98

Collection Development

Besides the titles listed above, most of the other titles mentioned throughout this book are needed at various times by genealogists. Very few public libraries can afford to acquire them all. The only sane approach to their acquisition is through cooperation. The larger public libraries of a cooperative system, network, or geographical area should band together and acquire as many of these titles as possible with as little duplication as possible. A simple network union catalog or mini-union catalog of holdings should be created to facilitate such collection development and use thereafter.

If a library needs to expand its collection beyond the above basic reference books, an evaluation should be made as to which states of the union and which foreign countries are being researched by their patrons. Then a priority list of these can be prepared and the selection of materials begun. The first materials selected should be how-to-do-it books or guides. Next select the necessary gazetteers from the how-to-do-it books for foreign countries.

Following this should be the purchase of statewide and countrywide indexes. Some genealogists and genealogical authors refer to these books as "locality finding aids." Of course, a statewide or countrywide index may be any book with names listed in alphabetical order that would, preferably, provide the researcher with a county, province, district, city, or town in which the person indexed resided. The following source lists several statewide indexes:

Vallentine, John F. LOCALITY FINDING AIDS FOR U.S. SURNAMES. 2d ed. Logan, Utah: Everton Publishers, 1977.

Federal census schedule indexes are also considered statewide indexes and are recommended purchases, particularly those for the years 1850, 1860, and 1870. In 1850 the census schedule started listing all members of households, but no Soundex (p. 144) was prepared for those years.

For other views on collection development, librarians may wish to consult any of the following:

Hartwell, J. Glenn, and Book, Betty L. "Genealogy," in COLLECTION DE-VELOPMENT, pp. 51-53. LJ Special Report, vol. 6. New York: Library Journal, 1978.

Kemp, Thomas J. "Inexpensive Items for Building Your Genealogical Library." CONNECTICUT ANCESTRY 19 (November 1976): 73-80.

Reed, Ronald D. "A Selected Bibliography for the Establishment of a Small Genealogy Collection for Medium-Size Public Libraries in Illinois." ILLINOIS LIBRARIES 59 (April 1977): 271-79.

Sinko, Peggy Tuck. "Building a Small Genealogy Collection in the Public Library." ILLINOIS LIBRARIES 59 (April 1977): 288-92.

ACQUISITION REFERENCE TOOLS

The hallmark of genealogical bibliographies is P. William Filby's AMERICAN & BRITISH GENEALOGY & HERALDRY: A SELECTED LIST OF BOOKS. 2d ed. Chicago: American Library Association, 1975. 1659712. 75-29383. 016. 929/1/097. Z5311.F55 1975 CS47.

Besides being of value as a reference tool, it can also be used for book selection and collection development. Filby solicited the assistance of many genealogical librarians to identify those books suitable for a small library. Those titles are identified throughout his book by an asterisk.

Another good source to check for the acquisition of genealogical materials is GENEALOGICAL & LOCAL HISTORY BOOKS IN PRINT, 1975-77. Volumes 1 and 2 list the names and addresses of vendors of genealogical materials. These lists represent the most comprehensive list of publishers, genealogical authors, and vendors that has ever been compiled. Volume 1 contains 1,159 and volume 2 contains 776. Only volume 2 is in alphabetical order.

There are no jobbers of genealogical books, and very few genealogical books are handled by the standard library jobbers. Therefore most orders must be placed directly with the publisher. Most genealogical publishers will honor library orders without advance payment. Many of these publishers also have large mailing lists and keep potential buyers well informed about their new publications and reprints.

The following are secondhand genealogical book dealers that publish sale catalogs and maintain want lists for persons searching for books such as family and local histories:

Charles E. Tuttle Co.
Rutland, Vt. 05701

Genealogical Publishing Co.
111 Water Street
Baltimore, Md. 21202

Goodspeeds Bookshop
18 Beacon Street
Boston, Mass. 02108

Some genealogists have developed a habit of reading genealogical book dealers' and publishers' catalogs. They may ask that the library acquire and add many such catalogs to the collection. Librarians should resist giving them any more attention than adding them to a pamphlet box. Catalogs are sometimes useful for keeping up-to-date on new publications, but too many genealogists rely on them and encourage others to do the same instead of reading journal reviews,

Collection Development

checking bibliographies, and consulting the LIBRARY OF CONGRESS CATA-
LOGS: SUBJECT CATALOG, 1950-- .

BOOK REVIEWS

Unfortunately most book reviews in genealogical periodicals are only book an-
nouncements. The following are the few genealogical periodicals that do contain bonafide book reviews:

AMERICAN GENEALOGIST. Des Moines: George E. McCracken, 1922-- .
Quarterly. 2444644. 78-4430. 929. F104.N6A64.

GENEALOGICAL JOURNAL. Salt Lake City: Utah Genealogical Association,
March 1972-- . Quarterly. 2250993. 78-96.

NATIONAL GENEALOGICAL SOCIETY QUARTERLY. Washington, D.C.:
National Genealogical Society, April 1912-- . 2321231. 1712813.
929.05. CS42.N4.

NEW ENGLAND HISTORICAL AND GENEALOGICAL REGISTER. Boston: New
England Historic Genealogical Society, January 1847-- . Quarterly. 2564052.
05-16188 rev. 593. 974/.005. FI.N56.

NEW YORK GENEALOGICAL AND BIOGRAPHICAL RECORD. New York:
New York Genealogical and Biographical Society, January 1870-- . Quarterly.
1760071. 05-37675 rev. F116.N28.

VIRGINIA GENEALOGIST. Washington, D.C.: J.F. Dorman, January-March
1957-- . Quarterly. 1769189. 60-17179.

EXCHANGE OF DUPLICATE GENEALOGICAL MATERIAL

It would be helpful for genealogical librarians to sponsor a special exchange
program for duplicate genealogical materials. Because of patron needs or geographical locale, an extraneous book to one library may be a pearl to another.

GIFTS

Collection development in some libraries entails the acceptance of gifts from
genealogical societies and patriotic organizations. Many of these gifts have
some **service-depriving** strings attached by the donor groups, such as demands
that the material not be permitted to circulate or that it be located in a special
room. Librarians should inform any organizations that make demands such as

these that the library sets its own circulation policies, arranges its collection
to best suit the needs of the patrons, and that all gifts are welcome, but without restrictions.

Many genealogical organizations abhor the restrictions imposed by libraries when
organization members try to borrow materials on interlibrary loan. Librarians
should enlighten these organizations that they, in fact, restrict their own research materials. In many cases, these organizations have created their own
problems of collection restrictions. The sad commentary is that librarians
have permitted them to do so.

Some gifts will be in such demand that they may require the same restricted
circulation as reference books. Regardless, most could circulate and, if listed
in national data bases and/or local union catalogs, could serve hundreds more
genealogists throughout the nation.

Not all gifts should be added to a collection. If they are not appropriate,
they should not be added; but an attempt should be made to get them into the
hands of a library that would find them useful.

If it is permissible for a library to solicit gifts, librarians should not hesitate
to indicate what titles are desired. Also, potential donors should be advised
that libraries are able to get discounts from dealers and publishers that may
make gifts of cash more economical. Of course, all genealogical and local
history gifts that are accepted should be appropriately acknowledged.

Some librarians may wish to prepare a news release that they would welcome
gift copies of genealogical books, including family histories. If library policy
permits memorial funds and/or matching funds, such programs may help fund
genealogical collection development.

SUMMARY

All libraries need a genealogical collection, even if it consists only of the
basic materials mentioned in this chapter. The collection should be scoped to
meet the research needs of the library's patrons.

Cooperative acquisitions are essential, as no library can afford all the materials
that genealogists need. Mini-union catalogs should be a part of planned cooperative acquisitions, to enable librarians and genealogists to know where research materials are locally available.

Chapter 3

THE LIBRARY'S ROLE IN
GENEALOGY AND LOCAL HISTORY

RESPONSIBILITY

The fifth article of the Library Bill of Rights states: "A person's right to use a library should not be denied or abridged because of origin, age, background, or views." Some librarians consider that genealogical research represents a "view." This may be true. Other genealogists may do research because of their origin. Regardless of why patrons do genealogical research, their rights to library use and services should not be denied or abridged. In the past there have been numerous examples of how the rights of genealogists to library service have been abridged, in some cases, and, in many cases, denied. Librarians should remember that the genealogist needs service, is a taxpayer that deserves service, and that one of our objectives is to get patron and research material together.

Librarians should see that library service to genealogists is as adequate as to any other segment of their public. This does not mean that every library has to have a large genealogical collection. Rather librarians should know something about genealogical research techniques and where materials can be consulted or obtained. A great deal of cooperation among librarians in collection development, use, and reference service should be fostered.

Librarians should develop and maintain basic reference collections for genealogists. Suggestions for collection development are covered in the preceding chapter. Many libraries already have basic materials needed to serve genealogists and may be serving them adequately. Others, perhaps, need to improve both their collections and services.

Many people in our transient society wish to discover their genealogical past. One sociological and psychological aspect of the desire for roots may be fulfilled through the genealogical and historical research of one's ancestors, thus learning about, if not knowing, one's extended family.

A 1978 questionnaire sent to patrons of the Modesto California Branch Genealogical Library by the librarian found that the majority of the seventy responding were doing genealogical research primarily to satisfy a desire to know something about their ancestors, and, secondly, to provide their descendants with a record or history of their ancestors. The survey excluded members of the Church of Jesus Christ of Latter-day Saints, as the majority of them would have answered that they were motivated for religious reasons. Another motive in genealogical research indicated by the responding patrons was that it satisfied a desire to do research. Very few answered that they were doing genealogical research to qualify for membership in a patronymic society, to find a coat of arms, to have a pedigree to show their friends, or to prove identity for an inheritance of money or property.

Regardless of their motives, many persons are doing it in every community. Librarians need to do their part in helping them. The rising interest in genealogy and, consequently, its impact on today's library service is very well expressed in Russell E. Bidlack's feature article, "Genealogy as it Relates to Library Service," in the 1978 ALA YEARBOOK, pages xxiii-xxx. It is impressive that this once librarian-neglected subject appears in the second of five feature articles in the yearbook.

REFERENCE LIBRARIAN PREPARATION

At least one librarian in each library should acquire the necessary skills to serve genealogists. These include knowing the fundamentals of genealogical research, the reference tools necessary and how to use them for genealogical research, how to assist genealogists, how to conduct a successful reference interview, and how to outline a search strategy for the patron. Librarians must also be able to refer them to additional materials in other libraries and archives. The specialist need not be a history major, but he or she must become interested in genealogical research. The librarian who pursues his or her own family research will soon come to understand the genealogist's needs, desires, and frustrations.

Other staff members should learn enough to help patrons a little and, in the interim, invite the more experienced librarian to assist them. Any referrals to another, more experienced librarian must be pleasantly made and never in a passing-the-buck, condescending, or indignant manner.

Another matter that reference librarians need to consider is developing an appearance of approachability. During a conversation with a technical services librarian of a large research library concerning some of the topics presented in this book, he requested that the author please tell librarians serving genealogists to "smile." The point, of course, is valid and applicable to all public service librarians. A close friend often relates how much she disliked librarians while she was a college student. One of the reasons her relationship with the reference librarians of her college was poor was because they never smiled. This is a simple problem for some librarians to overcome, but a giant barrier for some patrons. Please, colleagues, if you are not smiling and not appearing approachable and helpful, work hard at developing these traits.

Inservice can assist an entire library staff to be alert to genealogists' needs and and learn basic genealogical research service and reference interview techniques. This work could serve as a text for a detailed inservice program.

Librarians could provide themselves with an insight and understanding of county court house resources for use in genealogical research by arranging with their local county clerks, recorder, and land records staff to have an instructive tour of their facilities. They should learn how the vital records, deeds, wills, probates, civil and criminal court records are organized, indexed and housed. A knowledge of the public records of their own vicinity can assist in understanding how records are maintained generally throughout the country.

Brigham Young University provides correspondence courses in genealogy that can culminate in an associate of arts degree in genealogy. Additional information concerning their courses may be obtained by writing Brigham Young University, Independent Study Programs, 210 HRCB, Provo, Utah 84602. The university's department of family and local history studies sponsors an annual five-day Family History and Genealogical Research Seminar in August. The program and details may be obtained by writing Family History and Genealogical Research Seminar, Conferences and Workshops, 242 HRCB, Brigham Young University, Provo, Utah 84602.

The National Archives Trust Fund Board sponsors an annual three-week National Institute on Genealogical Research in July. Information concerning the institute is available by writing Genealogical Programs, Room 307, National Archives Trust Fund Board, Washington, D.C. 20408.

INTERLIBRARY LOAN

Adequate service to genealogists must include interlibrary loan. Nearly every chapter of this book includes something about the interlibrary loan of genealogical materials. The National Interlibrary Loan Code has recently been revised, and the discriminatory clause against the circulation of genealogical materials, added in 1968, has been eliminated. Those restrictions had been fostered by the librarians of the nation's largest genealogical collections, who do not circulate their collections. Fortunately, there were thousands of librarians that did not agree with the code and loaned their genealogical materials, refusing to abridge the rights of their genealogists to the library services provided any library patron.

With the advent of the interlibrary loan segment of OCLC, librarians can now identify the small and usually cooperative libraries that are willing to share their resources with larger libraries. Small libraries borrow so much more than they lend that lending is a privilege in which they are delighted to participate. They are usually flattered to be able to loan something to a larger library or to a library some distance away. If librarians will change their interlibrary loan request tactics to include as many small libraries as possible, the work load on the larger libraries may be cut to the point where they may relax some of their restrictions and reduce their charges.

THE LOCAL HISTORY COLLECTION

Librarians need to realize and respect the value of their local history collection. Most libraries have developed some kind of local history collection, and many of these are outstanding. Many of them contain the community's histories, the county's histories, the local newspapers and usually a back file of the newspaper on microfilm, the publications of the local genealogical or historical societies, city directories, telephone books, and, perhaps, some family histories of the community's prominent families. Some librarians have prepared card file indexes of newspapers or other items of the aforenamed sources. Other libraries have collected abstracts of the birth, marriage, death, and probate records of their counties; cemetery inscriptions and/or sexton records; plat books, maps, or atlases; census schedules; old tax records; voters records; and other miscellaneous historical records of local interest.

Most librarians are knowledgeable concerning the use of their fine local history collections and help to share it with those of their community and others who visit to use its special resources. These collections normally are full of genealogical materials that can help families of long residence in a community or relatives of residents of earlier years, visiting in search of their roots.

There are also people living elsewhere in the United States, or even in other countries, who would like to have access to these excellent resources but cannot afford to travel to the library. Librarians could share many of the resources of their local history collections with others all over the world if they would arrange to have some duplicate copies for circulation on interlibrary loan and/or acquire duplicate copies of those materials available in microform. Librarians should also prepare as many other genealogical materials in microform as is legally possible. The duplication of materials in microform will not only make materials available for interlibrary loan, but will provide a safeguard against a total loss of these rich resources in the case of fire, theft, or natural disasters.

Libraries should acquire copies of their city's directories already prepared in microform for circulation on interlibrary loan. Research Publications, 12 Lunar Drive, New Haven, Conn. 06525, has microfilmed many city directories from 1861 to 1901 and have microfiche for all of the directories listed in the following bibliography:

Spear, Dorothea N. BIBLIOGRAPHY OF AMERICAN DIRECTORIES THROUGH 1860. Worcester, Mass.: American Antiquarian Society, 1961. Reprint. Westport, Conn.: Greenwood Press, 1978. 577681. 3980848. 61-1054. 77-28204. 916.973/025. Z5771.S7.

Americana Unlimited has microfilmed many city directories for the years 1841 to 1942. Bay Microfilm, 737 Loma Verde Avenue, Palo Alto, Calif. 94303, is one marketing source for their directories. Librarians should attempt to have any city directories not in these collections microfilmed for availability on interlibrary loan.

If a library does not have adequate staff to assist genealogists by correspondence, librarians should develop a list of competent researchers that are willing and able to assist out-of-towners by mail, either free or for a fee. The librarians should not recommend any one person, but instead send the inquirer a list from which he or she can select a researcher.

In most cases genealogist patrons of communities will not find their own library's local history collection of any value to them because they need access to a local history collection in a library located several hundred or thousands of miles away. Librarians need to realize that materials similar to that which they have collected are also being collected all over the world and that library patrons in their community need access to them.

The librarian who understands his or her local history collection already has a good basic knowledge about genealogical research that can help patrons. There is, however, the necessity of determining the patron's needs and trying to apply the same solutions that would be applicable in the library's local history collection to a local history collection elsewhere.

In case there are some librarians who feel that their local history collections are inadequate, the following books may be of assistance in evaluating a local history collection and determining what should be done about it.

Suhler, Sam A. LOCAL HISTORY COLLECTION AND SERVICES IN A SMALL PUBLIC LIBRARY. American Library Association, Small Libraries Project. Pamphlets, no. 19. Chicago: American Library Association, 1970. 603174. Z688.L8S8.

Thompson, Enid T. LOCAL HISTORY COLLECTIONS: A MANUAL FOR LIBRARIANS. Nashville: American Association for State and Local History, 1978. 3609512. 77-28187. 026/.9877/82. Z688.L8T48.

The Local History Committee of the History Section, Reference and Adult Service Division, American Library Association, has developed "Guidelines for Establishing Local History Collections." These guidelines are very brief but useful and are published in RQ, 19 (Fall 1979): 29-30.

Genealogical and historical societies often have need of advice concerning projects and may ask librarians for ideas. Librarians should urge them to abstract and index local genealogical and historical resources. There is need for abstracts of births, marriages, deaths, divorces, civil and criminal court cases, wills, probates, sexton and cemetery records, and tax lists. Indexes are needed for any abstracts that are not arranged in alphabetical order, along with bride indexes for marriage abstracts. Indexes are also needed for all personal names in local histories, newspapers, and census schedules.

Chapter 17, "Abstracting Wills and Deeds," of Val Greenwood's THE RESEARCH-ER'S GUIDE TO AMERICAN GENEALOGY (1973), provides excellent instructions for the abstracting of records. The following work is recommended for indexing instructions:

Collison, Robert Lewis. INDEXING BOOKS: A MANUAL OF BASIC PRIN-CIPLES. New York: John De Graff, 1962. 1314592. 62-1822. 029.5. Z695.9 C64.

REFERRALS

Librarians need to learn what genealogical resources are near at hand to which patrons may be referred. Examples are branch libraries of the Genealogical Department, local genealogical society libraries, large genealogical collections in public or university libraries, or the location of particularly expensive or large indexes or reference materials in nearby libraries. Caution should be exercised so that any referral will not appear to be "passing the buck," nor should it be made with any derogatory attitude that serving genealogists is beneath the concept of library service, that it doesn't merit your attention, or is not worthy of serious consideration. Remember, genealogists' rights to library service must not be abridged.

It might be useful for librarians to annotate this book by adding the names of libraries in their vicinity that have specific titles to which genealogists may be referred. In addition, the call numbers for books that they have in their own libraries could be noted.

SUMMARY

It is really up to the librarians to see that genealogists are adequately served. If we do not do our job of providing them with adequate service, they may be forced to complain to governing boards. Genealogists are taxpayers and have a right to expect good library service to meet their research needs.

Chapter 4
THE REFERENCE INTERVIEW

The first essential step in the librarian's service to genealogists is to determine their needs through an effective reference interview. Librarians should feel free to ask genealogists if they have prepared a pedigree and family group sheets that illustrate their research to date. If they do not have these basic organizational charts, they should be informed as to where they can obtain them and how to complete them. It may also be appropriate to give them a very basic genealogical how-to-do-it book or pamphlet to assist them with the task of getting started and organized. Some librarians go a step further at this point and help the novice start to organize a pedigree from the papers that have been piled on the reference desk. This process may be especially necessary with the patron that is a slow learner.

Some libraries stock and sell genealogical forms. This is a helpful practice, where possible. If it is not provided, all librarians should know where the nearest stationery or book store is located that sells them; and the locality or the addresses of supply houses that sell them by mail should be readily available at the reference desk. Some supply houses advertise regularly in the genealogical journals.

While explaining to beginning genealogists that they need to prepare a pedigree and family group sheets, the librarian might add that they should prepare a family group sheet for every couple that appears on their pedigree. In addition, novice genealogists must go through all of their private papers, diaries, newspaper clippings, funeral programs, family birth, marriage and death certificates, family Bibles, baby books, and any other genealogical source that may be in their homes and add the required data on the pedigree and family group sheets. Genealogists should also be advised to visit or write their relatives for additional information taken from the private files and collections of their relatives' closets, bureau drawers, trunks, cedar chests, and file boxes. After this is done they should also be informed that the names of cities, counties, and states should be determined and recorded for all vital events appearing on their pedigree and family group sheets. This encouragement and instruction will keep them busy for a few weeks.

THE SECOND INTERVIEW

When the genealogist returns to the library after having completed the above work, the librarian really has his or her work cut out. The librarian must now direct a very enthusiastic genealogist to identify one single research problem. This often proves difficult because he or she has many problems and usually wants to attack them all at once, besides being so excited about all the newly found information and the organization thereof that he or she wants to tell all about it. Calmness must prevail with both parties, and attention must be given to one problem at a time. Normally this means one person at a time. However, it might mean one family or several families in the same town, county, or geographical area.

Another rule that must be adhered to right away is that genealogists work from the known to the unknown. An example of how this rule can be applied is if a genealogist knows the name and place and date of birth of his or her grandmother, but not her parents' names, finding a certificate or record of the grandmother's birth will normally provide this information. Beginning genealogists occasionally pick out some prominent person of an earlier period of history and, starting with them, try to prove that they are related. This approach has merit only in the rarest of circumstances.

One name or place at a time! Work from the known to the unknown. Like the journalist's who, what, why, how, and when, some genealogists like to use who, where, when, and what: who is being researched, where are they to be researched, when in the history of civilization, and what is the researcher looking for.

During the second interview the librarian will find that a check must be made to see that county names are included where required. This is very important, as most records of the nineteenth century in the United States are housed in county court houses. Therefore, it is essential that the county be known. If the patron has not completed this task, reference should be made to Rand McNally's COMMERCIAL ATLAS AND MARKETING GUIDE (1936-- .), and other appropriate gazetteers, place name literature, postal histories and directories, or ghost town books discussed in the chapter on identifying locations.

Genealogists need to survey the research that has already been done. They must be encouraged to first determine, if at all possible, if any research has been done concerning their ancestors by the Church of Jesus Christ of Latterday Saints (L.D.S.) or its members; and, likewise, if any family or local histories have been published that include their families. The completed L.D.S. or Mormon research can be determined by consulting the COMPUTER FILE INDEX (CFI) at one of the branch genealogical libraries of the Genealogical Department or at an L.D.S. meetinghouse library that has acquired the CFI. This index currently represents over 55 million names and is arranged by country, the United States being arranged by state and Great Britain by counties. Genealogists should also survey the L.D.S. Temple Records Index Bureau (TIB), a 30 million-name index in Salt Lake City. This may be done by acquiring a TIB form at a branch library of the Genealogical Department or a meetinghouse library and sending it in with the requested information and the small fee required. Additional information concerning this file and the CFI are contained in chapter 7 on "Vital Records."

The chapters dealing with family and local histories and periodical indexes cover the necessary aspects of the survey concerning published sources. Genealogists may be eager to use primary research materials as soon as possible. They should not be discouraged nor thwarted from doing so. It is very exciting and encouraging for the beginner to find his ancestor in an old record of some kind, even if it is only a census schedule. However, beginners must be encouraged to complete a survey as soon as possible.

Part of the reference interview technique is to make sure that the genealogists are asked why they want a particular record, thus evaluating whether they are pursuing the correct record for the information needed. Like the student who comes in asking for a "bibliographical sketch" about an author, genealogists will ask for sources that they do not understand. They may ask for Civil War military records or census schedules when looking for a birth date, and neither will give them that information. One interview problem that may be difficult for librarians is how to get away from the windy genealogist. Librarians manage this just like they do with the windy genealogist's counterparts in all disciplines or subject interests (i.e., bird watchers, all kinds of collectors, computer scientists, chess players, etc.). They excuse themselves as politely as possible to help others or to do something else.

The foregoing comment about talkative patrons does not mean that at this point the librarian has completed the reference interview. The librarian must now go on to an analysis of the research problem and determine and suggest resources that may help.

RESEARCH PROBLEM ANALYSIS

With a single research problem identified, the librarian is now challenged with the analysis of that problem. It is easy to ascertain what is known, as it should appear on the pedigree and family group. The next step is to determine what specific piece of information the genealogist needs to know or wants to pursue.

Then it must be determined what genealogical resources will answer the needs of this particular problem most economically and suitably. In order to complete this step, the librarian must know something about genealogical research. Librarians need not know the details of genealogical research for all states and countries, but they must know the logical sources usually found in all states and countries. They should also know the basic sources to identify what materials are available and how to obtain them. This book should help librarians not already prepared to assist the genealogist to do so.

SEARCH STRATEGY

One of this book's objectives is to help librarians develop a search strategy for the genealogist. However, regardless of all systematic search strategies and all logic, the patron should be provided a positive experience on each of his or her visits to the library. Every possible attempt should be made to help the genealogist find something or make some progress or hope for progress and success in the research, however small.

Librarians may, upon occasion, need to remind genealogists to be systematic and to follow some of the search strategies recommended in this book and elsewhere. However, librarians should not discipline them to the point of discouragement.

As research problems are analyzed and search strategies prepared, librarians should urge genealogists to make notes about the strategy. If the genealogist cannot be influenced to make notes, the librarian should then make some for him or her. It may be necessary to file a duplicate copy of such notes at the reference desk for future reference in case the genealogist returns asking the same questions or to say the notes were lost.

SUMMARY

Librarians need to learn some reference interview techniques that are unique to genealogists: consideration of one ancestor at a time; working from known to unknown; and encouraging the organization of family information on pedigrees and family group sheets. Furthermore, they need to instruct genealogists to collect data from home sources and relatives and help them learn the fundamentals of genealogical research.

These essential research steps must be taken: counties for the location of research must be identified; the COMPUTER FILE INDEX should be consulted, if at all possible; and the bibliographies of family and local histories and periodical indexes must be surveyed. Librarians should assist in the preparation of a search strategy and, finally, see that the genealogist's library experience is as positive as possible.

Chapter 5

IDENTIFYING THE COUNTIES FOR CITIES

One of the primary steps in genealogical research in the United States is for genealogists to identify the county in which their ancestors lived. This is essential because almost all vital records (birth, marriage, and death) before 1907 are housed in the county court house. Moreover, all census schedules are organized by county; the most helpful biographical sketches are found in county histories; and the records of probates and wills are maintained at the county court house.

SEARCH STRATEGY

Genealogists may begin at home to locate the counties for all the cities of their ancestors by consulting road maps and home atlases. A faster method is for them to use any of the following library reference materials (listed in order of comprehensiveness).

Rand McNally and Co. COMMERCIAL ATLAS AND MARKETING GUIDE. Chicago: 67th--, 1936-- . Annual. 1158319. G1019.R22.

> The index keys provide the best single source for genealogists to identify the counties for U.S. communities. It contains approximately 154,550 U.S. entries.

U.S. National Bureau of Standards. CODES FOR NAMED POPULATED PLACES AND RELATED ENTITIES OF THE STATES OF THE UNITED STATES. 2 vols. Federal Information Processing Standards, Publication no. 55. Springfield, Va.: National Technical Information Service, 1978. C13.52:55/ Paperbound and microfiche. Available from the NTIS, Springfield, Va. 22161.

> This list is another very good source for identifying the counties of cities, towns, townships, and villages in the United States. It contains an estimated 132,600 entries. It was created for data processing but is very useful to genealogists. All medium-sized libraries that do not have or cannot afford the COMMERCIAL ATLAS AND MARKETING GUIDE (above) should purchase the CODE and encourage its use for genealogical research.

It includes the populated cities, towns, villages, whether incorporated or unincorporated; important military and naval installations; townships; Indian reservations; named places that form parts of other places; places important for transportation, industrial or commercial purpose, for example, unpopulated railroad points, airports, and shopping centers listed in the COMMERCIAL ATLAS (above). It is arranged in alphabetical order by state and sub-arranged by city, town, and so on. It does not include the "physical features" listed in the COMMERCIAL ATLAS, nor, of course, maps. However, it costs considerably less.

LIPPINCOTT'S NEW GAZETTEER: A COMPLETE PRONOUNCING GAZETTEER OR GEOGRAPHICAL DICTIONARY OF THE WORLD, CONTAINING THE MOST RECENT AND AUTHENTIC INFORMATION RESPECTING THE COUNTRIES, CITIES, TOWNS, RESORTS, ISLANDS, RIVERS, MOUNTAINS, SEAS, LAKES, ETC., IN EVERY PORTION OF THE GLOBE. Edited by Angelo Heilprin and Louis Heilprin. Philadelphia: J.B. Lippincott Co., 1905, 1906, 1910, 1911, 1913, 1916, 1918, 1922.

Any edition of this gazetteer is more useful to genealogists than recently published gazetteers, as it includes more entries and many towns that no longer exist. The 1905 edition reviewed contains an estimated 67,750 U.S. entries and a total of 113,000 worldwide entries.

THE COLUMBIA LIPPINCOTT GAZETTEER OF THE WORLD. Edited by Leon E. Seltzer with the Geographical Research Staff of Columbia University Press and with the cooperation of the American Geographical Society. With 1961 Supplement. Morningside Heights, N.Y.: Columbia University Press, 1962. 273455. 62-4711. 910.3. G103.L7 1962.

This gazetteer provides the name of the county for each locality plus the direction and mileage of small towns to larger communities, enabling genealogists to identify on a map the location of a town, even if it does not appear on the map. It contains approximately 47,480 U.S. entries and a total of 164,000 worldwide entries.

DIRECTORY OF POST OFFICES (WITH ZIP CODES). Washington, D.C.: United States Postal Service, 1970--. Annual. 3697376. 73-644964. 383.42. HE6311 A312.

Besides being available in many libraries, this directory is, of course, available at all post offices. Old postal guides can also be helpful to genealogists. The 1977 DIRECTORY OF POST OFFICES contains about forty-seven thousand entries.

WEBSTER'S NEW GEOGRAPHICAL DICTIONARY. Springfield, Mass.: G. and C. Merriam Co., 1977. 2985183. 76-49519 rev. 78. 910.3. G103.5.W42 1977.

Contains an estimated eighteen thousand U.S. entries and a total of fifty-nine thousand worldwide entries. Of course, it is similar in function to THE COLUMBIA LIPPINCOTT GAZETTEER (above).

Andriot, John L., comp. and ed. TOWNSHIP ATLAS OF THE UNITED STATES, NAMED TOWNSHIPS. McLean, Va.: Andriot Associates, 1977. 3276140. 76-151923 MAP. 912.73. G1201.F7A5 1977.

This atlas contains current maps for twenty-three states showing the names and locations of counties, and county maps showing the names and locations of named townships. The 152-page index lists 1,411 counties and over 22,000 townships, towns, plantations, named precincts, gores, and others.

PLACE NAME LITERATURE

Place name literature likewise provides the name of a county for geographical locations. It also relates the reason why a town was given the name it has. The most comprehensive nationwide place name literature dictionary is the following.

Harder, Kelsie B., ed. ILLUSTRATED DICTIONARY OF PLACE NAMES, UNITED STATES AND CANADA. New York: Van Nostrand Reinhold, 1976. 1622195. 75-26907. 917.3/003. E155.H37.

This dictionary contains an estimated 18,720 U.S. entries and an additional 625 Canadian entries.

When none of the above sources provide the necessary information concerning a city or town in the United States, genealogists should search additional place name literature. The following bibliography and its supplements can help identify such literature:

Sealock, Richard Burl, and Seely, Pauline A. BIBLIOGRAPHY OF PLACE-NAME LITERATURE. 2d ed. Chicago: American Library Association, 1967. 557679. 67-2300. Z6824.S4 1967.

Included are old gazetteers and postal directories. This work and its supplements were helpful in preparation of the selected bibliography that appears at the end of this chapter.

Seely, Pauline A., and Sealock, Richard B. "Place-Name Literature, United States 1965-1967." NAMES 16 (June 1968): 146-60.

_____. "Place-Name Literature, United States 1967-1969." NAMES 18 (September 1970): 208-22.

_____. "Place-Name Literature, United States and Canada 1969-1971." NAMES 20 (December 1972): 240-65.

Sealock, Richard B., and Powell, Margaret S. "Place-Name Literature, United States and Canada 1971-1974." NAMES 22 (December 1974): 150-64.

_____. "Place-Name Literature, United States and Canada, 1975." NAMES 23 (1975): 296-99.

BOUNDARY CHANGES

Occasionally the change of a county boundary or the creation of a new county may confuse a genealogist trying to locate records at the county level. The following books provide the name of the county from which a county was created and its date of creation:

Everton, George B., ed. THE HANDY BOOK FOR GENEALOGISTS. 6th ed., rev. and enl. Logan, Utah: Everton Publishers, 1971. 197359. 72-169173. 929.3. CS16.E85 1971.

Jackson, Ronald Vern; Teeples, Gary Ronald; and Scharfermeyer, David, eds. U.S. COUNTIES. Encyclopedia of Local History and Genealogy, Series 1, vol. 1. Bountiful, Utah: Accelerated Indexing Systems, 1977. 3022231. 77-77313. D10.E525 Ser.1 v.I.

> This book also includes the names of progeny counties and the names of more than one parent county, if more than one county was involved.

There are some state guides that provide the history of county boundary changes. Several of these guides are included in the list of sources in this chapter. Many county histories also include boundary change information, as well as township boundary changes.

LOST CITIES

Genealogists with really tough places to find, such as ghost towns or places that no longer exist and are not listed in available sources, including the ghost town books listed at the end of this chapter, should write to the state library or the historical society library of the state involved. Most of these libraries maintain collections or card files for answering such questions.

A SELECTED BIBLIOGRAPHY OF STATEWIDE PLACE NAME LITERATURE, OLD GAZETTEERS, POSTAL SERVICE HISTORIES, GHOST TOWN DIRECTORIES AND HISTORIES, AND BOUNDARY CHANGE GUIDES

The titles selected for this list are those that the compiler considers to be the best single sources for each state. The ghost town books that are listed are those that include the most towns and may not be the best in quality in relationship to text and illustrations. The list is arranged by state and subarranged in the same order as the above subheading.

Alabama

Scruggs, J.H., Jr., comp. ALABAMA POSTAL HISTORY. Birmingham: Scruggs, 1950-59. 3750483. 77-377679. HE376.A1A22.

Harris, W. Stuart. DEAD TOWNS OF ALABAMA. University: University of Alabama Press, 1977. 2401765. 76-29655. 976.1. F328.H37.

> A collection of 242 Indian towns, fort sites, and towns are cited.

Alaska

Orth, Donald J. DICTIONARY OF ALASKA PLACE NAMES. U.S. Geological Survey. Professional Paper 567. Washington, D.C.: Government Printing Office, 1967. I 19.16:567. 1956142. F902.O7.

Schorr, Alan Edward. ALASKA PLACE NAMES. 2d ed. Juneau: University Library, University of Alaska, 1980. 1052452. 74-623028. 917.98/003. F902.S36.

> A supplement to Orth's DICTIONARY OF ALASKA PLACE NAMES (above).

Baker, Marcus. GEOGRAPHIC DICTIONARY OF ALASKA. 2d ed. Prepared by James McCormick. U.S. Geological Survey. Bulletin no. 299. Washington, D.C.: Government Printing Office, 1906.

> Issued also as House Document no. 938, 59th Congress, 1st session, 1906. Serial Set no. 5018.

Ricks, Melvin B. DIRECTORY OF ALASKA POSTOFFICES AND POSTMASTERS. Ketchikan, Alaska: Tongass Publishing Co., 1965. 6083777.

Balcom, Mary Gilmore. GHOST TOWNS OF ALASKA. Chicago: Adams Press, 1965. 1417147. 65-22673. F909.B27.

> Balcom cites 293 ghost towns.

Identifying the Counties for Cities

Arizona

Barnes, William Croft. ARIZONA PLACE NAMES. Rev. and enl. by Byrd H. Granger. Tucson: University of Arizona Press, 1960. 479862. 59-63657. F809.B27 1960.

Theobald, John, and Theobald, Lillian. ARIZONA TERRITORY: POST OFFICES AND POSTMASTERS. Phoenix: Arizona Historical Foundation, 1961. 4167847. 61-66266. 383.49791. HE6376.A1A77.

Murbarger, Nell. GHOSTS OF THE ADOBE WALLS: HUMAN INTEREST AND HISTORICAL HIGHLIGHTS FROM 400 GHOST HAUNTS OF OLD ARIZONA. Westernlore Ghost Town Series, vol. 3. Los Angeles: Westernlore Press, 1964. 2180747. 64-18546. F811.M98.

Dreyfuss, John J. A HISTORY OF ARIZONA'S COUNTIES AND COURTHOUSES. Tucson: National Society of the Colonial Dames of America in the State of Arizona, 1972. 309602. 79-170372. 979.1. F811.D7.

Walker, Henry Pickering, and Bufkin, Don. HISTORICAL ATLAS OF ARIZONA. Norman: University of Oklahoma Press, 1978. 4492419. 78-58086/MAP. 911/.791. G1510.W3 1978.

> "County Boundaries," plates 29-32.

Arkansas

Allsopp, Frederick William. "Arkansas Place Names." In his FOLKLORE OF ROMANTIC ARKANSAS, vol. 1, pp. 59-107. New York: Grolier Society, 1931. 1155039. 31-10247. 398.

California

Gudde, Erwin Gustav. CALIFORNIA PLACE NAMES: THE ORIGIN AND ETY-MOLOGY OF CURRENT GEOGRAPHICAL NAMES. Rev. and enl. 3d ed. Berkeley: University of California Press, 1969. 47781. 68-26528. 917.94/003. F859.G79 1969.

Salley, Harold E. HISTORY OF CALIFORNIA POST OFFICES, 1849-1976: INCLUDES BRANCHES AND STATIONS, NAVY NUMBERED BRANCHES, HIGH-WAY AND RAILWAY POST OFFICES. La Mesa, Calif.: Postal History Asso-ciates, 1977. 3542973. 77-26533. 383/.09794. HE6376.A1C37.

Nadeau, Remi A. GHOST TOWNS AND MINING CAMPS OF CALIFORNIA. Los Angeles: Ward Ritchie Press, 1965. 4219090. 65-13622. 979.404. F869.A15N29.

> Over 165 towns; counties not always given.

California. Historical Survey Commission. CALIFORNIA COUNTY BOUNDA-
RIES: A STUDY OF THE DIVISION OF THE STATE INTO COUNTIES AND THE
SUBSEQUENT CHANGES IN THEIR BOUNDARIES, WITH MAPS. By Owen C.
Coy, director of the Commission. Berkeley: 1923. Reprint. Fresno, Calif.:
Valley Publishers, 1973. 3439650. JS451.C2A5 1973.

Colorado

Eichler, George R. COLORADO PLACE NAMES: COMMUNITIES, COUNTIES,
PEAKS, PASSES: WITH HISTORICAL LORE AND FACTS, PLUS A PRONUN-
CIATION GUIDE. Boulder: Johnson Pub. Co., 1977. 3480351. 77-89726.
917.88/003. F774.E37.

Gannett, Henry. A GAZETTEER OF COLORADO. U.S. Geological Survey.
Bulletin no. 291. Washington, D.C.: Government Printing Office, 1906.
1969062. F774.G35.

   Issued also as House Document no. 839, 59th Congress, 1st session. 1906.
   Serial Set no. 5017.

Bauer, William H.; Ozment, James L.; and Willard, John H. COLORADO
POSTAL HISTORY: THE POST OFFICES. Crete, Nebr.: J-B Pub. Co., 1971.
257174. 70-182741. 383/.09788. HE6376.A1C62.

Eberhart, Perry. GUIDE TO THE COLORADO GHOST TOWNS AND MINING
CAMPS. 4th ed. Rev. Chicago: Swallow Press, 1969. 2718426. 917.88.
F776.E2 1969.

Connecticut

Hughes, Arthur H., and Allen, Morse S. CONNECTICUT PLACE NAMES.
Hartford: Connecticut Historical Society, 1976. 2423197. 75-43062. 917.46/
003. F92.H83.

Pease, John Chauncey. A GAZETTEER OF THE STATES OF CONNECTICUT
AND RHODE ISLAND. Hartford: Printed and published by William S. Marsh,
1819. 1017882. RCOO-3197. F92.P36.

Patera, Alan H. THE POST OFFICES OF CONNECTICUT. Burtonsville, Md.:
The Depot, 1977. 3505231.

Delaware

Heck, L.W. DELAWARE PLACE NAMES. U.S. Geological Survey. Bulletin
no. 1245. Washington, D.C.: Government Printing Office, 1966. 3673983.
GS66-305. 917.51003. QE75.B9 no. 1245 F162.H4.

Identifying the Counties for Cities

Gannett, Henry. A GAZETTEER OF DELAWARE. U.S. Geological Survey. Bulletin no. 230. Washington, D.C.: Government Printing Office, 1904. 290993. GS04-136. QE75.B9 no. 230.

> Issued also as House Document no. 725, 58th Congress, 2d session. 1904. Serial Set no. 4687.

Bounds, Harvey Cochran. A POSTAL HISTORY OF DELAWARE. Newark, Del.: Printed by Press of Kells, 1938. 3146976. 38-22844. 383.49751. HE6376.A1D32.

Florida

Morris, Allen Covington. FLORIDA PLACE NAMES. Coral Gables, Fla.: University of Miami Press, 1974. 984217. 74-13949. 917.59. F309.M67.

Hawks, John Milton, ed. THE FLORIDA GAZETTEER. New Orleans: Printed at the Bronze Pen Stfam [sic] Book and Job Office, 1871. Microfiche. Louisville, Ky.: Lost Cause Press, n.d. 1701887. 01-6899. F309.H41.

Bradbury, Alford G., and Hallock, Story. A CHRONOLOGY OF FLORIDA POST OFFICES. Florida Federation of Stamp Clubs. Handbook no. 2. Vero Beach, Fla.: n.p., 1962. 1579096. NUC64-7482. 383.4 B798.

Warnke, James R. GHOST TOWNS & SIDE ROADS OF FLORIDA. Combined titles and updated ed. Boynton Beach, Fla.: Roving Photographers and Assoc., 1978. 4641818. 78-111273. 917.59/04/6. F309.3.W36.

> A list of forty-one towns.

Georgia

Krakow, Kenneth K. GEORGIA PLACE-NAMES. Macon, Ga.: Winship Press, 1975. 1482211. 75-5230. 917.58/003. F284.K72.

Sherwood, Adiel. A GAZETTEER OF GEORGIA. 4th ed., rev. and cor. Atlanta: Cherokee Publishing Co., 1970. Microfiche. Chicago: Library Resources, 1971. 967189. 917.58. LAC 16943.

Bryant, Pat, comp. GEORGIA COUNTIES: THEIR CHANGING BOUNDARIES. Atlanta: State Printing Office, 1977. 3882856. 77-620036. JS451.G45B79.

Hawaii

Pukui, Mary Wiggin; Elbert, Samuel H.; and Mookini, Esther T. PLACE NAMES

OF HAWAII. Rev. and enl. ed. Honolulu: University Press of Hawaii, 1974. 104264. 73-85582. 919.69/003. DU622.P79 1974.

Coulter, John Wesley, comp. A GAZETTEER OF THE TERRITORY OF HAWAII. University of Hawaii. Research Publications, no. 11. Honolulu: University of Hawaii, 1935. Microfilm. Ann Arbor, Mich.: University Microfilms, n.d. 4764810. 35-28368. 919.69. DU622.C6.

Idaho

Kramer, Fritz L. "Idaho Town Names." In TWENTY-THIRD BIENNIAL REPORT, 1951-1952, of the Idaho State Historical Society, 23:14-114. 15-12386. F741.I18.

Schell, Frank R. GHOST TOWNS AND LIVE ONES: A CHRONOLOGY OF THE POSTOFFICE DEPT. IN IDAHO, 1861-1973. Twin Falls: n.p., 1973. 651354. 73-161365. 383/.42/09796. HE6376.A1 I28.

Miller, Don C. GHOST TOWNS OF IDAHO. Boulder: Pruett Publishing Co., 1976. 2463397. 76-42297. 979.6. F746.M5.

A list of 156 towns.

Illinois

Adams, James N., comp. ILLINOIS PLACE NAMES. Edited by William E. Keller. Illinois State Historical Society. Occasional Publications, no. 54. Springfield: Illinois State Historical Society, 1969. 105807. 75-633586. 917.73. F539.A3 1969.

"This special edition is reprinted for the members of the Illinois State Historical Society from ILLINOIS LIBRARIES, vol. 50, nos. 4, 5, 6 (April, May, June, 1968)."

Peck, John Mason. A GAZETTEER OF ILLINOIS IN THREE PARTS. Jacksonville, Ill.: R. Goudy, 1834. Microfiche. Louisville, Ky.: Lost Cause Press, 1977. Microfilm. New Haven, Conn.: Research Publications, n.d. 3354307. 4317800. 2746458. 05-33720. 917.73. F539.P36.

Illinois. Secretary of State. COUNTIES OF ILLINOIS: THEIR ORIGIN AND EVOLUTION, WITH TWENTY-THREE MAPS SHOWING THE ORIGINAL AND THE PRESENT BOUNDARY LINES OF EACH COUNTY OF THE STATE. Springfield: 1972. 1717416. F547.A15A32 1972.

Indiana

Baker, Ronald L., and Carmony, Marvin. INDIANA PLACE NAMES. Bloomington: Indiana University Press, 1975. 1530426. 74-17915. 917.72. F524.B34 1975.

Chamberlain, E. THE INDIANA GAZETTEER, OR TOPOGRAPHICAL DICTIONARY OF THE STATE OF INDIANA. 3d ed. Indianapolis: E. Chamberlain, 1849. Reprint. Knightstown, Ind.: Bookmart, 1977. 2659594. 3737103. 00-1620. 78-105809. 917.72/003. F524.C442.

Baker, J. David. THE POSTAL HISTORY OF INDIANA. 2 vols. Louisville, Ky.: Leonard H. Hartman, 1976. 3017903. 76-10531. 383.09772. HE6376. A1173.

Pence, George, and Armstrong, Nellie C. INDIANA BOUNDARIES, TERRITORIES, STATE, AND COUNTY. Indiana Historical Collections, vol. 19. Indianapolis: Indiana Historical Bureau, 1933. 2505399. 977.2.

Iowa

Hills, Leon Corning. HISTORY AND LEGENDS OF PLACE NAMES IN IOWA: THE MEANING OF OUR MAP. 2d ed. Omaha, Nebr.: Omaha School Supply Co., 1938. 4585464. 39-3588. 929.4 F619.H56 1938.

Hair, James T., comp. IOWA STATE GAZETTEER. Chicago: Bailey and Hair, 1865. Microfiche. Louisville, Ky.: Lost Cause Press, 1978. 4895586. 917.77. GD 982,200 Item 2.

Mott, David Charles. ABANDONED TOWNS, VILLAGES AND POST OFFICES OF IOWA. Council Bluffs, Iowa: J.W. Hoffman and S.L. Purington, 1973. 3596991. 977.7.

> Reprinted from THE ANNALS OF IOWA, vols. 17-18, 1930-1932.
> A list of 2,807 towns.

Kansas

Rydjord, John. KANSAS PLACE-NAMES. Norman: University of Oklahoma Press, 1972. 364106. 79-177346. 917.81. F679.R9.

Gannett, Henry. GAZETTEER OF KANSAS. U.S. Geological Survey. Bulletin no. 154. Washington, D.C.: Government Printing Office, 1898. GS5-175. QE75.B9.

> Issued also as House Document no. 571, 55th Congress, 2nd session. 1898. Serial Set no. 3703.

Baughman, Robert Williamson. KANSAS POST OFFICES, MAY 29, 1828-AUGUST 3, 1961. Topeka: Kansas Postal History Society, 1961. 1900803. 62-34174. 383.49781. HE6363.K2B3.

Fitzgerald, Daniel. GHOST TOWNS OF KANSAS. N.p.: 1976. 3120591. 77-150780. 978.1/03. F681.F57.

Includes 88 towns.

Gill, Helen Gertrude. THE ESTABLISHMENT OF COUNTIES IN KANSAS, 1855-1903. Topeka: n.p., 1904. 18-15315. F687.A18G4.

Reprinted from volume 8 of the Kansas Historical Society Collections, 1904.

Kentucky

Field, Thomas Parry. A GUIDE TO KENTUCKY PLACE NAMES. In cooperation with Department of Geography, University of Kentucky, Geological Survey. Series 10. Special publication 5. Lexington: College of Arts and Sciences, University of Kentucky, 1961. 1379630. 61-64281. 917.69. QE115.K42 no. 5.

Atkins, Alan T. POSTMARKED KENTUCKY: A POSTAL HISTORY OF THE COMMONWEALTH OF KENTUCKY FROM 1792 to 1900. Crete, Nebr.: J-B Publishing Co., 1975. 1364791. 74-21124. 383/.49/769. HE6184.C3A83.

Louisiana

Leeper, Clare D'Artois. LOUISIANA PLACES: A COLLECTION OF THE COLUMNS FROM THE BATON ROUGE SUNDAY ADVOCATE, 1960-1974. Baton Rouge: Legacy Publishing Co., 1976. 2197131. 76-3304. 917.63/003. F367.L43.

————. LOUISIANA PLACES. SUPPLEMENT. Baton Rouge: Legacy Publishing Co., 1975--. Irregular. 4180195. F367.L432

A collection of the columns from the BATON ROUGE SUNDAY ADVOCATE.

Historical Records Survey. Louisiana. COUNTY-PARISH BOUNDARIES IN LOUISIANA. New Orleans: Department of Archives, Louisiana State University, 1939. 4142357. 39-29350. 976.3. F377.A15H5.

Maine

Rutherford, Philip R. THE DICTIONARY OF MAINE PLACE-NAMES. Freeport,

Maine: Bond Wheelwright Co., 1971. 139012. 70-132915. 917.41. F17.R8.

Varney, George J. GAZETTEER OF THE STATE OF MAINE. Boston: Russell, 1886. 1729475. 974.1.

Dow, Sterling T. MAINE POSTAL HISTORY AND POSTMARKS. Lawrence, Mass.: Quarterman Publications, 1976. 2487942. 75-1790. 383/.09741. HE6376.A1M34 1976.

Attwood, Stanley Bearce. THE LENGTH AND BREADTH OF MAINE. Orono: University of Maine, 1973. 1278024. 73-622983. 917.41/003. F17.A8 1973.

Maryland

Fisher, Richard Swainson. GAZETTEER OF THE STATE OF MARYLAND. New York: J.H. Colton, 1852. 3456096. 917.52. GS 896,649 Item 2.

Associated Stamp Clubs of the Chesapeake Area. POSTAL MARKINGS OF MARYLAND, 1766-1855. Edited by Roger T. Powers. Towson, Md.: 1960. 63-30866. HE6185.U7M36.

Maryland. State Planning Department. THE COUNTIES OF MARYLAND AND BALTIMORE CITY: THEIR ORIGIN, GROWTH, AND DEVELOPMENT, 1634-1967. Publication no. 146. Baltimore: 1968. Microfiche. Greenwich, Conn.: Johnson Associates, 1976. 120690. 2945649. 72-630657. 917.52/03. F187.A15A58 1968.

Massachusetts

Writer's Program. Massachusetts. THE ORIGIN OF MASSACHUSETTS PLACE NAMES OF THE STATE, COUNTIES, CITIES, AND TOWNS. Sponsored by the State Librarian of the Commonwealth of Massachusetts. New York: Harian Publications, 1941. 2487552. 41-52742. 929.4. F62.W8.

Nason, Elias. A GAZETTEER OF THE STATE OF MASSACHUSETTS. Boston: B.B. Russell, 1874. 1728892. 01-12005. 974.4. F52.N26. GD 547,258.

Massachusetts. Secretary of the Commonwealth. HISTORICAL DATA RELATING TO COUNTIES, CITIES AND TOWNS IN MASSACHUSETTS. Boston: 1975. 2312811. 911/.744. F64.M5 1975.

Michigan

Romig, Walter. MICHIGAN PLACE NAMES: THE HISTORY OF THE FOUND-
ING AND THE NAMING OF MORE THAN FIVE THOUSAND PAST AND
PRESENT MICHIGAN COMMUNITIES. Grosse Pointe, Mich.: By the author,
1973. 663120. 73-161623. 917.74. F564.R6.

Blois, John T. GAZETTEER OF THE STATE OF MICHIGAN. 1838. Reprint.
New York: Arno Press, 1975. Knightstown, Ind.: Bookmark, 1979. Microfiche. Louisville, Ky.: Lost Cause Press, 1974. Chicago: Library Resources,
1971. 1218312. 75-87. 917.74/003. F564.B65 1975. LAC 11694.

Cole, Maurice F. MICHIGAN POSTAL MARKINGS. Ferndale, Mich.: 1955.
2495482. 55-42296. 383.22. HE6185.U7M53.

Dodge, Roy L. MICHIGAN GHOST TOWNS. Oscoda, Mich.: Books, Maps
and Periodicals Division, Amateur Treasure Hunters Association, 1970. 203149.
78-288013. 917.74/04/4. F566.D65.

   A list of 339 towns arranged by county with no index.

Welch, Richard W. COUNTY EVOLUTION IN MICHIGAN, 1790-1897.
Michigan. State Library Services. Occasional paper, no. 2. Lansing: State
Library Services, 1972. 701540. 72-612659. 911/.774. JS451.M55W44.

Minnesota

Upham, Warren. MINNESOTA GEOGRAPHIC NAMES: THEIR ORIGIN AND
HISTORIC SIGNIFICANCE. Publications of the Minnesota Historical Society,
vol. 17. 1920. Reprint. St. Paul: Minnesota Historical Society, 1969.
52304. 71-95570. 917.76. F604.U63 1969.

Patera, Alan H., and Gallagher, John S. THE POST OFFICES OF MINNE-
SOTA. Burtonville, Md.: The Depot, 1978. 4476765. HE6376.M5P38.

Lewis, Mary Ellen. "The Establishment of County Boundaries in Minnesota."
Master's thesis, University of Minnesota, 1946. 4322308. F612.B7L48.

Mississippi

Rowland, Dunbar. MISSISSIPPI: COMPRISING SKETCHES OF COUNTIES,
TOWNS, EVENTS, INSTITUTIONS, AND PERSONS, ARRANGED IN CYCLO-
PEDIC FORM. 4 vols. Atlanta: Southern Historical Publishing Association,
1907. Reprint. Spartanburg, S.C.: Reprint Co., 1976. Microfiche. Chicago:
Library Resources, 1971. 1994066. 76-73. 976.2/003. F339.R88 1976.
LAC 23430-32.

Oakley, Bruce C. A POSTAL HISTORY OF MISSISSIPPI STAMPLESS PERIOD, 1799-1860. Baldwyn, Miss.: Magnolia Publishers, 1969. 45896. 75-7488. 383/.09762. HE6184.C3035.

Missouri

Ramsay, Robert Lee. OUR STOREHOUSE OF MISSOURI PLACE NAMES. University of Missouri Bulletin, vol. 53, no. 34. Arts and Science Series, 1952. no. 7. Columbia: University of Missouri, 1952. 490478. 52-63016. F461. M79A8 no. 2.

Campbell, Robert Allen. CAMPBELL'S GAZETTEER OF MISSOURI. St. Louis: R.A. Campbell, 1874. Microfilm. Ann Arbor, Mich.: University Microfilms, n.d. 2650254. RCOO-1323. F464.C18. GD 897,468 Item I.

Montana

Cheney, Roberta Carkeek. NAMES ON THE FACE OF MONTANA: THE STORY OF MONTANA'S PLACE NAMES. Missoula: Printed by the Printing Department, University of Montana, 1971. 251818. 75-181582. 910/.3. F729.C5.

Lutz, Dennis, and Lutz, Meryl. "Montana Post Offices: 1864-1974." MONTANA POSTAL CACHE: RESEARCH JOURNAL OF THE MONTANA POSTAL HISTORY SOCIETY Part I, A-C, 1 (February 1975):Mi-M24; Part II, D-I, 1(May 1975):M25-49; Part III, J-P, 1(August 1975):M50-M74; Part IV, Q-Z, 1(November 1975):M75-M103.

Wolle, Muriel Vincent Sibell. MONTANA PAY DIRT: A GUIDE TO THE MINING CAMPS OF THE TREASURE STATE. Chicago: Swallow Press, 1971. 999560. F731.W6 1971.

Includes 380 towns and camps.

Montana. Laws, Statutes, etc. REVISED CODES OF MONTANA OF 1921.

Chapter 2, "County Boundaries." Quotes authority for county development and legal description.

Nebraska

Fitzpatrick, Lillian Linder. NEBRASKA PLACE-NAMES. INCLUDING SELECTIONS FROM THE ORIGIN OF THE PLACE-NAMES OF NEBRASKA. Lincoln: University of Nebraska Press, 1960. 1661718. 60-15471. 917.82. F664.F55 1960.

Rapp, William F. THE POST OFFICES OF NEBRASKA. Part I. TERRITORIAL POST OFFICES. Crete, Nebr.: J-B Publishing Co., 1971. 3582031. 383.

Nevada

Carlson, Helen S. NEVADA PLACE NAMES: A GEOGRAPHICAL DICTIONARY. Reno: University of Nevada Press, 1974. 984197. 74-13877. 917.93. F839.C37.

Harris, Robert P. NEVADA POSTAL HISTORY, 1861 TO 1972. Santa Cruz, Calif.: Bonanza Press, 1973. 763210. 73-176520. 383/.09793. HE6376. A1N33.

Paher, Stanley W. NEVADA GHOST TOWNS & MINING CAMPS. Berkeley, Calif.: Howell-North Books, 1970. 87644. 70-116733. 979.3/02. F842.P3.

Includes 497 towns and camps; Paher's preface claims over 575.

New Hampshire

Hunt, Elmer Munson. NEW HAMPSHIRE TOWN NAMES AND WHENCE THEY CAME. Peterborough, N.H.: Noone House, 1971. 127011. 79-125806. 917.42/003. F32.H85 1971.

Hayward, John. A GAZETTEER OF NEW HAMPSHIRE. Boston: J.P. Jewett, 1849. Microfiche. Louisville, Ky.: Lost Cause Press, 1975. 2126588. GD 823,666 Item 2.

Simonds, L.W. NEW HAMPSHIRE POST OFFICES, 1775-1978. New London, N.H.: Simonds, 1978. 4907503. 78-110757. 383/,42/09742. HE6376.A1 N467.

New Jersey

New Jersey. Public Library Commission. ORIGIN OF NEW JERSEY PLACE NAMES. Trenton, N.J.: 1945. 1835001. 929.4.

Gordon, Thomas Francis. GAZETTEER OF THE STATE OF NEW JERSEY. 1834. Reprint. Cottonport, La.: Polyanthos, 1973. Microfiche. Louisville, Ky.: Lost Cause Press, 1975. 1336133. 2736753. 01-7747REV. 73-90323. 974.9. F134.G66. GD 897,471 Item 1.

Kay, John L., and Smith, Chester M., Jr. NEW JERSEY POSTAL HISTORY: THE POST OFFICES AND FIRST POSTMASTERS, 1776-1976. Lawrence, Mass.:

Quarterman Publications, 1977. 3142233. 76-47325. 383/.42/09749. HE
6376.A1N54.

New Mexico

Pearce, Thomas Matthews; Cassidy, Ina Sizer; and Pearce, Helen S., eds.
NEW MEXICO PLACE NAMES: A GEOGRAPHICAL DICTIONARY. Albuquerque: University of New Mexico Press, 1975. 2009536. F794.P4 1975.

Dike, Sheldon Holland. THE TERRITORIAL POST OFFICES OF NEW MEXICO.
Albuquerque, N.Mex.: 1958. 58-19728. HE6376.A1N63.

Sherman, James E., and Sherman, Barbara H. GHOST TOWNS AND MINING
CAMPS OF NEW MEXICO. Norman: University of Oklahoma Press, 1975.
640228. 72-9525. 917.89. F796.S47.

> A list of 126 towns.

Coan, Charles Florus. THE COUNTY BOUNDARIES OF NEW MEXICO.
Santa Fe: Legislative Council Service, 1965. 3866149. 65-65108. F802.
B7C6 1965.

> First published in SOUTHWESTERN POLITICAL SCIENCE QUAR-
> TERLY 3 (December 1922): 252-86.

New York

French, John Homer, ed. GAZETTEER OF THE STATE OF NEW YORK. 7th
ed. Syracuse, N.Y.: R.P. Smith, 1860. Reprint. Port Washington, N.Y.:
I.J. Friedman, 1969. Knightstown, Ind.: Bookmark, 1977. 4669119. 24753.
4036079. 44-10783rev. 70-101018. 78-103033. 917.47. F117.F75 1977.
GD 599,141 Item 1.

Genealogical Department of the Church of Jesus Christ of Latter-day Saints.
COUNTY FORMATIONS AND MINOR CIVIL DIVISIONS OF THE STATE OF
NEW YORK. Genealogical Research Papers, Series B, no. 4. Salt Lake City:
1978.

North Carolina

Powell, William Stevens. THE NORTH CAROLINA GAZETTEER. Chapel Hill:
University of North Carolina Press, 1968. 444049. 68-25916. 917.56/003.
F252.P6.

Edwards, Richard, ed. STATISTICAL GAZETTEER OF THE STATES OF VIRGINIA AND NORTH CAROLINA. Richmond: Published for the Proprietor, 1856. RC2742. F224.E27.

North Carolina. State Department of Archives and History. THE FORMATION OF THE NORTH CAROLINA COUNTIES, 1663-1943. By David Leroy Corbitt. 1950. Reprint with supplementary data and corrections. Raleigh: North Carolina State Department of Archives and History. 1969. 1267765. 53514. 51-62165. 72-629414. 911/.756. F262.A15N63.

North Dakota

Williams, Mary Ann (Barnes). ORIGINS OF NORTH DAKOTA PLACE NAMES. Washburn, N.Dak.: Bismarck Tribune, 1966. 431626. 68-3032. 917.84/003. F634.W55.

Liddle, Janice. INDEX TO MARY ANN BARNES WILLIAMS' ORIGINS OF NORTH DAKOTA PLACE NAMES. Fargo: North Dakota Institute for Regional Studies, North Dakota State University, 1977. 3513236. 77-622724. 917. 84/003. F634.W552L5.

Phillips, George H. POSTOFFICES AND POSTMARKS OF DAKOTA TERRITORY. Postal History Monograph Series, no. 3. Crete, Nebr.: J-B Pub. Co., 1973. 800760. 73-8095rev.76. 383/.42/0978. HE6184.C3P45.

Ohio

Overman, William Daniel. OHIO TOWN NAMES. Akron, Ohio: Atlantic Press, 1958. 775429. 58-59837. F489.08.

Kilbourn, John, comp. THE OHIO GAZETTEER. 11th ed. Rev. and enl. Columbus: Scott and Wright, 1833. Reprint. Knightstown, Ind.: Bookmark, 1978. 2277854. RC01-2123. F489.K55. GD 476,928.

Gallagher, John S., and Patera, Alan H. THE POST OFFICES OF OHIO. Burtonsville, Md.: The Depot, 1979. 5625198. 383.097.

Downes, Randolph Chandler. EVOLUTION OF OHIO KENTUCKY BOUNDARIES. Columbus: Ohio Historical Society, 1970. 263098. F486.051 vol.36 1970.

   Originally published in OHIO ARCHAEOLOGICAL AND HIS-
   TORICAL PUBLICATIONS 36 (July 1927): 340-477.

Identifying the Counties for Cities

Oklahoma

Shirk, George H. OKLAHOMA PLACE NAMES. 2d ed., rev. and enl. Norman: University of Oklahoma Press, 1974. 960809. 74-170444. 917. 66/003. F692.S5 1974.

Gannett, Henry. A GAZETTEER OF INDIAN TERRITORY. U.S. Geological Survey. Bulletin no. 248. Washington, D.C.: Government Printing Office, 1905. 2937580. GS05-25. 557.3. QE75.B9 no. 248 F692.G19.

> Issued also as House Document no. 389, 58th Congress, 3d session 1905. Serial Set no. 4863.

Signorelli, Gaspare, and Caldwell, Tom J. INDIAN TERRITORY MAIL. New York: n.p., 1966. 433717. 68-5841. 383/.09766. HE6376.A1048.

Morris, John Wesley. GHOST TOWNS OF OKLAHOMA. Norman: University of Oklahoma Press, 1977. 3088685. 77-22439. 976.6. F694.M8195.

> Includes 130 towns.

Oregon

McArthur, Lewis Ankeny. OREGON GEOGRAPHIC NAMES. 4th ed., rev. and enl. Portland: Oregon Historical Society, 1974. 1156175. 72-86812. 917.95/003. F874.M16 1974.

Payne, Edwin R. OREGON POST OFFICES. 2d ed., rev. to January 1955. Salem: n.p., 1955.

Miller, Don C. GHOST TOWNS OF WASHINGTON AND OREGON. Boulder: Pruett Publishing Co., 1977. 3167272. 77-24428. 979.7. F891.M54.

> Includes 108 Oregon towns.

Brown, Erma Skyles. OREGON, COUNTY BOUNDARY CHANGE MAPS,1843-1916. Lebanon, Oreg.: End of Trail Researchers, 1970. 3151087. GD 908, 033 Item 2.

Pennsylvania

Espenshade, Abraham Howry. PENNSYLVANIA PLACE NAMES. Pennsylvania State College Studies in History and Political Science, no. 1. State College: Pennsylvania State College, 1925. Reprint. Baltimore: Genealogical Publishing Co., 1970. 91756. 71-112824. 917.48/003. F147.E75 1970.

Gordon, Thomas Francis. A GAZETTEER OF THE STATE OF PENNSYLVANIA. Philadelphia: T. Belknap, 1832. Reprint. New Orleans, La.: Polyanthos, 1975. Microfilm. New Haven: Research Publications, n.d. Microfiche. Louisville, Ky.: Lost Cause Press, 1976. 2897248. 1728538. 3087436. 01-10379. 917.48. F147.G66. GD 543,662.

Kay, John L., and Smith, Chester M. PENNSYLVANIA POSTAL HISTORY. Lawrence, Mass.: Quarterman Publications, 1976. 2086924. 75-1784. 383/.09748. HE6376.A1P454.

Rhode Island

Pease, John Chauncey. A GAZETTEER OF THE STATES OF CONNECTICUT AND RHODE ISLAND. Hartford: Printed and published by William S. Marsh, 1819. 1017882. RCOO-3197. F92.P36.

Merolla, Lawrence M.; Jackson, Arthur B.; and Crowther, Frank M. RHODE ISLAND POSTAL HISTORY: THE POST OFFICES. Providence: Rhode Island Postal History Society, 1977. 3914514. 77-85463. 383/.42/09745. HE7376. A1R45.

South Carolina

NAMES IN SOUTH CAROLINA. Vols. 1-12, 1954-1965. Edited by Claude Henry Neuffer. Columbia: Department of English, University of South Carolina, 1967. Reprint. Spartanburg, S.C.: Reprint Co., 1976. 2401705. 76-29026. 975.7. F267.N32 1976.

Black, James M. "The Counties and Districts of South Carolina." GENEA-LOGICAL JOURNAL 5 (September 1976): 100-113.

South Dakota

Sneve, Virginia Driving Hawk. SOUTH DAKOTA GEOGRAPHIC NAMES. Vermillion: University of South Dakota, 1941. Reprint. Sioux Falls, S.Dak.: Brevet Press, 1973. 3598112. 902460. 73-80523. 917.83. F649.S58.

Phillips, George H. THE POSTOFFICES OF SOUTH DAKOTA, 1861-1930. Postal History Monograph Series, no. 5. Crete, Nebr.: J-B Publishing Co., 1975. 1992911. 75-7209. 383/.09783. HE6376.A1S686.

Parker, Watson, and Lambert, Hugh K. BLACK HILLS GHOST TOWNS. Chicago: Sage Books, 1974. 1076704. 73-1501. 917.83/9. F657.B6P29.

A list of 585 South Dakota towns and 50 Wyoming towns.

Identifying the Counties for Cities

Tennessee

Fullerton, Ralph O. PLACE NAMES OF TENNESSEE. Tennessee. Division
of Geology. Bulletin, vol. 73. Nashville: State of Tennessee, Department
of Conservation, Division of Geology, 1974. 3018331. 75-621928. 917.
68/003. QE165.A2 no. 73 F434.

Morris, Eastin. THE TENNESSEE GAZETTEER, OR TOPOGRAPHICAL DICTION-
ARY. Nashville: W.H. Hunt and Co., 1834. Reprint. Nashville: Gazetteer
Press, 1971. Microfiche. Louisville, Ky.: Lost Cause Press, n.d. 1593981.
213539. 00-1271. 74-169152. 917.68/03/4. F434.M87.

Foster, Austin Powers. COUNTIES OF TENNESSEE. Nashville: Department
of Education, Division of History, State of Tennessee, 1923. 1977845. 23-
27331 rev. F436.F75.

Texas

Massengill, Fred I. TEXAS TOWNS: ORIGIN OF NAME AND LOCATION
OF EACH OF THE 2,148 POST OFFICES IN TEXAS. Terrell, Tex.: n.p.,
1936. 2535791. 36-18584. 929.4. F384.M35.

Gannett, Henry. A GAZETTEER OF TEXAS. 2d ed. U.S. Geological Survey.
Bulletin no. 224. Washington, D.C.: Government Printing Office, 1904.
2622266. 04-19124. 917.64. QE75.B9. F384.Q20. GD 896,651 Item 2.

> Issued also as House Document no. 676, 58th Congress, 2d session
> 1904. Serial Set no. 4685.

Konwiser, Harry Myron. TEXAS REPUBLIC POSTAL SYSTEM: A BRIEF HISTORY
RELATING TO THE POST OFFICE AND POSTAL MARKINGS OF THE REPUBLIC
OF TEXAS. New York: H.L. Lindquist, 1933. 1837186. 34-4509. 383.
49764. HE6376.A1T45.

Bartholomew, Ed Ellsworth. 800 TEXAS GHOST TOWNS. Fort Davis, Tex.:
Frontier Book, 1971. 942305. F391.B36.

Utah

Leigh, Rufus Wood. FIVE HUNDRED UTAH PLACE NAMES, THEIR ORIGIN
AND SIGNIFICANCE. Salt Lake City: n.p., 1961. 3412664. 61-34397/L.
917.92. F824.L4.

Gannett, Henry. A GAZETTEER OF UTAH. U.S. Geological Survey. Bulletin no. 166. Washington, D.C.: Government Printing Office, 1900. 4910954.
01-7923. 557.3 Un3b no. 166. QE75.B9 no. 166. F824.G19.

Issued also as House Document no. 715, 56th Congress, 1st session
1900. Serial Set no. 3951.

Gallagher, John S. THE POST OFFICES OF UTAH. Burtonsville, Md.: The
Depot, 1977. 4093366.

Carr, Stephen L. THE HISTORICAL GUIDE TO UTAH GHOST TOWNS. Salt
Lake City: Western Epics, 1972. 595478. 72-91023. 917.92/04/3. F826.
C27.

Includes 174 towns.

Vermont

Swift, Esther Monroe. VERMONT PLACE-NAMES: FOOTPRINTS OF HISTORY.
Brattleboro, Vt.: S. Greene Press, 1977. 2644095. 76-13815. 917.43/003.
F47.S84.

Hayward, John. A GAZETTEER OF VERMONT. Boston: Tappan, Whittemore
and Mason, 1849. Microfiche. Louisville, Ky.: Lost Cause Press, 1975.
2126665.

Slawson, George Clarke; Bingham, Arthur W.; and Drenan, Sprague W. THE
POSTAL HISTORY OF VERMONT. Collectors Club Handbook, no. 21. New
York: Collectors Club, 1969. 7681. 73-3546. 383/.09743. HE6185.U7V47.

Virginia

Hanson, Raus McDill. VIRGINIA PLACE NAMES: DERIVATIONS, HISTORICAL
USES. Verona, Va.: McClure Press, 1969. 13405. 69-20401. 917.55.
F224.H3.

Edwards, Richard, ed. STATISTICAL GAZETTEER OF THE STATE OF VIRGINIA.
Richmond: For the proprietor, 1855. Microfiche. Louisville, Ky.: Lost Cause
Press, 1975. 1672275. REOO-2741. F224.E26.

Robinson, Morgan Poitiaux. VIRGINIA COUNTIES: THOSE RESULTING FROM
VIRGINIA LEGISLATION. In BULLETIN, of the Virginia State Library, Rich-
mond. Richmond: 1916. Vol. 9, nos. 1-3, pp. 1-283. 506967. 16-27392.
Z881.V81B.

Washington

Meany, Edmond Stephen. ORIGIN OF WASHINGTON GEOGRAPHIC NAMES.
Seattle: University of Washington Press, 1923. Reprint. Detroit: Gale Research Co., 1968. 186185. 68-30593. 917.97/001/4. F889.M485 1968.

Phillips, James Wendell. WASHINGTON STATE PLACE NAMES. Seattle: University of Washington Press, 1971. 352325. 73-159435. 917.97/003. F889.P47.

Landes, Henry. A GEOGRAPHIC DICTIONARY OF WASHINGTON. Washington. Geological Survey. Bulletin no. 17. Olympia: F.M. Lamborn, Public Printer, 1917. GS18-101. QE175.A3 no. 17.

Landis, Robert L. POST OFFICES OF OREGON, WASHINGTON, AND IDAHO. Portland, Oreg.: Patrick Press, 1969. 18097. 76-83768. 383/.4. HE6376. A1075.

Miller, Don C. GHOST TOWNS OF WASHINGTON AND OREGON. Boulder: Pruett Publishing Co., 1977. 3167272. 77-24428. 979.7. F891.M54.

> Includes 101 Washington towns.

Abbott, Newton Carl, and Carver, Fred E. THE EVOLUTION OF WASHINGTON COUNTIES. Yakima, Wash.: Yakima Valley Genealogical Society, 1978. 4514595. 78-109940. 911/.797. F891.A23.

> Based on Abbott's thesis (M.A.), University of Washington, 1927.

West Virginia

Kenny, Hamill. WEST VIRGINIA PLACE NAMES, THEIR ORIGIN AND MEANING, INCLUDING THE NOMENCLATURE OF THE STREAMS AND MOUNTAINS. Piedmont, W.Va.: Place Name Press, 1945. 404442. 46-2004. F239.K4.

Gannett, Henry. THE GAZETTEER OF WEST VIRGINIA. U.S. Geological Survey. Bulletin, vol. 233. Washington, D.C.: Government Printing Office, 1904. Reprint. Baltimore: Genealogical Publishing Co., 1975. 272407. 1322154. GS04-152. 74-21655. 975.4/003. QE75.B9 no. 233. F224.G19 1975.

> Issued also as House Document no. 728, 58th Congress, 2d session 1904. Serial Set no. 4688.

Historical Records Survey. West Virginia. WEST VIRGINIA COUNTY FORMATIONS AND BOUNDARY CHANGES. Charleston, W.Va.: 1938. 3779121. 39-26066rev.43. 975.4. F247.A15H5.

Wisconsin

Gard, Robert Edward, and Sorden, L.G. THE ROMANCE OF WISCONSIN PLACE NAMES. New York: October House, 1968. 1995. 68-29817. 977. 5/003. F579.G3.

Hunt, John Warren. WISCONSIN GAZETTEER. Madison: B. Brown, printer, 1853. Reprint. Microfiche. Louisville, Ky.: Lost Cause Press, 1974. Microfilm. Ann Arbor, Mich.: University Microfilms, n.d. 1400205. GD 897,468 2d Item.

WISCONSIN POST OFFICE HANDBOOK, 1921-1971. Compiled by James B. Hale. Wisconsin Postal History Society. Bulletin no. 10. Madison: Wisconsin Postal History Society, 1971. 2128136. HE6363.W6W56.

Wyoming

Urbanek, Mae Bobb. WYOMING PLACE NAMES. 3d ed., rev. Boulder: Johnson Publishing Co., 1974. 2390334. F759.U7 1974.

Miller, Donald C. GHOST TOWNS OF WYOMING. Boulder, Colo.: Pruett Publishing Co., 1977. 3168406. 77-22097. 978.7/3. F765.M54.

> Lists 140 towns; counties not identified, but maps provided.

While reviewing many of the above postal histories in the stacks of the Library of Congress, the following bibliography was discovered. It, in turn, revealed some additional histories:

Rapp, William F. "A Bibliography of State and Territorial Books and Articles on Postal History." POSTAL HISTORY-U.S.A. 3 (December 1974): 67-68.

_____. "A Bibliography of State and Territorial Books and Articles on Postal History, Supplement 1." POSTAL HISTORY-U.S.A. 4 (March 1975): 7-8.

FOREIGN COUNTRIES

Most specific how-to-do-it books for foreign countries explain the use of that country's gazetteers and postal guides in genealogical research. If patrons do not have access to such guides or the gazetteers, explain to them that they should write the Genealogical Department in Salt Lake City for assistance.

COLLECTION DEVELOPMENT

All libraries should purchase THE HANDY BOOK FOR GENEALOGISTS and either the Rand McNally's COMMERCIAL ATLAS AND MARKETING GUIDE or the CODES FOR NAMED POPULATED PLACES. The purchase of a few titles from the foregoing selected bibliography of statewide place name literature, old gazetteers, postal service histories, ghost town directories and histories may be desirable for libraries because of strong local interest and need. Those titles that relate to the library's state might be of particular interest and may be acquired, if not already in the collection.

SUMMARY

It is essential for the genealogist to determine the county for every town and city of the United States that appears on his or her pedigree or family group sheets. The best single source for doing this is the Rand McNally's COMMER-CIAL ATLAS AND MARKETING GUIDE. The cheapest and perhaps the fastest way for genealogists to obtain this information for cities or towns not included in the COMMERCIAL ATLAS or any of the other sources mentioned in this chapter or are not readily available in local libraries, is to write the state library or state historical society in the state for which information is needed.

The most useful single source for boundary change information is THE HANDY BOOK FOR GENEALOGISTS. However, its information is limited to the date of the county's creation and the names of the county or counties from which it was formed.

Chapter 6

HOW-TO-DO-IT BOOKS

There are numerous how-to-do-it books and guides for genealogists. Beginners may need to be directed to a general how-to-do-it book. Care should be exercised not to give a too detailed or complicated guide to the novice. Such guides may discourage the beginning genealogist. On the other hand, a simplified guide may not only discourage but also frustrate the advanced researcher. Regardless of the expertise of a genealogist, how-to-do-it books for specific states or countries should be consulted as their research progresses.

A useful guide for the advanced genealogist is one that explains in detail types of records unique to a specific geographical location, and where these records are located, as well as how they are organized, their value or usefulness, shortcomings, if any, and how they are indexed. The guide should also tell how to gain access to them, either in person or by correspondence, and the cost. The best example of a how-to-do-it guide is Laureen Richardson Jaussi and Gloria Duncan Chaston's GENEALOGICAL RECORDS OF UTAH (Salt Lake City: Deseret Book Co., 1974). It includes an aspect of research evaluation that is lacking in most guides--the shortcomings of records.

Listed here are the best how-to-do-it books available. Included are a few resource inventories and bibliographies of genealogies. Those selected are included because of their comprehensiveness and statewide coverage.

GENERAL

American Society of Genealogists. GENEALOGICAL RESEARCH: METHODS AND SOURCES. Edited by Milton Rubincam and Kenn Stryker-Rodda. 2 vols. Washington, D.C.: 1960-71. 2655812. 60-919rev.72. 929/.1 CS16.A5.

> Some of the state guides listed in this bibliography are in these volumes. All medium-sized and larger libraries should have this excellent collection of papers.

Beard, Timothy Field, and Demong, Denise. HOW TO FIND YOUR FAMILY ROOTS. New York: McGraw-Hill, 1977. 3034553. 77-9411. 929/.1. CS16.B35.

Useful information for adoptees' genealogical research is found in chapter 15, "Adoptees in Search of Their Natural Parents," pp. 157-66. The other information presented in the book is too general, incomplete, and in some cases, incorrect or misleading for most libraries to justify its purchase.

Colket, Meredith Bright, and Bridgers, Frank E. GUIDE TO GENEALOGICAL RECORDS IN THE NATIONAL ARCHIVES. 1964. National Archives Publication no. 64-8. Reprint. Washington, D.C.: National Archives and Records Service, General Services Administration, 1979. 796624. 64-7048. CS15.C6. GS4. 6/2:G28.

Recommended for all collections.

Consumer Guide. TRACING YOUR ROOTS. New York: Bell Publishing Co., 1977. 3686429. 77-92416. 929.1.

Brief and simple for beginners. Recommended for all libraries.

Doane, Gilbert Harry, and Bell, James B. SEARCHING FOR YOUR ANCESTORS: THE HOW AND WHY OF GENEALOGY. 5th rev. ed. Minneapolis: University of Minnesota Press, 1980. 5894030. 79-27474. 929/.11/028. CS16-06. 1980.

Useful for beginners.

Everton, George B., ed. THE HANDY BOOK FOR GENEALOGISTS. 6th ed., rev. and enl. Logan, Utah: Everton Publishers, 1971. 197359. 72-169173. 929.3. CS16.E85 1971.

An essential source for all collections. Useful for addresses of courthouses and what records they have for genealogists.

Genealogical Department of the Church of Jesus Christ of Latter-day Saints. MAJOR GENEALOGICAL RECORD SOURCES IN THE UNITED STATES. Rev. Research Paper, Series B, no. 1. Salt Lake City: 1978. 929.173. CS1.6382 no. 1.

Greenwood, Val D. THE RESEARCHER'S GUIDE TO AMERICAN GENEALOGY. Baltimore: Genealogical Publishing Co., 1973. 624026. 73-6902. 929/.1/072073. CS47.G73.

The standard reference work of genealogical research. Absolutely essential for all collections and for all genealogists that have gotten started.

Helmbold, F. Wilbur. TRACING YOUR ANCESTRY: A STEP-BY-STEP GUIDE TO RESEARCHING YOUR FAMILY HISTORY. Birmingham, Ala.: Oxmoor House, 1976. 2555592. 76-14109. 929/.1072073. CS47.H44.

A good basic book for beginners.

Stevenson, Noel C. GENEALOGICAL EVIDENCE: A GUIDE TO THE STAN-
DARD OF PROOF RELATING TO PEDIGREES, ANCESTRY, HEIRSHIP AND
FAMILY HISTORY. Laguna Hills, Calif.: Aegean Park Press, 1979. 5591209.
79-53622. CS14.S74 1979.

National Archives and Records Service. GENEALOGICAL RECORDS IN THE
NATIONAL ARCHIVES. General Services Administration General Information
Leaflet, no. 5. Rev. Washington, D.C.: 1977. 3252143. GS 4.22:5/3.

GENERAL—YOUTH

Hilton, Suzanne. WHO DO YOU THINK YOU ARE?: DIGGING FOR YOUR
FAMILY ROOTS. Philadelphia: Westminister Press, 1976. Reprint. New
York: New American Library, 1978. 4788844. 75-40274. CS16.H541 1978.

> An excellent guide for young people interested in genealogical
> research.

Stryker-Rodda, Kenn. GENEALOGY. Boy Scouts of America. Merit Badge
Series, no. 3383. North Brunswick, N.J.: Boy Scouts of America, 1973.
815822. 74-155271. 929/.1/028. HS33313.Z95G42 CS16.

> Not necessary for the genealogical collection, but essential for
> scouting and for young people with a little interest in genealogy.

Weitzman, David L. THE BROWN PAPER SCHOOL PRESENTS MY BACKYARD
HISTORY BOOK. Boston: Little, Brown, 1975. 1254974. 75-6577. 973/
.07. E178.3.W45.

> An excellent juvenile book that is predominantly a genealogy
> how-to-do-it book.

UNITED STATES

Alabama

Stephenson, Jean. "Alabama." In GENEALOGICAL RESEARCH: METHODS
AND SOURCES. Edited by Kenn Stryker-Rodda, vol. 2, pp. 162-82. Washington, D.C.: American Society of Genealogists, 1971.

Arkansas

Perry, Larry S., comp. ARKANSAS GENEALOGY BIBLIOGRAPHY. Bibliographies Series, no. 25. Fayetteville: University of Arkansas, 1977. Microfiche. Educational Resources Information Center, ED 168 482. 3827611.
CS16.P46.

How-to-Do-It Books

This bibliography is not a how-to-do-it guide; rather, it contains citations to many excellent genealogical materials.

California

Parker, John Carlyle. SOURCES OF CALIFORNIANS: FROM PADRON TO VOTER REGISTRATION. World Conference on Records and Genealogical Seminar, Area I-34. Salt Lake City: Genealogical Society, 1969. GD 897,217 Item 31.

California. Historical Survey Commission. GUIDE TO THE COUNTY ARCH-IVES OF CALIFORNIA. By Owen C. Coy. Sacramento: California State Printing Office, 1919. 3787152. 20-27011. CD6111.A5 1919.

Colorado

Clint, Florence Runyan. COLORADO AREA KEY: A COMPREHENSIVE STUDY OF GENEALOGICAL RECORD SOURCES OF COLORADO, INCLUDING MAPS AND BRIEF GENERAL HISTORY. Denver: Eden Press, 1968. 2601307. F761.C55.

Connecticut

Kemp, Thomas Jay, ed. CONNECTICUT RESEARCHER'S HANDBOOK. Gale Genealogy and Local History Series. Detroit: Gale Research Co., forthcoming.

Sperry, Kip. CONNECTICUT SOURCES FOR FAMILY HISTORIANS AND GE-NEALOGISTS. Logan, Utah: Everton Publishers, 1980.

Delaware

Rubincam, Milton. GENEALOGICAL RESEARCH IN PENNSYLVANIA AND DELAWARE. World Conference on Records and Genealogical Seminar, Area I-23. Salt Lake City: Genealogical Society, 1969. GS 897,217 Item 21.

Georgia

Hathaway, Beverly West. PRIMER FOR GEORGIA GENEALOGICAL RESEARCH. West Jordan, Utah: Allstates Research Co., 1973. 875386. 74-161772. 929/.1. CS16.H37.

Hawaii

Conrad, Agnes C. "Genealogical Sources in Hawaii." HAWAII LIBRARY AS-SOCIATION JOURNAL 33 (June 1974): 3-10.

Illinois

Wolf, Joseph C. A REFERENCE GUIDE FOR GENEALOGICAL AND HIS-
TORICAL RESEARCH IN ILLINOIS. Detroit: Detroit Society for Genealogical
Research, 1963. 1725837. 65-9400. 977.3. Z1277.W65.

Indiana

Miller, Carolynne L. Wendel. AIDS FOR GENEALOGICAL SEARCHING IN
INDIANA, A BIBLIOGRAPHY. Detroit: Detroit Society for Genealogical
Research, 1970. 1739663. 929.3.

Iowa

McCracken, George E. "Iowa." In GENEALOGICAL RESEARCH: METHODS
AND SOURCES, edited by Kenn Stryker-Rodda, vol. 2, pp. 112-29. Washington, D.C.: American Society of Genealogists, 1971.

Kentucky

Hathaway, Beverly West. KENTUCKY GENEALOGICAL RESEARCH SOURCES.
West Jordan, Utah: Allstates Research Co., 1974. 1298894. 929.3769.
GD 928,177 Item 5.

_____. INVENTORY OF COUNTY RECORDS OF KENTUCKY. Salt Lake
City: Accelerated Indexing Systems, 1978. 4544479. 74-163601. 016.929
3769.

Not a how-to-do-it book, but a very good inventory.

Louisiana

DeVille, Winston. "Louisiana." In GENEALOGICAL RESEARCH: METHODS
AND SOURCES, edited by Kenn Stryker-Rodda, vol. 2, pp. 183-200. Washington, D.C.: American Society of Genealogists, 1971.

Maine

Fisher, Carleton E. RESEARCH IN MAINE. World Conference on Records and
Genealogical Seminar, Area I-22. Salt Lake City: Genealogical Society,
1969. GD 897,217 Item 20.

Maryland

Meyer, Mary Keysor. GENEALOGICAL RESEARCH IN MARYLAND: A GUIDE. Rev. and enl. Baltimore: Maryland Historical Society, 1976. 2457451. 76-21107. 929/.1/0720752. Z1293.M485 1976 F180.

Massachusetts

Wright, Norman Edgar. GENEALOGY IN AMERICA: MASSACHUSETTS, CONNECTICUT, AND MAINE. Vol. 1. Salt Lake City: Deseret Book Co., 1968. 21235. 68-8571. 929.2/0973. CS47.W7.

Bowen, Richard Le Baron. MASSACHUSETTS RECORDS: A HANDBOOK FOR GENEALOGISTS, HISTORIANS, LAWYERS, AND OTHER RESEARCHERS. Rehoboth, Mass.: n.p., 1957. 1284121. 57-11588. 929.1. CD3291.B6
> Very good inventory type book explaining what records are available, which have been burned, and so on.

Michigan

Williams, Ethel W. TRACING YOUR ANCESTORS IN MICHIGAN. World Conference on Records and Genealogical Seminar, Area 1-35. Salt Lake City: Genealogical Society, 1969. 3882836. 929.1. GS 897,217 Item 32.

Minnesota

Pope, Wiley R., and Wiener, Alissa L. TRACING YOUR ANCESTORS IN MINNESOTA: A GUIDE TO THE SOURCES. St. Paul: Pope Families Association, 1978. 4183572.

Mississippi

Lackey, Richard Stephen. "Mississippi." In GENEALOGICAL RESEARCH: METHODS AND SOURCES, edited by Kenn Stryker-Rodda, vol. 2, pp. 201-25. Washington, D.C.: American Society of Genealogists, 1971.

Missouri

Williams, Jacqueline Hogan, and Williams, Betty Harvey, comps. RESOURCES FOR GENEALOGICAL RESEARCH IN MISSOURI. Warrensburg, Mo.: n.p., 1969. 56361. 71-9142. 929.1/09778. CS16.W534. GS 824,284 Item 9.

Montana

Richards, Dennis L., ed. MONTANA'S GENEALOGICAL AND LOCAL HISTORY RECORDS: A SELECTED LIST OF BOOKS, MANUSCRIPTS AND PERIODICALS. Gale Genealogy and Local History Series. Detroit: Gale Research Co., forthcoming.

New Hampshire

Towle, Laird C. NEW HAMPSHIRE GENEALOGICAL RESEARCH GUIDE. Prince George's County Genealogical Society. Special Publication, no. 1. Bowie, Md.: Prince George's County Genealogical Society, 1973. 638688. 74-178207. 929/.1/09742. CD3371.T68.

New Jersey

Stryker-Rodda, Kenn. NEW JERSEY: DIGGING FOR ANCESTORS IN THE GARDEN STATE. Detroit: Detroit Society for Genealogical Research, 1970. 108875. 74-17944. 929.1. CS16.S86.

New York

Barck, Dorothy C. SOME REFERENCES FOR GENEALOGICAL SEARCHING IN NEW YORK STATE. Detroit: Detroit Society for Genealogical Research, 1965. 1727159. 974.7. GD 962,208 Item 10.

Clint, Florence Runyan. NEW YORK AREA KEY: A GUIDE TO THE GENEALOGICAL RECORDS OF THE STATE OF NEW YORK, INCLUDING MAPS, HISTORIES, CHARTS, AND OTHER HELPFUL MATERIALS. Elizabeth, Colo.: Keyline Publishers, 1979. 4961169. F118.C58.

North Carolina

Draughon, Wallace R., and Johnson, William Perry, comps. NORTH CAROLINA GENEALOGICAL REFERENCE: A RESEARCH GUIDE FOR ALL GENEALOGISTS, BOTH AMATEUR AND PROFESSIONAL. 2d ed. Durham: The Authors, 1966. Reprint. Durham: The Authors, 1973. 1437874. 3525451. 66-8377. 016.9291. Z5313.U6N63 1966.

Ohio

Douthit, Ruth Long. OHIO RESOURCES FOR GENEALOGISTS. WITH SOME REFERENCES FOR GENEALOGICAL SEARCHING IN OHIO. Rev. Detroit: Detroit Society for Genealogical Research, 1972. 640580. 72-171054. 929/.3771. F490.D68 1971.

Flavell, Carol Willsey, and Clint, Florence, comps. OHIO AREA KEY: A GUIDE TO GENEALOGICAL RECORDS OF THE STATE OF OHIO, INCLUDING MAPS, HISTORIES, CHARTS AND OTHER HELPFUL MATERIALS. Denver: Area Keys, 1977. 3024621. 929.1.

Flavell, Carol Willsey. OHIO GENEALOGICAL GUIDE. Youngstown, Ohio: Flavell, 1978. 3785571. 78-101048. 929/.3771. F490.F57. GD 1,036,398 Item 7.

Oregon

Genealogical Forum of Portland, Oregon. "Genealogical Research in Oregon." NATIONAL GENEALOGICAL SOCIETY QUARTERLY 47 (September 1959): 115-28.

Pennsylvania

Clint, Florence Runyan. PENNSYLVANIA AREA KEY: A GUIDE TO THE GENEALOGICAL RECORDS OF THE STATE OF PENNSYLVANIA, INCLUDING MAPS, HISTORIES, CHARTS, AND OTHER HELPFUL MATERIALS. 2d ed. Logan, Utah: Everton Publishers, 1976. 2747156. F148.C55 1976.

Rhode Island

Farnham, Charles W. RHODE ISLAND COLONIAL RECORDS. World Conference on Records and Genealogical Seminar, Area I-25. Salt Lake City: Genealogical Society, 1969. GD 897,217 Item 23.

South Carolina

Bryan, Evelyn McDaniel Frazier. HUNTING YOUR ANCESTORS IN SOUTH CAROLINA: A GUIDE FOR AMATEUR GENEALOGISTS. Rev. and enl. 2d ed. Jacksonville, Fla.: Florentine Press, 1974. 1532282. 75-318303rev.76. 929/.1/09757. CS16.B79 1974.

Tennessee

Hathaway, Beverly West. GENEALOGY RESEARCH SOURCES IN TENNESSEE. West Jordan, Utah: Allstates Research Co., 1972. 402759. 72-188904. 929/.3/025768. F435.H3.

Texas

Winfrey, Dorman. "GONE TO TEXAS": SOURCES FOR GENEALOGICAL RE-

SEARCH IN THE LONE STAR STATE. World Conference on Records and Genealogical Seminar, Area I-31. Salt Lake City: Genealogical Society, 1969. GD 897,217 Item 28.

Utah

Jaussi, Laureen Richardson, and Chaston, Gloria Duncan. GENEALOGICAL RECORDS OF UTAH. Salt Lake City: Deseret Book Co., 1974. 940385. 73-87713. 016.929/3792. CD3541.J38 1974.

Vermont

Hanson, Edward W. "Vermont Genealogy: A Study in Migration." NEW ENGLAND HISTORICAL AND GENEALOGICAL REGISTER 133 (January 1979): 3-19.

Virginia

McCay, Betty L. SOURCES FOR GENEALOGICAL SEARCHING IN VIRGINIA AND WEST VIRGINIA. Indianapolis: n.p., 1971. 142302. 72-24523. 929.3/755. Z5313.U6V78.

West Virginia

_____. SOURCES FOR GENEALOGICAL SEARCHING IN VIRGINIA AND WEST VIRGINIA. Indianapolis: n.p., 1971. 142302. 72-24523. 929.3/755. Z5313.U6V78.

Wisconsin

Ryan, Carol Ward. SEARCHING FOR YOUR WISCONSIN ANCESTORS IN THE WISCONSIN LIBRARIES. Green Bay, Wis.: Ryan, 1979. 4721364. 929.1.

ETHNIC, RELIGIOUS, AND POLITICAL

Black

Blockson, Charles L., and Fry, Ron. BLACK GENEALOGY. Englewood Cliffs, N.J.: Prentice-Hall, 1977. 2818073. 77-3150. 929/.1028. CS21.B55.

> Neither the Blockson-Fry nor the Walker guide (below) is as comprehensive as is needed, but they are all that is available at present. The Blockson-Fry guide is the more comprehensive of the two.

Walker, James D. BLACK GENEALOGY--HOW TO BEGIN. Athens: University of Georgia, Center for Continuing Education, 1977. 3465772. CS21.W3.

Rose, James, and Eichholz, Alice, eds. BLACK GENESIS. Gale Genealogy and Local History Series, vol. 1. Detroit: Gale Research Co., 1978. 4136972. 77-74819. 929/.1. CS21.R57.

An annotated bibliographic guide.

Catholic

Shellem, John J. CHURCH RECORDS OF THE UNITED STATES, PART A, PART I, ROMAN CATHOLIC SACRAMENTAL RECORDS. World Conference on Records and Genealogical Seminar, Area I-4 and 5a. Salt Lake City: Genealogical Society, 1969. GD 897,216 Item 31.

Huguenots

Allen, Cameron. RECORDS OF HUGUENOTS IN THE UNITED STATES, CANADA AND THE WEST INDIES WITH SOME MENTION OF DUTCH AND GERMAN SOURCES. World Conference on Records and Genealogical Seminar, Area F-10. Salt Lake City: Genealogical Society, 1969. GD 897,215 Item 29.

DuPasquier, J. Thierry. RECORDS OF HUGUENOTS IN FRANCE. World Conference on Records and Genealogical Seminar, Area F-8. Salt Lake City: Genealogical Society, 1969. GD 897,215 Item 27.

Gwynn, Robin D. RECORDS OF HUGUENOTS IN THE BRITISH ISLES. World Conference on Records and Genealogical Seminar, Area F-9. Salt Lake City: Genealogical Society, 1969. GD 897,215 Item 28.

Indians

Genealogical Department of the Church of Jesus Christ of Latter-day Saints. MAJOR GENEALOGICAL RECORD SOURCES OF THE INDIANS OF THE UNITED STATES. Rev. Research Paper, Series B, no. 2. Salt Lake City: Genealogical Department, 1977. 5968498. CSI.G382 1977.

Kirkham, E. Kay. OUR NATIVE AMERICANS: THEIR RECORDS OF GENEALOGICAL VALUE. Logan, Utah: Everton Publishers, 1980.

Parker, Jimmy B. "Sources of American Indian Genealogy." GENEALOGICAL JOURNAL 6 (September 1977): 120-25.

Japanese

Genealogical Society of the Church of Jesus Christ of Latter-day Saints. TRACING YOUR ANCESTORS TO JAPAN: A GUIDE FOR JAPANESE AMERICANS AND CANADIANS. Research Paper, Series J, no. 6. Salt Lake City: Genealogical Society, n.d.

Jewish

Rottenberg, Dan. FINDING OUR FATHERS: A GUIDEBOOK TO JEWISH GENEALOGY. New York: Random House, 1977. 2614220. 76-53493. 929/.1/028. CS21.R58.

Stem, Malcolm H. CHURCH RECORDS OF THE UNITED STATES, PART B, PART I, JEWISH SYNAGOGUE RECORDS. World Conference on Records and Genealogical Seminar, Area I-6 and 7a. Salt Lake City: Genealogical Society, 1969. GD 897,216 Item 35.

Loyalist

Kennedy, Patricia. HOW TO TRACE YOUR LOYALIST ANCESTORS: THE USE OF THE LOYALIST SOURCES IN THE PUBLIC ARCHIVES OF CANADA. Ottawa: Ontario Genealogical Society, 1971. 726133. 73-173763. 929/.1/07. CD3624.K46.

Leventhal, Herbert, and Mooney, James E. "A Bibliography of Loyalist Source Material in the United States. Parts I, II, & III." AMERICAN ANTIQUARIAN SOCIETY, PROCEEDINGS 85:73-308, 405-60; 86:343-90. 2532291. E172.A47.

Calder, Kathryn, and Fellows, Jo-Ann. "Bibliography of Loyalist Source Material in Canada." AMERICAN ANTIQUARIAN SOCIETY, PROCEEDINGS 82:67-256.

Mennonites

Gratz, Delbert. A CENTURY OF EMIGRATION FROM THE PALATINATE TO THE U.S.A. PART III: MENNONITES. World Conference on Records and Genealogical Seminar, Area D-3 and 4c. Salt Lake City: Genealogical Society, 1969. GD 897,214 Item 24.

Mexican Americans

Jenkins, Myra Ellen. TRACING SPANISH-AMERICAN PEDIGREES IN THE SOUTHWESTERN UNITED STATES. PART I: NEW MEXICO, TEXAS AND COLORADO. World Conference on Records and Genealogical Seminar, Area

F-14a. Salt Lake City: Genealogical Society, 1969. GD 897,215 Item 34.

Temple, Thomas Workman, II. SOURCES FOR TRACING SPANISH-AMERICAN PEDIGREES IN THE SOUTHWESTERN UNITED STATES: PART II: CALIFORNIA AND ARIZONA. World Conference on Records and Genealogical Seminar, Area F 14b. Salt Lake City: Genealogical Society, 1969. GD 897,215 Item 35.

Mormons

Jaussi, Laureen Richardson, and Chaston, Gloria Duncan, comps. REGISTER OF L.D.S. CHURCH RECORDS. CLASSIFIED BY THE LIBRARY OF THE GE-NEALOGICAL SOCIETY OF THE CHURCH OF JESUS CHRIST OF LATTER-DAY SAINTS. Salt Lake City: Deseret Book Co., 1968. 443797. 68-25348. 929.3. Z7845.M8 C48.

Quakers

Heiss, Willard. CHURCH RECORDS OF THE UNITED STATES. PART B, PART III: QUAKER RECORDS IN AMERICA: RECORDS WITH AN EXTRA DIMEN-SION. World Conference on Records and Genealogical Seminar, Area I-6 and 7c. Salt Lake City: Genealogical Society, 1969. GD 897,216 Item 37.

FOREIGN

Some authors and librarians seem to think that if they provide a genealogist with the name and address of an archives overseas, they have helped a great deal with his or her research need. Rarely is such information of much value. The genealogist requires just as much detailed information concerning overseas research as he or she does for any state in the union. In many cases there will be a language barrier for the genealogist to hurdle, as well, along with an in-creased difficulty in obtaining access to research material.

Most foreign reference sources cited in this list are those useful to residents of the United States who have to do their research without traveling. Cooperative library systems, networks, or several libraries in a geographical area may want to cooperate in the acquisition of foreign guides, interlibrary loaning them as needed to other libraries.

Several titles have been selected from the research papers of the Genealogical Department of the Church of Jesus Christ of Latter-day Saints. There are ad-ditional papers, a list of which may be obtained by writing the Genealogical Department, 50 East North Temple Street, Salt Lake City, Utah 84150. Many of them are now out-of-print.

Australia

Genealogical Society of the Church of Jesus Christ of Latter-day Saints. MA-JOR GENEALOGICAL RECORD SOURCES IN AUSTRALIA. Research Paper, Series E. no. 2. Salt Lake City: 1969. 2788776. 929.105.

Austria

Genealogical Society of the Church of Jesus Christ of Latter-day Saints. THE AUSTRO-HUNGARIAN EMPIRE BOUNDARY CHANGES AND THEIR EFFECT ON GENEALOGICAL RESEARCH. Research Paper, Series C, no. 18. Salt Lake City: n.d. 5877420. 929.105.

_____. MAJOR GENEALOGICAL RECORD SOURCES IN AUSTRIA. Research Paper, Series C, no. 16. Salt Lake City: 1971. 737835. 73-172317. 929/.3/436 CD1120.

Belgium

Genealogical Society of the Church of Jesus Christ of Latter-day Saints. MA-JOR GENEALOGICAL RECORD SOURCES IN BELGIUM. Research Paper, Series G, no. 3. Salt Lake City: 1976. 4836474. CD1670.G4.

Pardon, Jean-Michel. GENEALOGICAL RESEARCH RESOURCES IN THE FRENCH SPEAKING PARTS OF BELGIUM. World Conference on Records and Genea-logical Seminar, Area F-4a. Salt Lake City: Genealogical Society, 1969. GD 897,215 Item 22.

Canada

Baxter, Angus. IN SEARCH OF YOUR ROOTS: A GUIDE FOR CANADIANS SEEKING THEIR ANCESTORS. Toronto: MacMillan of Canada, 1978. 4134498. 78-315689. 929/.1/072071. CS82.B39.

Genealogical Society of the Church of Jesus Christ of Latter-day Saints. MA-JOR GENEALOGICAL RECORD SOURCES FOR CANADA. Rev. Research Papers, Series B, no. 3. Salt Lake City: 1976. 4915944. CS1.G3822 no.3.

Jonasson, Eric. THE CANADIAN GENEALOGICAL HANDBOOK: A COMPRE-HENSIVE GUIDE TO FINDING YOUR ANCESTORS IN CANADA. 2d ed. Rev. and enl. Winnipeg: Wheatfield Press, 1978. 4225522. 929/.1/0971. CS16.J66 1978.

MANITOBA

Jonasson, Eric. "Genealogical Sources in the Province of Manitoba." GE-
NEALOGICAL JOURNAL 8 (June 1979): 91-114.

NOVA SCOTIA

Punch, Terrence Michael. GENEALOGICAL RESEARCH IN NOVA SCOTIA.
Halifax, Nova Scotia: Petheric Press, 1978. 4741198.

ONTARIO

Kirk, Robert F.; Keffer, Marion C.; and Kirk, Audrey L., comps. SOME
ONTARIO REFERENCES AND SOURCES FOR THE FAMILY HISTORIAN. Rev.
and enl. Toronto: Ontario Genealogical Society, 1976. 3771380. 77-376702.
016.929/3713. Z1392.06 K57 1976 CS88.06.

China

Genealogical Society of the Church of Jesus Christ of Latter-day Saints. CHI-
NESE LOCAL HISTORIES AS A SOURCE FOR THE GENEALOGIST. Rev. Research Paper, Series J, no. 3. Salt Lake City: 1975. 4918472. CSl.G378
no. 3.

Czechoslovakia

Miller, Olga K., ed. GENEALOGICAL RESEARCH FOR CZECH AND SLOVAK
AMERICANS. Gale Genealogy and Local History Series, vol. 2. Detroit:
Gale Research Co., 1978. 4194320. 78-13086. 929/.1/09437. CS524.M54.

Denmark

Genealogical Society of the Church of Jesus Christ of Latter-day Saints. THE
CENSUS RECORDS OF DENMARK. Research Paper, Series D, no. 7. Salt
Lake City: n.d. 3701805. 929.3.

_____. THE CHURCH RECORDS OF DENMARK. Research Paper, Series D,
no. 6. Salt Lake City: n.d. 3701814. 929.3.

_____. DANISH-NORWEGIAN PALEOGRAPHY. Research Paper, Series D,
no. 16. Salt Lake City: n.d.

_____. MAJOR GENEALOGICAL RECORD SOURCES IN DENMARK. Rev.
Research Paper, Series D, no. 5. Salt Lake City: 1974. 3700560. 929.3.

_____. THE MILITARY LEVYING ROLLS OF DENMARK. Research Paper, Series D, no. 8. Salt Lake City: n.d. 3701819. 929.3.

_____. THE PROBATE RECORDS OF DENMARK. Rev. Research Paper, Series D, no. 9. Salt Lake City: 1977.

England

Gardner, David E., and Smith, Frank. GENEALOGICAL RESEARCH IN ENG-LAND AND WALES. Rev. ed. 3 vols. Salt Lake City: Bookcraft Publishers, 1956-1966. 2474776. 929.1.

Genealogical Society of the Church of Jesus Christ of Latter-day Saints. MA-JOR GENEALOGICAL RECORD SOURCES IN ENGLAND AND WALES. Rev. Research Paper, Series A, no. 1. Salt Lake City: 1973.

Finland

Genealogical Society of the Church of Jesus Christ of Latter-day Saints. MA-JOR GENEALOGICAL RECORD SOURCES IN FINLAND. Research Paper, Series D, no. 4. Salt Lake City: 1967. 2788865.

Walli, Harry. FINNISH GENEALOGICAL RESEARCH--METHODS AND PRO-CEDURES. World Conference on Records and Genealogical Seminar, Area E-15. Salt Lake City: Genealogical Society, 1969. GD 897,215 Item 16.

France

Durye, Pierre. GENEALOGICAL RESEARCH SOURCES IN FRANCE EXCEPT FOR PARIS AND ALSACE-LORRAINE. World Conference on Records and Genea-logical Seminar, Area F-1. Salt Lake City: Genealogical Society, 1969. GD 897,215 Item 19.

Genealogical Society of the Church of Jesus Christ of Latter-day Saints. MA-JOR GENEALOGICAL RECORD SOURCES IN FRANCE. Rev. Research Paper, Series G, no. 1. Salt Lake City: 1973.

Gut, Christian. GENEALOGICAL RESEARCH IN PARIS, FRANCE. World Con-ference on Records and Genealogical Seminar, Area F-2. Salt Lake City: Ge-nealogical Society, 1969. GD 897,215 Item 20.

Himly, Francois J. GENEALOGICAL RESEARCH SOURCES IN ALSACE-LORRAINE (FRANCE). World Conference on Records and Genealogical Seminar, Area F-3. Salt Lake City: Genealogical Society, 1969. GD 897,215 Item 21.

Germany

Genealogical Department of the Church of Jesus Christ of Latter-day Saints. GERMAN BOUNDARY AND LOCALITY NAME CHANGES. Research Paper, Series C, no. 4. Salt Lake City: 1978.

_____. MAJOR GENEALOGICAL RECORD SOURCES IN GERMANY. Rev. Research Paper, Series C, no. 1. Salt Lake City: 1977. 4918301. GSI. G3832 no. 1.

Genealogical Society of the Church of Jesus Christ of Latter-day Saints. THE CHURCH RECORDS OF GERMANY. Research Paper, Series C, no. 29. Salt Lake City: 1975. 6130605. 929.1.

Jensen, Larry O. A GENEALOGICAL HANDBOOK OF GERMAN RESEARCH. Rev. ed. Pleasant Grove, Utah: Jensen, 1979. 3763987. CS615.J36 1978.

Guatemala

Genealogical Society of the Church of Jesus Christ of Latter-day Saints. MA-JOR GENEALOGICAL RECORD SOURCES IN GUATEMALA. Research Paper, Series H, no. 1. Salt Lake City: 1970. 3700391. 929.3.

Hong Kong

Genealogical Society of the Church of Jesus Christ of Latter-day Saints. MA-JOR GENEALOGICAL RECORD SOURCES IN HONG KONG. Research Paper, Series J, no. 4. Salt Lake City: 1975. 4725035. 929.1.

Hungary

Genealogical Society of the Church of Jesus Christ of Latter-day Saints. THE AUSTRO-HUNGARIAN EMPIRE BOUNDARY CHANGES AND THEIR EFFECT ON GENEALOGICAL RESEARCH. Research Paper, Series C, no. 18. Salt Lake City: n.d. 5877420. 929.105.

_____. MAJOR GENEALOGICAL RECORD SOURCES IN HUNGARY. Research Paper, Series C, no. 17. Salt Lake City: 1972. 3825786. 929.3.

Iceland

Genealogical Society of the Church of Jesus Christ of Latter-day Saints. MA-JOR GENEALOGICAL RECORD SOURCES IN ICELAND. Research Paper, Series D, no. 2. Salt Lake City: 1967. 2788891.

Jonasson, Eric. TRACING YOUR ICELANDIC FAMILY TREE. Winnipeg: Jonasson, 1975. 3348163. 929.3094912.

Ireland

Falley, Margaret Dickson. IRISH AND SCOTCH-IRISH ANCESTRAL RESEARCH: A GUIDE TO THE GENEALOGICAL RECORDS, METHODS AND SOURCES IN IRELAND. 2 vols. Evanston, Ill.: n.p., 1962. 1423981. 62-51616. CS483.F32.

Genealogical Society of the Church of Jesus Christ of Latter-day Saints. BASIC GENEALOGICAL RESEARCH GUIDE FOR IRELAND. Research Paper, Series A, no. 58. Salt Lake City: 1978. 4754633. 929.1.

_____. MAJOR GENEALOGICAL RECORD SOURCES IN IRELAND. Rev. Research Paper, Series A, no. 2. Salt Lake City: 1974.

Isle of Man

Genealogical Society of the Church of Jesus Christ of Latter-day Saints. MAJOR GENEALOGICAL RECORD SOURCES IN THE ISLE OF MAN. Rev. Research Paper, Series A, no. 4. Salt Lake City: 1975.

Italy

Genealogical Department of the Church of Jesus Christ of Latter-day Saints. MAJOR GENEALOGICAL RECORD SOURCES FOR ITALY. Rev. Research Paper, Series G, no. 2. Salt Lake City: 1977. 4913707. CS1.G3872 no. 2.

Japan

Genealogical Society of the Church of Jesus Christ of Latter-day Saints. MAJOR GENEALOGICAL RECORD SOURCES IN JAPAN. Rev. Research Paper, Series J, no. 1. Salt Lake City: 1974. 4725043. 929.1.

Gubler, Greg. "Looking East: The Realities of Genealogical Research in Japan." GENEALOGICAL JOURNAL 8 (March 1979): 43-50.

Latin America

Platt, Lyman De, ed. GENEALOGICAL HISTORICAL GUIDE TO LATIN AMERICA. Gale Genealogy and Local History Series, vol. 4. Detroit: Gale Research Co., 1978. 4883104. 79-101158. 929/.1/07208. CS95.P58.

Mexico

Genealogical Society of the Church of Jesus Christ of Latter-day Saints. MAJOR GENEALOGICAL RECORD SOURCES IN MEXICO. Research Paper, Series H, no. 2. Salt Lake City: 1970. 206702. 70-29773. 929.3/025/72. CS101.G45.

The Netherlands

Genealogical Society of the Church of Jesus Christ of Latter-day Saints. CHURCH AND CIVIL RECORDS OF AMSTERDAM, THE NETHERLANDS, BEFORE 1811. Research Paper, Series C, no. 25. Salt Lake City: 1975. 4728952. 929.1.

_____. CHURCH RECORDS OF THE NETHERLANDS: DUTCH REFORMED. Research Paper, Series C, no. 22. Salt Lake City: 1974. 4721697. 929.1.

_____. CHURCH RECORDS OF THE NETHERLANDS: EVANGELICAL LUTHERAN AND RESTORED EVANGELICAL LUTHERAN. Research Paper, Series C, no. 24. Salt Lake City: 1974. 4741859. 929.1.

_____. CHURCH RECORDS OF THE NETHERLANDS: MENNONITES. Research Paper, Series C, no. 21. Salt Lake City: 1973. 4728955. 929.1.

_____. CHURCH RECORDS OF THE NETHERLANDS: REMONSTRANT CHURCH OF BROTHERHOOD. Research Paper, Series C, no. 20. Salt Lake City: 1972. 4728967. 929.1.

_____. CHURCH RECORDS OF THE NETHERLANDS: ROMAN CATHOLIC. Research Paper, Series C, no. 26. Salt Lake City: 1974. 4728974. 929.1.

_____. CHURCH RECORDS OF THE NETHERLANDS: WALLOON OR FRENCH REFORMED. Research Paper, Series C, no. 23. Salt Lake City: 1973. 4753307. 929.1.

_____. GUIDE TO GENEALOGICAL SOURCES IN THE NETHERLANDS: DRENTHE. Research Paper, Series C, no. 15. Salt Lake City: 1972. 4741847. 929.1.

_____. GUIDE TO GENEALOGICAL SOURCES IN THE NETHERLANDS: FRIESLAND. Research Paper, Series C, no. 7. Salt Lake City: 1971. 1215728. 949.2.

_____. GUIDE TO GENEALOGICAL SOURCES IN THE NETHERLANDS: GELDERLAND. Rev. Research Paper, Series C, no. 9. Salt Lake City: 1973.

_____. GUIDE TO GENEALOGICAL SOURCES IN THE NETHERLANDS: GRONINGEN. Research Paper, Series C, no. 6. Salt Lake City: 1971. 3653631. CS1.G383 no. 6.

_____. GUIDE TO GENEALOGICAL SOURCES IN THE NETHERLANDS: LIMBURG. Research Paper, Series C, no. 12. Salt Lake City: 1971. 3653588. CS1.G383 no. 12.

_____. GUIDE TO GENEALOGICAL SOURCES IN THE NETHERLANDS: NORTH BRABANT. Research Paper, Series C, no. 13. Salt Lake City: 1971. 3653544. CS1.G383 no. 13.

_____. GUIDE TO GENEALOGICAL SOURCES IN THE NETHERLANDS: NORTH HOLLAND. Research Paper, Series C, no. 10. Salt Lake City: 1971. 3653669. CS1.G383 no. 10.

_____. GUIDE TO GENEALOGICAL SOURCES IN THE NETHERLANDS: OVERIJSSEL. Rev. Research Paper, Series C, no. 8. Salt Lake City: 1974.

_____. GUIDE TO GENEALOGICAL SOURCES IN THE NETHERLANDS: SOUTH HOLLAND. Research Paper, Series C, no. 14. Salt Lake City: 1973. 4754807. 929.1.

_____. GUIDE TO GENEALOGICAL SOURCES IN THE NETHERLANDS: UTRECHT. Research Paper, Series C, no. 11. Salt Lake City: 1971. 4491201. 78-310488. 929/.3492/3. CS1.G383 no. 11.

_____. GUIDE TO GENEALOGICAL SOURCES IN THE NETHERLANDS: ZEELAND. Rev. Research Paper, Series C, no. 5. Salt Lake City: 1974.

_____. MAJOR GENEALOGICAL RECORD SOURCES IN THE NETHERLANDS. Rev. Research Paper, Series C, no. 3. Salt Lake City: 1972.

_____. THE ORIGINS OF NAMES IN THE NETHERLANDS AND THEIR EFFECT ON GENEALOGICAL RESEARCH. Research Paper, Series C, no. 28. Salt Lake City: 1975. 5295307. CS1.G38 ser.C, no. 28.

New Zealand

Genealogical Society of the Church of Jesus Christ of Latter-day Saints. MAJOR GENEALOGICAL RECORD SOURCES IN NEW ZEALAND. Research Paper, Series E, no. 1. Salt Lake City: 1967. 2788909.

Norway

Genealogical Society of the Church of Jesus Christ of Latter-day Saints. THE CENSUS RECORDS OF NORWAY. Research Paper, Series D, no. 12. Salt Lake City: n.d. 3701719. 929.3.

_____. THE CHURCH RECORDS OF NORWAY. Research Paper, Series D, no. 11. Salt Lake City: n.d. 2988616. CD1827.5.A1G4.

_____. DANISH-NORWEGIAN PALEOGRAPHY. Research Paper, Series D, no. 16. Salt Lake City: n.d.

_____. GUIDE TO GENEALOGICAL SOURCES IN NORWAY: AKERSHUS COUNTY. Research Paper, Series D, no. 23. Salt Lake City: n.d.

_____. GUIDE TO GENEALOGICAL SOURCES IN NORWAY: AUST-AGDER COUNTY. Research Paper, Series D, no. 21. Salt Lake City: n.d.

_____. GUIDE TO GENEALOGICAL SOURCES IN NORWAY: BUSKERUD COUNTY. Research Paper, Series D, no. 22. Salt Lake City: n.d.

_____. GUIDE TO GENEALOGICAL SOURCES IN NORWAY: HEDMARK COUNTY. Research Paper, Series D, no. 20. Salt Lake City: n.d.

_____. GUIDE TO GENEALOGICAL SOURCES IN NORWAY: TELEMARK COUNTY. Research Paper, Series D, no. 24. Salt Lake City: n.d.

_____. MAJOR GENEALOGICAL RECORD RESOURCES IN NORWAY. Research Paper, Series D, no. 1. Salt Lake City: n.d. 2788924.

_____. THE PROBATE RECORDS OF NORWAY. Rev. Research Paper, Series D, no. 13. Salt Lake City: 1973. 4914015. CS1.G384 no. 13.

Naeseth, Gerhard B. NORWEGIAN SETTLEMENTS IN THE UNITED STATES: A REVIEW OF PRINTED AND MANUSCRIPT SOURCES FOR THE STUDY OF NORWEGIAN SOURCES IN AMERICA. World Conference on Records and Genealogical Seminar, Area E-10. Salt Lake City: Genealogical Society, 1969. GD 897,215 Item 11.

Poland

Genealogical Society of the Church of Jesus Christ of Latter-day Saints. MA-JOR GENEALOGICAL RECORD SOURCES IN POLAND. Research Paper, Series C, no. 31. Salt Lake City: 1978. 4754723. 929.1.

Jensen, Larry O. "Genealogical Research in Eastern Europe." SASKATCHEWAN GENEALOGICAL SOCIETY BULLETIN 7 (Winter 1976): 15-37.

Portugal

De Faria, Antonio Machado. GENEALOGICAL RESEARCH SOURCES IN POR-TUGAL. World Conference on Records and Genealogical Seminar, Area F-12. Salt Lake City: Genealogical Society, 1969. GD 897,215 Item 31.

Samoa

Genealogical Society of the Church of Jesus Christ of Latter-day Saints. MA-JOR GENEALOGICAL SOURCES IN SAMOA. Research Paper, Series E, no. 3. Salt Lake City: 1969. 3653893. CS1.G385 no. 3.

Scandinavia

Johansson, Carl-Erik. THUS THEY WROTE: A GUIDE TO THE GOTHIC SCRIPT OF SCANDINAVIA--DENMARK, NORWAY, FINLAND, SWEDEN. Provo, Utah: Brigham Young University Press, 1970. 4793252. 929.3.

Scotland

Genealogical Society of the Church of Jesus Christ of Latter-day Saints. MA-JOR GENEALOGICAL RECORD SOURCES IN SCOTLAND. Rev. Research Paper, Series A, no. 3. Salt Lake City: 1972.

South Africa

Genealogical Department of the Church of Jesus Christ of Latter-day Saints. MAJOR GENEALOGICAL RECORD SOURCES IN SOUTH AFRICA. Research Paper, Series K, no. 1. Salt Lake City: 1976.

Sweden

Genealogical Society of the Church of Jesus Christ of Latter-day Saints. MA-JOR GENEALOGICAL RECORD SOURCES IN SWEDEN. Rev. Research Paper, Series D, no. 3. Salt Lake City: 1974.

Johansson, Carl-Erik. CRADLED IN SWEDEN: A PRACTICAL HELP TO GE-NEALOGICAL RESEARCH IN SWEDISH RECORDS. Logan, Utah: Everton Publishers, 1977. 3336092. CS2601.J6 1977.

Switzerland

Clottu, Olivier. GENEALOGICAL RESEARCH IN THE FRENCH SPEAKING PARTS OF SWITZERLAND, INCLUDING SWISS HUGUENOT RECORDS. World Conference on Records and Genealogical Seminar, Area F-5. Salt Lake City: 1969. GD 897,215 Item 24.

Genealogical Society of the Church of Jesus Christ of Latter-day Saints. MAJOR GENEALOGICAL RECORD SOURCES IN SWITZERLAND. Rev. Research Paper, Series C, no. 2. Salt Lake City: 1975.

Nielson, Paul Anthon. "Major Sources of Genealogical Information in Switzerland." In THE PROCEEDINGS OF THE FIRST SYMPOSIUM ON GENEALOGICAL AND HISTORICAL RESEARCH TECHNIQUES, THE SEATTLE GENEALOGICAL SOCIETY. Seattle: Seattle Public Library, 1971. Reprinted in the GENEALOGICAL JOURNAL 1 (June and September 1972): 43-46, 77-80.

Suess, Jared H. HANDY GUIDE TO SWISS GENEALOGICAL RECORDS. Logan, Utah: Everton Publishers, 1978.

Taiwan

Genealogical Department of the Church of Jesus Christ of Latter-day Saints. MAJOR GENEALOGICAL RECORD SOURCES IN TAIWAN. Rev. Research Paper, Series J, no. 2. Salt Lake City: 1976. 4754646. 929.1.

Wales

Gardner, David E., and Smith, Frank. GENEALOGICAL RESEARCH IN ENGLAND AND WALES. 3 vols. Rev. ed. Salt Lake City: Bookcraft Publishers, 1956-1966. 2474776. 929.1.

Genealogical Society of the Church of Jesus Christ of Latter-day Saints. WELSH PATRONYMICS & PLACE NAMES IN WALES AND MONMOUTHSHIRE. Research Paper, Series A, no. 6. Salt Lake City: 1967. 3664105. CS1.G38 no. 6.

Yugoslavia

Zontar, Joze. TRACING ANCESTRY IN YUGOSLAVIA. PART I: RESEARCH

IN YUGOSLAVIA. World Conference on Records and Genealogical Seminar, Area D-13 and 14a. Salt Lake City: Genealogical Society, 1969. GD 897,214 Item 37.

COLLECTION DEVELOPMENT AND SUMMARY

Every library should have Greenwood's RESEARCHER'S GUIDE TO AMERICAN GENEALOGY, GUIDE TO GENEALOGICAL RECORDS IN THE NATIONAL ARCHIVE, TRACING YOUR ROOTS, by Consumer Guide, and THE HANDY BOOK FOR GENEALOGISTS, by Everton. Other titles may be selected to meet patron needs. The number and variety of how-to-do-it books will depend on demand. Advanced researchers will need detailed guides, whereas beginners will need simplified books. How-to-do-it guides for foreign countries may be acquired cooperatively and interlibrary loaned as needed to other libraries in a geographical area.

Chapter 7

VITAL RECORDS

The basic data required for pedigree charts and family group sheets, besides names, are the dates and places of the vital events in the lives of the persons listed thereon. These events equal the vital statistics maintained in the state vital records office and the offices of civil registration of most western European countries. These records include birth, marriage, and death information supplied by local agencies and governments.

Genealogists need to know where to write for birth, marriage, and death certificates of ancestors. The following four pamphlets concerning U.S. vital records should be available at all public libraries:

U.S. Public Health Service. WHERE TO WRITE FOR BIRTH AND DEATH REC-ORDS, U.S. AND OUTLYING AREAS. Rev. DHEW Pub. No. HRA 78-1142. Washington, D.C.: Superintendent of Documents, 1978. HE20.6202:B53/.

> State registration, in general, started in 1907 in most states. However, it wasn't until 1911 that most states had 90 percent compliance with the laws requiring death registration and not until 1921 for birth registration. This compliance information was calculated from data compiled by state in the following article:
>
> Nichols, Elizabeth L. "Statewide Civil Vital Registration in the United States." GENEALOGICAL JOURNAL 8 (September 1979): 135-58. Reprinted GENEALOGICAL HELPER 34 (May-June 1980): 6-14.
>
> > Librarians should refer genealogists to this article for details concerning individual states.

_____. WHERE TO WRITE FOR MARRIAGE RECORDS, U.S. AND OUTLYING AREAS. Rev. DHEW Pub. No. HRA 78-1144. Washington, D.C.: Superintendent of Documents, 1978. HE20.6202:M34/.

> About 30 percent of the states have no centralized registration of marriages. Other states vary in beginning registration of marriages

from 1640 to 1968. Nine states began statewide registration
after 1941. Some have indexes and will forward inquiries to the
appropriate county.

_____. WHERE TO WRITE FOR DIVORCE RECORDS, U.S. AND OUTLYING
AREAS. Rev. DHEW Pub. No. PHS 78-1145. Washington, D.C.: Superintendent of Documents, 1978. HE20.6202:D64/.

Fifty percent of the states have no centralized registration
of divorces. Of those states that do, the beginning varies
from 1860 to 1968, fourteen states starting after 1941.
Some states have centralized indexes and will forward requests
to the appropriate county.

_____. WHERE TO WRITE FOR BIRTH AND DEATH RECORDS OF U.S. CITI-
ZENS WHO WERE BORN OR DIED OUTSIDE OF THE U.S. AND BIRTH CER-
TIFICATIONS FOR ALIEN CHILDREN ADOPTED BY U.S. CITIZENS. DHEW
Pub. No. HRA 77-1143. Washington, D.C.: 1977. HE20.6202:B53/2.

The above sources may be obtained free of charge from the Division of Vital
Statistics, National Center for Health Statistics, Public Health Service, DHEW,
Hyattsville, Md. 29782.

The first three of these pamphlets list the address of the Bureau of Vital Statistics (or its equivalent) in each state. Certificates are available in short and
full form. The short form is usually cheaper. These records cost from $1.00
to $4.00 per certificate. To obtain certificates before 1907, THE HANDY
BOOK FOR GENEALOGISTS must be consulted. It provides the names of the
counties of each state, their county seat, and zip code. It also includes some
information concerning the type, availability, and starting date of local records.

Normally birth records give the date and place of birth, the father's name and
mother's maiden name. Marriage records usually provide the names, including
the maiden name, the ages, and the date and place of marriage, as well as
the names of the witnesses. Death records usually give the date, place, and
cause of death; the name and relationship of the person providing the data; the
place and date of birth; and the names of parents. This latter information is
only as accurate as the knowledge of the person providing the data and is subject
to error almost to the degree of severity of the bereavement. An excellent
treatise on vital records is chapter 9, pages 113-38, of Val D. Greenwood's
THE RESEARCHER'S GUIDE TO AMERICAN GENEALOGY.

Some eastern seaboard vital records have been abstracted and published. They
are available in many large genealogical collections. Some of these published
records have been included in the LIBRARY OF AMERICAN CIVILIZATION
(LAC) collection that is available in some liberal arts colleges, universities,
and community college collections and listed in the NATIONAL REGISTER OF
MICROFORM MASTERS.

Some early American vital records are on microfilm and may be borrowed for use in any of the branch libraries of the Genealogical Department of the Church of Jesus Christ of Latter-day Saints. These microfilmed records do not infringe on the current rights of privacy, as they usually do not include any living persons. All genealogists should be encouraged to visit one of these branch libraries to check the Microfilm Card Catalog and send in a "Reference Questionnaire" to the Genealogical Department Library to determine if any vital records are available for the geographical locations of their ancestral events of vital importance.

The Genealogical Department considers all of the following as vital records in its subject cataloging: baptism records, Bible records, birth records, Bishop's transcripts, burial records, cemetery records, civil registration, death records, divorce records, marriage records, mortality schedules, mortuary records, obituaries, parish registers, and sexton records. Also, the subject subdivision, "Vital Records," is in the Microfilm Card Catalog with indirect subject headings that begin with the name of the state, then the county and city (e.g., NEW HAMPSHIRE, ROCKINGHAM, DERRY - VITAL RECORDS). Some records for a city, such as Derry, could also be found under the following indirect subject headings:

> NEW HAMPSHIRE, ROCKINGHAM - VITAL RECORDS
> NEW HAMPSHIRE - VITAL RECORDS

Genealogists should search these two additional headings if no records are found under the name of the city. Librarians should keep in mind that obtaining vital records on microfilm is much more economical than writing for numerous copies of certificates.

While at the branch library, genealogists should also check the COMPUTER FILE INDEX (CFI). The August 1978 edition of this microfiche index contains over 55 million names. The index is based primarily upon vital records from western Europe and the eastern United States. The CFI is published every two or three years by the Genealogical Department of the Church of Jesus Christ of Latter-day Saints.

After the CFI, genealogists should check the PARISH AND VITAL RECORDS LISTINGS. This microfiche catalog lists all vital records processed for the CFI or in process. It, also, is a publication of the Genealogical Department, issued nearly every six months.

Librarians who would like to have at hand some guides of partial holdings of the Genealogical Department should acquire the following, listed in order of importance.

Stemmons, John D., and Stemmons, E. Diane, comps. THE VITAL RECORD COMPENDIUM: COMPRISING A DIRECTORY OF VITAL RECORDS AND WHERE THEY MAY BE LOCATED. Logan, Utah: Everton Publishers, 1979. 5788107. 78-55686. 929.373.

Brown, Mary J. HANDY INDEX TO THE HOLDINGS OF THE GENEALOGICAL SOCIETY OF UTAH: COUNTIES OF THE UNITED STATES. Logan, Utah: Everton Publishers, 1971. 3060263. CS44.B87.

> Besides vital records this guide includes some biographical materials, census, emigration, land, military, and probate records.

Hale, Richard Walden, Jr., ed. GUIDE TO PHOTOCOPIED HISTORICAL MATERIALS IN THE UNITED STATES AND CANADA. Ithaca, N.Y.: Published for the American Historical Association by Cornell University Press, 1961. 577684. 61-17269. Z6209.H3.

> Out of date but still useful and possibly already in many general collections. It is not recommended for purchase if not already available in a library.

The University of Utah Press is now preparing "Finding Aids to the Microfilmed Manuscript Collection of the Genealogical Society of Utah." In some academic circles these aids are being well received. If a genealogist has access to a branch library and its MICROFILM CARD CATALOG, the purchase of a finding aid should not be necessary. In fact, they are inferior to the MCC, as they contain no microfilm call numbers. They are more up to date than the MCC; however, through the use of the "Reference Questionnaire" or a letter to the Genealogical Department, anyone can obtain an update of the library's holdings for a small photoduplication fee for copying a section of the library's card catalog of a specific geographical location. Some of the aids already published are as follow:

Cottler, Susan Muriel; Haigh, Roger M.; and Weather, Shirley A. PRELIMINARY SURVEY OF THE MEXICAN COLLECTION. Finding Aids to the Microfilmed Collection of the Genealogical Society of Utah, no. 1. Salt Lake City: University of Utah Press, 1978. 4674816. 78-71761. Z733.G45F4 no. 1.

Eakle, Arlene H.; Outsen, Arvilla; and Tompson, Richard S. DESCRIPTIVE INVENTORY OF THE ENGLISH COLLECTION. Findings Aids to the Microfilmed Manuscript Collection of the Genealogical Society of Utah, no. 3. Salt Lake City: University of Utah Press, 1979. 5742961. 79-51413. 016. 929/342. Z5313.G69E23. CS414.

Eakle, Arlene H., and Gunn, L. Ray. DESCRIPTIVE INVENTORY OF THE NEW YORK COLLECTION. Finding Aids to the Microfilmed Manuscript Collection of the Genealogical Society of Utah, no. 4. Salt Lake City: University of Utah Press, 1980. 6166909. 79-92984. Z5313.U6N73.

Jensen, Russell, et al. PRELIMINARY SURVEY OF THE FRENCH COLLECTION. Finding Aids to the Microfilmed Manuscript Collection of the Genealogical Society of Utah, no. 5. Salt Lake City: University of Utah Press, 1979.

Smelser, Ronald; Dullien, Thomas; and Hinrichs, Heribert. PRELIMINARY
SURVEY OF THE GERMAN COLLECTION. Finding Aids to the Microfilmed
Manuscript Collection of the Genealogical Society of Utah, no. 2. Salt Lake
City: University of Utah, 1979. 5517110. 79-51412. 929.343.

The subject headings relative to birth, marriage, and death records are as
follows:

Birth and Death Records

    LC   REGISTERS OF BIRTHS, ETC.--LINN COUNTY, IOWA

    Sears   REGISTERS OF BIRTHS, ETC.--LINN COUNTY, IOWA

    GD   IOWA, LINN - VITAL RECORDS

Marriage Records

    LC   MARRIAGE LICENSES--LINN COUNTY, IOWA p. 233.

    Sears   REGISTERS OF BIRTHS, ETC.--LINN COUNTY, IOWA

    GD   IOWA, LINN - VITAL RECORDS

HANDWRITING

Genealogists may ask librarians for assistance in deciphering handwriting, particularly on census schedules, vital records, and other older records, some of
which they may be using on microfilm. Librarians should simply encourage
patrons having such difficulties to prepare a table of samples from the record
of all the capital and lower-case letters of the alphabet. The table can then
be used to identify difficult letters of unrecognizable words.

The study of handwriting is paleography. There are many books on this skill
for many languages. A search of the LIBRARY OF CONGRESS CATALOGS:
SUBJECT CATALOG, 1950- under the subject heading, "PALEOGRAPHY--
HANDBOOKS, TREATISES, ETC." will produce a great variety. The following
few titles and parts of books in English will help the average genealogist:

Kirkham, E. Kay. THE HANDWRITING OF AMERICAN RECORDS FOR A
PERIOD OF 300 YEARS. Logan, Utah: Everton Publishers, 1973. 937978.
79-121378. 652/.1/0973. Z43.K55.

Gardner, David E., and Smith, Frank. GENEALOGICAL RESEARCH IN ENG-
LAND AND WALES. 3 vols. Salt Lake City: Bookcraft Publishers, 1956-
1966. 2474776. 929.1.

    See volume 3, chapters 1-8, pages 1-86 for handwriting information.

Jensen, Larry O. A GENEALOGICAL HANDBOOK OF GERMAN RESEARCH. Rev. ed. Pleasant Grove, Utah: Jensen, 1978. 3763987. CS614.J36 1978.

See chapters 14-16, "Handwriting and Terminology," pages 112-31.

Johansson, Carl-Erik. CRADLED IN SWEDEN: A PRACTICAL HELP TO GENEALOGICAL RESEARCH IN SWEDISH RECORDS. Logan, Utah: Everton Publishers, 1977. 3336092. CS2601.J6 1977.

See chapter 7, "Handwriting," pages 51-58.

_____. THUS THEY WROTE: A GUIDE TO THE GOTHIC SCRIPT OF SCANDINAVIA--DENMARK, NORWAY, FINLAND, SWEDEN. Provo, Utah: Brigham Young University Press, 1970. 4793252. 929.3.

See pages 1-5 on handwriting.

Miller, Olga K., ed. GENEALOGICAL RESEARCH FOR CZECH AND SLOVAK AMERICANS. Gale Genealogy and Local History Series, vol. 2. Detroit: Gale Research Co., 1978. 4194320. 78-13086. 929/.1/09437. CS524.M54.

Tables A, B, and C, pages 119-21, give samples of the difference between English and German script and modern writing of Czechoslovakia.

ADOPTION RECORDS

Adopted children usually have great difficulty in searching for information concerning their natural parents. Generally, adoption records are closed and are rarely opened by court order. Some additional information is provided in the "Missing Persons" section of the chapter, "Unique Research Services," p. 233.

CHURCH RECORDS

The next most reliable source for vital records, after the state and county vital records, is church records. Genealogists have not used these records extensively in the United States because of their inaccessability and the lack of comprehensive inventories and lists of availability. The majority of Greenwood's THE RESEARCHER'S GUIDE TO AMERICAN GENEALOGY, chapter 19, "Church Records," pages 358-99, is very useful for understanding church vital records. The following guides, listed in order of importance, are helpful in locating some of the church records that have been collected and consolidated in various archives and libraries:

Kirkham, E. Kay. A SURVEY OF AMERICAN CHURCH RECORDS: MAJOR AND MINOR DENOMINATIONS, BEFORE 1880-1890. 4th ed., rev. and enl. Logan, Utah: Everton Publishers, 1978. 4256260. 929.3.

Society of American Archivists. Church Archives Committee. A PRELIMINARY GUIDE TO CHURCH RECORDS REPOSITORIES. Comp. by Aug. R. Suelflow. St. Louis, Mo.: 1969. 2473755. BR133.U5S62.

Jaussi, Laureen Richardson, and Chaston, Gloria Duncan. REGISTER OF L.D.S. CHURCH RECORDS. CLASSIFIED BY THE LIBRARY OF THE GENEALOGICAL SOCIETY OF THE CHURCH OF JESUS CHRIST OF LATTER-DAY SAINTS. Salt Lake City: Deseret Book Co., 1968. 443797. 68-25348. 929.3. Z7845. M8C48.

Hebert, Donald J. A GUIDE TO CHURCH RECORDS IN LOUISIANA. Eunice, La.: Published by the author, 1975. 1894451. 75-329093. 929/.3763. CD3267.A1H4.

Lundeen, Joel W., comp. PRESERVING YESTERDAY FOR TOMORROW: A GUIDE TO THE ARCHIVES OF THE LUTHERAN CHURCH IN AMERICA. Chicago: Archives of the Lutheran Church in America, 1977. 3718272. Z7845.L9L8.

The subject headings relative to church records are as follows:

LC   CHURCH RECORDS AND REGISTERS

Sears   (By name of church)

GD   For birth, christening, marriage, death, and burial records:

    IOWA, LINN - VITAL RECORDS

    IOWA, LINN, ELY - VITAL RECORDS

  For church membership and minutes:

    IOWA - CHURCH RECORDS

CEMETERY RECORDS

Cemetery records are considered vital records by the Genealogical Department and consist of two different types of records: inscriptions and sexton records. The sexton records are considered to be the more accurate of the two. Greenwood also covers these records in chapter 23, pages 467-78 in his RESEARCHER'S GUIDE TO AMERICAN GENEALOGY. Many cemetery records have been copied by both state chapters of the Daughters of the American Revolution and the ward (local congregation) members of the Church of Jesus Christ of Latter-day Saints. All are available on microfilm from the Genealogical Department. Many of these microfilms are listed in the following guide:

Stemmons, John D., and Stemmons, E. Diane. THE CEMETERY RECORD COMPENDIUM: COMPRISING A DIRECTORY OF CEMETERY RECORDS AND WHERE THEY MAY BE LOCATED. Logan, Utah: Everton Publishers, 1979. 5576230. 78-55687. CS49.S7.

Vital Records

The subject headings relative to cemetery records are as follows:

    LC   CEMETERIES--IOWA--LINN COUNTY
              ELY, IOWA--CEMETERIES

    Sears CEMETERIES--IOWA--LINN COUNTY
              ELY, IOWA--CEMETERIES

    GD   IOWA, LINN - VITAL RECORDS
              IOWA, LINN, ELY - VITAL RECORDS

Another means of access to cemetery records is to write the cemetery's sexton. The following directory can assist in this correspondence.

DIRECTORY OF UNITED STATES CEMETERIES. San Jose, Calif.: Cemetery Research, 1974. 1915420. 74-647880. 363. RA626.3.D57.

The location of many old country cemeteries can be made through the use of topographical maps. Some college and university libraries have fine collections. However, many genealogists may not be able to travel to such institutions, and some will want to purchase their own copies. In order to purchase U.S. topographical maps, free state topographical map indexes and order forms must be requested from either of the following offices. For maps of areas east of the Mississippi River, including Minnesota: Branch Distribution, U.S. Geological Survey, 1200 South Eads Street, Arlington, Va. 22202. For maps of areas west of the Mississippi River: Branch Distribution, U.S. Geological Survey, Box 25286, Federal Center, Denver, Colo. 80225. Each state map index contains a list of "Map Reference Libraries" in the state.

MORTUARY RECORDS

A few mortuary records are also available through the Genealogical Department. Again, correspondence may be the only means of consulting some mortuary records. The following directory is owned by many mortuaries and may prove useful in obtaining addresses of mortuaries in other cities:

THE NATIONAL DIRECTORY OF MORTICIANS. Youngstown, Ohio 5740345. 53-31440. RA622.A7N37.

The subject headings relative to mortuary records are as follows:

    LC   MORTALITY--LINN COUNTY, IOWA

    Sears MORTALITY--LINN COUNTY, IOWA

    GD   IOWA, LINN - VITAL RECORDS
              IOWA, LINN, ELY - VITAL RECORDS

EPITAPHS

Every library should have at least one volume of epitaphs or tombstone inscriptions. These titles usually get lost in the literature classifications of libraries, so they should be brought to the attention of genealogists to add a little spice to genealogical research.

One of the enjoyable aspects of genealogical research is the occasional humorous, morbid, or thoughtful epitaph found while tramping through old cemeteries. The genealogist who does not have access to interesting old cemeteries can obtain some of the same enjoyment through books of epitaphs. Usually such books are of little research value. The following are a few books of epitaphs published in the United States:

Alden, Timothy. A COLLECTION OF AMERICAN EPITAPHS AND INSCRIPTIONS, WITH OCCASIONAL NOTES. 5 vols. New York: S. Marks, Printer, 1814. Reprint. 5 vols. in 2. New York: Arno, 1977. 176318. 16-5365. E176.A35.

Beable, William Henry. EPITAPHS: GRAVEYARD HUMOR & EULOGY. New York: Crowell, 1925. Reprint. Detroit: Singing Tree Press, 1971. 137721. 79-154494. 929.5. PN629.B4 1971.

COMIC EPITAPHS FROM THE VERY BEST OLD GRAVEYARDS. Mount Vernon, N.Y.: Peter Pauper Press, 1957. 381302. 57-41603. PN6291.C67.

Eills, Nancy, and Hayden, Parker. HERE LIES AMERICA: A COLLECTION OF NOTABLE GRAVES. New York: Hawthorn Books, 1978. 3958605. 77-72815. 920/.073. CT215.E38 1978.

Forbes, Harriette Merrifield. GRAVESTONES OF EARLY NEW ENGLAND, AND THE MEN WHO MADE THEM, 1653-1800. Boston: Houghton Mifflin, 1927. Reprint. Princeton: Pyne Press, 1973. 797964. 73-79521. 731/.549/0974. NB1855.F6 1973.

Hall, Alonzo C. GRAVE HUMOR, A COLLECTION OF HUMOROUS EPITAPHS. Charlotte, N.C.: McNally of Charlotte, 1961. 3218797. 62-11140/L. 827.088. PN6291.H26 1961.

Kippax, John Robert. CHURCHYARD LITERATURE: A CHOICE COLLECTION OF AMERICAN EPITAPHS, WITH REMARKS ON MONUMENTAL INSCRIPTIONS AND THE OBSEQUIES OF VARIOUS NATIONS. Chicago: S.C. Griggs, 1877. Reprint. Detroit: Singing Tree Press, 1969. Williamstown, Mass.: Corner House, 1978. 21454. 4419462. 68-22033. 929.5. PN6291.K6.

Mann, Thomas Clifford, and Greene, Janet. OVER THEIR DEAD BODIES:
YANKEE EPITAPHS & HISTORY. Brattleboro, Vt.: Stephen Greene Press, 1962.
789490. 62-17328. 929.5. PN6291.M33.

_____. SUDDEN & AWFUL: AMERICAN EPITAPHS AND THE FINGER OF
GOD. Brattleboro, Vt.: Stephen Greene Press, 1968. 428646. 68-54449.
929.5/0973. PN6291.M36.

Peterson, Gail. THE LAST LAUGH: A COMPLETELY NEW COLLECTION OF
FUNNY OLD EPITAPHS. Kansas City, Mo.: Hallmark Editions, 1968. 10184.
68-8777. 929.5. PN6291.P37.

Wallis, Charles Langworthy. STORIES ON STONE: A BOOK OF AMERICAN
EPITAPHS. New York: Oxford University Press, 1954. Reprint. New York:
Dover Publications, 1973. 5092987. 714465. 54-5297. 73-77790. 929/
.5/0973. E176.W18.

One or two of the above titles should be acquired for all collections. General
readers may use them as much or more than genealogists for recreational reading.

NEWSPAPERS AND PERIODICALS

Newspapers should only be relied upon for vital record data as a last resort.
Their use is explained in chapter 14. Many periodicals include vital record
abstracts and lists. The indexes for genealogical periodicals should be consulted as explained in chapter 10 on periodical indexes. That chapter also
explains their usefulness.

MORTALITY SCHEDULES

The Mortality Schedules of the U.S. federal censuses for 1850, 1860, 1870,
and 1880 are sometimes useful to genealogists if their ancestor or relative died
between June 1 of the preceding year and May 31 of the census year (e.g.
1 June 1849 - 31 May 1850). The information contained therein is the full
name of the deceased, age, sex, state of birth, month of death, and cause
of death. They are arranged by state and county.

There are several authors that explain the use and value of mortality schedules.
They are as follows:

Franklin, W. Neil. "Availability of Federal Mortality Census Schedules, 1850-
55." NATIONAL GENEALOGICAL SOCIETY QUARTERLY 52 (December 1964):
205-9.

_____. FEDERAL POPULATION AND MORTALITY CENSUS SCHEDULES, 1790-1890, IN THE NATIONAL ARCHIVES AND THE STATES: OUTLINE OF A LECTURE ON THEIR AVAILABILITY, CONTENT, AND USE. Special List, no. 24. Washington, D.C.: National Archives, 1971. 70-611467. 016. 312/0973. Z7554.U5F73.

    Consult pages 73-75.

"Genealogy Notes." PROLOGUE 4 (Winter 1972): 242-46.

    See table 3, "Available Mortality Census Schedules," page 245.

"Mortality Schedules." In THE RESEARCHER'S GUIDE TO AMERICAN GE-NEALOGY, by Val D. Greenwood, pages 178-85. Baltimore: Genealogical Publishing Co., 1973.

These same how-to-do-it aids also list which mortality schedules are available and where they are located. Some of the lists include information concerning indexes to the schedules. They all contain some errors and are unsatisfactory from a bibliographer's point of view. The following is an attempt to correct their errors, listing all known editions of copies of state mortality schedules and their statewide indexes in understandable bibliographical style. Some errors in this list may be perpetuated because of the transfer of schedules from one agency to another. An accurate report of exact locations would require a visit to each archives or library. This editor contacted several depositories in question and found many changes. The list is arranged by state, subarranged by census year, and then by author.

Alabama

Montgomery. Alabama Department of Archives and History. "Federal Mortality Census Schedules, 1850-80: Alabama."

Arizona

Washington, D.C. National Society, Daughters of the American Revolution, Genealogical Library (hereafter cited as DAR). "Federal Mortality Census Schedules and Indexes, 1870 (Mohave Co. - Yuma Co.) and 1880: Arizona."

    Indexes contain full names, 320 for 1870 and about 864 for 1880. Also available on microfilm: 1870 (Mohave Co. - Yuma Co.) at DAR; Washington, D.C. National Archives. T655:1; and Salt Lake City, Utah. Genealogical Department of the Church of Jesus Christ of Latter-day Saints 422,410 Item 1.

    1880 at DAR; NA T655:2; and GD 422,419 Item 2.

Jackson, Ronald Vern, ed. MORTALITY SCHEDULE, ARIZONA 1870. Salt Lake City: Accelerated Indexing Systems, 1980.

Vital Records

Jackson, Ronald Vern, ed. MORTALITY SCHEDULE, ARIZONA 1880. Salt Lake City: Accelerated Indexing Systems, 1980.

Arkansas

Fayetteville. University of Arkansas. Library. Special Collections. "Federal Mortality Census Schedules, 1850–80: Arkansas."

Also available on microfilm at Arkansas History Commission, Little Rock.

Jackson, Ronald Vern, ed. MORTALITY SCHEDULE, ARKANSAS 1850. Bountiful, Utah: Accelerated Indexing Systems, 1979. 6240353. 929.3.

McLane, Bobbie Jones, and Glazner, Capitola Hensley. 1850 MORTALITY SCHEDULES OF ARKANSAS. Hot Springs National Park, Ark.: n.p., 1968. 454991. 68-65578. 929.3 F410.M17.

A transcription of about 4,330 names in alphabetical order.

Glazner, Capitola Hensley, and McLane, Bobbie Jones, eds. 1860 MORTALITY SCHEDULES OF ARKANSAS. Hot Springs National Park, Ark.: n.p., 1974. 1210577. 976.7.

A transcription of about 5,184 names in alphabetical order.

Jackson, Ronald Vern, ed. MORTALITY SCHEDULE, ARKANSAS 1860. Bountiful, Utah: Accelerated Indexing Systems, 1979. 6240317. 929.3.

Glazner, Capitola Hensley, and McLane, Bobbie Jones. 1870 MORTALITY SCHEDULES OF ARKANSAS. Hot Springs National Park, Ark.: By the authors, 1971. 196963. 70-28898. 929.3/09767. F410.G45.

A transcription of about 4,368 names in alphabetical order.

Jackson, Ronald Vern, ed. MORTALITY SCHEDULE, ARKANSAS 1870. Bountiful, Utah: Accelerated Indexing Systems, 1979. 6240370. 929.3.

Glazner, Capitola Hensley, and McLane, Bobbie Jones. 1880 MORTALITY SCHEDULES OF ARKANSAS. Hot Springs National Park, Ark.: By the authors, 1975. 1226833. 976.7.

A transcription of about 10,665 names in alphabetical order.

California

Sacramento. California State Library. "Federal Mortality Census Schedules, 1850–80: California."

Also available on microfilm at the California State Library. The schedules were microfilmed by the University of California (Berkeley) Library, which has microfilm copies available in its Bancroft Library.

Daughters of the American Revolution. California. MORTALITY LIST: CALIFORNIA CENSUS OF PERSONS WHO DIED DURING THE YEAR ENDING JUNE 1, 1870. San Francisco: Genealogical Records Committee, California State Society, Daughters of the American Revolution, 1961.

Typed transcript with index of about 8,470 names. Available at the DAR and the California State Library.

Colorado

Washington, D.C. DAR. "Federal Mortality Census Schedules, 1870-80: Colorado."

Also available on microfilm at DAR; NA T655:3; and GD 422, 411 Items 1-2.

Jackson, Ronald Vern, ed. MORTALITY SCHEDULE, COLORADO 1870. Salt Lake City: Accelerated Indexing Systems, 1980.

_____. MORTALITY SCHEDULE, COLORADO 1880. Bountiful, Utah: Accelerated Indexing Systems, 1980.

Denver. Division of State Archives and Public Records. "1885 Colorado State Mortality Schedules."

Also available on microfilm at NA T655:4.

Connecticut

Hartford. Connecticut State Library.   "Federal Mortality Census Schedules and Indexes, 1850-80: Connecticut."

Schedules also available on microfilm: 1850-70 at GD 234,536 Items 1-3. 1880 at GD 234,537 Item 1.

Delaware

Dover. Delaware. State Bureau of Archives and Records. "Federal Mortality Census Schedules, 1850-80: Delaware."

Also available on microfilm at NA A1155.

Vital Records

District of Columbia

Washington, D.C. DAR. "Federal Mortality Census Schedules and Indexes, 1850-80: District of Columbia."

> Indexes contain full names; about 650 for 1850, 1,050 for 1860, 1,200 for 1870, and 2,800 for 1880.
>
> Also available on microfilm:
>
> 1850-70 at DAR; NA T655:5; and GD 422,412.
> 1880 at DAR; NA T655:6; and GD 874,320 (A-K), 874,321 (L-Z).

Florida

Tallahassee. Florida State University Library. "Federal Mortality Census Schedules, 1850-80: Florida."

Washington, D.C. NA. "1885 Florida State Mortality Schedules."

Georgia

Washington, D.C. DAR. "Federal Mortality Census Schedules and Indexes, 1850-70: Georgia." 3561890.

> Indexes are transcriptions in alphabetical order; about 440 for 1850, 590 for 1860, and 600 for 1870.
>
> Also available on microfilm:
>
> 1850 at DAR; NA T655:7; and GD 422,413.
> 1860 at DAR; NA T655:8; and GD 422,414.
> 1870 at DAR; NA T655:9; and GD 422,415.

Jackson, Ronald Vern, ed. MORTALITY SCHEDULE, GEORGIA 1850. Bountiful, Utah: Accelerated Indexing Systems, 1979. 6245050. 929.3.

Shaw, Aurora C. 1850 GEORGIA MORTALITY CENSUS. Jacksonville, Fla.: The Author, 1971. 281613. 72-178003. 929/.3/758. F285.A53.

> A transcription of about 4,140 names in alphabetical order.

Washington, D.C. DAR. "Federal Mortality Census Schedules, 1880: Georgia." 3561890.

> Also available on microfilm:
>
> Reel 1 Appling - Franklin Counties at DAR; NA T655:10; and GD 422,416.
> Reel 2 Fulton - Pulaski Counties at DAR; NA T655:11; and GD 422,417.

Reel 3 Putnam - Worth Counties at DAR; NA T655:12, and GD 422,418.

Idaho

Boise. Idaho State Historical Society. "Federal Mortality Census Schedules, 1870-80: Idaho."

Idaho Genealogical Society. IDAHO TERRITORY: FEDERAL POPULATION SCHEDULES AND MORTALITY SCHEDULES, 1870. Boise: Williams Printing Co., 1973. 886903. 74-161864. 929/.3796. F745.127 1973.

   A transcription with an index of about 1,566 surnames.

Jackson, Ronald Vern, ed. MORTALITY SCHEDULE, IDAHO TERRITORY 1870. Salt Lake City: Accelerated Indexing Systems, 1980.

Idaho Genealogical Society. IDAHO TERRITORY FEDERAL POPULATION SCHEDULES AND MORTALITY SCHEDULES, 1880. Boise: Williams Printing Co., 1976. 3133535.

   A transcription with an index of over 7,452 surnames.

Jackson, Ronald Vern, ed. MORTALITY SCHEDULE, IDAHO 1880. Bountiful, Utah: Accelerated Indexing Systems, 1979.

   A transcription of 320 names in alphabetical order.

"Mortality Census of Idaho--1880." IDAHO GENEALOGICAL SOCIETY QUAR-TERLY 8 (March 1965): 8-11; (June 1965): 11-15; (September 1965): 11-14; (December 1965): 12-15; 9 (March 1966): 5-10.

   A transcription of about 295 names.

MORTALITY SCHEDULE, IDAHO 1880. N.p.: n.d. GD 979.6 V23n (book number).

   Not indexed.

Illinois

Springfield. Illinois State Archives. "Federal Mortality Census Schedules, 1850-80: Illinois."

   Also available on microfilm: 1850 at NA T1133/58. 1860 at NA T1133/59-60. 1870 at NA T1133/59-60. 1880 at NA T1133/60-64.

Jackson, Ronald Vern, ed. MORTALITY SCHEDULE, ILLINOIS 1850. Salt Lake City: Accelerated Indexing Systems, 1980.

Vital Records

Volkel, Lowell M. 1850 ILLINOIS MORTALITY SCHEDULE. 3 vols. N.p.: 1972. 601411. 73-156332. 929/.3773. F450.V58.

A transcription of 6,048 names in three alphabets.

Indiana

Indianapolis. Indiana State Library. "Federal Mortality Census Schedules and Indexes, 1850-80: Indiana."

Jackson, Ronald Vern, ed. MORTALITY SCHEDULE, INDIANA 1850. Bountiful, Utah: Accelerated Indexing Systems, 1979. 5998384. 929.3772.

Volkel, Lowell M., comp. 1850 INDIANA MORTALITY SCHEDULE. 3 vols. Danville, Ill.: n.p. 1971. 163123. 71-28416rev.72. 929.3/772. F525.V6.

A transcription of about 12,045 names in three alphabets.

Iowa

Iowa City. State Historical Society of Iowa. "Federal Mortality Census Schedules, 1850-80: Iowa."

Also available on microfilm: 1850 at NA A1156/54. 1860 at NA A1156/55. 1870 at NA A1156/56-58. 1880 at NA A1156/59-62.

Kansas

Topeka. Kansas State Historical Society. "Federal Mortality Census Schedules, 1860-80: Kansas."

Typed transcript for 1860 prepared by Ruby G. Kistler, 1945-47, available at the DAR.

Also available on microfilm at Kansas State Historical Society; and NA (1860) T1130/1, (1870) T1130/3 and 5, and (1880) T1130/6-7.

Franklin, Helen H., and Carpenter, Thelma, comps. THE MORTALITY SCHEDULE OF THE TERRITORY OF KANSAS 1860; June 1, 1959 to May 31, 1860. Topeka: Topeka Genealogical Society, n.d. 5912580. 929.39781. GD 897, 418 Item 1; duplicate copy 924,501 Item 3.

A transcription of about 1,484 names in alphabetical order.

Jackson, Ronald Vern, ed. MORTALITY SCHEDULE, KANSAS 1860. Salt Lake City: Accelerated Indexing Systems, 1980.

Franklin, Helen H., and Carpenter, Thelma, comps. 1870 MORTALITY SCHED-
ULE OF KANSAS. Topeka: Topeka Genealogical Society, 1974. 1628304.
929.3.

A transcription with an index of 4,469 names.

Jackson, Ronald Vern, ed. MORTALITY SCHEDULE, KANSAS 1870. Bountiful,
Utah: Accelerated Indexing Systems, 1979. 6240998. 929.3.

Carpenter, Thelma, and Franklin, Helen, comps. 1880 MORTALITY SCHEDULE
OF KANSAS, DEATHS OCCURRING BETWEEN JUNE 1, 1879 TO MAY 31, 1880.
44 vols. in 3. Topeka: The Authors, 1973. GD 897,418 Items 2-11; 924,
098 Items 1-14; and 973,100 Items 1-19.

_____. INDEX TO 1880 MORTALITY SCHEDULE OF KANSAS. Topeka:
Topeka Genealogical Society, 1973. 1628415. 929.3. GD 973,266 Item 4.

An index of 14,805 names with references to county names.

Jackson, Ronald Vern, ed. MORTALITY SCHEDULE, KANSAS 1880. Bountiful,
Utah: Accelerated Indexing Systems, 1979. 6240336. 929.3.

Kentucky

Washington, D.C. DAR. "Federal Mortality Census Schedules and Indexes,
1850 (Pendleton Co.--Woodford Co.) and 1860-80: Kentucky."

Indexes contain about 1,786 names for 1850, 10,098 for 1870,
and 16,650 for 1880.

Also available on microfilm:

1850 at DAR; NA T655:13; and GD 422,419, Index 873,777
Item 1.
1860 at DAR; NA T655:14; and GD 422,420, Index 873,777
Item 1.
1870 at DAR; NA T655:15; and GD 422,421 (Adair Co.--Jefferson
Co.), 422,422 (Jessamine Co.--Woodford Co.), Index 873,
777 Item 1.
1880 at DAR; NA T655:16-20; and GD 422,425 (Adair Co.--
Jackson Co.), 422,426 (Jefferson Co.--Madison Co.), 422,
427 (Meade Co.--Woodford Co.), Index (1949-50) 422,423
(A--Mere), 422,424 (Meri--Z), Index (1956) 874,320 (A--K),
874,321 (La--Z).

Jackson, Ronald Vern, ed. MORTALITY SCHEDULE, KENTUCKY 1850. Bountiful,
Utah: Accelerated Indexing Systems, 1979. 5998303. 929.3769.

Smith, Randolph N., comp. FEDERAL MORTALITY CENSUS SCHEDULES, 1860,
1870, 1880: ABSTRACT AND INDEX, ADAIR, CLINTON, CUMBERLAND,

Vital Records

METCALFE, MONROE COUNTIES, KENTUCKY. Burkesville, Ky.: Smith, 1975. 2074792. 76-354174. 929/.3769. F450.S57.

>A transcription with several indexes. Not a statewide index.

Louisiana

Washington, D.C. DAR. "Federal Mortality Census Schedules and Indexes, 1850-80: Louisiana."

>Indexes contain about 550 names for 1850, 580 for 1860, 690 for 1870, and 4,823 for 1880.

>Also available on microfilm:

>1850 at DAR; NA T655:21; and GD 422,428, Index 976.3 V23d (Book).
>1860 at DAR; NA T655:22; and GD 422,429, Index 976.3 V23d (Book).
>1870 at DAR; NA T655:23; and GD 422,430, Index 976.3 V23d (Book).
>1880 at DAR; NA T655:24-25; and GD 422,431 (Ascension-- Natchitoches Parishes and Index A--Z), 422,432 (Orleans-- Winn Parishes).

Jackson, Ronald Vern, ed. MORTALITY SCHEDULE, LOUISIANA 1850. Bountiful, Utah: Accelerated Indexing Systems, 1979. 6245003. 929.3.

Achee, Benjamin E., and Wright, Margery. INDEX TO LOUISIANA 1860 MORTALITY SCHEDULE. Shreveport: n.p., 1969. 127390. 71-21789. 929. 3/.763. F368.A62.

>A transcription of about 2,655 names in alphabetical order.

Maine

Augusta. Office of the State Archivist of Maine. "Federal Mortality Census Schedules, 1850-80: Maine."

>Also available on microfilm: 1850 at the Office of the State Archivist of Maine; and GD 009,739. 1860 at the Office of the State Archivist of Maine; and GD 009,740. 1870 at GD 009,741.

Maryland

Annapolis. State Department of Legislative Reference, Maryland State Library. "Federal Mortality Census Schedules, 1850-80: Maryland."

Massachusetts

Boston. Massachusetts State Archives. "Federal Mortality Census Schedules, 1850–80: Massachusetts."

> The Massachusetts Daughters of the American Revolution, Genealogical Records Committee prepared a typewritten two-volume transcription and index for 1850 in 1947. The index contains about 17,292 names. It is available at the DAR. Also available on microfilm: 1850–70 at NA T1204 GR19/1-3. 1850–80 at Massachusetts State Archives.

Michigan

Lansing. Michigan State Library. "Federal Mortality Census Schedule, 1850: Michigan." (microfilm copy).

> Also available on microfilm at the State Library of Ohio; and NA T1163/1.

Jackson, Ronald Vern, ed. MORTALITY SCHEDULE, MICHIGAN 1850. Bountiful, Utah: Accelerated Indexing Systems, 1979. 6240977. 929.3.

Williams, Ethel W., and Williams, E. Gray, comps. "Michigan Mortality Records for Year Ending June 1, 1850." Indexed by Evelyn O'Rourke, Lansing Chapter of the Daughters of the American Revolution. Lansing: 1961. GD 927,685 Item 1.

> A transcription and index with about 5,025 names. Also available at the DAR and the Michigan State Library.

Lansing. Michigan State Archives. "Federal Mortality Census Schedules, 1860–80: Michigan."

> Also available on microfilm at the Michigan State Archives; Michigan State Library; DAR; and NA (1860) T1165/15, (1870) T1164/26-27, and (1880) T1164/74-77.

Minnesota

Saint Paul. Minnesota Historical Society. "Federal Mortality Census Schedules, 1850–80: Minnesota."

Janssen, Edith H., comp. MORTALITY RECORDS OF MINNESOTA BY COUNTIES FROM THE TERRITORIAL PERIOD OF 1850 TO THE END OF THE YEAR 1870 WITH THE RECORDS OF ST. LOUIS COUNTY TO THE END OF YEAR 1883. Duluth: Daughters of the American Revolution, Genealogical Records Committee, 1947. GD 977.6 V23d (book number).

> Also available at the DAR.

Vital Records

Jackson, Ronald Vern, ed. MORTALITY SCHEDULE, MINNESOTA 1850. Bountiful, Utah: Accelerated Indexing Systems, 1980.

Finnell, Arthur Louis, comp. INDEX TO THE 1860 MINNESOTA MORTALITY SCHEDULE. Marshall, Minn.: Finnell, 1978. 5022144.

Jackson, Ronald Vern, ed. MORTALITY SCHEDULE, MINNESOTA 1870. Salt Lake City: Accelerated Indexing Systems, 1979.

_____. MORTALITY SCHEDULE, MINNESOTA 1880. Bountiful, Utah: Accelerated Indexing Systems, 1979. 6364629. 929.3776.

Mississippi

Jackson. Mississippi Department of Archives and History. "Federal Mortality Census Schedules, 1850-80: Mississippi."

> Also available on microfilm at the Mississippi Department of Archives and History.

Gillis, Irene S., comp. MISSISSIPPI 1850 MORTALITY SCHEDULES. Shreveport: Gillis Publication, 1973. 829202. 74-155445. 929/.3762. F340.G474.

> A transcription of about 3,106 names in alphabetical order.

Jackson, Ronald Vern, ed. MORTALITY SCHEDULE, MISSISSIPPI 1850. Bountiful, Utah: Accelerated Indexing Systems, 1979. 6245072. 929.3.

Missouri

St. Louis. Missouri State Historical Society. "Federal Mortality Census Schedules, 1850-80: Missouri."

> Also available on microfilm at the State Historical Society of Missouri, Columbia.

Ellsberry, Elizabeth Prather, comp. MORTALITY RECORDS OF MISSOURI OF 1850. Chillicothe, Mo.: n.p., n.d.

> A transcription with an index of about 1,064 names.

_____. MORTALITY RECORDS OF MISSOURI OF 1860. Chillicothe, Mo.: n.p., n.d.

> A transcription with an index of over 1,020 names.

Montana

Helena. Montana Historical Society. "Federal Mortality Census Schedules, 1870-80: Montana."

> Also available on microfilm at NA GR6. Western Montana is part of the 1860 Washington Territory census schedules.

Nebraska

Lincoln. Nebraska State Historical Society. "Federal Mortality Census Schedules, 1860-70: Nebraska."

> Also available on microfilm: 1860 at NA T1128/1-2. 1870 at NA T1128/3-4.

James, Jane Emerson, comp. EIGHTH CENSUS OF THE UNITED STATES, 1860: NEBRASKA TERRITORY MORTALITY SCHEDULES. Huntsville, Ark.: Century Enterprises, 1972. 1224386. 929.4.

> A transcription of about 421 names in alphabetical order.

Lincoln. Nebraska State Historical Society. "Federal Mortality Census Schedules and Index, 1880: Nebraska."

> Also available on microfilm at NA T1128/14 (Adams Co.--Saunders Co.), T1128/15 (Seward Co.--York Co. and unorganized territory); Index T1128/42 (Allen--Ellsworth), T1128/43 (Foote--Morris), T1128/44 (Namaha--Wyanbotte).

Washington, D.C. NA. "1885 Nebraska State Mortality Schedules."

> NA Record Group M352.

Nevada

Reno. Nevada Historical Society. "Federal Mortality Census Schedules, 1870-80: Nevada."

> Also available on microfilm at the Nevada Historical Society.

Daughters of the American Revolution. Nevada. Sage Brush Chapter, Reno. "Federal Death Records of Nevada, June 1, 1869 to June 1, 1870." Reno: 1944-45.

> A typewritten transcription with an index of about 700 names. Available at the DAR; NA; and GD 979.3 V23f (Book number).

Jackson, Ronald Vern, ed. MORTALITY SCHEDULE, NEVADA 1870. Salt Lake City: Accelerated Indexing Systems, 1980.

Vital Records

New Hampshire

Concord. New Hampshire State Library. "Federal Mortality Census Schedules, 1850-80: New Hampshire."
   Also available on microfilm at GD 015,580 Items 1-3.

New Jersey

Trenton. New Jersey Archives and History Bureau. "Federal Mortality Census Schedules, 1850-80: New Jersey."
   Also available on microfilm:
   1850 at DAR; NA GR21:1; and GD 802,952.
   1860 at DAR; NA GR21:1; and GD 802,952.
   1870 at DAR; NA GE21:1-2; and GD 802,953.
   1880 at DAR; NA GR21:2-4; and GD 802,954-802,955.

New Mexico

Santa Fe. New Mexico Historical Society. "Federal Mortality Census Schedules, 1850-70: New Mexico."

Washington, D.C. NA. "1885 New Mexico State Mortality Schedules."

New York

Albany. New York State Library. "Federal Mortality Census Schedules, 1850-80: New York."

North Carolina

Raleigh. North Carolina Division of Archives and History. "Federal Mortality Census Schedules, 1850-80: North Carolina."
   Also available on microfilm: 1850 at NA GR1/1. 1860 at NA GR1/2. 1870 at NA GR1/3. 1880 at NA GR1/4-5.

North Dakota

Jackson, Ronald Vern, ed. MORTALITY SCHEDULE, DAKOTA TERRITORY 1880. Salt Lake City: Accelerated Indexing Systems, 1980.

Merrick, Velda, comp. "Mortality Records: Persons Who Died in the Year Ending 31 May 1880, Dakota Territory (North and South Dakota)." Boise, Idaho: 1953.

A transcription with an index of more than 1,020 surnames. Also available on microfilm at NA; and GD 020,156.

Bismarck. State Historical Society of North Dakota. "1885 Dakota Territory Mortality Schedules."

> May be a copy. Also available on microfilm at NA GR27/3-4 (may be incomplete).

Ohio

Columbus. State Library of Ohio. "Federal Mortality Census Schedules, 1850-60, 1880: Ohio" (microfilm copy).

> Also available on microfilm:

> 1850 at the Ohio Historical Society; NA T1159/14; and GD 978, 351 (Hamilton Co.--Marion Co.), 1,005,093 (Medina Co.--Wyandot Co.), Adams Co.--Guernsey Co. is missing.
> 1860 at the Ohio Historical Society; NA T1159/29-30; and GD 1,005,094 (Adams Co.--Huron Co.), 1,005,095 (Jackson Co.--Wyandot Co.).
> 1880 at the Ohio Historical Society; NA T1159/102-104; and GD 978,352 (Adams Co.--Clinton Co.), 978,353 (Columbiana Co.--Darke Co.), 978,354 (Defiance Co.--Geauga Co.), Greene Co.--Wyandot Co. is missing.

Jackson, Ronald Vern. MORTALITY SCHEDULE, OHIO 1850. Bountiful, Utah: Accelerated Indexing Systems, 1979. 5979521. 929.3771.

Oregon

Salem. Oregon State Archives Division. "Federal Mortality Census Schedules, 1850-80: Oregon."

> Also available on microfilm at the Oregon State Library.

Daughters of the American Revolution. Chemeketa Chapter. MORTALITY SCHEDULES FROM UNITED STATES CENSUS ORIGINAL RECORDS: 1850, TERRITORY OF OREGON, 1860, 1870, 1880 STATE OF OREGON. INDEX TO MORTALITY SCHEDULES FROM UNITED STATES CENSUS ORIGINAL RECORDS: 1850, TERRITORY OF OREGON, 1860, 1870, 1880 STATE OF OREGON. Compiled by the Oregon State Library. Salem: Oregon State Library, 1941. GD 897,219.

> One index of 1,440 names for all four schedules.

Goldmann, Judy. "Mortality Schedule: 1850 Federal Census, Territory of Oregon. Names of Persons Who Have Died in the Twelve Months Previous to the 1850 Census Enumeration." GENEALOGICAL FORUM OF PORTLAND, OREGON BULLETIN 23 (February 1974): 107-8.

A transcription of 47 names.

_____. "Mortality Schedule, 1860 Federal Census, State of Oregon." GE-NEALOGICAL FORUM OF PORTLAND, OREGON BULLETIN 25 (September 1975): 7-10, 29-32, 47-50, 69-71.

A transcription of about 455 names.

Pennsylvania

Harrisburg. Pennsylvania State Library. "Federal Mortality Census Schedules, 1850-80: Pennsylvania."

Also available on microfilm:

1850 at NA T956; and GD 899,736 (Adams Co.--Northumberland Co.), 899,737 (Philadelphia--York Co.).
1860 at NA T956; and GD 899,738 (Adams Co.--Erie Co.), 899,739 (Fayette Co.--York Co.).
1870 at NA T956; and GD 899,740 (Adams Co.--Elk Co.), 899, 741 (Erie Co.--Northumberland Co.), 899,742 (Perry Co.--York Co.).
1880 at NA T956; and GD 899,743-899,748.

Jackson, Ronald Vern, ed. MORTALITY SCHEDULE, PENNSYLVANIA 1870. Bountiful, Utah: Accelerated Indexing Systems, 1979. 6003157. 929.3748.

Rhode Island

Providence. Rhode Island State Library. "Federal Mortality Census Schedules, 1850-80: Rhode Island."

The Rhode Island Daughters of the American Revolution, Genealogical Records Committee prepared transcriptions and indexes for 1860-80 in 1946-47. The 1880 index contains about 3,840 names.

Daughters of the American Revolution. Rhode Island. MORTALITY SCHEDULES OF 1860-80 FOR RHODE ISLAND. Providence: Genealogical Records Committee, 1946-47.

A transcription and index available at the DAR. The 1880 index contains about 3,840 names. The Rhode Island State Library and the State Archives report that they do not have or know where the manuscript copies of the 1850-1880 mortality schedules are available.

South Carolina

Columbia. South Carolina Department of Archives and History. "Federal Mortality Census Schedules, 1850-80: South Carolina."

Also available on microfilm: 1850 at DAR; and NA GR22/1.
1860 at DAR; and NA GR22/1. 1870 at DAR; and NA GR22/2.
1880 at DAR; and NA GR22/3.

South Dakota

Pierre. South Dakota State Historical Society. "Federal Mortality Census
Schedules, 1870-80: Dakota."

Jackson, Ronald Vern, ed. MORTALITY SCHEDULE, DAKOTA TERRITORY
1880. Salt Lake City: Accelerated Indexing Systems, 1980.

Merrick, Velda, comp. "Mortality Records: Persons Who Died in the Year Ending
31 May 1880, Dakota Territory (North and South Dakota)." Boise, Idaho: 1953.

> A transcription with an index of more than 1,020 surnames. Also
> available on microfilm at NA; and GD 020,156.

Pierre. South Dakota State Historical Society. "1885 Dakota Territory Mortality Schedules."

> May be a copy. Also available on microfilm at NA GR27/3-4
> (may be incomplete).

Tennessee

Washington, D.C. DAR. "Federal Mortality Census Schedules and Indexes,
1850-60: Tennessee."

> Indexes contain full names, about 700 for 1850 and 930 for 1860.
> Also available on microfilm:
> 1850 at DAR; NA T655/26; and GD 422,433.
> 1860 at DAR; NA T655/27; and GD 422,434.

Jackson, Ronald Vern, ed. MORTALITY SCHEDULE, TENNESSEE 1850.
Bountiful, Utah: Accelerated Indexing Systems, 1979. 6184800. 929.3768.

Washington, D.C. DAR. "Federal Mortality Census Schedules, 1880: Tennessee."

> Also available on microfilm at DAR; NA T655/28-30; and GD
> 422,435 (Anderson Co.--Greene Co.), 422,436 (Grundy Co.--
> Moore Co.), 422,437 (Morgan Co.--Wilson Co.).

Texas

Austin. Archives Division, Texas State Library. "Federal Mortality Census
Schedules, 1850-80: Texas" (microfilm copy).

Vital Records

Also available on microfilm at: 1850 at NA T1134/53-54, GR 2/1-2. 1860 at NA T1134/54-55, GR2/2-3. 1870 at NA T11 34/55-56, GR2/3-4. 1880 at NA T1134/56-60, GR2/4-8.

Jackson, Ronald Vern, ed. MORTALITY SCHEDULE, TEXAS 1850. Bountiful, Utah: Accelerated Indexing Systems, 1979. 6240988. 929.3.

Woods, Frances Jerome. 1850 MORTALITY SCHEDULES OF TEXAS. Austin: Printing Craft, 1965. 1278792. NUC67-25267. 976.4. GD 1,000,607 Item 7.

A transcription of about twenty-three hundred names in alphabetical order.

Jackson, Ronald Vern, ed. MORTALITY SCHEDULE, TEXAS 1860. Bountiful, Utah: Accelerated Indexing Systems, 1979. 6364213. 929.3764.

Woods, Frances Jerome. 1860 MORTALITY SCHEDULES OF TEXAS. Austin: Printing Craft, 1966. GD 1,000,607 Item 8.

A transcription of about 6,256 names in alphabetical order.

Utah

Jackson, Ronald Vern, ed. MORTALITY SCHEDULE, UTAH 1850. Salt Lake City: Accelerated Indexing Systems, 1980.

_____. MORTALITY SCHEDULE, UTAH 1860. Salt Lake City: Accelerated Indexing Systems, 1980.

_____. MORTALITY SCHEDULE, UTAH 1870. Salt Lake City: Accelerated Indexing Systems, 1980.

Salt Lake City. Utah State Archives and Records Service. "Federal Mortality Census Schedules, 1870: Utah."

Also available on microfilm at NA GR7; GD 865,236; the Utah State Archives and Records Sercice; and the Archives Division, Texas State Library.

Vermont

Montpelier. Vermont Historical Society. "Federal Mortality Census Schedules, 1850-60, 1880: Vermont."

Daughters of the American Revolution. Vermont. MORTALITY SCHEDULES OF 1850. Copied from records at the State House by Miss Carrie Hollister and Mrs. U.W. Corker of the Marquis de Lafayette Chapter, Montpelier, National Society, Daughters of the American Revolution. 17th Book of Records, no. 3. Montpelier: Genealogical Records Committee, 1948.

Includes an index of about 3,375 names. Available at the Law and Documents Unit, Vermont Department of Libraries. Also available at the DAR in the Annual State Conference, Vermont Daughters of the American Revolution, 1948, vol. 17; and GD 850,115.

_____. MORTALITY SCHEDULES OF 1860. Copied from records at the State House by Miss Carrie Hollister and Mrs. U.W. Corker of the Marquis de Lafayette Chapter, Montpelier, National Society, Daughters of the American Revolution. 18th Book of Records, no. 3. Montpelier: Genealogical Records Committee, 1950.

Includes an index of about 3,108 names. Available at the Law and Documents Unit, Vermont Department of Libraries. Also available at the DAR in the Annual State Conference, Vermont Daughters of the American Revolution, 1950, vol. 18; and GD 850,115.

Montpelier. Vermont Historical Society. "Federal Mortality Census Schedules, 1870: Vermont" (microfilm copy).

Also available on microfilm at NA GR7; the Vermont State Library; and the Archives Division, Texas State Library.

Virginia

Richmond. Virginia State Library, Archives and Records Division. "Federal Mortality Census Schedules, 1850, 1870-80: Virginia" (microfilm copy).

Also available on microfilm: 1850 at NA T1132/1. 1870 at NA T1132/10. 1880 at NA T1132/18-19.

Durham, North Carolina. Duke University Library. "Federal Mortality Census Schedules, 1860: Virginia."

Also available on microfilm at NA T1132/5.

Washington

Olympia. Washington State Library. "Federal Mortality Census Schedules, 1860-80: Washington."

Also available on microfilm at NA T1154/3.

Daughters of the American Revolution. Washington. MORTALITY SCHEDULES OF WASHINGTON TERRITORY, FROM WASHINGTON STATE LIBRARY. Indexed by Mrs. Robert E. Clubb (Erma Chandler Clubb). n.p.: 1956.

Available at the DAR. The index contains 1,040 names in one alphabetical order for all three schedules, 1860-80.

Vital Records

Jackson, Ronald Vern, ed. MORTALITY SCHEDULE, WASHINGTON 1880. Bountiful, Utah: Accelerated Indexing Systems, 1979.

West Virginia

Charleston. West Virginia Archives and History Division. "Federal Mortality Census Schedules, 1850-80: West Virginia."

> Also available on microfilm: 1850 at GD 944,493 Item 1. 1860 at GD 944,493 Item 2.

Jackson, Ronald Vern, ed. MORTALITY SCHEDULE, WEST VIRGINIA 1850. Bountiful, Utah: Accelerated Indexing Systems, 1979. 5998158. 929.3754.

_____. MORTALITY SCHEDULE, WEST VIRGINIA 1860. Bountiful, Utah: Accelerated Indexing Systems, 1979. 5998226. 929.3754.

_____. MORTALITY SCHEDULE, WEST VIRGINIA 1870. Bountiful, Utah: Accelerated Indexing Systems, 1979. 5998093. 929.3754.

Wisconsin

Madison. State Historical Society of Wisconsin Library. "Federal Mortality Census Schedules, 1850-80: Wisconsin."

> Also available on microfilm at the State Historical Society of Wisconsin Library and Archives.

Daughters of the American Revolution. Wisconsin. John Bell Chapter. MORTALITY SCHEDULES OF 1850 FOR WISCONSIN. Madison: Genealogical Records Committee, 1945.

> Available at the DAR and the State Historical Society of Wisconsin Library.

_____. MORTALITY SCHEDULES OF 1860 FOR WISCONSIN. Madison: Genealogical Records Committee, 1947.

> Available at the DAR, the State Historical Society of Wisconsin Library, and the Milwaukee Public Library.

_____. MORTALITY SCHEDULES OF 1870 FOR WISCONSIN. Madison: Genealogical Records Committee, 1948.

> Available at the DAR, the State Historical Society of Wisconsin Library, and the Milwaukee Public Library.

Wyoming

Cheyenne. Wyoming State Archives, Museums and Historical Department, Archives and Records. "Federal Mortality Census Schedules, 1870-80: Wyoming."

> Transcriptions made by the Cheyenne Chapter of the Daughters of the American Revolution in 1944 and 1947 are available at the DAR.

> Also available on microfilm at the Wyoming State Archives, Museums and Historical Department, Archives and Records.

Jackson, Ronald Vern, ed. MORTALITY SCHEDULE, WYOMING 1880. Bountiful, Utah: Accelerated Indexing Systems, 1979.

The subject headings relative to mortality schedules are as follows:

LC	IOWA--GENEALOGY--SOURCES
	IOWA--CENSUS (year)
	MORTALITY
Sears	MORTALITY
GD	IOWA - VITAL RECORDS

WPA SURVEYS

The inventories of church, city, and county records of the Historical Records Surveys of the Work Project Administration are very incomplete. Those inventories that were completed and mimeographed or printed are listed in the following bibliography:

Child, Sargent Burrage, and Holmes, Dorothy P. CHECK LIST OF HISTORICAL RECORDS SURVEY PUBLICATIONS: BIBLIOGRAPHY OF RESEARCH PROJECTS REPORTS. W.P.A. Technical Series. Research and Records Bibliography, no. 7. Washington, D.C.: Historical Records Survey, 1943. Reprint. Baltimore: Genealogical Publishing Co., 1969. 47927. 69-17126. 016.973/08. Z1223. Z7C52.

Many inventories are also listed in Filby's AMERICAN & BRITISH GENEALOGY & HERALDRY (p. 11).

STATE ARCHIVES

No attempt has been made in this book to cover the holdings of the state archives of the nation. Many archives have guides to the collections, and many of these guides are listed in Filby's AMERICAN & BRITISH GENEALOGY & HERALDRY (p. 11).

Some of the materials in state archives are useful to genealogists. Most of the how-to-do-it books include some references to specific archival materials of value in genealogical research.

The following is the most comprehensive directory of the nation's archives:

U.S. National Historical Publications and Records Commission. DIRECTORY OF ARCHIVES AND MANUSCRIPT REPOSITORIES. Washington, D.C.: 1978. 4493072. 78-23870. 016.091/025/73. CD3020.U54.

However, the above work must be supplemented by the following directory that is still not superseded:

U.S. National Historical Publications Commission. A GUIDE TO ARCHIVES AND MANUSCRIPTS IN THE UNITED STATES. Edited by Phillip M. Hamer. New Haven: Yale University Press, 1961. 2594259. 61-6878. 025.171. CD3022.A45.

FOREIGN VITAL RECORDS

Civil registration, the equivalent of our vital statistics in many foreign countries, is usually carefully explained in the various how-to-do-it research guides for each country. Because of the widespread practice of state religions, the church records or parish registers that preceeded civil registration in most countries are also very useful and, again, are explained in the research guides.

Certificates may also be obtained from free western European countries. However, the cost in some countries is very high.

FOREIGN-LANGUAGE CORRESPONDENCE

Correspondence to foreign countries can be difficult for genealogists, as many have little or no language ability. Many countries have enough English language readers that letters in English will be answered.

Unless otherwise noted, all of the following articles, books, and parts of books contain sample letters for foreign research, along with an English translation of the correspondence.

Austria

"Instructions to Fill Out Form Letter." In HANDY GUIDE TO AUSTRIAN GENEALOGICAL RECORDS, by Dagmar Senekovic, p. 11. Logan, Utah: Everton Publishers, 1979. 5743248. 929.3426.

    Contains a sample letter to the parish priest.

Germany

Jensen, Larry O. A GENEALOGICAL HANDBOOK OF GERMAN RESEARCH.
Rev. ed. Pleasant Grove, Utah: Jensen, 1978. 3763987. CS614.J36 1978.

>   Appendix D, pages 198-200 has German letters that can be used
>   in Austria, Germany, and Switzerland.

Switzerland

"French Sample Letter to Swiss Registrar's Office." In HANDY GUIDE TO
SWISS GENEALOGICAL RECORDS, by Jared H. Suess, p. 21. Logan, Utah:
Everton Publishers, 1978.

"German Sample Letter to Send to Swiss Registrar's Office." In HANDY GUIDE
TO SWISS GENEALOGICAL RECORDS, by Jared H. Suess, pp. 19-20. Logan,
Utah: Everton Publishers, 1978.

Suess, Jared H. "Correspondence to Switzerland." GENEALOGICAL HELPER
33 (September-October 1979): 13, 93-94.

>   Contains sample German-language letters to offices of civil regis-
>   tration and to the parish priest.

Genealogical Department, 50 East North Temple Street, Salt Lake City, Utah
81450, has sample letters for the following countries and/or languages:

Finland	Parish Minister
French	Mayor
German	Parish Minister and Civil Registration Office
Italy	Registry Office, Office of Vital Statistics, and Parish Priest.

They are willing to share these letters with interested libraries and researchers.
They also have instructions on how to write the Embassies of Czechoslovakia
and the USSR for vital record information in these countries.

COLLECTION DEVELOPMENT

Every U.S. library should have the WHERE TO WRITE FOR pamphlets, along
with THE HANDY BOOK FOR GENEALOGISTS. Libraries serving many genealogists should also have the Stemmons books and Brown's HANDY INDEX.
Larger libraries, in addition, should acquire Kirkham's SURVEY OF AMERICAN
CHURCH RECORDS.

SUMMARY AND SEARCH STRATEGY

Genealogists should be encouraged to go to a branch library of the Genealogical Department and search first the COMPUTER FILE INDEX, the PARISH AND VITAL RECORDS LISTINGS, the MICROFILM CARD CATALOG, and submit a "Reference Questionnaire" inquiring about recent microfilming of vital records in their areas of interest. Then they should write either the state office of vital statistics or the county court house, for nineteenth-century records, as is necessary. Short form certificates should be requested when they are cheaper than the full form. However, genealogists may want to request full forms for direct line ancestors.

The family cards, arranged by geographical location, that are used for searching local history bibliographies, as explained in the next chapter, can also be used for searching the COMPUTER FILE INDEX, the PARISH AND VITAL RECORDS LISTINGS, and the MICROFILM CARD CATALOG. Genealogists may need to make additional cards for individuals in order to more successfully search the COMPUTER FILE INDEX.

Chapter 8

FINDING FAMILY HISTORIES

The beginning genealogist should be encouraged to determine if a family history of his family has been published or is available as a manuscript or part of an oral history interview. If a family history is well documented, a genealogist may find that a great deal of his research has been completed. If it is not well documented, then the data contained therein must be verified. Nevertheless, family histories can be a time saving asset to genealogists. The following bibliographies are listed in order of importance.

BIBLIOGRAPHIES

U.S. Library of Congress. GENEALOGIES IN THE LIBRARY OF CONGRESS: A BIBLIOGRAPHY. Edited by Marion J. Kaminkow. 3 vols. Baltimore: Magna Carta Book Co., 1972-77. 315166. 74-187078. 016.929/1. Z5319. U53. Vol. 3 Supplement only, 1977. 3120740. 76-151910.

> A search of this excellent bibliography is essential. It lists over twenty-three thousand family histories published in the United States, Great Britain, Germany, France, Scandinavia, Spain, Canada, Australia, Latin America, Poland, Netherlands, Italy, Portugal, and Asia. It also includes unpublished manuscripts and genealogical materials in books that are not especially genealogical in nature. It is arranged alphabetically by family surname with nearly thirty thousand references from variations in spelling and from one or two collateral family surnames to the surname for which the majority of a book is written. Each original volume has an addendum which must be checked. The materials listed therein do not circulate nor are they available on interlibrary loan from the Library of Congress. This bibliography supersedes the microcard edition of AMERICAN AND ENGLISH GENEALOGIES IN THE LIBRARY OF CONGRESS (Middletown, Connecticut, Godfrey Memorial Library, 1954, 21,218 entries) and the second edition (Washington, D.C., the Library of Congress, 1919; reprinted, Baltimore, Genealogical Publishing Co., 1967, 7,000 entries).

The LIBRARY OF CONGRESS SHELFLIST, MICROFICHE EDITION: C, GENEALOGY, HERALDRY, ARCHAEOLOGY, BIOGRAPHY, containing the majority of the Library of Congress' family histories, is available from University Microfilms International. It is inexpensive but difficult for patrons to use, as it contains no references. It also excludes some family histories that are classified in the CS portion of the Library of Congress classification scheme.

At least one set of Kaminkow's bibliography should be in every library cooperative, network, system, or local geographical area. Libraries that cannot afford Kaminkow might consider purchasing the LIBRARY OF CONGRESS SHELFLIST, MICROFICHE EDITION: C.

Genealogical Department of the Church of Jesus Christ of Latter-day Saints. MICROFILM CARD CATALOG: FAMILY HISTORY. 52 reels. Salt Lake City: 1974. Not for sale.

This catalog is available at all Genealogical Department branch libraries, and microfilm copies of family histories may be borrowed for use in these libraries for a small handling and postage fee. It is arranged alphabetically by family surname and contains an estimated twenty-one thousand titles and forty-two thousand added entries. The branch libraries may also send reference question- naires to the Genealogical Department requesting that indexes of specific books that are not yet on microfilm be checked for in- dividual names, requesting that a book be microfilmed if it is not copyrighted or no longer under copyright, or requesting that specific pages be photoduplicated for a small fee. Many of the branch libraries of the Genealogical Department are listed annually in the July-August issue of the GENEALOGICAL HELPER. A call to any Church of Jesus Christ of Latter-day Saints, listed in the white pages or in the yellow pages under "Churches," can also assist to determine the location of the nearest branch library. Genealogical Department, 50 East North Temple Street, Salt Lake City, Utah 84150, will, of course, send anyone, upon request, the location of local branch libraries in their area.

New York (City). Public Library. Local History and Genealogy Division. DICTIONARY CATALOG OF THE LOCAL HISTORY AND GENEALOGY DIVI- SION. 18 vols. Boston: G.K. Hall, 1974. 1661682. 75-307060. 016. 929/1. Z881.N59 1974.

The estimated twenty-six thousand family histories listed in this catalog are not available on interlibrary loan. Roger Scanland, in his article, "A Guide to the Use of Kaminkow's GENEALOGIES IN THE LIBRARY OF CONGRESS," GENEALOGICAL JOURNAL 6 (1977): 100, indicates that the New York Public Library catalog contains more foreign-language family histories than Kaminkow's bibliography, as well as many English-language family histories not listed in Kaminkow.

A comparative sample study of Kaminkow's bibliography and these catalogs and
the others listed in this chapter indicates that of the three largest Kaminkow's
bibliography is the most economical to own; the New York Public Library catalog has more family histories and more that are unique to their collection; and
that the Genealogical Department catalog has more added entries. Kaminkow
contains 40 percent of the family histories available and 18 percent of its titles
are unique to its collection. The New York Public Library catalog has 43
percent of the histories and 25 percent are unique. The Genealogical Department has 38 percent of the histories and 23 percent are unique. Details of
the study are given at the end of this chapter, p. 117.

SEARCH STRATEGY

In preparation for using these catalogs and the others listed in this chapter,
genealogists should be encouraged to prepare cards or single sheets of paper
for all families to be researched. Each should include, besides the surname,
the names of the counties and states in which the family has lived, and the
names and years of birth and death of prominent family members. Such data
often appear in the notes in these bibliographies and may assist in identifying
a researcher's family. A single family surname or all families may be searched
at any one time. Genealogists should search at least the three largest bibliographies listed above.

Genealogists should also be encouraged to prepare bibliographic cards or something similar for the entries that they find and may later wish to consult. The
call numbers and, when provided, the Library of Congress card order numbers
should be included to facilitate future interlibrary loans, research in any of
the above libraries, and the checking of additional library collections. Both
the author's name and the family surname should appear plainly enough on the
card so that the cards may be refiled either by author or surname. These cards
can later serve as a record of family histories consulted.

SUPPLEMENTAL CATALOGS AND BIBLIOGRAPHIES

U.S. Library of Congress. LIBRARY OF CONGRESS CATALOGS: SUBJECT
CATALOG. Washington, D.C.: 1950--. Quarterly.

> This catalog can be checked quarterly and/or annually for family
> histories that have been published since the latest supplement of
> GENEALOGIES IN THE LIBRARY OF CONGRESS: A BIBLIOG-
> RAPHY. The catalog includes family histories under the surnames
> (example: SMITH FAMILY).

Long Island Historical Society. Library. CATALOGUE OF THE AMERICAN
GENEALOGIES IN THE LIBRARY. Prepared under the direction of Emma
Toedteberg. Brooklyn: 1935. Reprint. Baltimore: Genealogical Publishing
Co., 1969. 34490. 79-81185. 916.9291/0973. Z5313.U5L8 1969.

Contains 9,051 noncirculating family histories. A search of its
supplement (pages 583–603) and the manuscript section (pages
605–60) is also necessary.

New England Historic Genealogical Society. THE CATALOG TO THE CIRCU-
LATING COLLECTION OF THE NEW ENGLAND HISTORIC GENEALOGICAL
SOCIETY. 2d ed. 3 vols. Boston: 1977. 3444620. 77-373861. 016.929/
373. Z5313.U5N38 1977.

Volumes 1 and 2 contain 5,724 family histories that are duplicate
copies of the society's collection and which circulate by mail to
its members for a service fee.

Barrett, Ellen C. A CATALOGUE OF PRINTED AND MANUSCRIPT GENE-
ALOGIES AVAILABLE IN THE LOS ANGELES PUBLIC LIBRARY. Los Angeles:
Los Angeles Public Library, 1965. 1727100. NUC 68-103340.

Contains about thirty-eight hundred family histories. Its supplement precedes the body of the catalog.

California. State Library. Sacramento. Sutro Branch, San Francisco. LOCAL
HISTORY AND GENEALOGY SHELFLIST. With a preface and introduction by
J. Carlyle Parker. 2 reels. Modesto, Calif.: Modesto Branch Geneal-
ogical Library, 1973.

Among the titles listed are about thirty-one hundred family histories. The shelf list contains no see references. Most materials
listed in this shelf list circulate on interlibrary loan within the
state of California. The state librarian has expressed her willing-
ness to circulate genealogical materials to other states if they
would reciprocate.

THE AMERICAN GENEALOGIST, BEING A CATALOGUE OF FAMILY HISTORIES.
A BIBLIOGRAPHY OF AMERICAN GENEALOGY, OR A LIST OF THE TITLE
PAGES OF BOOKS AND PAMPHLETS ON FAMILY HISTORY, PUBLISHED IN
AMERICA, FROM 1771 TO DATE. 5th ed. Albany, N.Y.: Joel Munsell's
Sons, 1900. Reprint. Detroit: Gale Research Co., 1975. Baltimore: Ge-
nealogical Publishing Co., 1971. 1176059. 159119. 74-34247. 74-27389.
016.9291. Z5313.U5A7.

Contains about 2,842 family histories but is out of date.

Draughon, Wallace R., and Johnson, William Perry, comps. NORTH CAROLINA
GENEALOGICAL REFERENCE: A RESEARCH GUIDE FOR ALL GENEALOGISTS,
BOTH AMATEUR AND PROFESSIONAL. 2d ed. Durham: The Authors, 1966.
Reprint. Durham: The Authors, 1973. 1437874. 3525451. 66-8377. 016.9291.
Z5313.U6N63 1966.

Pages 79–148 contain entries to 2,606 family histories and printed
genealogies that were housed in six North Carolina libraries in
1965. The libraries that hold the books are identified, and the

coverage is not limited to North Carolina families. There are numerous see references in the surname index to the collateral families that appear in most of the books. Pages 150-71 contain entries to 526 manuscript collections in the state with, again, in the surname index, many see references to collateral families.

St. Louis. Public Library. GENEALOGICAL MATERIAL AND LOCAL HISTORIES IN THE ST. LOUIS PUBLIC LIBRARY. Rev. ed. By Georgia Gambull. St. Louis Public Library, 1965. 432954. 68-4741. 016.9293. Z5319.S21 1966.

Contains approximately twenty-two hundred family histories (pp. 286-356). A few see references are included.

Glenn, Thomas Allen, comp. A LIST OF SOME AMERICAN GENEALOGIES WHICH HAVE BEEN PRINTED IN BOOK FORM. 1897. Reprint. Baltimore: Genealogical Publishing Co., 1969. 33387. 78-76815. 016.9291. Z5313. U5G5 1969.

Contains about 2,130 family histories. Use of this very out-of-date bibliography entails the checking of its two appendixes.

Thomson, Theodore Radford, comp. A CATALOGUE OF BRITISH FAMILY HISTORIES. 3d ed. Rutland, Vt.: Charles E. Tuttle Co., 1976. 2596090. 75-45516. 016.929/2/0941. Z5313.G69T4 1976 CS414.

Contains about twenty-one hundred English, Scots, Welsh, and Irish family histories.

Brown, Stuart E., Jr., comp. VIRGINIA GENEALOGIES, A TRIAL LIST OF PRINTED BOOKS AND PAMPHLETS. Berryville, Va.: Virginia Book Co., 1967. 1720173. 67-7956. 016.9292/0973. Z5313.U6V76.

Contains 1,962 family histories and numerous see references in its index.

MANUSCRIPT CATALOG

The personal papers, records, letters, Bibles, diaries, manuscript biographical sketches, and miscellaneous newspaper clippings that are found in a family home or the homes of relatives constitute excellent family research materials. Some of these materials find their way into the manuscript collections of research libraries and are listed in the following sources.

THE NATIONAL UNION CATALOG OF MANUSCRIPT COLLECTIONS. Washington, D.C.: Library of Congress, 1959-- . Annual. 1759448. 62-17486. 016.091. Z6620.U5N3.

Finding Family Histories

Most of the collections described in this catalog do not circulate. Those available on microfilm may be purchased and possibly are available on interlibrary loan. However, use of these materials more often requires traveling to the repository or the hiring of a researcher to consult the collection. Several cumulative indexes are available for this catalog. They can be searched by surname in the regular alphabetical order or under the "Genealogy" section which lists family genealogies by surname. Index entries refer to collection entries (examples: Cary family, Genealogy. 70-437; and Genealogy, Cary family. 70-437). The Library of Congress reports that at the present there are 37,600 collections in 990 repositories described in this catalog. There are over 5,100 family collections listed in its "Genealogy" sections.

SUPPLEMENTAL BIBLIOGRAPHIES, DIRECTORIES, AND GUIDES

U.S. National Historical Publication and Records Commission. DIRECTORY OF ARCHIVES AND MANUSCRIPT REPOSITORIES. Washington, D.C.: 1978. 4493072. 78-23870. 016.091/025/73. CD3020.U54.

This directory does not supersede the Hamer GUIDE TO ARCHIVES (below). It contains 2,675 depositories and lists many family manuscript collections in its index.

Hale, Richard Walden, Jr. GUIDE TO PHOTOCOPIED HISTORICAL MATERIALS IN THE UNITED STATES AND CANADA. Ithaca, N.Y.: Published for the American Historical Association by the Cornell University Press, 1961. 577684. 61-17269. Z6209.H3.

This guide includes a section of "personal papers" for many countries of the world and states and provinces of the United States and Canada. The index also identifies in one alphabetical order photocopied collections of letters and diaries by the name of the writer.

U.S. National Historical Publications Commission. A GUIDE TO ARCHIVES AND MANUSCRIPTS IN THE UNITED STATES. Edited by Philip M. Hamer. New Haven: Yale University Press, 1961. 2594259. 61-6878. 025.171. CD3022.A45.

This guide briefly reports the holdings of thirteen hundred depositories. The papers of over seventy-six hundred individuals of note are reported and listed in its index.

Matthews, William. AMERICAN DIARIES IN MANUSCRIPT, 1580-1954, A DESCRIPTIVE BIBLIOGRAPHY. Athens: University of Georgia Press, 1974. 987972. 73-76782. 016.92/0073. Z5305.U5M32.

Contains 5,022 diaries, of which an estimated 80 percent are not listed in the NATIONAL UNION CATALOG OF MANUSCRIPT COLLECTIONS.

_____. AMERICAN DIARIES: AN ANNOTATED BIBLIOGRAPHY OF AMERICAN DIARIES WRITTEN PRIOR TO THE YEAR 1861. Boston: J.S. Canner and Co., 1959. 577295. 59-13345. Z5305.U5M3 1959.

> Contains over twenty-four hundred diaries.

OTHER MANUSCRIPT CATALOGS

Many universities and archives have published catalogs of their holdings. Librarians should encourage interested genealogists to consult the card catalogs of large research libraries in their locale and check for such printed catalogs under the subject heading, "MANUSCRIPTS--(Name of state or country)--(Often subdivided again by the name of a city)--CATALOGS."

ORAL HISTORY

Another useful source for family history research is the tape recording of members of families and the utilization of oral history transcriptions that are available in many research collections.

Meckler, Alan, and McMullin, Ruth, comps. ORAL HISTORY COLLECTIONS. New York: Bowker, 1975. 1144745. 74-32128. 016.9098/025. A13.M4.

> This directory is the most comprehensive source for locating oral history transcriptions. It is not a bibliography but a subject index to oral history collections and their major holdings. Some oral history collections are included in the NATIONAL UNION CATALOG OF MANUSCRIPT COLLECTIONS (p. 109); however, at the present time the above work is superior in its coverage and should be used as the nearest source to a comprehensive bibliography of oral history.

The interlibrary loan of oral history transcriptions is limited; but some libraries do circulate them, and that information is included in the above directory. Some oral history transcriptions are also on microfilm and may be purchased. A few microfilm copies may be borrowed on interlibrary loan. The Microfilming Corporation of America, 21 Harristown Road, Glen Rock, New Jersey 07452 has produced in microform over one thousand oral history interviews. Many collections, however, can only be consulted by a visit or by hiring someone. Some additional information concerning oral histories is covered in the chapter, "Sources Listing Ancestors as Families."

INDEXES

Many family histories are indexed in various genealogical name indexes. Please consult the chapters "Genealogical Name Indexes" (p. 119) and "Genealogical

Periodicals and Periodical Indexes" (p. 125), for these indexes. Genealogists should be encouraged to consult name indexes, as many collateral families are indexed therein. As most bibliographies and catalogs do not contain references to all collateral families in a family history, indexing is necessary to provide genealogists with this needed information.

INTERLIBRARY LOAN

NATIONAL UNION CATALOG, PRE-1956 IMPRINTS: A CUMULATIVE AUTHOR LIST REPRESENTING LIBRARY OF CONGRESS PRINTED CARDS AND TITLES REPORTED BY OTHER AMERICAN LIBRARIES. London: Mansell, 1968-80. 67-30001. 021.64. Z881.A1U518.

NATIONAL UNION CATALOG. 1956-- . Monthly. 1759445. 56-60041 rev757. Z881.A1U372.

> The libraries reporting that they have books listed in these catalogs are, of course, identified at the end of an entry. Some of these libraries will circulate their books. Both catalogs are arranged alphabetically by author and should be consulted to locate books. Books published after 1956 should be searched for locations in the U.S. Library of Congress, Catalog Publications Division, NATIONAL UNION CATALOG REGISTER OF ADDITIONAL LOCATIONS, cumulative microform edition (Washington, D.C.: Library of Congress, 1976. 2988198).

It is assumed that librarians serving genealogists will try to obtain printed family histories on interlibrary loan for their patrons. Family histories are one type of library research material that should be shared as widely as possible on interlibrary loan.

The computer union catalogs are and will become an even greater asset to interlibrary loan and also useful in locating family histories. The two largest are OCLC and RLIN (Research Libraries Information Network). Both contain many family histories.

If the city of residence of a family for which a history was written can be determined from the bibliographic entry or the contents note, inquiry should be made to the public library in or near the place of residence to locate and borrow it. The book may have been presented to the local library by the author or members of the family.

Thomson, Sarah Katharine. INTERLIBRARY LOAN POLICIES DIRECTORY. Chicago: American Library Association, 1975. 1137996. 74-32182. 024/. 6/02573. Z713.5.U6T5.

This directory should be in every library that prepares interlibrary loan requests, as it reports which of the 276 surveyed libraries will or will not circulate genealogical materials on interlibrary loan.

PURCHASE

Many genealogists may want to acquire their family's histories. The following resources will help them.

GENEALOGICAL & LOCAL HISTORY BOOKS IN PRINT. 2 vols. Springfield, Va.: Netti Schreiner-Yantis, 6818 Lois Drive, 22150, 1975-77. 2998564. 77-648320. 016.929./1/0973. Z5313.U5G45.

The first two volumes list 993 family histories and family newsletters; 565 (pp. 183-249) and 428 (pp. 351-401) respectively. Each has a surname index and includes prices and the names and addresses of the publisher or vendor that sells each history or newsletter. Volume 1 is entitled GENEALOGICAL BOOKS IN PRINT. BOOKS IN PRINT also includes a few family histories, however, usually only of prominent families.

NATIONAL REGISTER OF MICROFORM MASTERS. Washington, D.C.: Library of Congress, 1965-- . Annual. 936298. 65-29419. 011. Z1033.M5N3.

The 1975 six-volume cumulation (1965-75) contains about 330,000 entries, some of which are family histories. Nearly all works found in this catalog may be purchased in microform. It is arranged alphabetically by author, with a brief entry for title, publisher, and date of publication.

Xerox University Microfilms. GENEALOGIES AND FAMILY HISTORIES: A CATALOG OF OUT-OF-PRINT TITLES. Ann Arbor, Mich.: 1973. OP. New ed. in progress. 1491817. Z5319.X4.

The approximately four hundred family histories in this catalog are also included in the above register. However, libraries that do not have the register may want to have this inexpensive catalog. All histories listed in this catalog may also be purchased as photoduplicate copies of the microfilm.

Philadelphia Bibliographical Center and Union Library Catalogue. Committee on Microphotography. UNION LIST OF MICROFILMS. Rev., enl. and cumulated ed. Ann Arbor: J.W. Edwards, 1951.

_____. UNION LIST OF MICROFILMS: CUMULATION 1949-1959. Ann Arbor: J.W. Edwards, 1961. 577764. 62-1343. 016.099. Z1033.M5P5 1961.

The above two volumes contain a few citations to family histories available on microfilm that are not cited in NATIONAL REGISTER OF MICROFORM MASTERS (p. 113). Entries are arranged by author.

SUBJECT GUIDE TO MICROFORMS IN PRINT. Englewood, Colo.: Microcard editions. 1962/63-- . Annual. 1641930. 62-21624. Z1033.M5G941.

The "Genealogy" section of this catalog lists some family histories that are not cited in any of the above catalogs.

RENTAL LIBRARIES

The previously mentioned catalog of the New England Historic Genealogical Society may be purchased by the society's members; and they may borrow by mail, for a fee, any of the over four thousand family histories listed therein. The society's address is: 101 Newbury Street, Boston, Mass. 02116. Additional rental services are listed in the chapter, "Unique Research Services."

USED BOOK DEALERS

The foremost dealers in used family histories are: Genealogical Publishing Company, 111 Water Street, Baltimore, Md. 21202; and Goodspeeds Bookshop, 18 Beacon Street, Boston, Mass. 02108.

CORRESPONDENCE

Cache Genealogical Library, Logan, Utah. HANDBOOK FOR GENEALOGICAL CORRESPONDENCE. Rev. ed. Logan, Utah: Everton Publishers, 1974. 996459. 929.1.

Genealogists should be referred to "Writing to Libraries, Public Archives and Historical Societies" in chapter 6, pp. 49-67, of the HANDBOOK. Correspondence to libraries and others should be restricted to one simple request for one person or family. Requests for photoduplication of vital pages may be included in correspondence. The maximum amount that the correspondent is willing to pay without consultation should be stated.

Recently published family histories that are not listed in GENEALOGICAL & LOCAL HISTORY BOOKS IN PRINT or in BOOKS IN PRINT may sometimes be acquired by writing the author, publisher, or printer. The addresses of publishers and printers may be easier to acquire. Of course, a telephone directory for the place of publication is the most useful source for obtaining publishers' addresses. Genealogists may have to rely on directory assistance and call in their order or inquire about availability of a family history direct to the source of sale or distribution.

RESEARCHERS FOR HIRE

Materials that cannot be obtained on interlibrary loan, purchased, nor the information acquired by correspondence, may necessitate the genealogist's visiting the library or hiring a researcher to do the same. The names of researchers may be obtained for a small fee by writing the Board of Certification of Genealogists, 1307 New Hampshire Avenue, N.W., Washington, D.C. 20036, or by requesting a free list of accredited genealogists from the Genealogical Department, 50 East North Temple Street, Salt Lake City, Utah 84150. Some archives and libraries maintain a list of researchers that they can recommend to corresponding genealogists to assist them with research. All archives and libraries should follow this practice.

The following article not only outlines for genealogists how to acquire the services of a professional genealogist, but how they should work with and evaluate his or her services:

> Wells, Jerry O. "Finding and Employing a Professional Genealogist," GENEALOGICAL JOURNAL 5 (March-June 1976): 12-17.

TRAVEL

Genealogists should be encouraged to check the card catalogs and the special genealogical and/or biographical indexes in libraries of interest when they travel on business, vacations, or genealogical research.

FOREIGN FAMILY HISTORIES

Besterman, Theodore. A WORLD BIBLIOGRAPHY OF BIBLIOGRAPHIES. 4th ed. Lausanne: Societas Bibliographica, 1965. 42965. 78-205303. 016.01. Z1002.B5685.

> In volume 3 of this bibliography, pages 2103-26 list several foreign library catalogs and bibliographies of family histories that have been published abroad. Genealogists with foreign research needs not too many generations removed or who have many relatives who remained in a foreign country should be referred to these bibliographies.

COLLECTION DEVELOPMENT

Librarians may only want to search out and acquire for their genealogical and local history collections those family histories written about local families. Libraries with adequate shelf space may want to select a few well written and researched family histories. Others may be able to add all family histories contributed to the library and openly solicit their donation.

Medium-sized and larger libraries should acquire GENEALOGIES IN THE LIBRARY OF CONGRESS and its supplement. Some libraries may want to substitute the LIBRARY OF CONGRESS SHELFLIST MICROFICHE EDITION: C.

SUMMARY

It is essential that genealogists search for printed histories. The best single source is GENEALOGIES IN THE LIBRARY OF CONGRESS. This bibliography should be in all but the smallest of collections. Librarians should attempt to obtain any desired family histories on interlibrary loan from the nearest available source. For noncirculating titles a request should be submitted that indexes be checked and pages photoduplicated.

Genealogists should also be encouraged to check the New York Public Library DICTIONARY CATALOG OF THE LOCAL HISTORY AND GENEALOGY DIVISION and the Genealogical Department's Dictionary Card Catalog or its MICROFILM CARD CATALOG at one of its branches. Librarians should be able to supply the nearest location of these catalogs and the cheapest means of consulting them, even if it includes the possibility of requesting a few photoduplicated catalog entries.

Librarians should also encourage genealogists to prepare bibliographic cards for each family history entry of interest that is found. Such a file will be invaluable to them as either they or libraries try to locate family histories. Later the file will be valuable as a record of sources consulted.

Genealogists should check the three major bibliographies systematically for all of their ancestral families. In practicality, most genealogists will check the bibliographies that are readily available for a few families of major interest and, perhaps, will check them later for other families as time permits, research progresses, and interests increase. Checking all of their families at one time may be very discouraging to some.

FAMILY HISTORY COMPARISON STUDY

(Based on one surname, a total of 92 titles.)

Title or Author	Estimated or Total Number of Family Histories Contained	Number of Titles in Study	Unique Titles Found Only in This Catalog	Number of References or Added Entries	Publication Date of Book	Publication Date of Latest History
New York Public Library	26,000	40	23	0	1974	1968
Genealogies in the Library of Congress and Supplement	23,000	37	17	20	1977	1975
Microfilm Card Catalog	21,000	35	21	33	1974	1973
Long Island Historical Society	9,051	15	5	0	1935	1923
New England Historic Genealogical Society	5,724	5	0	0	1978	1960
Los Angeles Public Library	3,800	4	2	1	1965	1955
Sutro Branch Library	3,100	4	1	0	1973	1955
American Genealogists	2,842	2	0	0	1900	1884
North Carolina Genealogical Reference	2,606	1	0	16	1966	1960
St. Louis Public Library	2,200	1	0	0	1965	1941
Glenn, Thomas Allen	2,130	2	0	2	1897	1879
Thomson, Theodore Radford	2,100	7	1	0	1976	1966
Brown, Stuart E.	1,962	2	0	4	1967	1960

Chapter 9

GENEALOGICAL NAME INDEXES

There are numerous indexes that identify individuals or family names that can save genealogists a great deal of research time. Librarians should learn what they are and how to use them and then encourage genealogists to use them. Genealogists will particularly need to use a name index if they do not know the city, town, or county of residence of some of their ancestors.

NATIONWIDE INDEXES

The usefulness of the BIO-BASE, Hyamson and Phillips' indexes to biographical dictionaries, is noted in chapter 11, "Sources Listing Ancestors as Families." Periodical indexes are also nationwide in scope and are explained in chapter 10 on "Genealogical Periodicals and Periodical Indexes."

The following indexes that also are nationwide in scope should be systematically checked by genealogists.

Newberry Library. Chicago. GENEALOGICAL INDEX. 4 vols. Boston: G.K. Hall, 1960. 1485754. 60-51633. 929.182. CS44.N42 1960a.

> This comprehensive index was prepared at the Newberry Library between the years 1896 and 1917. It was created as an index to the books and periodicals in their collection. Entries are very brief, arranged by surname and subarranged by general coverage, by state, and then by allied families. The Newberry Library does not circulate its materials and prefers not to respond to correspondence concerning index entries.
>
> This index contains 512 thousand entries. The bibliographic data concerning the source in which a name appears are very brief and often require the interpretation of an experienced librarian. The Newberry Library's unique call number can be ignored, unless someone is planning to visit the library in Chicago.
>
> The index's scope is national; but because of the library's location, the index is predominantly mid-western. It is also limited to books and periodicals published before 1918.

INDEX TO AMERICAN GENEALOGIES; AND TO GENEALOGICAL MATERIAL
CONTAINED IN ALL WORKS AS TOWN HISTORIES, COUNTY HISTORIES,
LOCAL HISTORIES, HISTORICAL SOCIETY PUBLICATIONS, BIOGRAPHIES,
HISTORICAL PERIODICALS, AND KINDRED WORKS, ALPHABETICALLY AR-
RANGED. 5th ed., rev., improved, and enl. With Supplement 1900 to 1908.
Albany: J. Munsell's Sons, 1900. Reprint. Detroit: Gale Research Co.,
1966. Baltimore: Genealogical Pub. Co., 1979. 553129. 5041804. 67-
2776. 67-19607. 016.929. Z5313.U515 1979.

THE AMERICAN GENEALOGIST, BEING A CATALOGUE OF FAMILY HISTORIES.
A BIBLIOGRAPHY OF AMERICAN GENEALOGY, OR A LIST OF THE TITLE
PAGES OF BOOKS AND PAMPHLETS ON FAMILY HISTORY, PUBLISHED IN
AMERICA, FROM 1771 TO DATE. 5th ed. Albany, N.Y.: Joel Munsell's
Sons, 1900. Reprint. Detroit: Gale Research Co., 1975. Baltimore: Ge-
nealogical Pub. Co., 1971. 1176059. 158119. 74-34247. 74-27389.
016.9291. Z5313.U5A7.

> The above two works should be used together. The second title
> in part is a bibliography of the family histories indexed in the
> first. The following article explains in detail the background
> of the index:
>
> Scanland, Roger. "The Munsell Genealogical Indexes." GE-
> NEALOGICAL JOURNAL 2 (September 1973): 103-8.

Stewart, Robert Armistead. INDEX TO PRINTED VIRGINIA GENEALOGIES,
INCLUDING KEY AND BIBLIOGRAPHY. Richmond, Va.: Old Dominion Press,
1930. Reprint. Baltimore: Genealogical Publishing Co., 1970. 92050.
73-119445. 016.9291. Z5313.U6V8.

> The definition of Virginia used in the preparation of this book
> is very broad and includes anyone from Virginia listed in any
> book the author checked in his nationwide search for Virginians.

THE AMERICAN GENEALOGICAL INDEX. Edited by Fremont River, 48 vols.
Middletown, Conn.: By a committee representing the Cooperating Subscribing
Libraries, 1942-52. 1216583. 42-14197. 016.92910973. CS44.A6.

THE AMERICAN GENEALOGICAL-BIOGRAPHICAL INDEX TO AMERICAN GE-
NEALOGICAL, BIOGRAPHICAL AND LOCAL HISTORY MATERIALS. Middletown, Conn.: Godfrey Memorial Library, 1952-- . Semiannual. 1479909.
53-1579. 929.A51. Z5313.U5A55.

> These indexes are often called the "Rider" indexes. They are
> detailed indexes to the names of individuals found in family and
> local histories, military histories, and other genealogical books.
> Entries include the birth date and state or country of birth if
> given in the book indexed.

McMullin, Phillip W., ed. GRASSROOTS OF AMERICA; A COMPUTERIZED INDEX TO THE AMERICAN STATE PAPERS: LAND GRANTS AND CLAIMS (1789-1837) WITH OTHER AIDS TO RESEARCH. (Government document serial set nos. 28-36). Salt Lake City: Gendex Corp., 1972. 369896. 71-186588. 333.1/0973. J33.M3.

> The use of this index is difficult for genealogists to understand. It is simply a personal name index to the sections on public land and claims in the AMERICAN STATE PAPERS.

> Librarians should ascertain where the nearest set of PAPERS is available and add a note someplace in GRASS ROOTS giving the name of the library that has the PAPERS, along with their call numbers or serial set numbers, such as:

	Index Entry	Serial Set no.
Public Lands	1	028
Public Lands	2	029
Public Lands	3	030
Public Lands	4	031
Public Lands	5	032
Public Lands	6	033
Public Lands	7	034
Public Lands	8	035
Claims	9	036

> In many cases the information found in the PAPERS is nothing more than a petition list or a list of landholders. However, the location and date are usually given; and these are useful for continued research, particularly if a county was previously unknown.

Daughters of the American Revolution. INDEX OF THE ROLLS OF HONOR (ANCESTOR'S INDEX) IN THE LINEAGE BOOKS OF THE NATIONAL SOCIETY OF THE DAUGHTERS OF THE AMERICAN REVOLUTION (VOL. 1-160). Reprint of vols. 1-4, 1916-40. 4 vol. in 2. Baltimore: Genealogical Pub. Co., 1972. 281324. 72-1819. 929/.373. E202.5.A15 1972.

> An index to nearly 25,000 revolutionary participants and nearly 160,000 of their descendants.

Kirkham, E. Kay. AN INDEX TO SOME OF THE FAMILY RECORDS OF THE SOUTHERN STATES: 35,000 MICROFILM REFERENCES FROM THE N.S.D.A.R. FILES AND ELSEWHERE. Logan, Utah: Everton Publishers, 1979.

> Indexes Bibles, family records, and family histories. Entries refer to the microfilm reel numbers of the Genealogical Department of the Church of Jesus Christ of Latter-day Saints.

Genealogical Department of the Church of Jesus Christ of Latter-day Saints. "Temple Records Index Bureau." Unpublished card file, 1927-1970.

This card file index (TIB) contains over 30 million entries. It includes the names of individuals who lived from 1501 to 1970, the majority born between 1501-1950. It is international in scope and arranged by country of birth, subarranged in alphabetical order.

The TIB may be consulted for direct-line ancestors by mail for a small fee. "The Temple Ordinance Indexes Request" form is required and may be obtained at the department's branch libraries or from the High Priest Group Leader of any L.D.S. congregation. A detailed pamphlet on its contents and use is as follows.

Genealogical Department of the Church of Jesus Christ of Latter-day Saints. A BRIEF GUIDE TO THE TEMPLE RECORDS INDEX BUREAU. Rev. Research Paper, Series F, no. 2. Salt Lake City: 1979.

STATEWIDE INDEXES

If a genealogist's ancestors were known to have lived in a specific state, there are numerous statewide indexes that may help locate and usually identify where they lived in the state. The following is the largest and most important index which genealogists should consult:

Genealogical Department of the Church of Jesus Christ of Latter-day Saints. COMPUTER FILE INDEX. Salt Lake City: 1978.

This microfiche index (CFI) was updated in August 1978 and is available at many of the Department's branch libraries. It is not available for sale. Because of its incredibly large number of entries, 55 million, it's absolutely essential that this index be checked by all genealogists. Moreover, it is international in scope, but each country is in one alphabetical order, with some exceptions. Each state of the United States is arranged in a separate alphabetical order, as are the provinces of Canada, and the counties of England.

The CFI lists only deceased persons and provides the names of parents or spouses, and the date and place where a birth, baptism, christening, marriage, or death took place from about 1500. It is organized such that the source used can be traced. Also, the names and addresses of many of the persons having submitted these names can be ascertained either by submitting a "Photoduplication Order" form to the Genealogical Department or by borrowing a microfilm copy of the research form submitted. Normally the "Photoduplication Order" form is the more economical. The CFI also may be consulted by mail for a small fee by using the same form used for the TIB mentioned above. The next edition of the CFI will be entitled, INTERNATIONAL GENEALOGICAL INDEX.

For more details the following pamphlet may be read: Gene-

alogical Society of the Church of Jesus Christ of Latter-day
Saints, THE GENEALOGICAL SOCIETY'S COMPUTER FILE IN-
DEX (Research Paper, Series F, no. 4, Salt Lake City: Ge-
nealogical Society, 1975).

The following bibliography lists many good statewide indexes:

Vallentine, John F. LOCALITY FINDING AIDS FOR U.S. SURNAMES. 2d ed.
Logan, Utah: Everton Publishers, 1977. 5988538. Z6824.V3 1977.

There are many more statewide indexes, some of which are listed in Filby's
AMERICAN & BRITISH GENEALOGY & HERALDRY and in the general state
sections of GENEALOGICAL & LOCAL HISTORY BOOKS IN PRINT. They
are not specifically identified in these sources other than by title. The card
catalogs of the Genealogical Department identify indexes on the collation line,
as will future cataloging of most libraries after the adoption of the ANGLO-
AMERICAN CATALOGUING RULES, 2d ed. (AACRII). Genealogists may use
the Department's MICROFILM CARD CATALOG at its branch libraries to assist
them in determining what general state genealogical books could be used as
statewide indexes. They simply look at the microfilm for a state of interest,
check the subjects "Genealogy," "Vital Records," and/or "History" and check
the collation line for an index statement.

Other excellent statewide indexes are the indexes to the federal census schedules.
They are explained and listed in chapter 12 about the census.

There are also a few statewide cumulative indexes to local histories. A few
are listed in chapter 13, "Finding County and City Histories." There are many
more such indexes needed.

OBITUARY INDEXES

Inquiries are often made by genealogists concerning obituary indexes. There
are many such indexes that have been prepared in and for libraries in card form
and in manuscript. Many may be found in the Genealogical Department's
MICROFILM CARD CATALOG. Ireland's LOCAL INDEXES IN AMERICAN
LIBRARIES lists others. The following are a few printed indexes:

American Antiquarian Society. Worcester, Massachusetts. INDEX OF OBIT-
UARIES IN MASSACHUSETTS CENTINEL AND COLUMBIAN CENTINEL, 1784-
1840. 5 vols. Boston: G.K. Hall, 1961. 1830193. G929.3.

Codman, Ogden. INDEX OF OBITUARIES IN BOSTON NEWSPAPERS, 1704-
1800; BOSTON ATHENAEUM. 3 vols. Boston: G.K. Hall, 1968. 27021.
72-6194. 929.3. F73.25.C6.

Haverford College. Library. QUAKER NECROLOGY. 2 vols. Boston: G.K. Hall, 1961. 1823687. 61-4958. 922.86. BX7791.

National Intelligencer. ABSTRACTS OF MARRIAGE AND DEATH NOTICES: FROM THE NATIONAL INTELLIGENCER. 3 reels of microfilm. Washington, D.C.: National Genealogical Society Library, n.d. 4623759. 929.373.

NEW YORK TIMES OBITUARIES INDEX, 1858-1968. New York: New York Times, 1970. 59713. 72-113422. 929.3. CT213.N47.

Virginia. State Library. Richmond. INDEX TO OBITUARY NOTICES IN THE RICHMOND ENQUIRER FROM MAY 9, 1804, THROUGH 1828, AND THE RICHMOND WHIG FROM JANUARY, 1824, THROUGH 1838. (Originally prepared by several Members of the Apprentice Class of the Virginia State Library, 1904, under the direction of Mr. John P. Kennedy, Librarian); edited by H.R. McIlwaine. Rev. ed. Richmond: Virginia State Library, 1923. Reprint. Baltimore: Genealogical Publishing Co., 1974. 1111288. 74-15235. 929/.3755. F225.V83.

COLLECTION DEVELOPMENT

Cooperative efforts should be made to acquire in a reasonable geographical area as many of these indexes as possible. Nearly all libraries should purchase a copy of Vallentine's LOCALITY FINDING AIDS.

SEARCH STRATEGY AND SUMMARY

Genealogists should be encouraged to check as many of the indexes mentioned in this chapter as possible and, particularly, the COMPUTER FILE INDEX. Searches can be made by using pedigrees or family group sheets or the card files mentioned in the searching for printed family histories or county histories.

Chapter 10

GENEALOGICAL PERIODICALS
AND PERIODICAL INDEXES

Many genealogical and historical periodicals contain abstracts of wills, probates, and vital records; cemetery records; family records; and summaries of family research. Indexes to these periodicals should be searched by genealogists. The following list is arranged in chronological order but should be checked by genealogists in reverse order except for Waldenmaier's Indexes which should be last.

INDEXES

INDEX TO AMERICAN GENEALOGIES: AND TO GENEALOGICAL MATERIAL CONTAINED IN ALL WORKS SUCH AS TOWN HISTORIES, COUNTY HISTORIES, LOCAL HISTORIES, HISTORICAL SOCIETY PUBLICATIONS, BIOGRAPHIES, HISTORICAL PERIODICALS, AND KINDRED WORKS, ALPHABETICALLY ARRANGED. 5th ed., rev., improved, and enl. With Supplement 1900 to 1908. Albany: J. Munsell's Sons, 1900. Reprint. Detroit: Gale Research Co., 1966. Baltimore: Genealogical Publishing Co., 1979. 553129. 5041804. 67-2776. 67-19607. 016.929. Z5315.U5I5.

> Indexes only nine genealogical periodicals and forty-three historical periodicals. Arranged by family surname.

Jacobus, Donald Lines. INDEX TO GENEALOGICAL PERIODICALS, TOGETHER WITH "MY OWN INDEX." New Haven, Conn.: Jacobus, 1932-53. Reprint. 3 vols. in 1. Baltimore: Genealogical Publishing Co., 1973. 1486343. 929.105. Z5313.U5J19.

ANNUAL INDEX TO GENEALOGICAL PERIODICALS & FAMILY HISTORIES. Washington, D.C.: I. Waldenmaier, 1957-1963. 4950588. 65-47890. 016.9293. CS45.A65.

GENEALOGICAL PERIODICAL ANNUAL INDEX. Bowie, Md.: Yankee Bookman, 1962-- . 4205809. 63-17702. 016.020105873. CS42.G467.

Periodicals and Periodical Indexes

These latter three indexes are arranged alphabetically by subject, including family surnames, geographical locations, and some individual names. In preparation for their use, genealogists should prepare a single alphabetical list of the geographical locations in which their ancestors have lived and of the surnames they are researching, including the complete names and years of birth and death of outstanding ancestors. The indexes of genealogical periodicals can then be checked against the prepared list for articles that may relate to the genealogist's research. When articles are found, cards or note paper should be prepared citing each article of interest. Genealogists may need to be instructed to copy the complete bibliographic entry.

The definitive work on the use of all of the above indexes is the following excellent guide:

Sperry, Kip, ed. A SURVEY OF AMERICAN GENEALOGICAL PERIODICALS AND PERIODICAL INDEXES. Gale Genealogy and Local History Series, vol. 3. Detroit: Gale Research Co., 1978. 4036318. 78-55033. 016.929/1/05. Z5313.U5S65 CS42.

SUPPLEMENTAL INDEXES

Barber, Gertrude A. NEW YORK GENEALOGICAL AND BIOGRAPHICAL RECORD: SUBJECT INDEX. VOLS. 77-94 INCLUSIVE. New York: New York Genealogical and Biographical Society, 1964. 2639375. 929.

Boston. Massachusetts Society of Mayflower Descendants. "Index to the Mayflower Descendants, a Quarterly Magazine of Pilgrim Genealogy and History." Compiled by Frank T. Calef. Filmed by the Genealogical Society at Rhode Island Historical Society. Providence, R.I.: July 1950. GD 1,335-1,377.

>   Patrons interested in this index should consult the MICROFILM CARD CATALOG under U.S. - PERIODICALS - INDEXES at a Branch Genealogical Library.

Broders, Nell Heaphy. CUMULATIVE SUBJECT INDEX OF THE LOUISIANA GENEALOGICAL REGISTER, 1954-1975, AND CUMULATIVE TABLE OF CONTENTS OF THE PROCEEDINGS OF THE ANNUAL GENEALOGICAL INSTITUTES, 1958-1975. Baton Rouge, La.: By the Author, 1976. 2614173. 76-45139. 016.929/3763. F366.B76.

CUMULATED MAGAZINE SUBJECT INDEX, 1907-1949: A CUMULATION OF THE F.W. FAXON COMPANY'S ANNUAL MAGAZINE SUBJECT INDEX. Edited by Frederick Winthrop Faxon, Mary E. Bates, and Anne C. Sutherland. Cumulated by G.K. Hall and Co. 2 vols. Boston. G.K. Hall, 1964. 3336859. 65-98. A13.C76.

>   A total of 27 percent of the periodicals indexed in this index are state and local historical periodicals of interest to genealogists.

Fisher, Carleton Edward, Comp. TOPICAL INDEX TO THE NATIONAL GE-
NEALOGICAL SOCIETY QUARTERLY. VOLS. 1-50, 1912-1962. Special
Publication of the National Genealogical Society, no. 29. Washington, D.C.:
National Genealogical Society, 1964.

Haverford College. Library. QUAKER NECROLOGY. 2 vols. Boston: G.K.
Hall, 1961. 1823687. 61-4958. 922.86. BX7791.

An index to four Quaker periodicals, 1827-1960:

THE FRIEND 1827-1955.
FRIENDS' WEEKLY INTELLIGENCER 1844-1955.
THE FRIENDS' REVIEW 1848-1894.
FRIENDS' JOURNAL 1955-1960.

NEW ENGLAND HISTORICAL AND GENEALOGICAL REGISTER INDEX OF
SUBJECTS, INDEX OF PLACES, INDEX OF PERSONS. Vols. 1-50. 4 vols.
Baltimore: Genealogical Publishing Co., 1972. 2364307. 72-1957.
929.374.

Parsons, Margaret Wellington, comp. INDEX (ABRIDGED) TO THE NEW ENG-
LAND HISTORICAL AND GENEALOGICAL REGISTER. Vols. 51-112: 1897-1958.
Marlborough, Mass.: Privately published by the compiler, 1959. 527836.
FI.N614.

New England Historic Genealogical Society. THE GREENLAW INDEX OF THE
NEW ENGLAND AND HISTORIC GENEALOGICAL SOCIETY. 2 vols. Boston:
G.K. Hall, 1979. 5765667. 929.016.

New Mexico Genealogical Society. INDEX TO THE NEW JERSEY GENESIS,
1953-1971. Edited by Mrs. Carl Nissen. Albuquerque: Hermosa Publishers,
1973. 1118054. 73-85622. 974.9.

Ray, Worth Stickley, comp. INDEX AND DIGEST TO HATHAWAYS NORTH
CAROLINA HISTORICAL AND GENEALOGICAL REGISTER, WITH GENEA-
LOGICAL NOTES AND ANNOTATIONS. Austin, Tex.: n.p., 1945. Reprint. Baltimore: Genealogical Publishing Co., 1971. 1805421. 67-121942.
975.6/005. F251.N8912.

Swem, Earl Gregg, comp. VIRGINIA HISTORICAL INDEX. Roanoke, Va.:
n.p., 1935. Reprint. 2 vols. in 4. Glouster, Mass.: P. Smith, 1965.
1723949. 66-520. 975.5016. F221.S93 1965.

Indexes one genealogical and four historical periodicals and two
primary Virginia historical collections.

There are also several cumulative indexes to additional periodicals, many of
which are listed under the subject "Genealogy," the names of localities, and

in the title index in the following: Ireland, Norma Olin. AN INDEX TO INDEXES: A SUBJECT BIBLIOGRAPHY OF PUBLISHED INDEXES. Useful Reference Series, no. 67. Boston: F.W. Faxon, 1942. Reprint. Boston: Gregg Press, 1972. 427532. 72-8745. 016.016. Z6293.I7 1972.

INTERLIBRARY LOAN

There are many system, network, region, and state union lists of periodicals besides the UNION LIST OF SERIALS and NEW SERIAL TITLES that include genealogical and historical periodicals and the libraries holding them. Any of these can be used for the interlibrary loan of genealogical and historical periodicals. Photoduplicated copies can usually be obtained free or for a small fee from the libraries reported holding the materials. Titles that are difficult to verify may be found in appendix 3, pages 127-81, "American Genealogical Periodicals: A Select List," of Kip Sperry's A SURVEY OF AMERICAN GE-NEALOGICAL PERIODICALS AND PERIODICAL INDEXES. Also the following bibliography may be of assistance:

Cappon, Lester Jesse. AMERICAN GENEALOGICAL PERIODICALS: A BIB-LIOGRAPHY WITH A CHRONOLOGICAL FINDING-LIST. New York: New York Public Library, 1964. 1855824. 016.9291.

If all of these fail to list the desired title and appropriate year, patrons should be referred to any branch genealogical library to use the Genealogical Depart-ment's microfiche copy of PERIODICALS AND SERIALS LIST. The branch ge-nealogical libraries also have a photoduplication form that patrons may utilize to order copies of desired articles for a small fee.

COLLECTION DEVELOPMENT

Most librarians are concerned about which periodicals they should have in their collections. The following are those of national and international scope that this author considers the best, or the most useful, listed in order of preference:

GENEALOGICAL HELPER. Logan, Utah: Everton Publishers, September 1947-- . Bimonthly. 1570534. 56-46837.

> The most popular and widely circulating genealogical periodical. Has many patron interest columns and functions. The book re-view column is actually only book notices. If a library can only afford one periodical, this is the one. Most novice ge-nealogists will find it the most useful for their needs.

NATIONAL GENEALOGICAL SOCIETY QUARTERLY. Washington, D.C.: Na-tional Genealogical Society, April 1912-- . 2321231. 17-12813. 929.05. CS42.N4.

> Contains scholarly articles and good reviews.

GENEALOGICAL JOURNAL. Salt Lake City: Utah Genealogical Association, March 1972-- . Quarterly. 2250993. 78-96.

Has been a very good, predominently how-to-do-it journal with quality reviews.

AMERICAN GENEALOGIST. Des Moines: George McCracken, July 1922-- . Quarterly. 2444644. 78-4430. 929. F104.N6A64.

Another journal of scholarly articles and reviews.

The genealogical indexes by Jacobus and the current indexes should be available in a geographical area within a reasonable driving radius. Kip Sperry's book, A SURVEY OF AMERICAN GENEALOGICAL PERIODICALS AND PERIODICAL INDEXES, should be in larger libraries.

SUMMARY AND SEARCH STRATEGY

Periodicals must be used at some point in a genealogist's search for ancestors. A systematic search should be made of all the major indexes mentioned, but particularly the GENEALOGICAL PERIODICAL ANNUAL INDEX (p. 125) and Jacobus' INDEX TO GENEALOGICAL PERIODICALS (p. 125). The family name cards prepared for the searching of the family history catalogs, local history bibliographies, and the MICROFILM CARD CATALOG of the Genealogical Department can also be used for searching periodical indexes. They will have to be arranged by family name for one search of the indexes and then geographically for a second search.

Chapter 11

SOURCES LISTING ANCESTORS AS FAMILIES

Records that group families together are very useful when no vital records have been found. These family-grouped records may help a genealogist discover the previously unknown parents of an ancestor.

The best of the family-grouped records are those that also indicate relationships. Probate records, wills, and land records, as well as the 1880 and 1900 census schedules, usually include relationships. County, city and family histories, biographical sketches and oral histories also give relationships. The census schedules for 1850, 1860, and 1870, and ship passenger lists group households and parties together but give no relationships.

PROBATES AND WILLS

Probates and wills are essential in almost all cases to establish some relation-ship of families. They also provide an interesting insight into the history of a family. Genealogists should be advised to consult them whenever possible.

However, caution should be given that photoduplicated copies of probates not be requested from the county court houses where most of them are housed. Court houses normally charge a great deal for photoduplication, and usually a probate contains many pages. Genealogists who are not able to obtain copies on microfilm loan, an abstracted published copy, or visit a court house should try to obtain the services, free or for a fee, of a person to abstract a probate or copy the will. Chapter 17 of Val D. Greenwood's THE RESEARCHER'S GUIDE TO AMERICAN GENEALOGY, pp. 316-33, provides excellent guide-lines for abstracting wills and deeds. Greenwood also explains in detail the use of probates and wills in chapters 12 through 14.

The probate also includes a long inventory that is of no genealogical value but rather of considerable historical value for the genealogist who desires to write a family history. Some inventories are short and simple, while others are very involved and long.

A few early wills and/or probates have been published. Some of them can be found in the genealogical bibliographies and catalogs, some are indexed in genealogical indexes, and others appear in genealogical periodical indexes. Many are available on microfilm through the branch libraries of the Genealogical Department.

The availability of some probates is noted in THE HANDY BOOK FOR GENEALOGISTS. Probates and wills available through the branch libraries of the Genealogical Department are listed on the MICROFILM CARD CATALOG geographically with the subject subdivision, "PROBATE RECORDS." Some are also noted in Richard Walden Hale's GUIDE TO PHOTOCOPIED HISTORICAL MATERIALS IN THE UNITED STATES AND CANADA (Ithaca, N.Y.: Published for the American Historical Association by Cornell University Press, 1961), and Mary J. Brown's HANDY INDEX TO THE HOLDINGS OF THE GENEALOGICAL SOCIETY OF UTAH: COUNTIES OF THE UNITED STATES (Logan, Utah: Everton Publishers, 1971).

Closely related to probates are guardianships, which can be a useful resource in some circumstances. Greenwood explains their value, use, and availability on pages 258-63 of his book.

The subject headings relative to probates and wills are as follows:

LC   PROBATE RECORDS--LINN COUNTY, IOWA
      WILLS--LINN COUNTY, IOWA

Sears WILLS--LINN COUNTY, IOWA

GD   IOWA, LINN - PROBATE RECORDS
      IOWA, LINN - PROBATE RECORDS - INDEXES

CENSUS SCHEDULES

The census schedules for the year 1850 on list the names of all household residents and, therefore, usually group families together. The census schedules and their use are covered in the following chapter. It is important for genealogists to be directed to the census schedules for their very useful grouping of families. The 1880 and 1900 census schedules also include relationships.

SHIP PASSENGER LISTS

Another source which lists families in groups, as long as they immigrated as a family, is the ship passenger lists. The official listing of immigration began in 1819, and most of the records date from 1820. A few lists have been lost or burned, others indexed, some partially indexed, and only five out of ninety-three ports have been microfilmed. Those microfilmed and available through the branch libraries of the Genealogical Department, but not yet through the National Archives branches, are as follows:

Baltimore	1820-91	Indexed
Boston	1820-74, 1883-91	Indexed, 1848-91
New Orleans	1820-1902	
New York	1820-1897	Indexed, 1820-46
Philadelphia	1800-1819 (manifests)	Indexed, 1800-1906

The branch libraries have registers that list the parts of the alphabet covered by each reel of the indexes and the ports and arrival dates covered by each reel of the lists, along with the Genealogical Department microfilm number. The lists include the names of all passengers and their age, sex, occupation, the country to which they belonged, and the state or place they planned to inhabit. Passengers are usually grouped together by family or party. At the beginning of each list is the name of the ship, the master's name, port of embarcation, and the port and date of arrival.

Additional details about the lists, other lists, and printed lists are given in the following guides:

"Passenger Arrival Lists." In GUIDE TO GENEALOGICAL RECORDS IN THE NATIONAL ARCHIVES, by Meredith B. Colket and Frank E. Bridgers, pp. 22-43. National Archives Publications, no. 64-8. Washington, D.C.: National Archives, 1979.

"American Aids to Finding the Home of the Immigrant Ancestor." In THE RESEARCHER'S GUIDE TO AMERICAN GENEALOGY, by Val D. Greenwood, pp. 400-413. Baltimore: Genealogical Publishing Co., 1973.

Ship passenger lists that are not available through the branch libraries of the Genealogical Department would have to be consulted at the National Archives in Washington, D.C. Some information can be obtained from the National Archives ship passenger lists by correspondence, but the exact date of arrival and port of entry have to be known. It would also be helpful if the name of the ship were known. A source that can be of assistance to some in solving these problems is the following:

MORTON ALLAN DIRECTORY OF EUROPEAN PASSENGER STEAMSHIP ARRIVALS FOR THE YEAR 1890 TO 1930 AT THE PORT OF NEW YORK AND FOR THE YEARS 1904 TO 1926 AT THE PORTS OF NEW YORK, PHILADELPHIA, BOSTON, AND BALTIMORE. New York: Immigration Information Bureau, Inc., 1931. Reprint. Baltimore: Genealogical Publishing Co., 1979. 4705572. 78-65163. 387.5/42. HE945.A2D5 1979.

Printed ship passenger lists for immigrants before 1820 are listed in the following bibliography that now, unfortunately, is incomplete and out-of-date:

Lancour, Harold. A BIBLIOGRAPHY OF SHIP PASSENGER LISTS, 1538-1825:
BEING A GUIDE TO PUBLISHED LISTS OF EARLY IMMIGRANTS TO NORTH
AMERICA. 3d ed., rev. and enl. by Richard J. Wolfe. New York: New
York Public Library, 1978. 4518219. 63-18141. Z7164.I3L2 1978.

Lancour's bibliography (above) cites ship arrivals by date in chronological order.
It is based on lists published in periodicals and books. It is updated and
superceded by the following work:

Filby, P. William, and Meyer, Mary K., eds. PASSENGER AND IMMIGRA-
TION LISTS INDEX: A GUIDE TO PUBLISHED ARRIVAL RECORDS OF 300,000
PASSENGERS WHO CAME TO THE UNITED STATES AND CANADA IN THE
SEVENTEENTH, EIGHTEENTH, AND NINETEENTH CENTURIES. 3 vols.
Detroit: Gale Research Co., 1980.

> Entries name the precise books, magazines, or documents to
> consult for further details. Filby unearthed over 750 sources
> not in Lancour. With Filby and Meyer's index, a genealogist
> no longer needs to borrow on interlibrary loan the items listed
> in Lancour.

The following books also have reprinted some of the lists cited in Lancour:

Boyer, Carl, ed. SHIP PASSENGER LISTS: NATIONAL AND NEW ENGLAND
(1600-1825). Newhall, Calif.: Boyer, 1977. 3353223. 76-37355. 929.
373016.

_____. SHIP PASSENGER LISTS: NEW YORK AND NEW JERSEY (1600-
1825). Newhall, Calif.: Boyer, 1978. 4303619. 929.373016.

_____. SHIP PASSENGER LISTS: PENNSYLVANIA AND DELAWARE (1641-
1825). Newhall, Calif.: Boyer, 1980. 6258594. 79-57204. 929/.3748.
F148.B76.

_____. SHIP PASSENGER LISTS: THE SOUTH, 1538-1825. Newhall, Calif.:
Boyer, 1979. 5103305. 78-52618. 929/.373. CS68.B75.

EMIGRANTS TO PENNSYLVANIA, 1641-1819: A CONSOLIDATION OF SHIP
PASSENGER LISTS FROM THE PENNSYLVANIA MAGAZINE OF HISTORY AND
BIOGRAPHY. Edited by Michael Tepper. Baltimore: Genealogical Publishing
Co., 1975. 4464026. 78-322609. 929/.3. F148.E5 1975.

IMMIGRANTS TO THE MIDDLE COLONIES: A CONSOLIDATION OF SHIP
PASSENGER LISTS AND ASSOCIATED DATA FROM THE NEW YORK GENE-
ALOGICAL AND BIOGRAPHICAL RECORD. Edited by Michael Tepper.
Baltimore: Genealogical Publishing Co., 1978. 3690105. 77-15281. 929/.
37. F106.147.

NEW WORLD IMMIGRANTS: A CONSOLIDATION OF SHIP PASSENGER LISTS AND ASSOCIATED DATA FROM PERIODICAL LITERATURE. Edited by Michael Tepper. 2 vols. Baltimore: Genealogical Publishing Co., 1979. 5246065. 79-84392. 929/.373. CS68.N48.

PASSENGERS TO AMERICA: A CONSOLIDATION OF SHIP PASSENGER LISTS FROM THE NEW ENGLAND HISTORICAL AND GENEALOGICAL REGISTER. Edited by Michael Tepper. Baltimore: Genealogical Publishing Co., 1977. 3205345. 77-72983. 929/.373. CS68.P37 1977.

The subject headings relative to ship passenger lists are as follows:

LC   U.S.--EMIGRATION AND IMMIGRATION (names of national groups, e.g., MEXICANS IN THE U.S.)

Sears   U.S.--IMMIGRATION AND EMIGRATION (names of nationality groups)

GD   U.S. - EMIGRATION AND IMMIGRATION
        U.S. - EMIGRATION AND IMMIGRATION - INDEXES

COUNTY AND FAMILY HISTORIES

Mug books and family histories have been covered in other chapters. Both are good secondary sources for family groupings. Librarians should not let genealogists overlook them.

DIVORCE RECORDS

Couples that are divorced after they have had children leave an informative family record for their genealogist descendants. Genealogists could write court clerks to check indexes for an ancestor. However, in most cases they would have to visit the appropriate county court house or else hire someone to do the research for them.

A brief description of these records appears in chapter 18, "Court Records," of Greenwood's THE RESEARCHER'S GUIDE TO AMERICAN GENEALOGY, pages 345-49, 352-57. THE HANDY BOOK FOR GENEALOGISTS also reports the availability of divorce records of many counties. The following guide should also be consulted:

U.S. Public Health Service. WHERE TO WRITE FOR DIVORCE RECORDS, U.S. AND OUTLYING AREAS. Rev. DHEW Pub. no. HRA. 78-1145. Washington, D.C.: Superintendent of Documents, 1978. HE20.6202:D64/

LAND RECORDS

Genealogists should be reminded to consult land records not only because of the land transactions that were made between relatives, but also for their historical value. Again, Greenwood provides three excellent chapters (15, 16, and 17) on the subject in his RESEARCHER'S GUIDE TO AMERICAN GENEALOGY, pages 264-333.

Many land records are available on microfilm through the branch libraries of the Genealogical Department. Their availability may be ascertained by consulting the MICROFILM CARD CATALOG at a branch library by the subject subdivision, "LAND RECORDS," following the name of the state and county. The majority, however, are only available in the court houses. THE HANDY BOOK FOR GENEALOGISTS includes notes concerning their availability.

Nearly all land records are indexed in some manner. Both those at the court houses and those court house records that have been microfilmed by the Genealogical Department will have grantee and grantor indexes that should be consulted first in searching land records.

The subject headings relative to land records are as follows:

<blockquote>

LC   DEEDS--LINN COUNTY, IOWA
LAND TITLES--LINN COUNTY, IOWA--INDEXES

Sears   REAL ESTATE--LINN COUNTY, IOWA

GD   IOWA, LINN - LAND AND PROPERTY
</blockquote>

BIOGRAPHICAL SOURCES

Most librarians are aware of the excellent general biographical indexes. These biographical indexes can also serve as genealogical research tools, as names of spouses, parents, and children are sometimes found therein.

The following are the four principal biographical indexes, listed in order of importance:

BIO-BASE: A PERIODIC CUMULATIVE MASTER INDEX IN MICROFICHE TO SKETCHES FOUND IN 500 CURRENT AND HISTORIC BIOGRAPHICAL DICTIONARIES. Detroit: Gale Research Co., 1978-- . Irregular. 5214949. 016.02.

Hyamson, Albert Montefiore. A DICTIONARY OF UNIVERSAL BIOGRAPHY OF ALL AGES AND OF ALL PEOPLES. 2d ed., entirely rewritten. New York: Dutton, 1951. Reprint. Detroit: Gale Research Co., 1980. 1098216. 51-14243. 920.02. CT103.H9 1951.

An index to twenty-four early twentieth-century biographical dictionaries and encyclopedias.

Phillips, Lawrence Barnett. THE DICTIONARY OF BIOGRAPHICAL REFERENCE; CONTAINING OVER ONE HUNDRED THOUSAND NAMES; TOGETHER WITH A CLASSED INDEX OF THE BIOGRAPHICAL LITERATURE OF EUROPE AND AMERICA. New ed., rev., cor. and augm. with supplement ot date, by Frank Weitenkampf. London: S. Low, Marston and Co., 1889. Reprint. Graz, Austria: Akademische, Druck-u Verlagsanstalt, 1966. 1000374. 147211. 02-3274. 920.03. CT102.P5.

An index to forty-two nineteenth-century biographical diction- aries and encyclopedias.

BIOGRAPHY INDEX: A CUMULATIVE INDEX TO BIOGRAPHICAL MATERIAL IN BOOKS AND MAGAZINES. New York: H.W. Wilson Co., 1946-- . Quarterly. 1536408. 47-6532. Z5301.B5.

For ascertaining what additional biographical directories are available, the fol- lowing bibliographies must be consulted:

Slocum, Robert B. BIOGRAPHICAL DICTIONARIES AND RELATED WORKS: AN INTERNATIONAL BIBLIOGRAPHY OF COLLECTIVE BIOGRAPHIES, BIO- BIBLIOGRAPHIES, COLLECTIONS OF EPITAPHS, SELECTED GENEALOGICAL WORKS, DICTIONARIES OF ANONYMS AND PSEUDONYMS, HISTORICAL AND SPECIALIZED DICTIONARIES, BIOGRAPHICAL MATERIALS IN GOVERN- MENT MANUALS, BIBLIOGRAPHIES OF BIOGRAPHY, BIOGRAPHICAL IN- DEXES, AND SELECTED PORTRAIT CATALOGS. Detroit: Gale Research Co., 1967. 367212. 67-27789/rev782. 916.92. Z5301.S55.

_____. BIOGRAPHICAL DICTIONARIES AND RELATED WORKS: AN INTERNA- TIONAL BIBLIOGRAPHY OF COLLECTIVE BIOGRAPHIES, BIO-BIBLIOGRAPHIES, COLLECTIONS OF EPITAPHS, SELECTED GENEALOGICAL WORKS, DICTION- ARIES OF ANONYMS AND PSEUDONYMS, HISTORICAL AND SPECIALIZED DICTIONARIES, BIOGRAPHICAL MATERIALS IN GOVERNMENT MANUALS, BIBLIOGRAPHIES OF BIOGRAPHY, BIOGRAPHICAL INDEXES, AND SELECTED PORTRAIT CATALOGS: SUPPLEMENT. Detroit: Gale Research Co., 1972--. Irregular. 4337031. 67-27789. Z5301S55 Suppl.

For other notables of a particular state, the state library can be of assistance through correspondence. Many State Bars have excellent records of their mem- bers, both current and deceased. Businesses are proud of their early executives and have materials that they are happy to share.

The subject headings relative to biographical dictionaries are as follows:

LC   IOWA--BIOGRAPHY--DICTIONARIES
LINN COUNTY, IOWA--BIOGRAPHY

Sears IOWA--BIOGRAPHY--DICTIONARIES
       LINN COUNTY, IOWA--BIOGRAPHY

GD   IOWA - BIOGRAPHY
       IOWA, LINN - BIOGRAPHY
       IOWA, LINN - BIOGRAPHY - INDEXES

ORAL HISTORY

Oral histories are more limited in their coverage of the general populace than
biographical directories; however, the introductory material of most transcriptions
does include some genealogical information about the interviewee. Oral history
is now expanding to local history and will, in the future, acquire great quan-
tities of genealogy and family history as it includes more common folks. Its
significance to genealogical research will increase in the future. Nevertheless,
the following directory includes many names of individuals who have provided
in their interviews some data concerning their families:

Meckler, Alan M., and McMullin, Ruth, comps. ORAL HISTORY COLLEC-
TIONS. New York: Bowker, 1975. 1144745. 74-32128. 016.9098/025.
A13.M4.

Additional information concerning oral histories is covered in chapter 8, "Finding Family Histories." The subject headings relative to oral history are as
follows:

LC   ORAL HISTORY

Sears ORAL HISTORY

GD   (None)

COLLECTION DEVELOPMENT

Many of the titles mentioned in this chapter have been recommended for purchase in other chapters. It is recommended that all medium-sized and larger
libraries acquire Filby and Meyer's PASSENGER AND IMMIGRATION LISTS
INDEX.

SUMMARY

Researching the family as a group is essential. Regardless of how complete
genealogists' records may be, there is still need to look at census schedules,
ship passenger lists, and county histories, if appropriate. Genealogists should
be influenced to search particularly for wills and probates, as well as land
records.

Chapter 12

CENSUS SCHEDULES

The most genealogically useful U.S. federal census schedules are those for 1850, 1860, 1870, 1880, and 1900. These schedules contain the names of and demographic information about all residents of households at the time the census was taken.

Census schedules are not arranged in alphabetical order, but rather in house-to-house order, as the census taker made his circuit. Data obtained includes the age of each one enumerated at the time of the census, as well as sex, occupation, and the state or country of birth. Some of the census schedules also include information concerning the value of personal and real property, literacy, and other miscellaneous information. Although these schedules list all the members of a household, only 1880 and 1900 specify relationship to the head of the house. The 1880 and 1900 census schedules, in addition, include the name of the state or country of birth of the parents of each person enumerated. Of the census taken in 1890 the only schedules remaining and available are parts of seventeen counties in ten states and part of the District of Columbia. The rest were destroyed by fire in 1921.

The earlier census schedules, for the years 1790, 1800, 1810, 1820, 1830, and 1840, include only the heads of households. They do list the numbers of males and females within specified age groups living in each household. Slave schedules were also created for these years, as well as 1850 and 1860, listing the owner and the number of slaves by sex and age groups. There are many statewide indexes published of the heads of households listed in the schedules for these years.

The simplest, yet most adequate, explanation of the variations in the census schedules and their miscellaneous information is an anonymous article entitled "Genealogy Notes," PROLOGUE 4 (Winter 1972): 242-46. For additional useful detail consult chapters 10 and 11 of Greenwood's, THE RESEARCHER'S GUIDE TO AMERICAN GENEALOGY.

The census schedules for 1910 to 1970 may be consulted by mail for a fee, but only under certain circumstances. Use Form BC-600, available from the Bureau of the Census, Personal Census Service Branch, Pittsburg, Kansas 66762. Because of the confidential nature of the records, either the person whom the record concerns or his or her next-of-kin must sign the form and, in some cases, meet other requirements explained on the form.

MICROFILM FOR INTERLIBRARY LOAN

The census schedules have been microfilmed by the National Archives and are available for use by the public at the National Archives in Washington, D.C. and its eleven Regional Branch Archival Centers. Census schedules may also be borrowed through interlibrary loan from the following center: Chief, Archives Branch, Federal Archives and Records Center, P.O. Box 6216, Fort Worth, Texas 76115. The addresses of the other centers are listed below. In order to borrow census schedules, the requesting library needs to provide the Fort Worth Branch with year, the name of the state, county, reel number, and the record number desired on an American Library Association Interlibrary Loan Form. The reel and record number may be obtained from the catalogs listed below. The record number is found at the beginning of each census year (e.g., M432).

U.S. National Archives and Records Service. FEDERAL POPULATION CENSUSES, 1790-1890: A CATALOG OF MICROFILM COPIES OF THE SCHEDULES. Pub. 71-3. Washington, D.C.: The Service, 1979. GS4.2:P81/2 790-890. 5041352. 72-610891. 016.312. Z7554.U5U72.

_____. 1900 FEDERAL POPULATION CENSUS. Washington, D.C.: 1979. 4525931. 72-610891. 317.3. HA37.U548F442.

These catalogs may be acquired free from the Fort Worth Archives Branch. All libraries should have them.

The addresses and service areas of the National Archives Branch Archival Centers are as follows (For each of the following, address inquiries to: Chief, Archives Branch, Federal Archives and Records Center, GSA):

ATLANTA

1557 St. Joseph Avenue
East Point, Ga. 30344
Telephone: 404-763-7477

Serves Alabama, Florida, Georgia, Kentucky, Mississippi, North Carolina, South Carolina, and Tennessee.

BOSTON

380 Trapelo Road
Waltham, Mass. 02154
Telephone: 617-223-2657

Serves Connecticut, Maine, Massachusetts, New Hampshire, Rhode Island, and Vermont.

CHICAGO

7358 South Pulaski Road
Chicago, Ill. 60629
Telephone: 312-353-0160

Serves Illinois, Indiana, Michigan, Minnesota, Ohio, and Wisconsin.

DENVER

Building 48, Denver Federal Center
Denver, Colo. 80225
Telephone: 303-234-5271

Serves Colorado, Montana,
North Dakota, South Dakota,
Utah, and Wyoming.

FORT WORTH

4900 Hemphill St. (street address)
P.O. Box 6216 (mailing address)
Fort Worth, Tex. 76115
Telephone: 817-334-5515

Serves Arkansas, Louisiana,
New Mexico, Oklahoma,
and Texas.

KANSAS CITY

2306 East Bannister Road
Kansas City, Mo. 64131
Telephone: 816-926-7271

Serves Iowa, Kansas,
Missouri, and Nebraska.

LOS ANGELES

24000 Avila Road
Laguna Niguel, Calif. 92677
Telephone: 714-831-4220

Serves Arizona; the southern
California counties of Imperial,
Inyo, Kern, Los Angeles,
Orange, Riverside, San
Bernardino, San Diego,
San Louis Obispo, Santa
Barbara, and Ventura; and
Clark County, Nevada.

NEW YORK

Building 22-MOT
Bayonne, N.J. 07002
Telephone: 201-858-7164

Serves New Jersey, New
York, Puerto Rico, and the
Virgin Islands.

PHILADELPHIA

5000 Wissahickon Avenue
Philadelphia, Pa. 19144
Telephone: 215-951-5588

Serves Delaware and Penn-
sylvania; for the loan of
microfilm, also serves the
District of Columbia,
Maryland, Virginia, and
West Virginia.

SAN FRANCISCO

1000 Commodore Drive
San Bruno, Calif. 94066
Telephone: 415-876-9001

Serves California (except
southern California), Hawaii,
Nevada (except Clark County),
and the Pacific Ocean area.

SEATTLE

6125 Sand Point Way N.E.
Seattle, Wash. 98115
Telephone: 206-442-4502

Serves Alaska, Idaho,
Oregon, and Washington.

A special census was taken in 1890 of Union Civil War veterans; however, the results are available only for part of Kentucky through Wyoming, plus the District of Columbia. The schedules for the other states were destroyed by fire.

PURCHASE

Patrons that have a great deal of research to do in one county or on one reel of microfilm may find it more convenient to purchase that reel. They may be purchased from the Cashier, National Archives (GSA), Washington, D.C. 20408.

SEARCH STRATEGY

Librarians might need to suggest to some genealogists who have only fragmented data concerning their progenitors that they conduct a systematic search of all their ancestors who can be found in the census schedules. This could be done through the use of pedigree charts or by the biographical cards prepared for the search of family histories, rearranged by state, county, and city. In most cases, genealogists need only search for those families wherein they lack the names and places of birth of some family members, places of birth of their direct line ancestors, their occupations, personal or property value, literacy, or other miscellaneous characteristics and data.

DIFFICULTIES IN USE

One difficulty in the use of the 1810-1900 census schedules is that many counties are contained on more than one reel of microfilm. The National Archives has provided no means of determining on which reel a city, town or township appears. Therefore it may be necessary to order several reels for some genealogists to complete their research in one county. In the case of the 1850 schedules, however, genealogists can be assisted by the following to locate cities, towns and townships on the reels:

Parker, J. Carlyle, ed. CITY, COUNTY, TOWN, AND TOWNSHIP INDEX TO THE 1850 FEDERAL CENSUS SCHEDULES. Gale Genealogy and Local History Series, vol. 6. Detroit: Gale Research, 1979. 4804899. 79-11644. 929/.373. CS65.P37.

Another difficulty in the use of the 1820-1900 census schedules is that many of the larger cities are divided by wards. There are statewide indexes and some city indexes that will solve most of these problems and eliminate lengthy searches of several wards or reels of microfilm. Genealogists searching schedules of large cities should be encouraged to determine the address of their ancestor from another source. They may be able to discover the address from relatives or from family letters. Some may need to be referred to the city directories of the city involved and directed to write the public library of that city, requesting their assistance in checking the directories. Some large libraries have microfiche copies of the city directories listed in the following bibliography:

Spear, Dorothea N. BIBLIOGRAPHY OF AMERICAN DIRECTORIES THROUGH 1860. Worcester, Mass.: American Antiquarian Society, 1961. Reprint. Westport, Conn.: Greenwood Press, 1978. 577681. 3980848. 61-1054. 77-28204. 016.973/025. Z5771.S7.

Additional information concerning city directories is covered in chapter 11, "Sources Listing Ancestors as Families."

Once the address is known, the genealogist should consult the ward maps in the following:

Kirkham, E. Kay. HANDY GUIDE TO RECORD-SEARCHING IN LARGER CITIES OF THE UNITED STATES. Logan, Utah: Everton Publishers, 1974. 5831424. 79-121132. 016.929/1/0973. Z5305.U5K57 CS47.

If a ward map is not available in Kirkham (above), a genealogist may have to write the Correspondence Branch, National Archives (NNCC), Washington, D.C., 20408, for assistance. They have reference sources that can be consulted through correspondence. Genealogists who find a ward problem with the 1900 census schedules should first consult the Soundex and then, if necessary, the above resources.

Librarians in large metropolitan libraries that haven't already acquired ward census maps for their cities should purchase copies from either the National Archives or the Library of Congress. Listed in the following bibliography are 232 ward maps for thirty-five cities available from the Library of Congress.

U.S. Library of Congress. WARD MAPS OF UNITED STATES CITIES: A SE-LECTIVE CHECKLIST OF PRE-1900 MAPS IN THE LIBRARY OF CONGRESS. Compiled by Michael H. Shelley. Washington, D.C.: Government Printing Office, 1975. 1094899. 74-23316. 016.912/73. Z6028.U572 1975.

Still another problem sometimes encountered in using census schedules is that the ink on many schedules has faded and is nearly impossible or impossible to read. When provided the name of the state, county, year, page and name desired, the staff of the National Archives will consult the original schedules and try to read the paper impressions for researchers. Persons in need of this service should write the Correspondence Branch, National Archives (NNCC), Washington, D.C. 20408.

Librarians may occasionally be confronted with another problem when genealo-gists are reading census schedules: how to read handwriting that may be next to illegible. The simplest thing to do is to instruct the genealogist to create a table of examples of the handwriting, letter by letter, both capitals and lower case from A to Z. This can be done from the words that are identifiable. With this newly created table in hand, they usually can proceed to unravel the scribe's penmanship.

A how-to-do-it book that can provide much more help than this simple suggestion is the following:

Kirkham, E. Kay. THE HANDWRITING OF AMERICAN RECORDS FOR A PERIOD OF 300 YEARS. Logan, Utah: Everton Publishers, 1973. 937978. 79-121378. 652.1/0973. Z43.K55.

CENSUS SCHEDULE INDEXES

If a genealogist knows only that an ancestor was from somewhere in a state, a census schedule index may help by identifying the county and town where the ancestor lived. One type of index, the Soundex, is arranged in the order of phonetic pronunciations and has been made for the 1880 schedules for families with children under ten and for the 1900 schedules for all those enumerated. Microfilm copies of these, also, may be obtained from the National Archives branches through interlibrary loan by determining the Soundex code for the names desired from the soundex code table on the last page of the catalogs and then finding the reel number needed and the record number from the preceeding catalog pages. Other useful indexes are the statewide indexes to the 1850-1870 census schedules. However, most of these index only the head of a household and persons with different surnames living in the same household.

There have been several expensive reprints made of the printed edition of the 1970 census schedules that include statewide indexes. Medium-sized libraries should purchase the entire set on microfilm from the National Archives, at a substantial savings (T498, reels 1-3), Cashier, National Archives (GSA), Washington, D.C. 20408. The National Archives has prepared a complete index for the 6,160 legible entries that survived for the 1890 census. This index is available at the National Archives branches and from the Fort Worth branch on interlibrary loan.

Many of the National Archives branches, the Genealogical Department, and other large genealogical libraries have collected numerous statewide census schedule indexes. Most libraries will not circulate census schedule indexes because of their reference value. However, many of them are willing to photoduplicate needed pages from them. The Genealogical Department branch libraries have a photoduplication form for requesting this service from the main library for a small fee.

Librarians should prepare mini-union lists of federal census schedule indexes for the libraries of networks, cooperatives, or geographical areas for the use of genealogists in obtaining photoduplicated pages as needed through the services of interlibrary loan or by visiting those libraries which have the needed indexes.

Where such lists already exist, they have proven to be effective and efficient.

There has been some controversy over the accuracy of some of the statewide census schedule indexes. Some criticism has been justified; but like the imperfections of numerous abstracts, indexes, and reference tools that librarians are forced to use, they are accepted and welcomed despite their failings because they are the only tools we have. Most census indexes have been made from microfilm copies of the original schedules. Microfilm does not provide the indexer the opportunity to study the paper impresses of faded entries. The penmanship and spelling that abound throughout the schedules are additional problems that cause imperfect indexes. Of course, the human error of the indexer and the task of alphabetizing thousands of names are other negative factors that create errors.

The census index list at the end of this chapter is an attempt to cite the statewide census schedule indexes that are now available. Concerted effort has been made to determine or estimate the number of names indexed in each. In some cases a comparison of the quantity of names may assist librarians in the selection of a preferred index where several are available. However, no qualitative study has been attempted in this bibliography. The author recommends that all indexes for any given state and year be consulted if a name is not found in the first index used.

The subject headings relative to census schedules and their indexes are as follows:

      LC   IOWA--CENSUS (year)

      Sears   IOWA--CENSUS

      GD   IOWA - CENSUS
             IOWA - CENSUS - INDEXES
             IOWA - LINN - CENSUS
             IOWA, LINN - CENSUS - INDEXES

STATE CENSUS SCHEDULES

State census schedules are available for some of the states. Most of them are for mid-decade years and contain information similar to the federal schedules. The following list the state census schedules:

U.S. Library of Congress. Census Library Project. STATE CENSUSES: AN ANNOTATED BIBLIOGRAPHY OF CENSUSES OF POPULATION TAKEN AFTER THE YEAR 1790 BY STATES AND TERRITORIES OF THE UNITED STATES. Prepared by Henry J. Dubester. Washington, D.C.: Government Printing Office, 1948. Reprint. American Classics in History and Social Science, 72. Burt Franklin Bibliography and Reference Series, 238. New York: B. Franklin, 1969. 47804. 68-58215. 016.312. Z7554.U5U63 1969.

Census Schedules

Vallentine, John F. "State and Territories Census Records in the United States." GENEALOGICAL JOURNAL 2 (December 1973): 133-39.

> List of state and territory census schedules. Arranged by state indicating year, type of census (federal, Spanish padron, state and territorial), location of original schedules, special information and availability in the Genealogical Department and Brigham Young University libraries.

The availability of many state census schedules, as well as federal census schedules and some of their indexes, are listed in the following:

Stemmons, John D., comp. THE UNITED STATES CENSUS COMPENDIUM: A DIRECTORY OF CENSUS RECORDS, TAX LISTS, POLL LISTS, PETITIONS, DIRECTORIES, ETC. WHICH CAN BE USED AS A CENSUS. Logan, Utah: Everton Publishers, 1973. 714466. 73-77805. 016.929/3/73. Z1250.S83.

MORTALITY CENSUS SCHEDULES

Mortality schedules make it possible for genealogists to try to locate ancestors that died in the census year. Details of their value, use, and availability are given in the chapter, "Vital Records."

AGRICULTURAL CENSUS SCHEDULES

Some patrons may inquire as to the use, value, and availability of the agricultural census schedules of the U.S. federal census, 1850-1880. These schedules are of historical but not genealogical value. They include the names of farmers and ranchers, their property values, number of various animals, and measurements of production.

FOREIGN CENSUS SCHEDULES

The Public Archives of Canada will circulate microfilm copies of their 1851, 1861, and 1871 census schedules to libraries in the United States on interlibrary loan. Participating libraries may use American Library Association interlibrary loan forms but must provide reel numbers of desired films. In order to ascertain the reel numbers the CENSUS RETURNS: 1825-1871 (catalogue number SA 2095-1978) must be consulted. A copy of it may be acquired for a small fee by writing the Publishing Centre, Department of Supplies and Services, Mail Order Service, 270 Albert Street, Ottawa, Ontario, Canada K1A 0S9.

Likewise, the Genealogical Department has some copies of Canadian census schedules that may circulate to their branches. In addition, the Genealogical Department has microfilm copies of census schedules of many Western European countries that are available for use through its branches. The branch libraries have either microfilm copies of the Genealogical Department's card catalog or separate registers that list its holdings and the microfilm call numbers for them.

COLLECTION DEVELOPMENT AND SUMMARY

All libraries, including the smallest branches, should have copies of the federal census schedule catalogs in order to obtain microfilm copies of the schedules on interlibrary loan. Larger libraries should acquire some census schedule indexes as needed for the majority of their patrons. Cooperative acquisitions should be undertaken and a mini-union catalog prepared to assist patrons to gain access to other indexes.

PUBLISHED STATEWIDE CENSUS SCHEDULE INDEXES

Unless otherwise stated all annotations in the following bibliography refer to listing of full names of the heads of households and other surnames within each household in the schedule. Some of the census indexes in this list are transcriptions of the census schedules, arranged in alphabetical order by name. Other transcriptions are arranged in the same order as the schedules, with full name or surname indexes with page references to the printed transcription. A transcription contains all of the information reported in the census schedule that relates to persons enumerated.

With the exception of their introduction, the indexes of the Accelerated Indexing Systems are uniform in their format and coverage. They index all names, and many are transcriptions of the census data in the 1800 through 1840 census schedules. The indexes for the 1850-70 census schedules include only the heads of households and anyone living within the household with a different surname. Entries include the given names, the first four letters of the name of the county (exceptions are noted), the stamped number for each leaf, and eight letters of the census division (e.g., township, city, ward, district, etc.). Other publishers have used a similar indexing system but refer to the handwritten page numbers that assign each leaf two page numbers, like a published book.

The 1790 census schedule transcriptions and indexes have been reprinted many times. Some indexes that are not statewide have been included in order to identify their incompleteness. A few large city indexes have also been included.

Alabama

Boise. Idaho Genealogical Society. "Index to Alabama Census Returns, 1820, by Alabama State Department of Archives and History, Montgomery, Alabama, 1960." Typewritten. 1974. GD 962,911 Item 2.

   Contains about 3,520 names.

Montgomery. Alabama State Department of Archives and History. "Index to Alabama Census Returns, 1820." Typewritten.

> Contains about 410 names. Copy also available at the National Society, Daughters of the American Revolution, Genealogical Library.

Alabama. Department of Archives and History. ALABAMA CENSUS RETURNS, 1820, AND AN ABSTRACT OF FEDERAL CENSUS OF ALABAMA, 1830. Baltimore: Genealogical Publishing Co., 1967. 953374. 67-28599. 317.61. F325.A28 1967. GD 824,280 Item 8.

> Not indexed and not in alphabetical order. Contains more than 4,860 names. Reprinted from the ALABAMA HISTORICAL QUARTERLY, vol. 6, no. 3, 1944.

Gandrud, Pauline Myra, comp. ALABAMA: AN INDEX TO THE 1830 UNITED STATES CENSUS. Hot Springs National Park, Ark.: B. Jones McLane, 1973. 596623. 73-154733. 929/.3761. F326.G3.

> Contains 33,839 names with counties of residence.

Jackson, Ronald Vern; Teeples, Gary Ronald; and Schaefermeyer, David, eds. ALABAMA 1830 CENSUS INDEX. Bountiful, Utah: Accelerated Indexing Systems, 1976. 2669573. F326.J33.

> Contains 32,440 names.

Jackson, Ronald Vern, and Teeples, Gary Ronald. ALABAMA 1840 CENSUS INDEX. Bountiful, Utah: Accelerated Indexing Systems, 1977. 3713698. 976.1.

> Contains 56,421 names.

Posey, Betty Sue Drake, and Posey, Seth A.R., comps. ALABAMA 1840 CENSUS INDEX. Hattiesburg, Miss.: n.p., 1973. 746488. 73-174905. 016.929/ 3761. F325.P67.

> Only one volume, transcription with index, containing twelve of the state's thirty-seven counties; 4,400 names.

Jackson, Ronald Vern, Schaefermeyer, David; and Teeples, Gary Ronald, eds. ALABAMA 1850 CENSUS INDEX. Bountiful, Utah: Accelerated Indexing Systems, 1976. 2231934. 976.1.

> Contains 100,011 names.

Kilduff, Eleanor M. CENSUS-1850, CITY OF MOBILE, ALABAMA. Mobile: Mobile Genealogical Society, 1966. 2025874. F334.M6K5.

Alaska

Jackson, Ronald Vern, and Teeples, Gary Ronald, eds. ALASKAN CENSUS RECORDS, 1870-1907. Bountiful, Utah: Accelerated Indexing Systems, 1976. 3661860. 929.3798.

Contains 5,097 names.

Arizona

Jackson, Ronald Vern, and Teeples, Gary Ronald, eds. ARIZONA 1860 TERRITORIAL CENSUS INDEX. Bountiful, Utah: Accelerated Indexing Systems, 1978. 4285380. F810.J32.

Contains 2,117 names.

_____. ARIZONA 1864 TERRITORIAL CENSUS INDEX. Bountiful, Utah: Accelerated Indexing Systems, 1978. 4285389. F810.J323.

Contains 3,156 names.

Schreier, Jim, and Schreier, Mary. AN INDEX TO THE TERRITORIAL MANU-SCRIPT OF THE 1864 CENSUS OF ARIZONA, CORRELATED TO THE HISTORICAL RECORDS SURVEY OF 1938 AND THE U.S. SENATE DOCUMENT NUMBER 13, 1965: DRAWN FROM THE ORIGINAL DOCUMENT IN THE DEPARTMENT OF LIBRARY AND ARCHIVES, ARIZONA. Phoenix: J. Schreier, 1975. 1602683. 75-320665. 312/.09791. F810.S37.

Contains about 4,320 names and page references.

_____. AN INDEX TO THE 1866 CENSUS OF THE ARIZONA TERRITORY. Phoenix: Arizona Territorial Genealogy, 1975. 2284296. 76-361792. 929/. 3791. F810.S36.

Contains about 5,124 names and page references.

Jackson, Ronald Vern, and Teeples, Gary Ronald, eds. ARIZONA 1870 TERRI-TORIAL CENSUS INDEX. Bountiful, Utah: Accelerated Indexing Systems, 1978. 4285393. F810.J325.

Contains 6,657 names.

Jackson, Ronald Vern. ARIZONA 1880 TERRITORIAL CENSUS INDEX. Salt Lake City: Accelerated Indexing Systems, 1979.

Southern Arizona Genealogical Society. TERRITORY OF ARIZONA, INDEX TO 1880 FEDERAL CENSUS. 4 reels of microfilm. Tucson: Southern Arizona Genealogical Society, 1962. GD 882,917-20.

Census Schedules

Arkansas

Jackson, Ronald Vern, and Teeples, Gary Ronald, eds. ARKANSAS SHERIFF'S CENSUSES, 1823 AND 1829. Salt Lake City: Accelerated Indexing Systems, 1976. 4810013. 78-112554. 929/.3767/86. F417.A65J3.

   Contains 2,605 names.

McLane, Bobbie Jones, and Cline, Inez Evelyn. AN INDEX TO FIFTH UNITED STATES CENSUS OF ARKANSAS. Fort Worth, Tex.: Arrow Printing Co., 1963. 1573817. 65-27148. 929.3767. GD 1,036,552 Item 3.

   Contains 4,425 names. The 1830 Federal Census.

Presley, Leister E., Mrs., comp. TERRITORY OF ARKANSAS, UNITED STATES CENSUS 1830. Searcy, Ark.: n.p., 1970. 2027131. F411.T33P7. GD 908,037 Item 5 (index only).

   Transcription with a surname index to each county; about 2,960 names.

Jackson, Ronald Vern, and Teeples, Gary Ronald, eds. ARKANSAS 1840 CENSUS INDEX. Bountiful, Utah: Accelerated Indexing Systems, 1976. 2675828. 78-112536. 929/.3761. F410.J177.

   Contains 12,962 names.

McLane, Bobbie Jones. AN INDEX TO 1840 UNITED STATES CENSUS OF ARKANSAS. Arkansas: n.p., 1967. 1451879. 976.7. GD 897,455 Item 1.

   Contains 1,270 names and counties of residence.

Presley, Leister E., Mrs., comp. FEDERAL POPULATION SCHEDULES, ARKANSAS CENSUS 1840. Searcy, Ark.: Presley, 1971.

   Transcription with a surname index for each county; about 7,960 names.

Jackson, Ronald Vern; Schaefermeyer, David; and Teeples, Gary Ronald, eds. ARKANSAS 1850 CENSUS INDEX. Bountiful, Utah: Accelerated Indexing Systems, 1976. 2303076. 929.3767.

   Contains 40,387 names.

Presley, Leister E., Mrs., comp. ARKANSAS CENSUS, 1850: SURNAME INDEX. Searcy, Ark.: Presley, 1974. 1207092. 74-195996. 929/.3767. F410.P73.

   Contains more than 22,260 surnames with county and page references.

California

Bowman, Alan P. INDEX TO THE 1850 CENSUS OF THE STATE OF CALIFORNIA. Baltimore: Genealogical Publishing Co., 1972. 266697. 70-148609. 929/.3794. F860.B6.

> Not a statewide index. Contains just under 30,200 names in twenty-four alphabetical listings by county.

Jackson, Ronald Vern, and Teeples, Gary Ronald. CALIFORNIA 1850 CENSUS INDEX. Bountiful, Utah: Accelerated Indexing Systems, 1978. 4252800. 77-85788. 979.4.

> Contains 59,594 names.

U.S. Bureau of the Census. CENSUS OF THE CITY AND COUNTY OF LOS ANGELES, CALIFORNIA, FOR THE YEAR 1850; TOGETHER WITH AND AN ANALYSIS AND AN APPENDIX BY MAURICE H. NEWMARK AND MARCO R. NEWMARK. Los Angeles: Times-Mirror Press, 1929. 497557. HA730.L7A45 1929.

> Copy of schedule with very incomplete index to heads of households.

Colorado

Denver. Colorado Historical Society Library. "Index to the 1860 Territorial Census of Colorado." Card index.

Genealogical Society of Weld County, Colorado. 1870 CENSUS OF THE TERRITORY OF COLORADO. Greely, Colo.: Weld County Genealogical Society, 1977. 3585768. 978.8. GD 1,036,745 Item 2.

> Contains a little less than 39,104 names.

Jackson, Ronald Vern, ed. COLORADO 1880 CENSUS INDEX. Salt Lake City: Accelerated Indexing Systems, 1979.

Connecticut

Holbrook, Jay Mack. CONNECTICUT 1670 CENSUS. Oxford, Mass.: Holbrook Research Institute, 1977. 3183313. 77-152342. 929/.3746. F93.H73.

> Contains 2,522 names with county and township references.

U.S. Bureau of the Census. HEADS OF FAMILIES AT THE FIRST CENSUS OF THE UNITED STATES TAKEN IN THE YEAR 1790: CONNECTICUT. Washington, D.C.: Government Printing Office, 1908. Reprint. Spartanburg, S.C.:

Reprint Co., 1964; Baltimore: Genealogical Publishing Co., 1966; and Bountiful, Utah: Accelerated Indexing Systems, 1978. Microfilm. T498 reel 1. Washington, D.C.: National Archives, 1960; and New Haven, Conn.: Research Publications, 1972. 2531640. 64-62655. 929/.3746. F93.U5. GD 874,192 Item 3.

> Index contains about 41,538 names.

Jackson, Ronald Vern; Teeples, Gary Ronald; and Schaefermeyer, David, eds. CONNECTICUT 1800 CENSUS INDEX. Bountiful, Utah: Accelerated Indexing Systems, 1977. 2865815. 974.6.

> A transcription of 41,808 names in alphabetical order.

Volkel, Lowell M., comp. AN INDEX TO THE 1800 FEDERAL CENSUS OF THE STATE OF CONNECTICUT. 3 vols. Danville, Ill.: 1968. 8407. 46650. 106642. 76-2721. 71-7984. 70-17908. 929.3. F93.V65.

> Not a statewide index. Consists of three indexes, with about 43,680 names.

Jackson, Ronald Vern; Teeples, Gary Ronald; and Schaefermeyer, David, eds. CONNECTICUT 1810 CENSUS INDEX. Bountiful, Utah: Accelerated Indexing Systems, 1976. 2666081. 929.3746.

> Contains 45,046 names.

_____. CONNECTICUT 1820 CENSUS INDEX. Bountiful, Utah: Accelerated Indexing Systems, 1977. 2908988.

> Contains 49,954 names.

Jackson, Ronald Vern, and Teeples, Gary Ronald, eds. CONNECTICUT 1830 CENSUS INDEX. Bountiful, Utah: Accelerated Indexing Systems, 1977. 3341477. 929.3746.

> Contains 53,693 names.

_____. CONNECTICUT 1840 CENSUS INDEX. Bountiful, Utah: Accelerated Indexing Systems, 1978. 3936239. F93.J2 1840.

> Contains 60,538 names.

_____. CONNECTICUT 1850 CENSUS INDEX. Bountiful, Utah: Accelerated Indexing Systems, 1978. 3936357. F93.J2 1850.

> Contains 134,211 names.

Connecticut. State Library. "U.S. Census Index for Connecticut, 1790-1850, Hartford." Microfilm. Hartford: Connecticut State Library, filmed by the Genealogical Society, n.d. GD 3,434-3,479.

Interfiled with other Connecticut cities, A to, but not including, New Haven.

_____. "U.S. Census Index for Connecticut, 1790-1850, New Haven." Microfilm. Hartford: Connecticut State Library, filmed by the Genealogical Society, n.d. GD 3,480-3,483.

_____. "U.S. Census Index for Connecticut, 1790-1850, New London-Stratford." Microfilm. Hartford: Connecticut State Library, filmed by the Genealogical Society, n.d. GD 3,484-3,511.

Contains indexes for the cities of New London-Stratford in separate alphabets for each city.

Delaware

Jackson, Ronald Vern, and Teeples, Gary, Ronald, eds. EARLY DELAWARE CENSUS RECORDS, 1665-1697. Bountiful, Utah: Accelerated Indexing Systems, 1977. 3715055. 975.1.

Contains 1,850 names.

De Valinger, Leon. RECONSTRUCTED 1790 CENSUS OF DELAWARE. Special Publications of the National Genealogical Society, no. 10. Reprinted from the NATIONAL GENEALOGICAL SOCIETY QUARTERLY, September 1948-December 1953. Washington, D.C.: National Genealogical Society, 1962. 1281176. 975.1. Cox Library, Del., Reel 2, no. 13. GD 1,000,156 Item 6.

Not a statewide index. Arranged in alphabetical order by hundred. Contains about 830 names.

Jackson, Ronald Vern; Teeples, Gary Ronald; and Schaefermeyer, David, eds. DELAWARE 1800 CENSUS INDEX. Bountiful, Utah: Accelerated Indexing Systems, 1977. 2979140. 929.3751.

A transcription of 9,337 names in alphabetical order.

Maddux, Gerald, and Maddux, Doris Ollar, comps. 1800 CENSUS OF DELAWARE. Montgomery, Ala.: n.p., 1964. Reprint. Baltimore: Genealogical Publishing Co., 1976. 2295772. 76-3095. 929.375.

Arranged by county and hundred in schedule order with three indexes to 8,084 surnames only.

Jackson, Ronald Vern, and Teeples, Gary Ronald, eds. DELAWARE 1810 CENSUS INDEX. Bountiful, Utah: Accelerated Indexing Systems, 1976. 4810072. 78-112449. 929/.3751. F163.J32.

Contains 10,566 names.

Jackson, Ronald Vern; Teeples, Gary Ronald; and Schaefermeyer, David, eds. DELAWARE 1820 CENSUS INDEX. Bountiful, Utah: Accelerated Indexing Systems, 1974. 2908956.

>   Contains 10,854 names.

Jackson, Ronald Vern, and Teeples, Gary Ronald, eds. DELAWARE 1830 CENSUS INDEX. Bountiful, Utah: Accelerated Indexing Systems, 1977. 4833905. 78-112639. 929/.3751. F163.J34.

>   Contains 12,357 names.

_____. DELAWARE 1840 CENSUS INDEX. Bountiful, Utah: Accelerated Indexing Systems, 1977. 3725168. 77-85945. 929/.3751. F163.J327.

>   Contains 13,504 names.

_____. DELAWARE 1850 CENSUS INDEX. Bountiful, Utah: Accelerated Indexing Systems, 1977. 4809988. 78-112568. 929/.3751. F163.J33.

>   Contains 31,640 names.

Olmstead, Virginia Langham, comp. INDEX TO THE 1850 CENSUS OF DELAWARE. Baltimore: Genealogical Publishing Co., 1977. 3294372. 77-76790. 929/.3751. F163.045.

>   Not a statewide index. Contains 90,774 names in three lists of the state's three counties in alphabetical order.

District of Columbia

Jackson, Ronald Vern, and Teeples, Gary Ronald, eds. DISTRICT OF COLUMBIA 1800 CENSUS INDEX. Bountiful, Utah: Accelerated Indexing Systems, 1977. 4225306. 929/.3753. F193.J33.

>   A transcription of 1,167 names in alphabetical order.

_____. DISTRICT OF COLUMBIA 1820 CENSUS INDEX. Bountiful, Utah: Accelerated Indexing Systems, 1976. 2623492. 78-112494. 929/.3753. F193.J333.

>   Contains 5,128 names.

_____. DISTRICT OF COLUMBIA 1830 CENSUS INDEX. Bountiful, Utah: Accelerated Indexing Systems, 1977. 4809949. 78-112640. 312/.09753. F193.J334.

>   Contains 6,546 names.

_____. DISTRICT OF COLUMBIA 1840 CENSUS INDEX. Bountiful, Utah: Accelerated Indexing Systems, 1977. 3804187. 77-85903. 929/.3753. F193.J335.

Contains 7,290 names.

_____. DISTRICT OF COLUMBIA 1850 CENSUS INDEX. Bountiful Utah: Accelerated Indexing Systems, 1977. 3804193. 77-85904. 929/.3753. F193.J336.

Contains 17,385 names.

Florida

Jackson, Ronald Vern, and Teeples, Gary Ronald, eds. FLORIDA 1830 CENSUS INDEX. Bountiful, Utah: Accelerated Indexing Systems, 1976. 2743398. 78-112447. 929/.3759. F310.J3.

Contains 3,696 names.

Shaw, Aurora C., comp. 1830 FLORIDA U.S. CENSUS INDEX. Jacksonville, Fla.: Southern Genealogist's Exchange Quarterly, 1969. 3983163. F310.S56x 1830.

Contains about 3,626 heads of households with counties of residence.

Jackson, Ronald Vern, and Teeples, Gary Ronald, eds. FLORIDA 1840 CENSUS INDEX. Bountiful, Utah: Accelerated Indexing Systems, 1976. 4810069. 78-112460. 929/.3759. F310.J32.

Contains 4,595 names.

Mallon, Lucille S., comp. 1840 INDEX TO FLORIDA CENSUS. N.p.: B.M. Taylor, n.d. 2874170. 77-352479. 312/.09759. F310.M245. GD 940,013 Item 7.

Not a statewide index. Arranged alphabetically by county. Contains about 4,031 names.

Shaw, Aurora C. FLORIDA U.S. CENSUS, 1840. A STATEWIDE INDEX OF ALL HEADS OF HOUSEHOLDS IN ALL TWENTY COUNTIES FORMED BY 1840 SHOWING COUNTIES IN WHICH THEY RESIDED. Jacksonville, Fla.: Southern Genealogists Exchange Quarterly, 1968. 1851043.

Contains 4,840 names with counties of residence.

Jackson, Ronald Vern; Teeples, Gary Ronald; and Schaefermeyer, David, eds. FLORIDA 1850 CENSUS INDEX. Bountiful, Utah: Accelerated Indexing Systems, 1976. 2636125. 975.9.

Contains 14,439 names.

Census Schedules

Southern Genealogist's Exchange Society. INDEX TO 1850 FLORIDA CENSUS. Jacksonville, Fla.: Southern Genealogists Exchange Society, 1976. 2401761. 76-29651. 929/.3759. F310.S68 1976.

    Contains about 8,646 surnames with counties of residence.

Georgia

Georgia Historical Society. INDEX TO UNITED STATES CENSUS OF GEORGIA FOR 1820. 2d ed., with additions and corrections by Mrs. Eugene A. Stanley. Baltimore: Genealogical Publishing Co., 1969. 50782. 79-90052. 929.3. F285.G38 1969.

    Contains about 30,378 complete names with county, without pages or data.

Jackson, Ronald Vern, and Teeples, Gary Ronald, eds. GEORGIA 1820 CENSUS INDEX. Bountiful, Utah: Accelerated Indexing Systems, 1976. 4810008. 78-112559. 929/.3758. F285.J28.

    Contains 52,296 names.

Delwyn Associates. INDEX TO HEADS OF FAMILIES 1830 CENSUS OF GEORGIA. Albany, Ga.: Delwyn Associates, 1974. 1311003.

    Contains about 55,062 names with county and page references.

Jackson, Ronald Vern, and Teeples, Gary Ronald eds. GEORGIA 1830 CENSUS INDEX. Bountiful, Utah: Accelerated Indexing Systems, 1976. 2674081. 78-112667. 929/.3758. F285.J29.

    Contains 52,295 names.

Register, Alvaretta Kenan, comp. INDEX TO THE 1830 CENSUS OF GEORGIA. Baltimore: Genealogical Publishing Co., 1974. 940318. 73-22267. 016. 9293/758. F285.R39.

    Contains about 55,014 names with county and page references.

Jackson, Ronald Vern, and Teeples, Gary Ronald, eds. GEORGIA 1840 CENSUS INDEX. Bountiful, Utah: Accelerated Indexing Systems, 1977. 3722880. 77-85914. 929.3.

    Contains 69,997 names.

Sheffield, Eileen, and Woods, Barbara. 1840 INDEX TO GEORGIA CENSUS. Baytown, Tex.: By the authors, 1971. 160536. 70-27869. 929.3. F285.S5 1971.

    Not a statewide index. All names are arranged by county; about 75,800 names.

Jackson, Ronald Vern, and Teeples, Gary Ronald, eds. GEORGIA 1840 CEN-
SUS INDEX. Bountiful, Utah: Accelerated Indexing Systems, 1976. 4810052.
78-112490. 929/.3758. F285.J32.

Contains 123,242 names.

Otto, Rhea Cumming, comp. 1850 CENSUS OF GEORGIA: INDEX TO 25
COUNTIES. Savannah, Ga.: Otto, 1975. 1365465. 75-311342. 929/.3758.
F285.087.

Not a statewide index.

Idaho

Idaho Genealogical Society. IDAHO TERRITORY: FEDERAL POPULATION
SCHEDULES AND MORTALITY SCHEDULES, 1870. Boise: Williams Printing
Co., 1973. 886903. 74-161864. 929/.3796. F745.127 1973.

A transcription with an index of over 1,566 surnames.

Jackson, Ronald Vern, ed. IDAHO 1870 TERRITORIAL CENSUS INDEX. Salt
Lake City: Accelerated Indexing Systems, 1979. 5082424. F745.J32.

Contains 15,504 names.

Idaho Genealogical Society. IDAHO TERRITORY: FEDERAL POPULATION
SCHEDULES AND MORTALITY SCHEDULES, 1880. Boise: Williams Printing
Co., 1976. 3204651. 77-359716. 929/.3796. F745.127 1976.

A transcription with an index of over 7,452 surnames.

Jackson, Ronald Vern, ed. IDAHO 1880 TERRITORIAL CENSUS INDEX. Salt
Lake City: Accelerated Indexing Systems, 1979. 5082452. F745.J325.

Contains 31,944 names.

Illinois

Springfield. Illinois State Archives. "Name Index to Early Illinois Records."
248 reels of 16mm. microfilm. Springfield: Illinois State Archives, filmed by
the Genealogical Society, 1975. GD 1,001,592-1,001,801.

Index to the state and federal censuses of 1810, 1818, 1820,
1825, 1830, 1835, 1840, 1845, 1850, and 1855 and other state
public documents.

Norton, Margaret Cross, ed. ILLINOIS CENSUS RETURNS, 1810 AND 1818.
Baltimore: Genealogical Publishing Co., 1969. 47987. 70-75351. 312/.09773.
HA346.N63. GD 798,331 Item 2.

Originally published as Collections of the Illinois State Historical
Library, volume 24. Statistical series, volume 2. Springfield,
1935. A transcription with an index of over 5,708 names.

Jackson, Ronald Vern; Teeples, Gary Ronald; and Schaefermeyer, David, eds.
ILLINOIS 1830 CENSUS INDEX. Bountiful, Utah: Accelerated Indexing
Systems, 1977. 3447823. 929.3.

Contains 9,097 names.

Norton, Margaret Cross, ed. ILLINOIS CENSUS RETURNS, 1820. Baltimore:
Genealogical Publishing Co., 1969. 50523. 77-75350. 317.73. F536.
I34543N6. GD 874,431 Item 2.

Originally published as Collections of the Illinois State Historical Library, volume 26. Statistical series, volume 3. Not
a statewide index. Contains about 9,400 names arranged by
county.

Volkel, Lowell M., and Gill, James V., comps. 1820 FEDERAL CENSUS OF
ILLINOIS. Thomson, Ill.: Heritage House, 1977. 3307248. F540.V6 1977.

Contains 8,816 names with county, township, page and line
references.

Gill, James V., and Gill, Maryan R., comps. INDEX TO THE 1830 FEDERAL
CENSUS, ILLINOIS. 4 vols. in 1. Danville, Ill.: Heritage House, 1968-
1976. 3141420. 929.3.

Not a statewide index. Contains 26,162 names in four indexes
with county, page, and line references.

Jackson, Ronald Vern; Teeples, Gary Ronald; and Schaefermeyer, David, eds.
ILLINOIS 1830 CENSUS INDEX. Bountiful, Utah: Accelerated Indexing
Systems, 1976. 2738357. 929.3773.

Contains 25,949 names.

Jackson, Ronald Vern, and Teeples, Gary Ronald, eds. ILLINOIS 1840 CEN-
SUS INDEX. Accelerated Systems, 1977. 3760382. 77-85919. 929/.3773.
F540.J33.

Contains 79,334 names.

Wormer, Maxine E., comp. ILLINOIS 1840 CENSUS INDEX. 4 vols. Thomas,
Ill.: Heritage House, 1973. 1157188. 929.3773.

Not a statewide index. Contains an index to each volume.
About 57,960 names.

Jackson, Ronald Vern, and Teeples, Gary Ronald, eds. ILLINOIS 1850 CEN-
SUS INDEX. Bountiful, Utah: Accelerated Indexing Systems, 1976. 3713624.
77-85920. 977.3.

> Contains 236,348 names.

Indiana

Indianapolis. Indiana State Library. "Indexes to the 1820, 1830, 1840, and
1850 Censuses of Indiana." Card index. 1970.

Heiss, Willard, comp. 1820 FEDERAL CENSUS FOR INDIANA. Indianapolis:
Genealogy Section of the Indiana Historical Society, 1966. 1726157. 977.2.

> A transcription of 23,957 names in alphabetical order.

Jackson, Ronald Vern; Teeples, Gary Ronald; and Schaefermeyer, David, eds.
INDIANA 1820 CENSUS INDEX. Bountiful, Utah: Accelerated Indexing
Systems, 1976. 4809947. 78-112645. 929/.3772. F525.J317.

> Contains 23,842 names.

Jackson, Ronald Vern, and Teeples, Gary Ronald, eds. INDIANA 1830 CEN-
SUS INDEX. Salt Lake City: Accelerated Indexing Systems, 1978. 4556819.
77-85922. F525.J253.

> Contains 56,395 names.

Indiana. State Library, Indianapolis. Genealogy Division. INDEX, 1840
FEDERAL POPULATION CENSUS. Indianapolis: Genealogy Section of the
Indiana Historical Society, 1975. 1992273. 75-332011. 929/.3772. F525.I52
1975.

> Contains about 115,383 names with county and page references.

Jackson, Ronald Vern, and Teeples, Gary Ronald, eds. INDIANA 1840 CEN-
SUS INDEX. Bountiful, Utah: Accelerated Indexing Systems, 1976. 4810034.
78-112525. 929/.3773. F525.J33.

> Contains 113,316 names.

Indiana. State Library, Indianapolis. Genealogical Division. INDEX TO 1850
UNITED STATES FEDERAL CENSUS OF INDIANA. 15 vols. Indianapolis:
Indiana State Library, 1970. GD 962,904-909.

Jackson, Ronald Vern, and Teeples, Gary Ronald, eds. INDIANA 1850 CEN-
SUS INDEX. Bountiful, Utah: Accelerated Indexing Systems, 1976. 3713635.
77-85926. 977.2.

> Contains 255,983 names.

Census Schedules

Pickrell, Martha M. "Index to the 1880 Federal Census of the City of Elkhart." Typewritten. 1979. 4771994. 929.3.

Iowa

Jackson, Ronald Vern; Teeples, Gary Ronald; and Schaefermeyer, David, eds. IOWA 1836 TERRITORIAL CENSUS INDEX. Bountiful, Utah: Accelerated Indexing Systems, 1976. 4810025. 78-112542. 929/.377. F620.J33.

A transcription of 2,064 names in alphabetical order.

Jackson, Ronald Vern, ed. IOWA 1840 TERRITORIAL CENSUS INDEX. Salt Lake City: Accelerated Indexing Systems, 1979. 5082360. F620.J29.

Contains 8,780 names.

Obert, Rowene T.; Blumbagen, Helen M.; and Adkins, Wilms. THE 1840 IOWA CENSUS. CENSUS OF THE 18 ORIGINAL COUNTIES AND SEVERAL PRECINCTS WHICH COMPRISED THE AREA THEN KNOWN AS IOWA. Salt Lake City, Utah: 1968. 1746315. 929.3. GD 844,885 Item 3.

A transcription with an index of over 8,466 names.

Jackson, Ronald Vern, ed. IOWA CENSUS RECORDS, 1841-1849. Salt Lake City: Accelerated Indexing Systems, 1979. 5082349. F620.J295.

A transcription of 7,702 names in alphabetical order.

Jackson, Ronald Vern, and Teeples, Gary Ronald, eds. IOWA 1850 CENSUS INDEX. Bountiful, Utah: Accelerated Indexing Systems, 1976. 4309162. 77-85928.

Contains 47,242 names.

Kansas

Topeka. Kansas State Historical Society. "Indexes to the 1855, 1859, and 1860 Censuses of Kansas." Card index.

Heiss, Willard C., ed. THE CENSUS OF THE TERRITORY OF KANSAS, FEBRUARY, 1855: WITH INDEX AND MAP OF KANSAS ELECTION DISTRICTS IN 1854. Knightstown, Ind.: Bookmark, 1973. 1739261. 929.3781. GD 896, 835 Item 5.

A partial transcription, with an index of about 14,418 names.

Jackson, Ronald Vern; Teeples, Gary Ronald; and Schaefermeyer, David, eds. KANSAS 1855 TERRITORIAL CENSUS INDEX. Bountiful, Utah: Accelerated Indexing Systems, 1977. 2841863. 929.377.

Contains 6,287 names.

Jackson, Ronald Vern, and Teeples, Gary Ronald, eds. KANSAS 1860 TERRI-
TORIAL CENSUS INDEX. Bountiful, Utah: Accelerated Indexing Systems,
1978. 4810026. 78-112539. 929/.3781. F680.J35.

> Contains 63,259 names.

Kentucky

Hainemann, Charles Brunk, comp. FIRST CENSUS OF KENTUCKY, 1790.
Washington, D.C.: M. Brumbaugh, 1940. Reprint. Baltimore: Genealogical
Publishing Co., 1971. 629987. F450.H45 1971.

> Contains 9,100 names in alphabetical order with county and
> tax list data references.

Clift, Garrett Glenn, comp. "SECOND CENSUS" OF KENTUCKY, 1800: A
PRIVATELY COMPILED AND PUBLISHED ENUMERATION OF TAXPAYERS AP-
PEARING IN THE 79 MANUSCRIPT VOLUMES EXTANT OF TAX LISTS OF THE
42 COUNTIES OF KENTUCKY IN EXISTENCE IN 1800. Frankfort: n.p., 1954.
Reprint. Baltimore: Genealogical Publishing Co., 1970. 2779217. GD 390,
838.

> Contains thirty-two thousand names in alphabetical order, with
> county and tax list data references.

Bell, Annie Walker Burns. THIRD CENSUS OF THE UNITED STATES, 1810,
STATE OF KENTUCKY. Indexed by the Genealogical Society of Utah. Wash-
ington: Bell, 1936. 5907254. 312. Index: GD 8,657. Transcription:
GD 8,658 Adair-Harden; GD 8,659 Harrison-Montgomery; GD 8,660 Muhlenberg-
Woodford.

> A transcription with an index of more than 37,920 names.

Jackson, Ronald Vern, and Teeples, Gary Ronald, eds. KENTUCKY 1810
CENSUS. Bountiful, Utah: Accelerated Indexing Systems, 1978. 4559119.
77-85932.

> Contains 52,017 names.

Volkel, Lowell M. AN INDEX TO THE 1810 FEDERAL CENSUS OF KENTUCKY.
4 vols. Springfield, Ill.: n.p., 1971-1972. 139352. 72-23952rev.72.
929/.3769. F450.V6.

> Not a statewide index. Contains four indexes of about 53,486
> names with county and page references.

Jackson, Ronald Vern; Teeples, Gary Ronald; and Schaefermeyer, David, eds.
KENTUCKY 1820 CENSUS INDEX. Bountiful, Utah: Accelerated Indexing
Systems, 1976. 2918329. 929.3.

> Contains 66,847 names.

Volkel, Lowell M. AN INDEX TO THE 1820 FEDERAL CENSUS OF KENTUCKY. 4 vols. Thomson, Ill.: Heritage House, 1974. 1576391. 929.3769.

> Not a statewide index. Contains four indexes of 68,310 names with county and page references.

Jackson, Ronald Vern, and Teeples, Gary Ronald, eds. KENTUCKY 1830 CENSUS INDEX. Bountiful, Utah: Accelerated Indexing Systems, 1976. 4809972. 78-112588. 929/.3769. F450.J316.

> Contains 85,070 names.

Smith, Dora Wilson, comp. KENTUCKY 1830 CENSUS INDEX. 6 vols. Thomson, Ill.: Heritage House, 1973. 1286961. 929.3769.

> Not a statewide index. Contains six indexes. About 85,848 names.

Jackson, Ronald Vern, and Teeples, Gary Ronald, eds. KENTUCKY 1840 CENSUS INDEX. Bountiful, Utah: Accelerated Indexing Systems, 1976. 4701394. 77-85936. F450.K450 1840.

> Contains 102,463 names.

_____. KENTUCKY 1850 CENSUS INDEX. Bountiful, Utah: Accelerated Indexing Systems, 1976. 4833909. 78-112589. 929/.3769. F450.J322.

> Contains 193,957 names.

McDowell, Sam, comp. A SURNAME INDEX TO THE 1850 FEDERAL POPULATION CENSUS OF KENTUCKY. 20 vols. Hartford, Ky.: McDowell, 1974-- . 1031802. 74-176028rev.79. 929/.3769. F450.M16. GD 962,205 Item 1 (3 counties), 962,324 Items 2-3 (7 counties).

> Not a statewide index. Contains twenty volumes but is not yet complete.

Louisiana

Maduell, Charles R., comp. THE CENSUS TABLES FOR THE FRENCH COLONY OF LOUISIANA FROM 1699 THROUGH 1732. Baltimore: Genealogical Publishing Co., 1972. 369902. 72-1355. 929/.3763. F368.M3.

> Miscellaneous lists with a surname index of over forty-one hundred names.

Jackson, Ronald Vern, and Teeples, Gary Ronald, eds. LOUISIANA 1810 CENSUS INDEX. Bountiful, Utah: Accelerated Indexing Systems, 1976. 4833755. 78-113475. 929/.3763. F368.J28.

> Transcription of 8,864 entries in alphabetical order.

_____. LOUISIANA 1820 CENSUS INDEX. Bountiful, Utah: Accelerated Indexing Systems, 1976. 4833916. 78-112540. 929/.3763. F368.J29.

Contains 13,285 names.

Sanders, Mary Elizabeth. AN INDEX TO THE 1820 CENSUS OF LOUISIANA'S FLORIDA PARISHES AND 1812 ST. TAMMANY PARISH TAX LIST. Lafayette, La.: n.p., 1972. 572973. 73-151480. 929/.3763/1. F377.F6S26. GD 1,036,558 Item 3.

Contains about 2,924 names.

Jackson, Ronald Vern; Teeples, Gary Ronald; and Schaefermeyer, David, eds. LOUISIANA 1830 CENSUS INDEX. Bountiful, Utah: Accelerated Indexing Systems, 1976. 2909182.

Contains 19,622 names.

Jackson, Ronald Vern, and Teeples, Gary Ronald, eds. LOUISIANA 1840 CENSUS INDEX. Bountiful, Utah: Accelerated Indexing Systems, 1978. 3889567. 77-85942.

Contains 33,340 names.

_____. LOUISIANA 1850 CENSUS INDEX. Bountiful, Utah: Accelerated Indexing Systems, 1978. 3889578. 77-85943. HA402.A4.

Contains 106,615 names.

Maine

U.S. Bureau of the Census. HEADS OF FAMILIES AT THE FIRST CENSUS OF THE UNITED STATES TAKEN IN THE YEAR 1790: MAINE. Washington, D.C.: Government Printing Office, 1908. Reprint. Spartanburg, S.C.: Reprint Co., 1963; Baltimore: Genealogical Publishing Co., 1966; and Bountiful, Utah: Accelerated Indexing Systems, 1978. Microfilm. T498 reel 1. Washington, D.C.: National Archives, 1960. and New Haven, Conn.: Research Publications, 1972. 2531660. 64-60351. 929/.3741. F24.U5. GD 874,191 Item 3.

Index contains about 17,495 names.

Jackson, Ronald Vern; Teeples, Gary Ronald; and Schaefermeyer, David, eds. MAINE 1800 CENSUS INDEX. Bountiful, Utah: Accelerated Indexing Systems, 1977. 4810045. 78-112504. 929/.3741. F18.J29.

A transcription of 25,123 names in alphabetical order.

Jackson, Ronald Vern, and Teeples, Gary Ronald, eds. MAINE 1810 CENSUS INDEX. Bountiful, Utah: Accelerated Indexing Systems, 1976. 4809969.

78-112595. 929/.3741. F18.J293.

Contains 34,681 names.

_____. MAINE 1820 CENSUS INDEX. Bountiful, Utah: Accelerated Indexing Systems, 1976. 4641502. 78-112466. 929/.3741. F18.J3.

Contains 48,088 names.

_____. MAINE 1830 CENSUS INDEX. Bountiful, Utah: Accelerated Indexing Systems, 1977. 4810053. 78-112489. 929/.3741. F18.J32.

Contains 64,739 names.

_____. MAINE 1840 CENSUS INDEX. Bountiful, Utah: Accelerated Indexing Systems, 1978. 4641497. 78-112491. 929/.3741. F18.J33.

Contains 84,751 names.

_____. MAINE 1850 CENSUS INDEX. Bountiful, Utah: Accelerated Indexing Systems, 1978. 4202760. 929.1.

There are some names for Virginia that were inadvertently published in this index--GENEALOGICAL HELPER 33 (1979): 107.

Maryland

Brumbaugh, Gaius Marcus. MARYLAND RECORDS: COLONIAL, REVOLUTIONARY COUNTY AND CHURCH, FROM ORIGINAL SOURCES. 2 vols. Baltimore: Williams and Wilkins, 1915. Reprint. Baltimore: Genealogical Publishing Co., 1975. 1596979. 67-24374. F180.B89 1967 GD 873,779 Items 1-2.

Contains a 1776 census.

Carothers, Bettie Stirling, comp. 1776 CENSUS OF MARYLAND. Chesterfield, Mo.: n.p., 1972. 676658. F180.C28 1972. GD 928,227 Item 2.

Transcription arranged by county and hundred with an index of 10,584 names.

_____. 1778 CENSUS OF MARYLAND. Chesterfield, Mo.: n.p., 1972. 598766. 929.3752. F180.C3 1972. GD 908,123 Item 3.

Transcription of over 3,500 names in alphabetical order.

U.S. Bureau of the Census. HEADS OF FAMILIES AT THE FIRST CENSUS OF THE UNITED STATES TAKEN IN THE YEAR 1790: MARYLAND. Washington, D.C.: Government Printing Office, 1907. Reprint. Spartanburg, S.C.:

Reprint Co., 1964; Baltimore: Genealogical Publishing Co., 1965; and Bountiful, Utah: Accelerated Indexing Systems, 1978. Microfilm. T498 reel 1.
Washington, D.C.: National Archives, 1960; and New Haven, Conn.: Research Publications, 1972. 2531678. 64-61300. 929/.3752. F185-U5.
GD 874,193 Item 3.

    Index contains about 33,898 names.

Jackson, Ronald Vern, and Teeples, Gary Ronald, eds. MARYLAND 1800
CENSUS INDEX. Bountiful, Utah: Accelerated Indexing Systems, 1978.
4400353. 77-85953. 929/.3752. F180.J32.

    Transcription of 37,406 names in alphabetical order.

_____. MARYLAND 1810 CENSUS INDEX. Bountiful, Utah: Accelerated
Indexing Systems, 1976. 4810048. 78-112501. 929/.3752. F180.J323.

    Contains 42,753 names.

_____. MARYLAND 1820 CENSUS INDEX. Accelerated Indexing Systems,
1977. 4641496. 78-112495. 929/.3752. F180.J325.

    Contains 49,794 names.

Jackson, Ronald Vern; Schaefermeyer, David; and Teeples, Gary Ronald, eds.
MARYLAND 1830 CENSUS INDEX. Bountiful, Utah: Accelerated Indexing
Systems, 1976. 2231926. 975.2.

    Contains 48,973 names.

Jackson, Ronald Vern, and Teeples, Gary Ronald, eds. MARYLAND 1840
CENSUS INDEX. Bountiful, Utah: Accelerated Indexing Systems, 1977.
3760503. 77-85957. 929.3752.

    Contains 65,037 names.

_____. MARYLAND 1850 CENSUS INDEX. Bountiful, Utah: Accelerated
Indexing Systems, 1976. 4810036. 78-112516. 929/.3752. F180.J333.

    Contains 170,128 names.

Massachusetts

U.S. Bureau of the Census. HEADS OF FAMILIES AT THE FIRST CENSUS OF
THE UNITED STATES TAKEN IN THE YEAR 1790: MASSACHUSETTS. Wash-
ington, D.C.: Government Printing Office, 1908. Reprint. Spartanburg,
S.C.: Reprint Co., 1964; Baltimore: Genealogical Publishing Co., 1973; and
Bountiful, Utah: Accelerated Indexing Systems, 1978. Microfilm. T498 reel 1.
Washington, D.C.: National Archives, 1960; and New Haven, Conn.: Re-
search Publications, 1972. 2531697. 64-62657. 929/.3744. F63.U5. GD
874,192 Item 1.

Index contains about 65,960 names.

Bentley, Elizabeth Petty, comp. INDEX TO THE 1800 CENSUS OF MASSA-
CHUSETTS. Baltimore: Genealogical Publishing Co., 1978. 4242580. 78-
58855. 929/.3744. F63.B46.

Contains about 70,455 names.

Jackson, Ronald Vern, and Teeples, Gary Ronald, eds. MASSACHUSETTS
1800 CENSUS INDEX. Bountiful, Utah: Accelerated Indexing Systems, 1977.
4809967. 78-112597. 929/.3744. F63.J27.

A transcription of 67,356 names in alphabetical order.

_____. MASSACHUSETTS 1810 CENSUS INDEX. Bountiful, Utah: Accel-
erated Indexing Systems, 1976. 4810061. 78-112471. 929/.3744. F63.J28.

Contains 79,232 names.

_____. MASSACHUSETTS 1820 CENSUS INDEX. Bountiful, Utah: Accel-
erated Indexing Systems, 1976. 4641481. 78-112560. 929/.3744. F63.J3.

Contains 91,830 names.

_____. MASSACHUSETTS 1830 CENSUS INDEX. Bountiful, Utah: Accel-
erated Indexing Systems, 1976. 4810019. 78-112550. 929/.3744. F63.J32.

Contains 105,101 names.

_____. MASSACHUSETTS 1840 CENSUS INDEX. Bountiful, Utah: Accel-
erated Indexing Systems, 1978. 4269587. 77-85964. 974.4.

Contains 142,002 names.

_____. MASSACHUSETTS 1850 CENSUS INDEX. Bountiful, Utah: Accel-
erated Indexing Systems, 1978. 4283644. 77-85963. F63.J33 1850.

Contains 369,507 names.

Michigan

Jackson, Ronald Vern, and Teeples, Gary Ronald, eds. EARLY MICHIGAN
CENSUS RECORDS. Bountiful, Utah: Accelerated Indexing Systems, 1976.
3341151. 929.3774.

Contains 752 names.

Kresge, Mrs. E.B.; McGlynn, Mrs. James D.; and Davis, Mrs. Elvert M.
MICHIGAN TERRITORY FEDERAL CENSUS, 1820. Copied from DETROIT SO-
CIETY FOR GENEALOGICAL RESEARCH MAGAZINE, v. 12-15. GD 927,678
Item 1.

A transcription of about 1,700 names in alphabetical order.

Wiedeman, Ruby, and Bohannan Larry, comps. FEDERAL POPULATION CEN-
SUS: 1820 MICHIGAN. Huntsville, Ark.: Century Enterprises Genealogical
Services, 1968. 1196241. 977.4. GD 927,678 Item 2.

A transcription of schedules with a 5,456 name index.

Not a statewide index but a transcription of about 1,456 names
arranged in eight alphabets.

Harland, Elizabeth Taft; Millbrook, Minnie Dubbs; and Irwin, Elizabeth Case.
1830 FEDERAL CENSUS, TERRITORY OF MICHIGAN AND A GUIDE TO AN-
CESTRAL TRAILS IN MICHIGAN. By Lucy Mary Kellogg. 4th ed. Detroit:
Detroit Society for Genealogical Research, 1975. 3010964. 929.3774.
GD 928,352 Item 6; duplicate copy 926,745 Item 1.

A transcription of schedules with a 5,456 name index.

Jackson, Ronald Vern, and Teeples, Gary Ronald, eds. MICHIGAN 1830
CENSUS INDEX. Bountiful, Utah: Accelerated Indexing Systems, 1976.
4809968. 78-112596. 929/.3774. F565.J33.

Contains 5,811 names.

_____. MICHIGAN 1840 CENSUS INDEX. Bountiful, Utah: Accelerated
Indexing Systems, 1977. 4667649. 77-85969. 929/.3774. F565.J332.

Contains 36,810 names.

McGlynn, Estelle A., ed. INDEX TO 1840 FEDERAL POPULATION CENSUS
OF MICHIGAN. Detroit: Detroit Society for Genealogical Research, 1977.
3204631. 77-151248. 929/.3774. F565.M32.

Contains 36,415 names.

Jackson, Ronald Vern, and Teeples, Gary Ronald, eds. MICHIGAN 1850
CENSUS INDEX. Bountiful, Utah: Accelerated Indexing Systems, 1978.
4426707. 977.4.

Contains 118,233 names.

Michigan Genealogical Council. INDEX TO THE 1850 FEDERAL POPULATION
CENSUS OF MICHIGAN. Lansing: Michigan Society Daughters of the American
Revolution and the Michigan Genealogical Council, 1976. 2312457. F566.
M6765.

Contains 113,775 names.

Stuart, Donna Valley, ed. INDEX TO THE 1860 FEDERAL POPULATION CEN-
SUS OF DETROIT AND WAYNE COUNTY, MICHIGAN. Detroit: Detroit Society for Genealogical Research, 1979. 4566950.

Census Schedules

Minnesota

St. Paul. Minnesota Historical Society. "Indexes of the 1850, 1857, and 1860 Censuses of Minnesota." Card index.

Harpole, Patricia C., and Nagle, Mary D., eds. MINNESOTA TERRITORIAL CENSUS, 1850. Publications of the Minnesota Historical Society. St. Paul: Minnesota Historical Society, 1972. 323719. 70-188492. 929/.3776. F605.H3.

> A transcription of over 2,040 surnames.

Rotzel, Myra Durand, and Hyde, Edith Drake. "The Federal Census of Minnesota Territory for 1850." Typewritten. DAR Library, n.d.

> Transcription with an index of many more than 1,825 names.

Jackson, Ronald Vern, ed. MINNESOTA 1860 CENSUS INDEX. Salt Lake City: Accelerated Indexing Systems, 1979. 6161505. 977.6.

_____. MINNESOTA 1870 CENSUS INDEX. Salt Lake City: Accelerated Indexing Systems, 1979. 5020410. F605.M76.

> Contains 423,812 names.

Mississippi

Jackson. Mississippi Department of Archives and History. "Indexes to the 1816 and 1820 Censuses of Mississippi." Card index.

Gillis, Irene S., and Gillis, Norman E. MISSISSIPPI 1820 CENSUS. Baton Rouge, La.: n.p., 1963. 942076. 64-225. HA466.G5.

> A transcription of 7,314 names in alphabetical order.

Jackson, Ronald Vern; Teeples, Gary Ronald; and Schaefermeyer, David, eds. MISSISSIPPI 1820 CENSUS INDEX. Accelerated Indexing Systems, 1976. 4809931. 78-112669. 929/.3762. F340.J328.

> Contains 7,437 names.

McEllhiney, Wilda Blewett, and Thomas, Elizabeth Wood. 1820 CENSUS OF MISSISSIPPI. Tuscaloosa, Ala.: Willo Publishing Co., 1964. 3261167. 939.3762.

> A transcription by county with a surname index to each county. Contains more than 2,688 names.

Gillis, Irene S., and Gillis, Norman E. MISSISSIPPI 1830 CENSUS. Baton Rouge, La.: 1965. 942069. 65-56450. F340.G47.

Transcription of about 11,450 names in alphabetical order.

Jackson, Ronald Vern, and Teeples, Gary Ronald, eds. MISSISSIPPI 1830 CENSUS INDEX. Bountiful, Utah: Accelerated Indexing Systems, 1976. 4810054. 78-112488. 929/.3762. F340.J33.

Contains 11,654 names.

Platt, Gwen; Lannart, Annabel; and Peer, Marian. MISSISSIPPI NORTHERN DISTRICT: INDEX TO THE UNITED STATES CENSUS OF 1840. Santa Ana, Calif.: G.A.M. Publications, 1970. 2115191. HA466.P5 1840. GD 496, 891 Item 6.

Contains many more than 4,788 names.

_____. MISSISSIPPI SOUTHERN DISTRICT: INDEX TO THE UNITED STATES CENSUS OF 1840. Santa Ana, Calif.: G.A.M. Publications, 1970. 2115199. HA466.P55 1840. GD 908,533 Item 2.

Contains many more than 5,814 names.

Gillis, Irene S. MISSISSIPPI 1850 CENSUS: SURNAME INDEX. Shreveport, La.: n.p., 1972. 521108. 72-169087. 929/.3762. F340.G473.

Contains 52,057 names.

Jackson, Ronald Vern, and Teeples, Gary Ronald, eds. MISSISSIPPI 1850 CENSUS INDEX. Bountiful, Utah: Accelerated Indexing Systems, 1977. 4810046. 78-112503. 929/.3762. F340.J34.

Contains 76,037 names.

Missouri

Glazner, Capitola Hensley, and McLane, Bobbie Jones. AN INDEX TO FIFTH CENSUS OF THE UNITED STATES, 1830: POPULATION SCHEDULES, STATE OF MISSOURI. Hot Springs National Park, Ark.: Published by the Authors, 1966. 209622. 75-23051. F466.G42. GD 1,000,307 Item 4.

Contains 19,119 names.

Jackson, Ronald Vern, and Teeples, Gary Ronald, eds. MISSOURI 1830 CENSUS INDEX. Bountiful, Utah: Accelerated Indexing Systems, 1976. 4641491. 78-112518. 929/.3778. F465.J3.

Contains 19,213 names.

Census Schedules

Stercula, Beverly Margaret. HEADS OF FAMILIES 1830 CENSUS OF MISSOURI. Fullerton, Calif.: Genealogems Publications, 1966. 2531847. 317.3.

Full name listing with a surname index of over 3,933 entries.

Jackson, Ronald Vern, and Teeples, Gary Ronald, eds. MISSOURI 1840 CENSUS INDEX. Bountiful Utah: Accelerated Indexing Systems, 1976. 4810076. 78-112439. 929/.3778. F465.J32.

Contains 53,961 names.

Nelson, Frances, and Brouse, Gwen. THE INDEX TO THE FEDERAL CENSUS OF MISSOURI FOR 1840: A GUIDE TO THE COUNTY BY COUNTY ENUMERATION. 3 vols. Riverside, Calif.: Ancestor's Attic, 1977. 3456957. 929.3778.

Contains 55,296 names.

Jackson, Ronald Vern, and Teeples, Gary Ronald, eds. MISSOURI 1850 CENSUS INDEX. Bountiful, Utah: Accelerated Indexing Systems, 1976. 3713597. 77-85978. 977.8.

Contains 166,696 names.

St. Louis Genealogical Society. INDEX OF 1850 U.S. CENSUS, ST. LOUIS & ST. LOUIS COUNTY, MO. St. Louis: n.p., 1969. 75262. 75-12565. 929.3. F474.S3S283.

Contains 99,661 names.

Montana

Jackson, Ronald Vern, ed. MONTANA 1870 TERRITORIAL CENSUS INDEX. Salt Lake City: Accelerated Indexing Systems, 1979. 5088373. F730.J32.

Contains 19,935 names.

Marshall, Thelma Leasure. MONTANA TERRITORY 1870 CENSUS INDEX. Great Falls, Mont.: The Author, 1979.

Contains nearly 20,600 names.

Nebraska

Cox, E. Evelyn, ed. 1854, 1855, 1856 NEBRASKA TERRITORY CENSUSES. 3 vols, in 1. Ellensburg, Wash.: Cox, 1977. 3179715.

Contains three surname indexes in rough alphabetical order. Index for 1854 has more than 648 names; 1855, 702 names; and 1856, 2,214 names.

_____. 1860 NEBRASKA TERRITORY CENSUS: INDEX TO HEADS-OF-FAMILIES. Ellensburg, Wash.: Ancestree House, 1979. 5049881. 929.3782. F665.668 1860.

Jackson, Ronald Vern, and Teeples, Gary Ronald, eds. NEBRASKA 1860 TERRITORIAL CENSUS INDEX. Bountiful, Utah: Accelerated Indexing Systems, 1978. 4810058. 78-112478. 929/.3782. F665.J33.

> Contains 27,658 names.

Cox, E. Evelyn. 1870 NEBRASKA CENSUS. Ellensburg, Wash.: Ancestree House, 1979. 4791588. F665.6682.

> Includes index.

Nevada

Jackson, Ronald Vern, ed. NEVADA 1870 TERRITORIAL CENSUS INDEX. Salt Lake City: Accelerated Indexing Systems, 1979. 5088381. F840.J32.

> Contains 61,705 names.

_____. NEVADA 1880 TERRITORIAL CENSUS INDEX. Salt Lake City: Accelerated Indexing Systems, 1979. 5086894. F840.J325.

> Contains 43,499 names.

New Hampshire

Holbrook, Jay Mack. NEW HAMPSHIRE 1776 CENSUS. Oxford, Mass.: Holbrook Research Institute, 1976. 2619932. 76-151110. F33.H64.

> Contains 47,242 names.

U.S. Bureau of the Census. HEADS OF FAMILIES AT THE FIRST CENSUS OF THE UNITED STATES TAKEN IN THE YEAR 1790: NEW HAMPSHIRE. Washington, D.C.: Government Printing Office, 1907. Reprint. Spartanburg, S.C.: Reprint Co., 1964; Baltimore: Genealogical Publishing Co., 1972; and Bountiful, Utah: Accelerated Indexing Systems, 1978. Microfilm. T498 reel 1. Washington, D.C.: National Archives, 1960; and New Haven, Conn.: Research Publications, 1972. 2785043. 64-61301. 929/.3742. F38.U5. GD 874,191 Item 4.

> Index contains about 24,675 names.

Gill, James V., and Gill, Maryan, comp. AN INDEX TO THE 1800 FEDERAL CENSUS OF NEW HAMPSHIRE. 3 vols. in 1. Danville, Ill.: Illiana Genealogical Publishing Co., 1967-1973. 1750840. 929.3742.

> Contains about 19,836 names.

Jackson, Ronald Vern, and Teeples, Gary Ronald, eds. NEW HAMPSHIRE 1800 CENSUS INDEX. Bountiful, Utah: Accelerated Indexing Systems, 1977. 4810028. 78-112537. 929/.3742. F33.J298 1977.

Contains 25,842 names.

Threlfall, John Brooks, comp. HEADS OF FAMILIES AT THE SECOND CENSUS OF THE UNITED STATES TAKEN IN THE YEAR 1800, NEW HAMPSHIRE. Madison, Wis.: n.p., 1973. 947653. 73-86863. 929/.3742. F33.T47.

Transcription with index of more than 20,425 names.

Jackson, Ronald Vern, and Teeples, Gary Ronald, eds. NEW HAMPSHIRE 1810 CENSUS INDEX. Bountiful, Utah: Accelerated Indexing Systems, 1976. 4810049. 78-112497. 929/.3742. F33.J3.

Contains 34,883 names.

_____. NEW HAMPSHIRE 1820 CENSUS INDEX. Bountiful, Utah: Accelerated Indexing Systems, 1976. 4810056. 78-112481. 929/.3742. F33.J314.

Contains 27,112 names.

_____. NEW HAMPSHIRE 1830 CENSUS INDEX. Bountiful, Utah: Accelerated Indexing Systems, 1877. 3341085. 78-113329. 929/.3742. F33.J318.

Contains 63,311 names.

_____. NEW HAMPSHIRE 1840 CENSUS INDEX. Bountiful, Utah: Accelerated Indexing Systems, 1978. 3949456. 77-85984. 929/.3742. F33.J32.

Contains 40,775 names.

_____. NEW HAMPSHIRE 1850 CENSUS INDEX. Bountiful Utah: Accelerated Indexing Systems, 1978. 4031237. 77-86133. 929/.3742. F33.J323.

Contains 105,835 names.

New Jersey

Stryker-Rodda, Kenn. REVOLUTIONARY CENSUS OF NEW JERSEY: AN INDEX, BASED ON RATABLES, OF THE INHABITANTS OF NEW JERSEY DURING THE PERIOD OF THE AMERICAN REVOLUTION. Cottonport, La.: Polyanthos, 1972. 538760. 70-180475. 929/.3749. F133.S77.

Three alphabetical lists.

Jackson, Ronald Vern, ed. NEW JERSEY 1830 CENSUS. Bountiful, Utah: Accelerated Indexing Systems, 1974. 1812069. 78-112444. 929/.3749. F133.J33.

Contains 60,500 names.

Jackson, Ronald Vern, and Teeples, Gary Ronald, eds. NEW JERSEY 1840 CENSUS INDEX. Bountiful, Utah: Accelerated Indexing Systems, 1978. 4641500. 78-112469. 929/.3749. F133.J335.

> Contains 65,660 names.

_____. NEW JERSEY 1850 CENSUS INDEX. Bountiful, Utah: Accelerated Indexing Systems, 1976. 4833774. 78-112967. 929/.3749. F133.J336.

> Contains 159,778 names.

Tanco, Barbrae Owens. THE 1850 CENSUS TOGETHER WITH INDEX . . . NEW JERSEY; INCLUDING THE 1840 LIST OF REVOLUTIONARY AND MILITARY PENSIONERS. . . . Fort Worth, Tex.: Printed by Millican Press, 1973. 63714. 73-16108rev.72. 929.3749. F133.T36.

> Incomplete; each volume indexed.

New Mexico

Olmstead, Virginia L., comp. SPANISH AND MEXICAN COLONIAL CENSUSES OF NEW MEXICO, 1790, 1823, 1845. Albuquerque: New Mexico Genealogical Society, 1975. 2118554. 75-23853. 929/.3789. F795.S67.

> Contains many more than one thousand surnames.

Jackson, Ronald Vern, and Teeples, Gary Ronald, eds. NEW MEXICO 1850 CENSUS INDEX. Bountiful, Utah: Accelerated Indexing Systems, 1978. 4641483. 78-112541. 929/.3789. F795.J33.

> Contains 19,874 names.

Windham, Margaret Leonard, ed. NEW MEXICO 1850 TERRITORIAL CENSUS. 4 vols. Albuquerque: New Mexico Genealogical Society, 1976. 3033077. 76-5820rev.78. 312/.09789. F795.W56.

Jackson, Ronald Vern, ed. NEW MEXICO 1860 TERRITORIAL CENSUS INDEX. Salt Lake City: Accelerated Indexing Systems, 1979.

New York

Meyers, Carol M., comp. EARLY NEW YORK STATE CENSUS RECORDS. Gardena, Calif.: RAM Publishers, 1965. 128906. 72-271070. 929/.3/747. F118.M6 1965.

> Transcription of over 7,020 names in alphabetical order.

U.S. Bureau of the Census. HEADS OF FAMILIES AT THE FIRST CENSUS OF

Census Schedules

THE UNITED STATES TAKEN IN THE YEAR 1790: NEW YORK. Washington, D.C.: Government Printing Office, 1908. Reprint. Spartanburg, S.C.: Reprint Co., 1964; Baltimore: Genealogical Publishing Co., 1976; and Bountiful, Utah: Accelerated Indexing Systems, 1978. Microfilm. T498 reel 2. Washington, D.C.: National Archives, 1960; and New Haven, Conn.: Research Publications, 1972. GD 874,192 Item 4 and 874,193 Item 1.

Index contains about 55,214 names.

Jackson, Ronald Vern, and Teeples, Gary Ronald, eds. NEW YORK 1800 CENSUS INDEX. Bountiful, Utah: Accelerated Indexing Systems, 1977. 4810062. 78-112468. 929/.3747. F118.J28 1977.

A transcription pf 102,911 names in alphabetical order.

McMullin, Phillip W., ed. NEW YORK IN 1800: AN INDEX TO THE FEDERAL CENSUS SCHEDULES OF THE STATE OF NEW YORK, WITH OTHER AIDS TO RESEARCH. Provo, Utah: Gendex Corp., 1971. 205461. 74-172992rev.73. 929/.3747. F118.M17.

Contains 97,801 names with page and reel.

Jackson, Ronald Vern; Teeples, Gary Ronald; and Schaefermeyer, David, eds. NEW YORK 1810 CENSUS INDEX. Bountiful, Utah: Accelerated Indexing Systems, 1976. 2231897. 974.7.

A transcription of 150,321 names in alphabetical order.

Jackson, Ronald Vern, and Teeples, Gary Ronald, eds. NEW YORK 1820 CENSUS INDEX. Bountiful, Utah: Accelerated Indexing Systems, 1977. 2902846. 78-112593. 929/.3747. F118.J29.

Contains 217,306 names.

_____. NEW YORK 1830 CENSUS INDEX. Bountiful, Utah: Accelerated Indexing Systems, 1977. 3779849. 77-86117. F188.J33 1830.

Contains 315,070 names.

_____. NEW YORK 1840 CENSUS INDEX. Salt Lake City: Accelerated Indexing Systems, 1978. 4269618. 77-81843. 974.7.

Contains 408,345 names.

_____. NEW YORK 1850 CENSUS. 2 vols. Bountiful, Utah: Accelerated Indexing Systems, 1977. 3128876. 77-81842. 929/.3747. F118.J3.

Contains 806,399 names.

_____. NEW YORK CITY 1850 CENSUS INDEX. Bountiful, Utah: Accel-

erated Indexing Systems, 1976. 2079528. 78-112567. 929/.3747/1. F128.
25.J33.

Contains 210,351 names.

North Carolina

North Carolina. State Department of Archives and History. STATE CENSUS
OF NORTH CAROLINA, 1784-1787. Transcribed and indexed by Alvaretta
Kenan Register. 2d ed., rev. Baltimore: Genealogical Publishing Co., 1973.
677297. 73-3664. 929/.3756. F258.N9 1971a. GD 897,274 Item 2.

A transcription with full name index.

U.S. Bureau of the Census. HEADS OF FAMILIES AT THE FIRST CENSUS OF
THE UNITED STATES TAKEN IN THE YEAR 1790: NORTH CAROLINA.
Washington, D.C.: Government Printing Office, 1908. Reprint. Spartanburg,
S.C.: Reprint Co., 1974; Baltimore: Genealogical Publishing Co., 1973;
and Bountiful, Utah: Accelerated Indexing Systems, 1978. Microfilm T498
reel 2. Washington, D.C.: National Archives, 1960; and New Haven, Conn.:
Research Publications, 1972. 2531745. 61-60771. 929/.3756. F251.U5.
GD 873,671 Item 3.

Index contains about 53,475 names.

Bentley, Elizabeth Petty, comp. INDEX TO THE 1800 CENSUS OF NORTH
CAROLINA. Baltimore: Genealogical Publishing Co., 1977. 2847689.
76-53969. 929/.3/756. F253.B46.

Contains about 62,370 names.

Jackson, Ronald Vern, and Teeples, Gary Ronald, eds. NORTH CAROLINA
1800 CENSUS INDEX. Bountiful, Utah: Accelerated Indexing Systems, 1977.
4810078. 78-112438. 929/.3756. F253.J22.

A transcription of 61,592 names in alphabetical order.

Johnson, William Perry, and Potter, Dorothy Williams, eds. 1800 NORTH
CAROLINA CENSUS. Tullahoma, Tenn.: Johnson, 1975. 2089925. 76-
354354. 929/.3756. F253.U54 1800.

A transcription with an index for each county in separate
volumes.

Bentley, Elizabeth Petty, comp. INDEX TO THE 1810 CENSUS OF NORTH
CAROLINA. Baltimore: Genealogical Publishing Co., 1978. 3621908.
77-88140. 929/.3756. F253.B462.

Contains about 21,791 names.

Jackson, Ronald Vern, and Teeples, Gary Ronald, eds. NORTH CAROLINA 1810 CENSUS INDEX. Bountiful, Utah: Accelerated Indexing Systems, 1976. 4809986. 78-112574. 929/.3756. F253.J23.

Contains 63,161 names.

Smith, Dora Wilson, comp. NORTH CAROLINA 1810 CENSUS INDEX. Thomson, Ill.: Heritage House, 1977. 3258953. 77-79657. 929.3.

Contains six indexes.

Jackson, Ronald Vern, and Teeples, Gary Ronald, eds. NORTH CAROLINA 1830 CENSUS INDEX. Bountiful, Utah: Accelerated Indexing Systems, 1976. 4809954. 78-112623. 929/.3756. F253.J233.

Contains 22,944 names.

Potter, Dorothy Williams, ed. INDEX TO 1820 NORTH CAROLINA CENSUS: SUPPLEMENTED FROM TAX LISTS AND OTHER SOURCES. Tullahoma, Tenn.: n.p., 1974. Reprint. Baltimore: Genealogical Publishing Co., 1978. 4492185. 78-58459. 929/.3756. F253.P67 1978.

Contains 69,224 names.

Jackson, Ronald Vern, and Teeples, Gary Ronald, eds. NORTH CAROLINA 1830 CENSUS INDEX. Bountiful, Utah: Accelerated Indexing Systems, 1976. 4311923. 78-112414. 929/.3756. F253.J234.

Contains 84,930 names.

_____. NORTH CAROLINA 1840 CENSUS INDEX. Bountiful, Utah: Accelerated Indexing Systems, 1978. 3889619. 78-112467. 929/.3756. F253.J235.

Contains 88,977 names.

Petty, Gerald McKinney, comp. INDEX OF THE 1840 FEDERAL CENSUS OF NORTH CAROLINA. Columbus, Ohio: Petty, 1974. 1205936. 74-10113. 929/.3756. F253.P47.

Contains about 97,920 names.

Jackson, Ronald Vern, and Teeples, Gary Ronald, eds. NORTH CAROLINA 1850 CENSUS INDEX. Bountiful, Utah: Accelerated Indexing Systems, 1976. 4810044. 78-112505. 929/.3756. F253.J236.

Contains 141,293 names.

North Dakota

Jackson, Ronald Vern, ed. DAKOTA 1870 TERRITORIAL CENSUS INDEX. Salt Lake City: Accelerated Indexing Systems, 1979. 5082375. F650.J3.

Contains 13,602 names.

_____. DAKOTA 1880 TERRITORIAL CENSUS INDEX. Salt Lake City: Accelerated Indexing Systems, 1979. 5082386. F650.J35.

Contains 133,208 names.

Ohio

Jackson, Ronald Vern, and Teeples, Gary Ronald, eds. EARLY OHIO CENSUS RECORD. Bountiful, Utah: Accelerated Indexing Systems, 1976. 4884690. 77-86110. 929/.3771. F490.J27.

Contains 3,759 names.

_____. OHIO 1820 CENSUS INDEX. Bountiful, Utah: Accelerated Indexing Systems, 1977. 4810029. 78-112533. 929/.3771. F490.J32.

Contains 89,729 names.

Ohio Library Foundation. Columbus. 1820 FEDERAL POPULATION CENSUS, OHIO: INDEX. Columbus: 1964. 839246. 65-1168. F490.0367.

Contains 89,727 names.

Jackson, Ronald Vern, and Teeples, Gary Ronald, eds. OHIO 1830 CENSUS INDEX. Bountiful, Utah: Accelerated Indexing Systems, 1976. 3762286. 78-112659. 929/.3771. F490.J325.

Contains 153,222 names.

Ohio Family Historians. 1830 FEDERAL POPULATION CENSUS, OHIO: INDEX. 2 vols. Columbus: Ohio Library Foundation, 1964. 839247. 65-1172. F490.0363.

Contains 148,845 names.

Jackson, Ronald Vern, and Teeples, Gary Ronald, eds. OHIO 1840 CENSUS INDEX. Bountiful, Utah: Accelerated Indexing Systems, 1978. 4340006. 77-86102. 929.3771.

Contains 244,504 names.

Census Schedules

Wilkens, Cleo Goff, comp. INDEX TO 1840 FEDERAL POPULATION CENSUS OF OHIO. 4 vols. Fort Wayne, Ind.: n.p., 1969. 116833. 72-18004. 929.3. F490.W67. GD 873,934 vol 1 Adams–Delaware Co.; GD 873,934 vol. 2 Erie–Knox Co.; GD 873,935 vol. 3 Lake–Putnam Co.; GD 908,930 vol. 4 Richland–Wood Co.

Contains four different alphabets of an estimated 28,000 names.

Jackson, Ronald Vern, and Teeples, Gary Ronald, eds. OHIO 1850 CENSUS INDEX. Salt Lake City: Accelerated Indexing Systems, 1978. 4555960. 77-85103. F495.J34 1850.

Contains 572,035 names.

Ohio Family Historians. INDEX TO THE 1850 FEDERAL POPULATION CENSUS OF OHIO. Mineral Ridge, Ohio: L.F. Harshman, 1972. 3207998. 74-151178. 929/.3771. F495.035.

Contains 526,819 names.

Harshman, Lida Flint, comp. INDEX TO THE 1860 FEDERAL POPULATION CENSUS OF OHIO. 2 vols. Mineral Ridge, Ohio: Harshman, 1979. 5590630. 317.71.

Contains 650,449 names.

Oklahoma

Woods, Frances Jerome. INDIAN LANDS WEST OF ARKANSAS (OKLAHOMA) POPULATION SCHEDULE OF THE UNITED STATES CENSUS OF 1860. N.p.: Arrow Printing Co., 1964. 1499380. 67-27953. 929.3766. GD 1,000,357 Item 1.

Contains more than 567 names.

Oklahoma Genealogical Society. AN INDEX TO THE 1890 U.S. CENSUS OF UNION VETERANS AND THEIR WIDOWS IN OKLAHOMA. Special Publication, no. 3. Oklahoma City: 1970. GD 496,937 Item 1.

Contains about three thousand names.

Oregon

Jackson, Ronald Vern, and Teeples, Gary Ronald, eds. OREGON 1850 TERRITORIAL CENSUS INDEX. Bountiful, Utah: Accelerated Indexing Systems, 1978. 3936233. 77-86104. 929/.3795. F875.J3.

Contains 4,980 names.

Oregon. State Library, Salem. Division of State Archives. PIONEER FAMI-
LIES OF THE OREGON TERRITORY 1850. 2d ed. Oregon State Archives.
Bulletin no. 3, Publication no. 17. Salem: 1961. 4758258. 929.3.

> Contains about 5,120 names using the name of county, schedule
> page number and name of the type of schedule (population,
> mortality, agriculture and industry).

Youngberg, Elsie, comp. 1850 OREGON TERRITORIAL CENSUS. Lebanon,
Oreg.: End of Trail Researchers, 1970. 4828290. HA592.Y6. GD 897,219
Item 3.

> Transcription by county with a surname index of about 2,916
> names.

Pennsylvania

Stemmons, John D., and Stemmons, E. Diane, comps. PENNSYLVANIA IN
1780: A STATEWIDE INDEX OF CIRCA 1780 PENNSYLVANIA TAXLISTS.
Salt Lake City: Stemmons, 1978. 4288558. 78-55688. F148.S8.

> Contains more than 48,240 names.

U.S. Bureau of the Census. HEADS OF FAMILIES AT THE FIRST CENSUS OF
THE UNITED STATES TAKEN IN THE YEAR 1790: PENNSYLVANIA. Washington, D.C.: Government Printing Office, 1908. Reprint. Spartanburg,
S.C.: Reprint Co., 1971; Baltimore, Genealogical Publishing Co., 1977;
and Bountiful, Utah: Accelerated Indexing Systems, 1978. Microfilm. T498
reel 2. Washington, D.C.: National Archives, 1960; and New Haven, Conn.: Research Publications, 1972. 2531760. 63-62362. 929/.3748. F153.U5.
GD 874,193 Item 2.

> Index contains about 87,923 names.

Jackson, Ronald Vern, and Teeples, Gary Ronald, eds. PENNSYLVANIA
1800 CENSUS INDEX. Salt Lake City: Accelerated Indexing Systems, 1972.
4324401. 77-86105.

> Contains 96,368 names.

Stemmons, John D., ed. PENNSYLVANIA IN 1800: A COMPUTERIZED IN-
DEX TO THE FEDERAL POPULATION SCHEDULES OF THE STATE OF PENN-
SYLVANIA, WITH OTHER AIDS TO RESEARCH. Salt Lake City: n.p.,
1972. 652294. 72-88048. 929/.3748. F158.4.S8.

> Contains 96,071 names.

Jackson, Ronald Vern, and Teeples, Gary Ronald, eds. PENNSYLVANIA 1810
CENSUS INDEX. Bountiful, Utah: Accelerated Indexing Systems, 1976.
4641495. 78-112506. 929/.3748. F148.J3.

> Contains 129,923 names.

Census Schedules

Ohio Family Historians. INDEX TO 1810 CENSUS OF PENNSYLVANIA.
Cleveland: Micro Photo Division, Bell and Howell Co., 1966. 1137336.
67-2600. 929.3. F148.05. GD 496,937 Items 2-3; Duplicate copy, 590,430.

 Contains about 122,140 names.

Jackson, Ronald Vern; Teeples, Gary Ronald; and Schaefermeyer, David, eds.
PENNSYLVANIA 1820 CENSUS INDEX. Accelerated Indexing Systems, 1978.
4234658. 77-86095. F148.J32.

 Contains 164,271 names.

_____. PENNSYLVANIA 1830 CENSUS INDEX. Bountiful, Utah: Accelerated
Indexing Systems, 1976. 2452721. F153.J27 1830.

 Contains 219,668 names.

Jackson, Ronald Vern, and Teeples, Gary Ronald, eds. PENNSYLVANIA 1840
CENSUS INDEX. Bountiful: Accelerated Indexing Systems, 1978. 4336762.
77-86097. 974.8.

 Contains 295,347 names.

_____. PENNSYLVANIA 1850 CENSUS INDEX. 2 vols. Bountiful, Utah:
Accelerated Indexing Systems, 1976. 2910474. 78-112461. 929/.3748.
F148.J33.

 Contains 687,237 names.

Penrose, Maryly Barton. "HEADS OF FAMILIES" INDEX, 1850 FEDERAL CEN-
SUS, CITY OF PHILADELPHIA. 2d ed., rev. Franklin Park, N.J.: Liberty
Bell Associates, 1974. 1104463. 74-84454. 929/.3748/11. F158.25.P45
1974. GD 392,914.

 Contains about 25,690 names.

Rhode Island

Calef, Frank T. A CENSUS OF THE FREEMEN OF 1747 AS FOUND IN THE
SUPPLEMENT TO THE RHODE ISLAND COLONIAL RECORDS. N.p.: 1928.
GD 22,390 Item 2.

 Contains 1,848 names.

Providence. Rhode Island Historical Society. "Indexes to 1774, 1782, 1850,
1860, and 1865 Censuses of Rhode Island." Card index.

Rhode Island (Colony) General Assembly. CENSUS OF THE INHABITANTS OF
THE COLONY OF RHODE ISLAND AND PROVIDENCE PLANTATIONS, 1774.
Arr. by John R. Bartlett. With index by E.E. Brownell. 1858. Reprint.

Baltimore: Genealogical Publishing Co., 1969. 5748. 69-17130. 929.3. F78.A59 1969.

A transcription that contains a 9,450 name index.

Stewart, Gertrude. CENSUS OF RHODE ISLAND, 1782. Providence: Rhode Island Historical Society, 1950. GD 22,390 Item 1.

Arranged by town. Contains 1,624 surnames.

U.S. Bureau of the Census. HEADS OF FAMILIES AT THE FIRST CENSUS OF THE UNITED STATES TAKEN IN THE YEAR 1790: RHODE ISLAND. Washington, D.C.: Government Printing Office, 1908. Reprint. Spartanburg, S.C.: Reprint Co., 1963; Baltimore: Genealogical Publishing Co., 1966; and Bountiful, Utah: Accelerated Indexing Systems, 1978. Microfilm. T498 reel 3. Washington, D.C.: National Archives, 1960; and New Haven, Conn.: Research Publications, 1972. GD 874,192 Item 2.

Index contains about 12,015 names.

Jackson, Ronald Vern, ed. RHODE ISLAND 1800 CENSUS. Salt Lake City: Accelerated Indexing Systems, 1972. 415994. 72-190122rev.73. 929/.3745. F78.J3.

A transcription of 12,417 names in alphabetical order.

Volkel, Lowell M., comp. AN INDEX TO THE 1800 FEDERAL CENSUS OF RHODE ISLAND. N.p.: 1970. 140721. 71-23199. 929.3745. F78.V6.

Contains about 8,288 names.

Jackson, Ronald Vern, and Teeples, Gary Ronald, eds. RHODE ISLAND 1810 CENSUS INDEX. Bountiful, Utah: Accelerated Indexing Systems, 1976. 4809960. 78-112607. 929/.3745. F78.J32.

Contains 13,267 names.

_____. RHODE ISLAND 1820 CENSUS INDEX. Bountiful, Utah: Accelerated Indexing Systems, 1976. 4810035. 78-112524. 929/.3745. F78.J322.

Contains 14,549 names.

_____. RHODE ISLAND 1830 CENSUS INDEX. Bountiful, Utah: Accelerated Indexing Systems, 1977. 4810037. 78-112514. 929/.3745. F78.J325.

_____. RHODE ISLAND 1840 CENSUS INDEX. Bountiful, Utah: Accelerated Indexing Systems, 1976. 3936367. 78-112513. 929/.3745. F78.J327.

Contains 19,730 names.

_____. RHODE ISLAND 1850 CENSUS INDEX. Bountiful, Utah: Accelerated Indexing Systems, 1976. 4641492. 78-112511. 929/.3745. F78.J33.

A transcription of 12,417 names in alphabetical order.

Rhode Island. Secretary of State. CENSUS OF 1865. INDEX. 24 reels of 16mm. microfilm. Providence: 1974. GD 934,776-934,799.

South Carolina

U.S. Bureau of the Census. HEADS OF FAMILIES AT THE FIRST CENSUS OF THE UNITED STATES TAKEN IN YEAR 1790: SOUTH CAROLINA. Washington, D.C.: Government Printing Office, 1908. Reprint. Spartanburg, S.C.: Reprint Co., 1960. Baltimore: Genealogical Publishing Co., 1978; and Bountiful, Utah: Accelerated Indexing Systems, 1978. Microfilm. T498 reel 3. Washington, D.C.: National Archives, 1960; and New Haven, Conn.: Research Publications, 1972. GD 1,036,840 Item 3.

Index contains about 27,246 names.

Holcomb, Brent H. INDEX TO THE 1800 CENSUS OF SOUTH CAROLINA. Baltimore: Genealogical Publishing Co., 1980. 79-93028.

Contains thirty thousand names.

Jackson, Ronald Vern, and Teeples, Gary Ronald, eds. SOUTH CAROLINA 1800 CENSUS. 2d ed. Bountiful, Utah: Accelerated Indexing Systems, 1975. 4810055. 78-112485. 929/.3757. F268.J33 1975.

A transcription of 34,855 names in alphabetical order.

Rainwater, Margaret. 1800 CENSUS SOUTH CAROLINA. Houston, Tex.: n.p., 1964-67.

Contains about 32,670 names.

Jackson, Ronald Vern, and Teeples, Gary Ronald, eds. SOUTH CAROLINA 1810 CENSUS INDEX. Bountiful, Utah: Accelerated Indexing Systems, 1976. 4383025. 77-86086.

A transcription of 39,860 names in alphabetical order.

Platt, Gwen. SOUTH CAROLINA INDEX TO THE UNITED STATES CENSUS OF 1820. Tustin, Calif.: Published by G.A.M., 1972. 3625017. GD 873,981 Item 1.

A transcription with surname index of many more than 12,100 names.

Jackson, Ronald Vern, and Teeples, Gary Ronald, eds. SOUTH CAROLINA 1820 CENSUS INDEX. Bountiful, Utah: Accelerated Indexing Systems, 1976. 4309195. 77-86087. 929/.3757. F268.J334.

A transcription of 42,904 names in alphabetical order.

Hazlewood, Jean Park; Hazlewood, Fred L., Jr.; and Smith, T.L. INDEX, 1830 CENSUS--SOUTH CAROLINA. Forth Worth, Tex.: GenRePut, 1973.

Contains 47,570 names.

Jackson, Ronald Vern, and Teeples, Gary Ronald, eds. SOUTH CAROLINA 1830 CENSUS INDEX. Bountiful, Utah: Accelerated Indexing Systems, 1976. 2303043. 78-112562. 929/.3757. F268.J335.

Contains 45,545 names.

_____. SOUTH CAROLINA 1840 CENSUS INDEX. Bountiful, Utah: Accelerated Indexing Systems, 1977. 4810041. 78-112508. 929/3757. F268.J337.

Contains 47,838 names.

_____. SOUTH CAROLINA 1850 CENSUS INDEX. Bountiful, Utah: Accelerated Indexing Systems, 1976. 2079519. 78-112552. 929/.3757. F268.J34.

Contains 72,014 names.

South Dakota

Jackson, Ronald Vern, ed. DAKOTA 1870 TERRITORIAL CENSUS INDEX. Salt Lake City: Accelerated Indexing Systems, 1979. 5082375. F650.J3.

Contains 13,602 names.

_____. DAKOTA 1880 TERRITORIAL CENSUS INDEX. Salt Lake City: Accelerated Indexing Systems, 1979. 5082386. F650.J35.

Contains 133,208 names.

Tennessee

Jackson, Ronald Vern, and Teeples, Gary Ronald, eds. TENNESSEE 1820 CENSUS. ed ed. Bountiful, Utah: Accelerated Indexing Systems, 1974. 4810075. 78-112441. 929/.3768. F435.J3 1974.

A transcription of 35,200 names in alphabetical order.

_____. TENNESSEE 1830 CENSUS INDEX. Bountiful, Utah: Accelerated Indexing Systems, 1976. 3760491. 78-112529. 929/.3768. F435.J32.

Contains 86,088 names.

Sistler, Byron, comp. 1830 CENSUS TENNESSEE. 3 vols. Evanston, Ill.: Byron Sistler and Associates, 1969-1971. 4032112. 929.3768. GD 924,404 Items 1-3.

> Contains more than 73,980 names.

Jackson, Ronald Vern, and Teeples, Gary Ronald, eds. TENNESSEE 1840 CENSUS INDEX. Bountiful, Utah: Accelerated Indexing Systems, 1976. 4810042. 78-112507. 929/.3768. F435.J33.

> Contains 107,312 names.

_____. TENNESSEE 1850 CENSUS INDEX. Bountiful, Utah: Accelerated Indexing Systems, 1977. 3760466. 77-86075. 929.3768.

> Contains 178,732 names.

Sistler, Byron, comp. 1850 CENSUS TENNESSEE. 8 vols. Evanston, Ill.: n.p., 1974. 1144210. 976.8.

> Eight separate transcriptions with indexes containing about 139,800 names.

Texas

White, Gifford E., ed. THE 1840 CENSUS OF THE REPUBLIC OF TEXAS. Austin, Tex.: Pemberton Press, 1966. 969238. 67-5982. 317.64. F390.W59. GD 1,000,607 Item 6.

> Prepared from tax lists and other records, arranged by county with an index of 14,048 names.

Austin. University of Texas. "Indexes to the 1850 and 1860 Censuses of Texas." Card index.

Carpenter, V.K., comp. THE STATE OF TEXAS FEDERAL POPULATION SCHEDULES: SEVENTH CENSUS OF THE UNITED STATES, 1850. 5 vols. Huntsville, Ark.: Century Enterprises, 1969. 23896. 70-6196rev.782. 312/.09764. F385.U54 1850. GD 823,884.

> A transcription with an index of many more than 19,656.

Jackson, Ronald Vern, and Teeples, Gary Ronald, eds. TEXAS 1850 CENSUS INDEX. Bountiful, Utah: Accelerated Indexing Systems, 1976. 4641498. 78-112483. 929/.3764. F385.J16.

> Contains 44,471 names.

Utah

Bell, Annie Walker Burns. FIRST FAMILIES OF UTAH AS TAKEN FROM THE 1850 CENSUS OF UTAH. Washington, D.C.: n.p., 1949. 4293008. 49-5579. 929.1. F825.B46. GD 56,534.

A transcription with a surname index of more than 13,250 names.

Jackson, Ronald Vern, and Teeples, Gary Ronald, eds. UTAH 1850 CENSUS INDEX. Bountiful, Utah: Accelerated Indexing Systems, 1978. 4031268. 78-112585. 929/.3792. F825.J33.

Contains 9,766 names.

Bowen, William. 1851 CENSUS OF UTAH. Northridge: California State University, 1972. GD 924,039 Item 3.

A transcription of 11,380 names in alphabetical order.

Jackson, Ronald Vern, ed. UTAH 1860 TERRITORIAL CENSUS INDEX. Salt Lake City: Accelerated Indexing Systems, 1979. 5122856. F825.J325.

Contains 44,876 names.

U.S. Bureau of the Census. INDEX TO THE 1880 CENSUS OF UTAH. Compiled by the Brigham Young University Research Center. 7 reels of microfilm. Salt Lake City. Filmed by the Genealogical Society, 1970. GD 538,587-538,593.

Contains 144,000 names.

Vermont

U.S. Bureau of the Census. HEADS OF FAMILIES AT THE FIRST CENSUS OF THE UNITED STATES TAKEN IN THE YEAR 1790: VERMONT. Washington, D.C.: Government Printing Office, 1907. Reprint. Spartanburg, S.C.: Reprint Co., 1963; Baltimore: Genealogical Publishing Co., 1966; and Bountiful, Utah: Accelerated Indexing Systems, 1978. Microfilm. T498 reel 3. Washington, D.C.: National Archives, 1960; and New Haven, Conn.: Research Publications, 1972. 2531834. 64-60350. 929/.3743. F52.U5. GD 974,191 Item 5.

Index contains about 15,577 names.

United States. Census Office. 2d Census, 1800. HEADS OF FAMILIES AT THE SECOND CENSUS OF THE UNITED STATES TAKEN IN THE YEAR 1800: VERMONT. Montpelier: Vermont Historical Society, 1938. Reprint. Baltimore: Genealogical Publishing Co., 1972. 240180. 71-39493. 929.3. F48.A43 1972. GD 928,125 Item 1.

Census Schedules

A transcription with index. 25,603 families were reported in this census.

Jackson, Ronald Vern, and Teeples, Gary Ronald, eds. VERMONT 1810 CENSUS INDEX. Bountiful, Utah: Accelerated Indexing Systems, 1976. 4641504. 78-112440. 929/.3743. F48.J3.

Contains 34,124 names.

_____. VERMONT 1820 CENSUS INDEX. Bountiful, Utah: Accelerated Indexing Systems, 1978. 4641511. 78-112428. 929/.3743. F48.J32.

Contains 38,846 names.

_____. VERMONT 1830 CENSUS INDEX. Bountiful, Utah: Accelerated Indexing Systems, 1977. 4810084. 78-112429. 929/.3743. F48.J325.

Contains 45,719 names.

_____. VERMONT 1840 CENSUS INDEX. Bountiful, Utah: Accelerated Indexing Systems, 1978. 3936212. 77-86070. 929/.3743. F48.J33.

Contains 52,839 names.

_____. VERMONT 1850 CENSUS INDEX. Bountiful, Utah: Accelerated Indexing Systems, 1978. 4029050. 77-86071. 929.3.

Contains 99,593 names.

Virginia

Fothergill, Augusta Bridgland, and Naugle, John Mark. VIRGINIA TAX PAYERS, 1782-87; OTHER THAN THOSE PUBLISHED BY THE UNITED STATES CENSUS BUREAU. Richmond, Va.: n.p., 1940. Reprint. Baltimore: Genealogical Publishing Co., 1974. 1666542. 66-30321. 929.3. F225.F6 1967.

An alphabetical list of 32,376 full names with references to county of residence and number of slaves.

U.S. Bureau of the Census. HEADS OF FAMILIES AT THE FIRST CENSUS OF THE UNITED STATES TAKEN IN THE YEAR 1790: RECORDS OF THE STATE ENUMERATIONS 1782-1785, VIRGINIA. Washington, D.C.: Government Printing Office, 1908. Reprint. Spartanburg, S.C.: Reprint Co., 1961; Baltimore: Genealogical Publishing Co., 1970; and Bountiful, Utah: Accelerated Indexing Systems, 1978. Microfilm. T498 reel 3. Washington, D.C.: National Archives, 1960; and New Haven, Conn.: Research Publications, 1972. 1065090. 77-111630. 929.3755. F230.U5. GD 029,681.

Index contains about 39,370 names.

Bentley, Elizabeth Petty, comp. INDEX TO THE 1810 CENSUS OF VIRGINIA. Baltimore: Genealogical Publishing Co., 1980. 6035922. F225.B46.

Contains eighty-five thousand names.

Crichard, Madeline W., comp. INDEX TO THE 1810 VIRGINIA CENSUS: HEADS OF FAMILIES LISTED IN THE THIRD CENSUS OF THE UNITED STATES. Parson, W. Va.: n.p., 1971. 159472. 73-159522. 016.9293/755. F230.C765.

Contains 81,760 names.

Jackson, Ronald Vern, and Teeples, Gary Ronald, eds. VIRGINIA 1810 CEN-SUS INDEX. Bountiful, Utah: Accelerated Indexing Systems, 1978. 4531285. 77-86062.

A transcription of 85,704 names in alphabetical order.

Felldin, Jeanne Robey, comp. INDEX TO THE 1820 CENSUS OF VIRGINIA. Baltimore: Genealogical Publishing Co., 1976. 2112214. 75-45757. 929/. 3755. F225.F4.

Contains 110,000 names with schedule leaf numbers.

Jackson, Ronald Vern, and Teeples, Gary Ronald, eds. VIRGINIA 1820 CEN-SUS INDEX. Bountiful, Utah: Accelerated Indexing Systems, 1976. 4809987. 78-112569. 929/.3755. F225.J32.

Contains 110,450 names.

_____. VIRGINIA 1830 CENSUS INDEX. Bountiful, Utah: Accelerated Indexing Systems, 1976. 4810050. 78-112493. 929/.3755. F225.J33.

Contains 127,728 names.

_____. VIRGINIA 1840 CENSUS INDEX. Bountiful, Utah: Accelerated Indexing Systems, 1978. 3889734. 77-86066. 929/.3755. F225.J332.

Contains 137,088 names.

_____. VIRGINIA 1850 CENSUS INDEX. Bountiful, Utah: Accelerated Indexing Systems, 1976. 2406435. 78-112653. 929/.3755. F225.J333.

Contains 257,851 names. There are some entries for Maine that were inadvertently published in this index--GENEALOGICAL HELPER 33 (1979): 107.

Washington

Jackson, Ronald Vern, ed. WASHINGTON 1860 TERRITORIAL CENSUS INDEX. Salt Lake City: Accelerated Indexing Systems, 1979. 5088356. F890.J32.

Contains 11,595 names.

Census Schedules

Stucki, J.W. INDEX TO THE FIRST FEDERAL CENSUS, TERRITORY OF WASH-INGTON (1860). Huntsville, Ark.: Century Enterprises, Genealogical Services, 1972. 320262. 72-181249. 929.3/797. F890.S8.

> Contains about 6,720 names.

Jackson, Ronald Vern, ed. WASHINGTON 1870 TERRITORIAL CENSUS INDEX. Salt Lake City: Accelerated Indexing Systems, 1979. 5088362. F890.J325.

> Contains 24,854 names.

_____. WASHINGTON 1880 TERRITORIAL CENSUS INDEX. Salt Lake City: Accelerated Indexing Systems, 1979.

Wisconsin

Wisconsin. State Historical Society, Library. INDEX TO 1820-1870 FEDERAL CENSUSES OF WISCONSIN. 268 reels of 16mm. microfilm. Madison: Filmed by the University of Wisconsin, 1971. GD 933,597-933,859.

Jackson, Ronald Vern, and Teeples, Gary Ronald, eds. WISCONSIN 1836 CENSUS INDEX. Bountiful, Utah: Accelerated Indexing Systems, 1976. 4809970. 78-112592. 929/.3775. F580.J317.

> Contains 1,781 names.

_____. WISCONSIN 1840 CENSUS INDEX. Bountiful, Utah: Accelerated Indexing Systems, 1978. 3917654. 77-86058. 929/.3775. F580.J32.

> Contains 5,774 names.

_____. WISCONSIN 1850 CENSUS INDEX. Bountiful, Utah: Accelerated Indexing Systems, 1978. 3917614. 78-112512. 929/.3775. F580.J34.

> Contains 91,339 names.

Wyoming

Laramie. Wyoming State Archives and Historical Department. "Indexes to the 1870 and 1880 Censuses of Wyoming." Card index.

> Copy also available at the Library of Congress.

Jackson, Ronald Vern, and Teeples, Gary Ronald, eds. WYOMING 1870 TERRITORIAL CENSUS INDEX. Bountiful, Utah: Accelerated Indexing Systems, 1978. 4268579. F760.J33.

> Contains 4,324 names.

Jackson, Ronald Vern, ed. WYOMING 1880 TERRITORIAL CENSUS INDEX.
Salt Lake City: Accelerated Indexing Systems, 1979.

Chapter 13

FINDING COUNTY AND CITY HISTORIES

COUNTY HISTORIES

County histories are useful in genealogical research for several reasons. First, of course, is their historical coverage of a county. Many also include the names, origin, and boundary changes of the county's townships. Foremost, however, is that most of them include biographical sketches of early settlers, prominent citizens, county officials, and anyone who could afford to subscribe to the county history. Those written, published, and sold by subscription between 1875 and 1930 usually include a great deal of biographical and genealogical data concerning the subscriber and his family. Historians refer to the county histories of this period as "mug books" because of their numerous portraits and illustrations. They contain biographical sketches of anyone that paid the price for inclusion. The result was usually a large volume containing from several hundred to over a thousand pages.

The biographical data contained in most county histories must be verified. Often they serve only as sources of clues for the genealogist. Nevertheless, they should be consulted for any geographical area in which a person may have resided, particularly if ancestors lived in the area during the period when the history was published. The following is the most economical and useful bibliography of county histories:

Peterson, Clarence Stewart. CONSOLIDATED BIBLIOGRAPHY OF COUNTY HISTORIES IN FIFTY STATES IN 1961, CONSOLIDATED 1935-1961. 2d ed. Baltimore: Genealogical Publishing Co., 1973. 730705. 73-8036. 016. 929/3. Z1250.P47.

> This bibliography lists many county histories, but not all that are published. It is arranged alphabetically by state and then alphabetically by county under each state.

CITY HISTORIES

City histories are also useful for genealogical research, but their biographical sketches are not as voluminous as those in county histories. City histories were not normally prepared and marketed by subscription; therefore, their biographical sketches are usually restricted to prominent citizens. The following is the best list of nineteenth-century city histories:

Bradford, Thomas Lindsley, comp. BIBLIOGRAPHER'S MANUAL OF AMERICAN HISTORY, CONTAINING AN ACCOUNT OF ALL STATE, TERRITORY, TOWN AND COUNTY HISTORIES RELATING TO THE UNITED STATES OF NORTH AMERICA, WITH VERBATIM COPIES OF THEIR TITLES, AND USEFUL BIBLIO-GRAPHICAL NOTES, TOGETHER WITH THE PRICES AT WHICH THEY HAVE BEEN SOLD FOR THE LAST FORTY YEARS, AND WITH AN EXHAUSTIVE IN-DEX BY TITLES, AND AN INDEX BY STATES. 5 vols. Philadelphia: S.V. Henkels, 1907-10. Reprint. Detroit: Gale Research Co., 1968. Microfiche or microfilm. New York: AMS Press, 1974. 582669. 67-14023. 016.973. Z1250.B852.

> This work is not a complete bibliography of city histories and must be supplemented by other bibliographies. It is arranged alphabetically by author. The index (volume 5) must be used for finding books by city. County histories are included, but Peterson's bibliography is more useful.

SEARCH STRATEGY

In preparation for using Peterson, Bradford, and the other bibliographies of this chapter, the cards of all families prepared for searching family histories should be arranged by state, county, and city. All of the counties may be searched at one time or specific counties of interest may be searched individually.

Genealogists should be encouraged to record the standard bibliographic informa-tion on separate cards for each title found. Librarians may have to remind genealogists to select only those titles published during the period when their ancestors lived in a county or town, except if other members of the family continued to live there.

SUPPLEMENTAL BIBLIOGRAPHIES AND CATALOGS

U.S. Library of Congress. UNITED STATES LOCAL HISTORIES IN THE LIBRARY OF CONGRESS: A BIBLIOGRAPHY. Edited by Marion J. Kaminkow. 5 vols. Baltimore: Magna Carta Book Co., 1975-76. 1365920. 74-25444. 016.973. Z1250.U59 1975.

> This bibliography is excellent, but comparison with Peterson (p. 191) reveals the incompleteness of the Library of Congress holdings. However, it has somewhat better coverage than Bradford (above). Some libraries may prefer to use this bib-liography rather than Peterson or Bradford because of its more complete and correct bibliographic citations. It is arranged in

shelf list order by Library of Congress classification scheme number.

Each state is subdivided by its counties in alphabetical order, followed by cities and towns in alphabetical order. It also includes county history indexes.

The LIBRARY OF CONGRESS SHELFLIST, MICROFICHE EDITION: F 1-975, HISTORY: STATES OF THE U.S. contains the same material as in the above bibliography. It is available from University Microfilm International. However, it would be harder for genealogists to use.

New York (City). Public Library. Local History and Genealogy Division. UNITED STATES LOCAL HISTORY CATALOG: A MODIFIED SHELF LIST ARRANGED ALPHABETICALLY BY STATE, AND ALPHABETICALLY BY LOCALITY WITHIN EACH STATE. 2 vols. Boston: G.K. Hall, 1974. 1926539. 75-313771. 019.1097471. Z881.N59 1974a.

Arranged by state, subarranged by city and county interfiled in alphabetical order, this catalog, again, is not as comprehensive as Peterson (p. 191) nor quite as good as Bradford (p. 192).

WRITINGS ON AMERICAN HISTORY. 1902-1961, 1974-- . Washington, D.C.: Government Printing Office and American Historical Association, 1903-1972, 1973-74--. 973.

The first part of this bibliography includes books and periodical articles that relate to the history of cities and counties. It was an annual publication with a cumulative index compiled by the American Historical Association for the years 1902-1940. Publication was suspended from 1941 to 1947 and for the years 1962 to 1973. Since 1974 it covers only periodical articles. It is arranged geographically by regions and by the states therein. The cumulative index is arranged alphabetically by city, county, state, author, and subject.

U.S. Library of Congress. LIBRARY OF CONGRESS CATALOGS: SUBJECT CATALOG. Washington, D.C.: 1950-- . Quarterly.

This catalog includes city and county histories and their indexes and should be searched periodically for recent publications. It may be used to update all of the above bibliographies and catalogs. It is arranged alphabetically by subject in five-year accumulations with annual and quarterly issues.

Genealogical Department of the Church of Jesus Christ of Latter-day Saints. MICROFILM CARD CATALOG. 88 reels. Salt Lake City: Genealogical Department, 1973.

This catalog is available at all Genealogical Department Branch Libraries, and microfilm copies of county and city histories may be borrowed for use in these libraries for a small handling and postage fee. County histories are listed by subject following the name of the state (e.g., MISSOURI, BENTON--HISTORY). The MICROFILM CARD CATALOG also includes indexes to county histories. Indexes found in county histories or reprints of county histories are identified in this catalog with the notation "index" on the collation line. Any of these indexes that are not on microfilm may be consulted by genealogists by completing a branch library reference questionnaire requesting that a specific book's index be checked for a specific name or family name. The reference questionnaire may also be used to request that materials not under copyright be microfilmed.

The subject headings relative to county and city histories are as follows:

    City Histories

LC	ELY, IOWA--HISTORY
Sears	ELY, IOWA--HISTORY
GD	IOWA, LINN, ELY - HISTORY

    County Histories

LC	LINN COUNTY, IOWA--HISTORY
Sears	LINN COUNTY, IOWA--HISTORY
GD	IOWA, LINN - HISTORY

STATE LOCAL HISTORY BIBLIOGRAPHIES

Local history bibliographies are available for some states that not only supplement the above works, but in some cases surpass or supersede them. The following are the best of these bibliographies. They are arranged in alphabetical order by state.

Ricks, Melvin Byron. MELVIN RICKS' ALASKA BIBLIOGRAPHY: AN INTRODUCTORY GUIDE TO ALASKAN HISTORICAL LITERATURE. Edited by Stephen W. Haycox and Betty J. Haycox. Portland, Oreg.: Published by Binford and Mort for the Alaska Historical Commission, 1977. 3383655. 77-80570. Z1255.R5 F904.

Clark, Georgia H., and Parham, R. Bruce, comps. ARKANSAS COUNTY AND LOCAL HISTORIES: A BIBLIOGRAPHY. Fayetteville: University of Arkansas, 1976. 3465266. 976.7.

Rocq, Margaret Miller, ed. CALIFORNIA LOCAL HISTORY: A BIBLIOGRAPHY

AND UNION LIST OF LIBRARY HOLDINGS. Edited for the California Library
Association. 2d ed., rev. and enl. Stanford, Calif.: Stanford University
Press, 1970. 86426. 70-97912. 016.9794. Z1261.R63 1970.

_____, ed. CALIFORNIA LOCAL HISTORY: A BIBLIOGRAPHY AND UNION
LIST OF LIBRARY HOLDINGS: SUPPLEMENT TO THE SECOND EDITION
COVERING WORKS PUBLISHED 1961 THROUGH 1970. Edited for the California Library Association. Stanford, Calif.: Stanford University Press, 1976.
2894383. 76-383888. 016.9794. Z1261.R63 1970 Suppl. F861.

Wilcox, Virginia Lee. COLORADO: A SELECTED BIBLIOGRAPHY OF ITS
LITERATURE, 1858-1952. Denver: Sage Books, 1954. 1441284. 54-35636.
016.9788. Z1263.W5.

Kemp, Thomas Jay, ed. CONNECTICUT RESEARCHER'S HANDBOOK. Gale
Genealogy and Local History Series. Detroit: Gale Research Co., forthcoming.

Schnare, Robert E. LOCAL HISTORICAL RESOURCES IN CONNECTICUT: A
GUIDE TO THEIR USE. Darien: Connecticut League of Historical Societies,
1975. 1862982. 78-309060. 016.9746. Z1265.S35F94.

Reed, Henry Clay, and Reed, Marion Bjhomason, comps. A BIBLIOGRAPHY
OF DELAWARE THROUGH 1960. Newark: Published for the Institute of
Delaware History and Culture by the University of Delaware Press, 1966.
1020070. 66-18259. 016.91751. Z1267.R4.

Hugh M. Morris Library. Reference Department. BIBLIOGRAPHY OF DELA-
WARE, 1960-1974. Newark: University of Delaware, 1976. 3223035. 77-
151378. 016.9751/04. Z1267.H84 1976 F164.

    Supplement to H.C. Reed and M.B. Reed's A BIBLIOGRAPHY
    OF DELAWARE THROUGH 1960 (above).

Harris, Michael H., comp. FLORIDA HISTORY: A BIBLIOGRAPHY. Metuchen,
N.J.: Scarecrow Press, 1972. 328979. 72-4222. 016.9759. Z1271.H35.

    "Cities and Towns," pages 197-217; and "County Histories,"
    pages 217-20.

Rowland, Arthur Ray, and Dorsey, James E. A BIBLIOGRAPHY OF THE WRIT-
INGS ON GEORGIA HISTORY, 1900-1970. Rev. and enl. ed. Spartanburg,
S.C.: Reprint Co., 1978. 3169227. 77-21733. 016.0758. Z1273.R6 1977
F286.

Warren, Mary Bondurant. GEORGIA GENEALOGICAL BIBLIOGRAPHY, 1968.
Danielsville, Ga.: Heritage Papers, 1969. 46744. 72-7727. 016.9293.
Z5313.U6G47.

Yenawine, Wayne S. "A Checklist of Source Materials for Counties of Georgia." GEORGIA HISTORICAL QUARTERLY 32 (September 1948): 179-229.

Nelson, Milo G., and Webbert, Charles A., eds. IDAHO LOCAL HISTORY: A BIBLIOGRAPHY WITH A CHECKLIST OF LIBRARY HOLDINGS. Edited for the Idaho Library Association. Moscow: University Press of Idaho, 1976. 3474214. 76-48614. Z1275.N45.

Buck, Solon Justus. TRAVEL AND DESCRIPTION, 1765-1865, TOGETHER WITH A LIST OF COUNTY HISTORIES, ATLASES, AND BIOGRAPHICAL COLLECTIONS AND A LIST OF TERRITORIAL AND STATE LAWS. Springfield: The Trustees of the Illinois State Historical Library, 1914. Reprint. Burt Franklin Research and Source Works Series, no. 827. New York: B. Franklin, 1971. 388470. 71-147150. 016.91773. Z1277.B83 1971.

> Illinois.

Wendel, Carolynne L. AIDS FOR GENEALOGICAL SEARCHING IN INDIANA, A BIBLIOGRAPHY. Detroit: Detroit Society for Genealogical Research, 1962. 1723957. 62-53173. 977.2. Z5313.U6157.

Petersen, William John. IOWA HISTORY REFERENCE GUIDE. Iowa City: State Historical Society of Iowa, 1952. 1510975. 52-62980. 016.9777. Z1283.P46 1952.

> "Cities and Towns," pages 83-95; no county histories.

Anderson, Lorene, and Farley, Alan W. "A Bibliography of Town and County Histories of Kansas." KANSAS HISTORICAL QUARTERLY 21 (Autumn 1955): 513-51.

Coleman, John Winston. A BIBLIOGRAPHY OF KENTUCKY HISTORY. Lexington: University of Kentucky Press, 1949. 1720103. 49-11965. 016.769. Z1287.C6.

> "County Histories," pages 193-202; "Municipal History," pages 340-48; and plat books, pages 10-14.

Yoes, Henry E., III, comp. BIBLIOGRAPHY OF LOUISIANA MATERIALS. Hahnville, La.: n.p., 1973. 699388. 73-166327. 016.91763/03/6. Z1289.Y63.

Committee for a New England Bibliography. MAINE, A BIBLIOGRAPHY OF ITS HISTORY. Edited by John D. Haskell, Jr. Bibliographies of New England History, vol 2. Boston: G.K. Hall, 1977. 3071838. 77-9072. 016.9741. Z1291.C65 1977 F19.

Finding County and City Histories

Meyer, Mary Keysor. GENEALOGICAL RESEARCH IN MARYLAND: A GUIDE. Rev. Baltimore: Maryland Historical Society, 1976. 2457451. 76-21107. 929/.1/0720752. Z1293.M485 1976 F180.

> "Bibliography," pages 62-89, is a selected bibliography, arranged by county, and includes county and city histories.

Committee for a New England Bibliography. MASSACHUSETTS, A BIBLIOGRAPHY OF ITS HISTORY. Edited by John D. Haskell, Jr. Bibliographies of New England History, vol. 1. Boston: G.K. Hall, 1976. 1735501. 75-33285. 016.9744. Z1295.C65 1976 F64.

Michigan. Bureau of Library Services. MICHIGAN COUNTY HISTORIES: A BIBLIOGRAPHY. Lansing: Michigan Department of Education, Bureau of Library Services, 1978. 4103504. Z1297.A5 1978.

Brook, Michael. REFERENCE GUIDE TO MINNESOTA HISTORY: A SUBJECT BIBLIOGRAPHY OF BOOKS, PAMPHLETS, AND ARTICLES IN ENGLISH. St. Paul: Minnesota Historical Society, 1974. 841697. 74-4222. 016.91776. Z1299.B76.

Selby, Paul Owen. A BIBLIOGRAPHY OF MISSOURI COUNTY HISTORIES AND ATLASES. Kirksville: Northeast Missouri State Teachers College, 1966. 30139. 75-6117. 016.9778. Z1303.S43.

Richards, Dennis L., ed. MONTANA'S GENEALOGICAL RECORDS. Gale Genealogy and Local History Series, vol. 11. Detroit: Gale Research Co., 1981.

White, John Browning. PUBLISHED SOURCES ON TERRITORIAL NEBRASKA, AN ESSAY AND BIBLIOGRAPHY. Nebraska State Historical Society. Publications, vol. 23. Lincoln: Nebraska State Historical Society, 1956. 2771633. 56-63172. 016.9782. F661.N3 vol. 23.

Elliott, Russell R., and Poulton, Helen J. WRITINGS ON NEVADA: A SELECTED BIBLIOGRAPHY. Nevada Studies in History and Political Science, no. 5. University of Nevada Press. Bibliographical Series, no. 2. Reno: University of Nevada Press, 1963. 2476986. 63-64667. 016.91793. Z1309.E4.

Committee for a New England Bibliography. NEW HAMPSHIRE, A BIBLIOGRAPHY OF ITS HISTORY. Edited by John D. Haskell, Jr. Bibliographies of New England History, vol. 3. Boston: G.K. Hall, 1979. 5493861. 79-22253. 016.9742. Z1311.C65 1979 F34.

Burr, Nelson Rollin. A NARRATIVE AND DESCRIPTIVE BIBLIOGRAPHY OF NEW JERSEY. New Jersey Historical Series, vol. 21. Princeton, N.J.: Van Nostrand, 1964. 860386. 65-862. 016.91749. Z1313.B8.

Finding County and City Histories

"Counties," pages 82-87; and "Cities and Towns," pages 88-99.

Saunders, Lyle. A GUIDE TO MATERIALS BEARING ON CULTURAL RELA-
TIONS IN NEW MEXICO. New Mexico. University. School of Inter-American
Affairs. Inter-Americana Series. Bibliographies, III. Albuquerque: University
of New Mexico Press, 1944. 1100334. 44-53707. 016.9789. Z1315.S35.

Nestler, Harold. A BIBLIOGRAPHY OF NEW YORK STATE COMMUNITIES,
COUNTIES, TOWNS, VILLAGES. Empire State Historical Publications Series,
51. Port Washington, N.Y.: J. Friedman, 1968. 440382. 68-18353.
Z1317.N45.

Powell, William Stevens. NORTH CAROLINA COUNTY HISTORIES: A BIB-
LIOGRAPHY. University of North Carolina. Library Studies, no. 1. Chapel
Hill: University of North Carolina Library, 1958. 1068663. 58-62746.
016.9756. Z1319.P6 1958.

Thornton, Mary Lindsay. A BIBLIOGRAPHY OF NORTH CAROLINA, 1589-
1956. Westport, Conn.: Greenwood Press, 1973. 57621. 73-441. 015/.756.
Z1319.T495 1973.

North Dakota. State Library Commission. NORTH DAKOTA HISTORY: A
CATALOG OF BOOKS AVAILABLE ON LOAN FROM THE STATE LIBRARY
THROUGH YOUR SCHOOL, PUBLIC, COLLEGE, UNIVERSITY, OR SPECIAL
LIBRARY. Bismarck: 1979. 5283524. Z1321.N67 1979.

Douthit, Ruth Long. OHIO RESOURCES FOR GENEALOGISTS. WITH SOME
REFERENCES FOR GENEALOGICAL SEARCHING IN OHIO. Rev. Detroit:
Detroit Society for Genealogical Research, 1971. 640580. 72-171054.
929/.3771. F490.D68 1971.

> County bibliographies, pp. 40-129; and town and township
> histories, pp. 130-33.

Ohio. State Library. Columbus. COUNTY BY COUNTY IN OHIO GENE-
ALOGY. By Petta Khouw and Genealogy Staff. Rev. Columbus: 1978.
Microfiche. Educational Resources Information Center, ED 160 094. 3899318.
016.9771. Z1323.044.

Pennsylvania. Historical and Museum Commission. BIBLIOGRAPHY OF PENN-
SYLVANIA HISTORY. Compiled by Norman B. Wilkinson; edited by S.K.
Stevens and Donald H. Kent. 2d ed. Harrisburg: 1957. 4681577. 58-9079.
016.9748. Z1329.A5 1957.

> "County and Local History," pages 550-632.

_____. BIBLIOGRAPHY OF PENNSYLVANIA HISTORY: A SUPPLEMENT.
Edited by Carol Wall. Harrisburg: 1976. 3650450. 77-624218. 016.9748.
Z1329.A5 1957 Suppl F149.

Smith, Sam B., ed. TENNESSEE HISTORY, A BIBLIOGRAPHY. Luke H. Banker, assistant editor. Knoxville: University of Tennessee Press, 1974. 902881. 74-8504. 016.91768. Z1337.S55.

> "County Histories," pages 320-452; not many mug books.

"Tennessee County Histories." In GENEALOGY RESEARCH SOURCES IN TENNESSEE, by Beverly West Hathaway, pages 88-94. West Jordan, Utah: All-states Research, 1972.

Tennessee. State Library and Archives, Nashville. TENNESSEE COUNTY DATA FOR HISTORICAL AND GENEALOGICAL RESEARCH. Nashville: 1966. 146902. 68-65823. F443.A15A57.

Tennessee. State Library and Archives, Nashville. State Library Division. Reference Department. WRITINGS ON TENNESSEE COUNTIES AVAILABLE ON INTERLIBRARY LOAN FROM THE TENNESSEE STATE LIBRARY DIVISION. Nashville: 1971. 298312. 72-610145. 016.9768. Z1337.A513 1971.

Jenkins, John Holmes. CRACKER BARREL CHRONICLES: A BIBLIOGRAPHY OF TEXAS TOWN AND COUNTY HISTORIES. Austin, Tex.: Pemberton Press, 1965. 845496. 65-8617. 016.91764. Z1339.J4.

Jaussi, Laureen Richardson, and Chaston, Gloria Duncan. GENEALOGICAL RECORDS OF UTAH. Salt Lake City: Deseret Book Co., 1974. 940385. 73-87713. 016.929/3792. CD3541.J38 1974.

> "History of Utah Counties: Locality Histories," pages 14-25.
> There are no traditional mug books of Utah's counties.

Virginia. State Library, Richmond. VIRGINIA LOCAL HISTORY, A BIBLIOGRAPHY. Richmond: 1971. 416272. 72-611228. 016.01755/03. Z1345.A56.

Shetler, Charles. GUIDE TO THE STUDY OF WEST VIRGINIA HISTORY. Morgantown: West Virginia University Library, 1960. 2218554. 60-9691. Z1349.S45.

Gleason, Margaret. PRINTED RESOURCES FOR GENEALOGICAL SEARCHING IN WISCONSIN: A SELECTIVE BIBLIOGRAPHY. Detroit: Detroit Society for Genealogical Research, 1964. 1726921. 977.5.

INDEXES

Many county histories have been indexed, some for all names contained therein and others only for the biographees or persons for whom biographical sketches have been written. The majority of the complete name indexes are published, and citations for them may be found in the above bibliographical tools. The majority of the biographee-only indexes are found as cumulative card indexes to multiple histories located in various libraries. The following are a few that have been published:

THE LIBRARY OF CONGRESS INDEX TO BIOGRAPHIES IN STATE AND LOCAL HISTORIES. Microfilm. 40 reels. Baltimore: Magna Carta Book Co., 1979.

> This index contains approximately 170,000 entries to biographees of volumes in the Library of Congress. It is, of course, very useful and the most comprehensive index available for the mug books of the United States. However, it indexes 340 titles which only includes a small percentage of the state, county and local histories in the Library of Congress. Kentucky has the largest number of titles indexed with 50; Georgia has 36; California, 34; Tennessee, 32; Texas, 27; Louisiana, 21; Mississippi and South Carolina, 13; Idaho, 12; Nevada, 11; Arkansas and North Carolina, 10; Alabama, 8; Arizona, 6; Alaska, Connecticut, Delaware, District of Columbia, Hawaii, North Dakota, and Oklahoma, 3; Maryland, New York, and Ohio 2; and the other 26 states are represented by only 1 title.

California

Parker, J. Carlyle, ed. AN INDEX TO THE BIOGRAPHEES IN 19TH CENTURY CALIFORNIA COUNTY HISTORIES. Gale Genealogy and Local History Series, vol. 7. Detroit: Gale Research Co., 1979. 4832150. 79-11900. 979.4/04/0922. Z5313.U6C36 F860.

> Contains approximately 16,500 entries for sixty-one county histories.

Colorado

Bromwell, Henriette Elizabeth. "Colorado Portrait and Biography Index." 5 vols. Denver: n.p., 1935. 4044268. F775.B76.

> Available at the Colorado Historical Society and the Western History Department of the Denver Public Library.

Indiana

Indianapolis. Public Library. A CONSOLIDATED INDEX TO THIRTY-TWO HISTORIES OF INDIANAPOLIS AND INDIANA. Indianapolis: 1939. 40-5807. 016.9772. Z1282.I414.

Iowa

Morford, Charles. BIOGRAPHICAL INDEX TO THE COUNTY HISTORIES OF IOWA. Baltimore: Gateway Press, 1979. 5336698. 79-87902. 977.7/00992. Z1283.M55 F620.

> Contains 40,540 entries of the biographees in 131 of the 251 county histories for all of Iowa's ninety-nine counties.

Michigan

Loomis, Frances, comp. MICHIGAN BIOGRAPHY INDEX. Detroit: Detroit Public Library, 1946. Microfilm. 4 reels. Woodbridge, Conn.: Research Publications, 1973. 3646166.

> Contains approximately seventy-three thousand names of the biographees in 361 biographical directories, city and county directories and histories.

New York

"The New York State Biographical, Genealogical and Portrait Index." Personal index of Gunther E. Pohl, 24 Walden Place, Great Neck, N.Y. 11020.

> This index contains entries to the biographical sketches and portraits in about nine hundred New York state, county, city, and community histories. Pohl will consult this index for patrons and provide them with bibliographic citations and page numbers for a moderate fee. All correspondence to him must include a self-addressed stamped envelope.

Oregon

Brandt, Patricia, and Guilford, Nancy, eds. OREGON BIOGRAPHY INDEX. Oregon State University Bibliographic Series, no. 11. Corvallis: Oregon State University, 1976. 2388703. 76-366322. 920/.9795. Z5305.U5B7 CT256.

> Contains over 2,600 names to biographees from forty-six histories.

Some libraries holding card indexes to county histories are listed in the following:

American Library Association. Junior Members Round Table. LOCAL INDEXES IN AMERICAN LIBRARIES: A UNION LIST OF UNPUBLISHED INDEXES. Edited by Norma Olin Ireland and the National Editorial Committee of Junior Members. Boston: Faxon, 1947. Reprint. Boston: Gregg Press, 1972. 388782. 72-6992. 017/.5. Z6293.A5 1972.

> This book is arranged alphabetically by the name of the county. Inquiries for a single name to be checked in these indexes are usually honored.

Finding County and City Histories

The following supplements this list for two states:

California

Dillon, Richard H. "Local Indexes in California Libraries." NEWS NOTES OF CALIFORNIA LIBRARIES 49 (October 1954): 501-42.

Ohio

Hoagland, Joan, and Adams, Marie. LOCALLY PREPARED INDEXES IN OHIO LIBRARIES. Columbus: Ohio Library Association, 1973. 796488. 016.027. Z1002.H6.

Many of the biographies in local histories are also indexed in various genealogical name indexes. Please consult the chapter on "Indexes" for them.

INTERLIBRARY LOAN

Much of the information concerning how to obtain family histories on interlibrary loan, purchase, and rental, or information from family histories gained through correspondence, hire, or travel also applies to local histories. Additional sources for the obtaining of local histories are as follows:

AMERICAN LIBRARY DIRECTORY. 32d ed. New York: Bowker, 1979. 5770387. 021/.0025/73. Z731.A512 1979.

> Many county and city libraries listed in this directory will circulate on interlibrary loan their duplicate copies of city or county histories that relate to their locale. If no response is obtained from a city or county library, an interlibrary loan request should be sent to the regional library or academic library in the area.

All libraries should acquire microform copies of their own county histories for circulation on interlibrary loan. The NATIONAL REGISTER OF MICROFORM MASTERS, of course, lists many of these county histories. Nearly all of the county histories published before 1907 have been microfilmed for the states of California, Illinois, Indiana, Michigan, New York, Ohio, Pennsylvania, and Wisconsin by Research Publications, 12 Lunar Drive, Woodbridge, Connecticut 06525.

Another publisher that, unfortunately, is not listed in GENEALOGICAL & LOCAL HISTORY BOOKS IN PRINT, BOOKS IN PRINT, nor in GUIDE TO REPRINTS is Unigraphic, 1401 North Fares Avenue, Evansville, Indiana 47711. The publisher has printed over 144 county histories, primarily of the midwestern states. Librarians should encourage genealogical and/or historical societies to investigate the utilization of this firm's excellent reprint program. The program provides a fund raising opportunity for a society through pre-publication sales at a good profit, yet a reasonable price for the consumer.

An additional source for gaining access to local histories of the eastern seaboard states is found in the microbook collection, LIBRARY OF AMERICAN CIVILIZA- TION (LAC) by the Encyclopedia Britannica. The collection contains about fourteen thousand volumes of primarily American history and literature books published before 1906. A small percentage of its titles are local and state histories. Many libraries throughout the United States have acquired this col- lection and some will circulate individual titles on interlibrary loan. The best reader for LAC books is the Microbook reader; however; some of them can also be read on 45x or 48x readers. The collection's titles are also listed in the NATIONAL REGISTER OF MICROFORM MASTERS.

The following is a large collection that may be of assistance for interlibrary loan of county histories:

Americana Unlimited. THE COX LIBRARY: COUNTY, STATE & LOCAL HIS- TORIES: A MICROFILM OFFERING FROM AMERICANA UNLIMITED. Parts I-IV. Tucson, Ariz.: Americana Unlimited, 1976. 5250361.

   615 reels of 16mm. microfilm.

   Parts I-IV of this collection contain 1,979 titles; 1,323 of them are county histories, and 153 are city histories. The number of county histories for each of the thirty-five states represented is as follows:

Arkansas	2	New Jersey	15
California	65	New York	102
Colorado	2	North Carolina	9
Connecticut	9	Ohio	168
Georgia	5	Oregon	3
Illinois	209	Pennsylvania	89
Indiana	90	South Carolina	5
Iowa	140˙	South Dakota	3
Kansas	35	Tennessee	2
Kentucky	7	Texas	13
Maine	7	Utah	1
Maryland	3	Vermont	12
Massachusetts	13	Virginia	17
Michigan	71	Washington	9
Minnesota	50	West Virginia	17
Missouri	73	Wisconsin	54
Nebraska	29	Wyoming	2
New Hampshire	7		

Part V contains some United States military histories and Canadian histories. Parts VI and VII contain 1,370 U.S. city directories from 1841-1942. The collection is sold by Bay Microfilm, 737

Loma Verde Avenue, Palo Alto, California 94303. Some libraries, including the Genealogical Department, have acquired it.

The following bibliography lists the collection's holdings. It is arranged by region, then alphabetically by state therein. Unfortunately, it has no index and no see references to identify all counties in multi-county volumes.

Americana Unlimited. THE COX LIBRARY: COUNTY, STATE & LOCAL HISTORIES: A MICROFILM OFFERING FROM AMERICANA UNLIMITED. Tucson, Ariz.: Americana Unlimited; Glendale, Calif.: Distribution by A.H. Clark Co., 1974. 2165136. 76-358242. 016.973. Z1250.A44 1974 E180.

RENTAL LIBRARIES

The New England Historic Genealogical Society has a fine collection of New England and New York county and city histories that it will circulate by mail to its members for a fee. The society's address is 101 Newbury Street, Boston, Massachusetts 02116. They will sell interested members their circulating collection catalog.

New England Historic Genealogical Society. THE CATALOG TO THE CIRCULATING COLLECTION OF THE NEW ENGLAND HISTORIC GENEALOGICAL SOCIETY. 2d ed. 3 vols. Boston: 1977. 3444620. 77-373861. 016.929/373. Z5305.U5N38 1977.

Additional rental services are listed in the chapter, "Unique Research Services."

FOREIGN CITY AND COUNTY HISTORIES

County and city histories for other countries generally do not contain the same volume of biographical sketches as do U.S. county histories. Our county histories are a product of the nation's capitalistic free enterprise system.

COLLECTION DEVELOPMENT

If all libraries of the nation would conscientiously collect the local historical materials of their service areas and make available as much of it as possible for interlibrary loan, there would be no need for libraries to purchase local history materials for areas outside their own. However, some large libraries may want to cooperatively purchase microfilm collections of local histories that could be shared. Peterson's CONSOLIDATED BIBLIOGRAPHY OF COUNTY HISTORIES should be in all libraries down to and including the medium-sized library.

SUMMARY

Peterson's CONSOLIDATED BIBLIOGRAPHY OF COUNTY HISTORIES is the best single source that genealogists can consult to determine what county histories or "Mug Books" are available for U.S. counties in which their ancestors lived. Genealogists ought to be encouraged to check also the LOCAL HISTORIES IN THE LIBRARY OF CONGRESS for additional county histories, when the opportunity arises. Researchers definitely need to consult Bradford for town histories. Bibliographic cards should be made for all titles that are of interest. Librarians should try to obtain these materials on interlibrary loan from the nearest available source or from the city, county, or regional library of the locale about which the history is written.

Genealogists should at least check Peterson and Bradford for histories of the genealogical locations of their ancestors. However, in practice, most of them will check only a few of interest at the time they are first introduced to the two bibliographies. Librarians then need to remind them to continue a comprehensive search at a later date.

Chapter 14

NEWSPAPERS

Newspapers may be the only source available to a genealogist for both history and vital data concerning his or her ancestors. In some newspapers vital statistic information was not published until after 1875. The lists of unclaimed mail, delinquent taxes, and business advertisements or directory information may also be useful to genealogists. A newspaper is a secondary source filled with errors; nevertheless, the use of newspapers must be considered to help solve some genealogical research problems. In preparation for use of newspapers, the dates and places of a genealogist's ancestor's residence must be determined as precisely as possible.

NATIONAL UNION LISTS

The following union lists are arranged in reverse chronological order.

NEWSPAPERS IN MICROFORM. Washington, D.C.: Library of Congress, 1973. 1354452. 75-644000. 016.05. Z663.733.N46.

> The main volume of this work is entitled, NEWSPAPERS IN MICROFORM: UNITED STATES, 1948-1972 with a supplement for 1973-1979. The dates refer to the years of data collection, not to the years of coverage. Newspaper holdings of small libraries normally will not be reported in this union list. Nevertheless, librarians should request newspapers in microform from the libraries of the community in which the newspaper was published. Those libraries will probably have the newspaper in microform and will be willing to interlibrary loan it.

> Many of the libraries listed in this catalog will lend their microfilm files of newspapers on interlibrary loan. Requests for interlibrary loan of newspapers that are listed as only available from commercial firms should, nevertheless, be made to the libraries of the city in which the newspaper was published or to larger libraries in the area or state.

Newspapers

AMERICAN NEWSPAPERS, 1821-1936: A UNION LIST OF FILES AVAILABLE IN THE UNITED STATES AND CANADA. Edited by Winifred Gregory under the auspices of the Bibliographical Society of America. New York: H.W. Wilson Co., 1937. Reprint. New York: Kraus Reprint, 1967. 1805017. 579985. 37-12783. 016.071. Z6945.A53.

> Many of the newspapers reported in the foregoing catalog are now available on microfilm. Some, however, will not be reported as such in NEWSPAPERS IN MICROFORM. Therefore, librarians should still try to request microfilm copies of the needed newspapers reported in AMERICAN NEWSPAPERS.

Brigham, Clarence Saunders. HISTORY AND BIBLIOGRAPHY OF AMERICAN NEWSPAPERS, 1690-1820. 2 vols. Worcester, Mass.: American Antiquarian Society, 1947. Reprint. Westport, Conn.: Greenwood Press, 1976. 1973968. 789013. 75-40215. 47-4111. 016.071/3. Z6951.B86.

_____. ADDITIONS AND CORRECTIONS TO HISTORY AND BIBLIOGRAPHY OF AMERICAN NEWSPAPERS, 1690-1820. Worcester, Mass.: American Antiquarian Society, 1961. 1609882 071.01.

> Reprinted from the PROCEEDINGS OF THE AMERICAN ANTIQUARIAN SOCIETY 71, no. 1 (1961): 15-62.

Many of the newspapers reported in this catalog will also be on microfilm and may be borrowed, even if not reported in NEWSPAPERS IN MICROFORM.

All of the union catalogs listed above include the names of libraries where backfiles of a specific newspaper are available and what dates each library has. They are all arranged alphabetically by state and then alphabetically by city.

STATE UNION LISTS

Often state union lists of newspapers are more comprehensive than the above national union lists. The following are those that are fairly up to date and the majority of which include microfilm holdings:

Davis, Phyllis. A GUIDE TO ALASKA'S NEWSPAPERS. Compiled by Phyllis Davis for the Alaska Division of State Libraries and Museums; with some vignettes in Alaskan journalism by Evangeline Atwood. Alaska State Library Historical Monograph, no. 4. Juneau: Gastineau Channel Centennial Association, 1976. 3627105. 77-620967. 071/.98. Z6952.A6D38 PN4897.A64.

Arizona. Department of Library and Archives. A UNION LIST OF ARIZONA NEWSPAPERS IN ARIZONA LIBRARIES. Phoenix: 1965. 66-63164. Z6945.A776.

Newspapers

Worley, Ted R., comp. ARKANSAS NEWSPAPERS ON MICROFILM. Little
Rock, Ark.: Arkansas History Commission, 1957.

California State University and Colleges. UNION LIST OF NEWSPAPERS ON
MICROFORMS IN THE CALIFORNIA STATE UNIVERSITY AND COLLEGES LI-
BRARIES. Fullerton, Calif.: 1973. 1683738. Z6945.C3.

Oehlerts, Donald E., comp. GUIDE TO COLORADO NEWSPAPERS, 1859-
1963. Denver: Bibliographical Center for Research, Rocky Mountain Region,
1964. 683401. 64-2489. 016.07188. Z6952.C703.

Gustafson, Don. A PRELIMINARY CHECKLIST OF CONNECTICUT NEWS-
PAPERS, 1755-1975. 2 vols. Hartford: Connecticut State Library, 1978.
5943957. 79-622877. 071.46. Z6952.C8G87.

Delaware. University, Newark. Library. UNION LIST OF NEWSPAPERS IN
MICROFORM. Newark: 1964. 20685. 65-63236. Z6945.D32.

Mookini, Esther K. THE HAWAIIAN NEWSPAPERS. Honolulu: Topgallant
Publishing Co., 1974. 1009863. 74-80373. 079/.969. Z6952.H3M66.

Idaho. University. Library. UNIVERSITY OF IDAHO NEWSPAPER HOLDINGS
AS OF JULY 1, 1975. Compiled by Charles Webbert, Head, Special Collections, University of Idaho Library. University of Idaho Library Publication,
no. 17. Moscow: The Library, 1975. 2092416. 76-620581. 016.05.
Z6945.I25 1975 PN4731.

"Newspapers in the Illinois State Historical Library." ILLINOIS LIBRARIES 61
(February 1979): 81-194.

Iowa. State Historical Society. NEWSPAPER COLLECTION OF THE STATE
HISTORICAL SOCIETY OF IOWA. Compiled by L.O. Cheever. Studies in
Iowa History, vol. 1, no. 2. Iowa City: 1969. 130239. 70-631616/r75.
016.071/77. F621.S87 vol. 1, no. 2.

McMullan, T.N., ed. LOUISIANA NEWSPAPERS, 1794-1961: A UNION
LIST OF LOUISIANA NEWSPAPER FILES AVAILABLE IN PUBLIC, COLLEGE,
AND UNIVERSITY LIBRARIES IN LOUISIANA. Editor: T.N. McMullan, in
cooperation with the Louisiana Library Association. Rev. Baton Rouge: Louisiana State University Library, 1965. 2028089. 67-64803. Z6952.L8M25.

Hofstetter, Eleanore O., and Eustis, Marcella, eds. NEWSPAPERS IN MARY-
LAND LIBRARIES: A UNION LIST. Compiled under the auspices of the Academic and Research Division of the Maryland Library Association. Baltimore:
Division of Library Development Services, Maryland State Department of Education, 1977. 3160087. 78-620563. 016.07. Z6945.H635 PN4801.

Michigan. State Library Services. MICHIGAN NEWSPAPERS ON MICROFILM: WITH A DESCRIPTION OF THE "MICHIGAN NEWSPAPERS ON MICROFILM" PROJECT. 4th ed. Lansing: 1973. 803634. 73-622650. 071/.74. Z6952. M45M53 1973.

Mississippi. State Library Commission. MISSISSIPPIANA. 2 vols. Jackson: Mississippi Library Commission, 1971. 1253772. 72-170842. 016.91762. Z1301.A5.

Taft, William Howard. MISSOURI NEWSPAPERS: WHEN AND WHERE, 1808-1963. Columbia: State Historical Society of Missouri, 1964. 2892596. 64-63090. Z6952.M6T3.

UNION LIST OF MONTANA SERIALS: A SUB-SET OF THE MINNESOTA UNION LIST OF SERIALS--MULS. Minneapolis: University of Minnesota Library, 1977. Microfiche.

Nebraska State Historical Society. A GUIDE TO THE NEWSPAPER COLLECTION OF THE STATE ARCHIVES, NEBRASKA STATE HISTORICAL SOCIETY. Compiled by Anne P. Diffendal. Lincoln: 1977. 3611731. Z6952.N2N43 1977. GD 1,036,134 Item 7.

Folkes, John Gregg. NEVADA'S NEWSPAPERS: A BIBLIOGRAPHY; A COMPILATION OF NEVADA HISTORY, 1854-1964. Nevada Studies in History and Political Science, no. 6. University of Nevada Press. Bibliographical series, no. 3. Reno: University of Nevada Press, 1964. 1556585. 65-63210. 016. 07193. Z6952.N49F6.

DIRECTORY OF NEW JERSEY NEWSPAPERS, 1765-1970. Edited by William C. Wright and Paul A. Stellhorn. Trenton: New Jersey Historical Commission, 1977. 2048211. 76-4077. 016.071/49. Z6952.N54D57.

Grove, Pearce S.; Barnett, Becky J.; and Hansen, Sandra J., eds. NEW MEXICO NEWSPAPERS: A COMPREHENSIVE GUIDE TO BIBLIOGRAPHICAL ENTRIES AND LOCATION. Albuquerque: University of New Mexico Press, 1975. 1531635. 74-84232. 016.071/89. Z6952.N55G75.

North Carolina. State Department of Archives and History. UNION LIST OF NORTH CAROLINA NEWSPAPERS, 1751-1900. Edited by H.G. Jones and Julius H. Avant, in cooperation with the Committee on the Conservation of Newspaper Resources of the North Carolina Library Association. Raleigh: 1963. 2632280. 63-63845. 016.0756. Z6952.N6A58.

Ohio Historical Society. GUIDE TO OHIO NEWSPAPERS, 1793-1973: UNION BIBLIOGRAPHY OF OHIO NEWSPAPERS AVAILABLE IN OHIO LIBRARIES.

Edited by Stephen Gutgesell. Columbus: Ohio Historical Society, 1976. 2274046. 75-225. 071/.71. Z6952.04044 1976 PN4897.033.

> Expanded second edition of UNION LIST OF OHIO NEWS-PAPERS AVAILABLE IN OHIO, prepared by Ohio Historical Society Library and published in 1946.

Oklahoma. Department of Libraries. GUIDE TO OKLAHOMA MANUSCRIPTS, MAPS, AND NEWSPAPERS ON MICROFILM IN THE OKLAHOMA DEPART-MENT OF LIBRARIES. Compiled and edited by Robert L. Clark, Jr. Oklahoma City: 1970. 1601782. 72-634928. 016.9766. Z1325.044 1970.

Oregon. State Library, Salem. OREGON NEWSPAPERS; HOLDINGS OF: LIBRARY ASSOCIATION OF PORTLAND, OREGON HISTORICAL SOCIETY LIBRARY, OREGON STATE LIBRARY, UNIVERSITY OF OREGON LIBRARY. Salem: 1963. 20669. 64-64057. Z6952.07A5.

Rossell, Glenora E., ed. PENNSYLVANIA NEWSPAPERS: A BIBLIOGRAPHY AND UNION LIST. Edited under the auspices of the Pennsylvania Library Association. 2d ed. Pittsburgh: Pennsylvania Library Association, 1978. 4834243. 78-71000. 016.071/48. Z6952.P4S3 1978 PN4897.P38.

> Edition for 1969 edited by R. Salisbury.

CHECKLIST OF SOUTH DAKOTA NEWSPAPERS IN THE SOUTH DAKOTA STATE HISTORICAL SOCIETY AND THE HISTORICAL RESOURCE CENTER AT PIERRE, SOUTH DAKOTA: A BICENTENNIAL PROJECT. Pierre: South Dakota State Historical Society, 1976. 3310189. 77-622091. 016.071/83. Z6952.S8C45 PN4897.S65.

Tennessee. State Library and Archives, Nashville. State Library Division. TENNESSEE NEWSPAPERS: A CUMULATIVE LIST OF MICROFILMED TENNES-SEE NEWSPAPERS IN THE TENNESSEE STATE LIBRARY, AUGUST 1969, PRO-GRESS REPORT. Nashville: 1969. 2198591. Z6952.T3A5 1969.

Murphy, Virginia B.; Ashford, Daisy; and Covington, Pamela B., eds. NEWS-PAPER RESOURCES OF SOUTHEAST TEXAS. Houston: University of Houston Libraries, 1971. 496863. 75-637140. 016.071/3. Z6945.M93.

Wittenmyer, Mary Oleta, ed. A UNION LIST OF NEWSPAPERS IN THE LI-BRARIES OF THE FORT WORTH-DALLAS MAJOR RESOURCE CENTERS. Fort Worth: Texas Christian University Press, 1969. 728551. Z6945.W87.

"Bibliography--Newspapers." In GENEALOGICAL RECORDS OF UTAH, by Laureen Richardson Jaussi and Gloria Duncan Chaston, pages 98-123. Salt Lake City: Deseret Book, 1974.

> Includes holdings for nine Utah libraries.

Mills, Hazel E., and Kloostra, Georgia M., comps. NEWSPAPERS ON MI-
CROFILM IN THE LIBRARIES OF THE STATE OF WASHINGTON: A UNION
LIST. Olympia: Washington State Library, 1974. 1274141. 75-315011.
016.07. Z6945.M634.

West Virginia. University. Library. NEWSPAPERS IN THE WEST VIRGINIA
UNIVERSITY LIBRARY. Compiled by Lorise C. Boger. Morgantown: 1964.
66-63039. Z6945.W45.

Wisconsin. State Historical Society. GUIDE TO WISCONSIN NEWSPAPERS,
1833-1957. Compiled by Donald E. Oehlerts. Madison: 1958. 189548.
58-62501. Z6952.W8W76.

Homsher, Lola M. GUIDE TO WYOMING NEWSPAPERS, 1867-1967. Cheyenne:
Wyoming State Library, 1971. 195211. 75-634149. 016.071/87. Z6952.
W9H65.

NATIONAL OR ETHNIC GROUP UNION LISTS OF NEWSPAPERS

Wynar, Lubomyr R., and Wynar, Anna T. ENCYCLOPEDIC DIRECTORY OF
ETHNIC NEWSPAPERS AND PERIODICALS IN THE UNITED STATES. 2d ed.
Littleton, Colo.: Libraries Unlimited, 1976. 76-23317. 070.4/84/02573.
Z6953.5.A1W94 1976 PN4882.

Arndt, Karl John Richard, and Olson, May E. GERMAN-AMERICAN NEWS-
PAPERS AND PERIODICALS, 1732-1955; HISTORY AND BIBLIOGRAPHY. 2d
rev. ed. New York: Johnson Reprint Corp., 1965. 682999. 66-2897.
016.0713. Z6953.5.G3A7 1965.

Hebrew Union College, Jewish Institute of Religion. American Jewish Periodical
Center. JEWISH NEWSPAPERS AND PERIODICALS ON MICROFILM, AVAIL-
ABLE AT THE AMERICAN JEWISH PERIODICAL CENTER. Cincinnati: 1957.
Supplement. 1960. 1866686. 57-13466rev. 016.0713. Z6944.J4H4.

Minnesota. University. Immigration History Research Center. NEWSPAPERS
ON MICROFILM. St. Paul: 1970. 2959795. PN4731.M5.

INDEXES

Indexes to newspapers are additional reference sources that may be helpful in
obtaining information from newspapers. The following are a few lists of indexes
that include newspaper indexes which may be of assistance to genealogists.
Many of the libraries that have newspaper indexes will normally cooperate in
answering single name mail inquiries.

Milner, Anita Cheek. NEWSPAPER INDEXES: A LOCATION AND SUBJECT
GUIDE FOR RESEARCHERS. Metuchen, N.J.: Scarecrow Press, 1977-- .
Irregular. 3003179. 77-7130rev.80. 016.071. Z6951.M635A13.

American Library Association. Junior Members Round Table. LOCAL INDEXES
IN AMERICAN LIBRARIES: A UNION LIST OF UNPUBLISHED INDEXES. Edited
by Norma Olin Ireland and National Editorial Committee of Junior Members.
Useful Reference Series, no. 73. Boston: F.W. Faxon, 1947. Reprint.
Boston: Gregg Press, 1972. 388782. 72-6992. 017/.5. Z6293.A5 1972.

New England Library Association. Bibliography Committee. A GUIDE TO
NEWSPAPER INDEXES IN NEW ENGLAND. N.p.: 1978. 3956101. Z6952.
A11N48.

Dillon, Richard H. "Local Indexes in California." NEWS NOTES OF CALI-
FORNIA LIBRARIES 49 (October 1954): 501-42.

"A Union List of Indexes to Michigan Newspapers." FAMILY TRAILS 3 (Fall-
Winter 1971-72): 13-15.

"Indexes and Abstracts in the Michigan State Library of Vital Records Extracted
from Michigan Newspapers." FAMILY TRAILS 3 (Fall-Winter 1971-72): 16-17.

Hoagland, Joan, and Adams, Marie. LOCALLY PREPARED INDEXES IN OHIO
LIBRARIES. Columbus: Ohio Library Association, 1973. 796488. 016.027.
Z1002.H6.

An occasional mail inquiry may meet with some success for historical and genealogical purposes if the newspaper has a librarian that maintains an index,
file, or morgue of obituaries. Several obituary indexes are listed in the chapter,
"Genealogical Name Indexes."

The subject headings relative to newspapers and their indexes are as follows:

LC   IOWA--NEWSPAPERS

Sears   NEWSPAPERS--IOWA

GD   IOWA - NEWSPAPERS
        IOWA - NEWSPAPERS - INDEXES
        IOWA, LINN, ELY - NEWSPAPERS
        IOWA, LINN, ELY - NEWSPAPERS - INDEXES

GENEALOGICAL NEWSPAPER COLUMNS

Genealogists will inquire about genealogical newspaper columns. There have
been many genealogical columns in various newspapers throughout the nation,
and there are many still published today. Most of them are columns of inquiry

that are generated from the readers of a particular city and its limited circulation area. The most popular and widely circulated inquiry publication is the GENEALOGICAL HELPER. Nevertheless, for the genealogists that inquire, the following checklist will be of assistance.

Milner, Anita Cheek, comp. NEWSPAPER GENEALOGY COLUMNS: A PRELIMINARY CHECKLIST. Escondido, Calif.: Milner, 1975. 76-350128. 929.1/0973. CS44.M5.

The following are two genealogical newspaper columns that have been compiled into collections and published:

Boston Transcript. GENEALOGY: NEWSPAPER COLUMNS, JAN.1, 1904-APR. 30, 1941. Microcard edition arranged by Carlos Parsons Darling, Lawrenceville, Pa. N.P.: n.d. 2129984. 929.05.

Hartford Times. GENEALOGICAL COLUMNS FROM THE HARTFORD TIMES, HARTFORD, CONNECTICUT, FEBRUARY 1934-May 1967. Collected by Jean R. Rentmeister. Fond du Lac, Wis.: J.R. Rentmeister, 1978. 424036.

ADVERTISEMENTS FOR LOST RELATIVES

Another useful service that newspapers can provide genealogists is to place an advertisement in their newspaper announcing a person's desire to contact a distant relative or a descendant of a common ancestor. Some such advertisements have led to articles in small town papers and very meaningful results for the genealogists. AYER DIRECTORY OF PUBLICATIONS (Philadelphia: Ayer Press, 1972-- .) is the most useful source for providing genealogists with the addresses of town and city newspapers.

INTERLIBRARY LOAN

The interlibrary loan of newspapers on microfilm has already been mentioned in this chapter. A few years ago this editor tried to borrow an 1860 reel of an Eastern newspaper and was rejected by three large libraries in the city in which the newspaper has been published. Letters to the three library directors pleading that one of their institutions should surely lend it resulted in a successful transaction and a happy genealogical researcher. Such a plea should not be necessary. Nevertheless, librarians should not hesitate to challenge their uncooperative colleagues.

If a librarian is not successful in obtaining a newspaper on microfilm on interlibrary loan, the genealogist may have to hire a researcher or travel to consult the bound or paper files of a library or archive. If an exact date of a newspaper account or report can be ascertained, some small libraries may be willing to consult the newspaper for a genealogist and/or photoduplicate the desired information.

COLLECTION DEVELOPMENT

Librarians should see that some library in the community has microfilm copies of the local papers. If possible, circulating microfilm copies should also be available. If more than one library has microfilm copies, a cooperative agreement should be made designating which library will fill all of the interlibrary loan requests for a town's or a city's newspapers.

If the local newspapers are not available on microfilm, librarians should try to get them microfilmed by negotiating with microfilming firms, the publishers of newspapers still being published, or libraries that have complete or substantial holdings. This may involve agreements by several libraries to purchase copies if a microfilming firm will microfilm the newspapers.

SUMMARY

For the interlibrary loan of newspapers the only practical source is NEWSPAPERS IN MICROFORM. Librarians should encourage genealogists to consult newspapers when appropriate and request them on interlibrary loan from libraries in or near the city of origin, even if they are not listed in NEWSPAPERS IN MICROFORM.

Chapter 15

SOURCES LISTING ANCESTORS AS INDIVIDUALS

If ancestors are not found in records that list them with families, then genealogists may have to turn to records that list people individually. Such records
include federal census schedules, 1790-1840; military records; tax lists; poll
lists; city directories; civil and criminal court records; and naturalization records.

CENSUS SCHEDULES

The 1790-1840 federal census schedules are described in the chapter, "Census
Schedules." These early schedules have been completely indexed by the Accelerated Indexing System, and some states' schedules have also been indexed
by other publishers and/or societies. The schedules list only the heads of households and others in the household with a different surname. The schedules include tables of figures that give the ages of the members of the household.
This information can help some genealogists calculate, by elimination, which
individuals may be their ancestors. Verification of such calculations would have
to be made in other sources.

MILITARY RECORDS

There are three military records that can be of value to genealogists: service
records, pension applications, and bounty land warrant applications. Their
respective information will be outlined here.

Military service records normally include the place of birth, age, and occupation. Besides this genealogical data, they also include various other data of
historical interest. These include the places mustered in and out, equipment
lost, places of muster, rank, unit, hospital records, and prison records.

The pension application may contain information about older veterans, widows,
and orphans. The most informative of the applications is the widow's, because
she had to prove her marriage; the documentation thereof is often very helpful
to genealogists.

The bounty land warrant applications inform genealogists of some westward emigration. These records may also include widows' or heirs' applications.

For more detailed information concerning military records, the following sources should be consulted (listed in order of importance):

U.S. National Archives and Records Service. MILITARY SERVICE RECORDS IN THE NATIONAL ARCHIVES OF THE UNITED STATES. General Services Administration General Information Leaflet, no. 7. Washington, D.C.: 1977. GS4.22:7.

Greenwood, Val D. THE RESEARCHER'S GUIDE TO AMERICAN GENEALOGY. Baltimore, Genealogical Publishing Co., 1973. 624026. 73-6902. 929/.1/ 072073. CS47.G73.

> Chapter 21, "Military Records: Colonial Wars and the American Revolution," pages 414-43, and chapter 22, "Military Records: After the Revolution," pages 444-66, contain good explanations of the records and bibliographies of other useful sources.

Colket, Meredith Bright, and Bridgers, Frank E. GUIDE TO GENEALOGICAL RECORDS IN THE NATIONAL ARCHIVES. National Archives Publication no. 64-8. Washington, D.C.: National Archives, 1964. Reprint. National Archives and Records Service, General Services Administration, 1979. 796624. 64-7048. CS15.C6. GS4.6/2:G28.

Beers, Henry Putney. GUIDE TO THE ARCHIVES OF THE GOVERNMENT OF THE CONFEDERATE STATES OF AMERICA. U.S. National Archives Publication no. 68-15. Washington, D.C.: National Archives, National Archives and Records Service, General Services Administration, 1968. 390979. CD3053.B4.

Munden, Kenneth White, and Beers, Henry Putney. GUIDE TO FEDERAL ARCHIVES RELATING TO THE CIVIL WAR. National Archives Publication no. 63. Washington, D.C.: National Archives, National Archives and Records Service, General Services Administration, 1962. 795805. 62-9432. CD3047.M8.

To assist genealogists in gaining access to copies of the military service records available from the National Archives, librarians should have on hand a supply of the GSA Form 6751, "Order and Billing for Copies of Veteran's Records," for distribution to genealogists. These forms may be obtained free from Military Service Records (NNCC), National Archives (GSA), Washington, D.C. 20408. This form is to be used for records that are 75 years old or older. Librarians should also have a supply of Standard Form 180, "Request Pertaining to Military Personnel Records," for requesting information from records that are less than 75 years old. Form 180 is available from the National Personnel Records Center (MPRC), GSA, 9700 Page Boulevard, St. Louis, Missouri 63132.

Librarians should be aware that the Genealogical Department has many of the
National Archives military records on microfilm. They are, of course, available to genealogists through branch genealogical libraries. The National
Archives' branches also have some military records that relate to their jurisdictions. Librarians may borrow many of these records for genealogists through
interlibrary loan from any of the National Archives branches.

The following catalog lists records that are available through the Genealogical
Department's branches but not the National Archives' branches:

U.S. National Archives and Records Service. REVOLUTIONARY WAR PENSION
AND BOUNTY-LAND-WARRANT APPLICATION FILES. National Archives
Microfilm Publications Pamphlet Describing M804. Washington, D.C.: 1974.

> This catalog contains the microfilm reel numbers for eighty
> thousand pension and bounty-land-warrant application files.
> The Genealogical Department microfilm numbers for this collec-
> tion start with 970,001 for the first item in the catalog and
> end with 972,625 for reel 2,625.

The Genealogical Department also has prepared a register of this collection.
It may be available at some of the Department's branch libraries.

Genealogical Society of the Church of Jesus Christ of Latter-day Saints.
REGISTER OF FILM NUMBERS: FOR REVOLUTIONARY WAR PENSION AND
BOUNTY-LAND-WARRANT APPLICATION FILES. Salt Lake City: 1975.
GD 908,690 Item 1.

The Genealogical Department has, in addition, the indexes and compiled service
records of Confederate soldiers and the indexes to the compiled service records
of volunteer Union soldiers, 1861-65. The National Archives' branches have
these same records for their respective jurisdictions. The Union service records
have not been microfilmed and are available only at the National Archives.
The Genealogical Department register for the microfilm numbers of the consolidated index of these service records is as follows:

Workman, Beth B. CONFEDERATE SOLDIERS SERVICE RECORD REGISTER.
Salt Lake City: Genealogical Society, 1964. GD 908,646.

The following are a few selected indexes that are very useful for identifying
service men:

National Genealogical Society. INDEX OF REVOLUTIONARY WAR PENSION
APPLICATIONS IN THE NATIONAL ARCHIVES. Special Publication, no. 40.
Washington, D.C.: 1976. 2211855. 75-43393. 929.3.

Daughters of the American Revolution. DAR PATRIOT INDEX. Washington, D.C.: National Society of the Daughters of the American Revolution, 1966. Supplement. Washington, D.C.: 1969-- . 1361754. 67-27776. 929.3. E255.D36.

Brigham Young University. Library. REVOLUTIONARY SOLDIERS GRAVE LISTS INDEX. 3 x 5 cards.

> This index of about sixty-seven thousand names found on the DAR Revolutionary Soldiers Grave Lists from 1898 through 1972 was prepared from the annual report of the National Society of the Daughters of the American Revolution published in the U.S. Congress, Serial Set. It contains the name, place of burial, birth and death dates, service, and additional facts. The index may be consulted by writing the History and Genealogy Department, Harold B. Lee Library, Brigham Young University, Provo, Utah 84602.

United States. Census Office. 6th Census, 1840. A CENSUS OF PENSIONERS FOR REVOLUTIONARY OR MILITARY SERVICES: WITH THEIR NAMES, AGES, AND PLACES OF RESIDENCE AS RETURNED BY THE MARSHALS OF THE SEVERAL JUDICIAL DISTRICTS, UNDER THE ACT FOR TAKING THE SIXTH CENSUS. Bound with a General Index. Prepared by the Genealogical Society of the Church of Jesus Christ of Latter-day Saints. 2 vols. in 1. Baltimore: Genealogical Publishing Co., 1974. 2135663. 351/.5/0973. E255.U42 1974.

Smith, Clifford Neal. FEDERAL LAND SERIES: A CALENDAR OF ARCHIVAL MATERIALS ON THE LAND PATENTS ISSUED BY THE UNITED STATES GOVERNMENT, WITH SUBJECT, TRACT, AND NAME INDEXES. Chicago: American Library Association, 1972-- . 548057. 72-3238rev.74. 333.1/6/0973. KF675.A73S6.

> Volume 1. 1788-1810. Volume 2. FEDERAL BOUNTY-LAND WARRANTS OF THE AMERICAN REVOLUTION, 1799-1835.

There are many state lists and indexes of veterans of different wars. Some are listed in Greenwood. Other lists and indexes can be found in the following:

GENEALOGICAL & LOCAL HISTORY BOOKS IN PRINT. 2 vols. Springfield, Va.: Netti Schreiner-Yantis, 6818 Lois Drive, 22150, 1975-77. 2998564. 77-648320. 016.929/1/0973. Z5313.U5G45 CS47.

> Volume 1 is entitled GENEALOGICAL BOOKS IN PRINT.

Filby, P. William, comp. AMERICAN & BRITISH GENEALOGY & HERALDRY: A SELECTED LIST OF BOOKS. 2d ed. Chicago: American Library Association, 1975. 1659712. 75-29383. 016.929/1/097. Z5311.F55 1975 CS47.

Curtis, Mary Barnett, comp. BIBLIOGRAPHY OF THE AMERICAN REVOLUTION.
3 vols. Fort Worth, Tex.: Magazine of Bibliographies, 1973. Reprint from
MAGAZINE OF BIBLIOGRAPHIES; vol. 1, no. 4, vol. 2, nos. 1-2. 4316822.
016.97334.

Rosters and lists; battles and eyewitness accounts; general history.

The subject headings relative to military records for genealogical research are
as follows:

Military History

LC   ELY, IOWA--HISTORY, MILITARY
EUROPEAN WAR, 1914-1918--REGIMENTAL
HISTORIES--UNITED STATES
U.S.--HISTORY--FRENCH AND INDIAN WAR, 1755-
1763--REGIMENTAL HISTORIES
U.S.--HISTORY--REVOLUTION--REGIMENTAL
HISTORIES
U.S.--HISTORY--WAR OF 1812--REGIMENTAL
HISTORIES
U.S.--HISTORY--WAR WITH MEXICO, 1845-1848--
REGIMENTAL HISTORIES
U.S.--HISTORY--WAR WITH MEXICO, 1845-1848--
REGISTERS, LISTS, ETC.
U.S.--HISTORY--WAR WITH MEXICO, 1845-1848--
REGISTERS OF DEAD
U.S.--HISTORY--CIVIL WAR, 1861-1865--REGIMENTAL
HISTORIES
U.S.--HISTORY--WAR OF 1898--REGIMENTAL
HISTORIES
WORLD WAR, 1939-1945--REGIMENTAL HISTORIES--
UNITED STATES

Sears   WORLD WAR, 1939-1945--REGIMENTAL HISTORIES

GD   IOWA - MILITARY RECORDS - CIVIL WAR - REGIMENTAL
HISTORIES

Military Records

LC   EUROPEAN WAR, 1914-1918--REGISTERS OF DEAD
IOWA--MILITIA
KOREAN WAR, 1950-1953--REGISTERS OF DEAD
PENSIONS, MILITARY--IOWA
PENSIONS, MILITARY--UNITED STATES
PENSIONS--(by war)
U.S.--ARMED FORCES--REGISTERS OF DEAD
U.S. ARMY--REGISTERS OF DEAD
U.S.--HISTORY--FRENCH AND INDIAN WAR, 1755-
1763--REGISTERS, LISTS, ETC.
U.S.--HISTORY--FRENCH AND INDIAN WAR, 1755-
1763--REGISTERS OF DEAD

U.S.--HISTORY--REVOLUTION--REGISTERS, LISTS, ETC.
U.S.--HISTORY--WAR OF 1812--REGISTERS, LISTS, ETC.
U.S.--HISTORY--WAR OF 1812--REGISTERS OF DEAD
U.S.--HISTORY--WAR WITH MEXICO, 1845-1848--
  REGISTERS, LISTS, ETC.
U.S.--HISTORY--WAR WITH MEXICO, 1845-1848--
  REGISTERS OF DEAD
U.S.--HISTORY--CIVIL WAR, 1861-1865--REGISTERS,
  LISTS, ETC.
U.S.--HISTORY--CIVIL WAR, 1861-1865--REGISTERS
  OF DEAD
U.S.--HISTORY--WAR OF 1898--REGISTERS, LISTS, ETC.
U.S.--HISTORY--WAR OF 1898--REGISTERS OF DEAD
U.S. NAVY--REGISTERS OF DEAD
WORLD WAR, 1939-1945--REGISTERS OF DEAD--U.S.

Sears   IOWA--MILITIA
PENSIONS, MILITARY--IOWA

GD   IOWA - MILITARY RECORDS - REVOLUTION
IOWA - MILITARY RECORDS - WAR OF 1812
IOWA - MILITARY RECORDS - WAR WITH MEXICO,
  1845-1848
IOWA - MILITARY RECORDS - CIVIL WAR
IOWA - MILITARY RECORDS - CIVIL WAR - INDEXES
IOWA - MILITARY RECORDS - EUROPEAN WAR,
  1914-1918

CITY DIRECTORIES

City directories can serve the useful purpose of providing the street address of
an ancestor in a large city so that the search of a census schedule can be
shortened. Also they may be the only source for substantiating an ancestor's
residence. The following bibliography lists all known directories published before 1860 for 1,646 communities. It is arranged alphabetically by city and
includes library holdings.

Spear, Dorothea N. BIBLIOGRAPHY OF AMERICAN DIRECTORIES THROUGH
1860. Worcester, Mass.: American Antiquarian Society, 1961. Reprint.
Westport, Conn.: Greenwood Press, 1978. 577681. 3980848. 61-1054.
77-28204. 016.973/025. Z5771.S7.

Librarians should try to obtain microform copies of city directories on interlibrary
loan. When necessary, genealogists might be encouraged to write the directory-
holding library and request that a specific directory be checked for a given
ancestor. Research Publications of New Haven, Connecticut, has reproduced
on microfiche the directories that are listed in the above bibliography. Many
libraries have purchased this collection, and some will circulate directories on
interlibrary loan. Librarians should try to determine which libraries have cir-

culating collections and whether there is a library in their vicinity to which they can refer genealogists. The OCLC entry for this collection is as follows:

CITY AND BUSINESS DIRECTORIES OF THE UNITED STATES THROUGH 1860. New Haven, Conn.: Research Publishing, 1966. 1580855. 016.9173.

> Based on the book by Dorothea N. Spear, BIBLIOGRAPHY OF AMERICAN DIRECTORIES THROUGH 1860 (p. 222).

Research Publications has extended its city directories collection to include 1861-1881 for seventy-three cities and for sixty-seven cities from 1881-1901. These two collections are available on microfilm.

Another publisher has microfilmed city directories for ninety cities for the years 1841 to 1900 and twenty-four cities for 1901 to 1942. The collection is sold on 16mm. microfilm by Bay Microfilm, 737 Loma Verde Avenue, Palo Alto, California 94303. The collection is listed in parts 6 and 7 of the following bibliography:

Americana Unlimited. THE COX LIBRARY: COUNTY, STATE & LOCAL HISTORIES: A MICROFILM OFFERING FROM AMERICANA UNLIMITED. Tucson, Ariz.: Americana Unlimited; Glendale, Calif.: distribution by A.H. Clark Co., 1974. 2165136. 76-358242. 016.073. Z1250.A44 1974 E180.

The subject headings relative to city directories are as follows:

LC	ELY, IOWA--DIRECTORIES
Sears	ELY, IOWA--DIRECTORIES
GD	IOWA, LINN, ELY - DIRECTORIES

NATURALIZATION RECORDS

The declaration of intention for naturalization in most cases contains very little useful information for genealogists. However, some of them do contain the place and date of birth, occupation, date and port of entry, and the name of the ship. In some cases genealogists will find it necessary to try to obtain a naturalization record of the ancestor in an attempt to find their place of birth or residence before coming to the United States. These records are in various federal and state courts throughout the country. The best guide for determining where to write and how to obtain naturalization records is the following:

Neagles, James C., and Neagles, Lila Lee. LOCATING YOUR IMMIGRANT ANCESTOR: A GUIDE TO NATURALIZATION RECORDS. Logan, Utah: Everton Publishers, 1975. 1280724. JK1811.N435.

The subject headings relative to naturalization records are as follows:

LC   NATURALIZATION RECORDS

Sears   NATURALIZATION

GD   U.S. - EMIGRATION AND IMMIGRATION

REAL PROPERTY MAPS

Occasionally a genealogist will express an interest in plat books, county atlases, or land ownership maps. All of these are land and property maps that identify owners and can be helpful in some difficult research problems as well as being of historical interest. Collectively, they are considered real property maps by the Library of Congress.

The following are the principal bibliographies for these maps and atlases:

U.S. Library of Congress. Map Division. A LIST OF GEOGRAPHICAL AT-LASES IN THE LIBRARY OF CONGRESS, WITH BIBLIOGRAPHICAL NOTES. Compiled under the direction of Philip Lee Phillips and Clara Egli Le Gear. Washington, D.C.: Government Printing Office, 1909-- . Reprint of vols. 1-4 in 2. Amsterdam: Theatrum Orbis Terrarum, 1971. 1583643. 525252. 09-35009 r 752. 74-165906. 016.912. Z6028.U56.

_____. UNITED STATES ATLASES: A LIST OF NATIONAL, STATE, COUNTY, CITY, AND REGIONAL ATLASES IN THE LIBRARY OF CONGRESS. Compiled by Clara Egli Le Gear, Division of Maps. 2 vols. Washington, D.C.: 1950-1953. Reprint. New York: Arno Press, 1971. 1842965. 152647. 50-62950. 71-154058. 016.91273. Z881.U5.

U.S. Library of Congress. Geography and Map Division. LAND OWNERSHIP MAPS, A CHECKLIST OF NINETEENTH CENTURY UNITED STATES COUNTY MAPS IN THE LIBRARY OF CONGRESS. Compiled by Richard W. Stephenson. Washington, D.C.: Government Printing Office, 1967. LC5.2:L22. 735029. 67-60091. Z6027.U5U54.

The following are three good state bibliographies of real property maps:

Miles, William, comp. MICHIGAN ATLASES AND PLAT BOOKS: A CHECK-LIST 1872-1973. Lansing: Michigan Dept. of Education, State Library Services, 1975. 1915223. 75-623304. 016.912/774. Z6027.U5M65 GA431.

Fox, Michael J., comp. MAPS AND ATLASES SHOWING LAND OWNERSHIP IN WISCONSIN: IN THE COLLECTIONS OF THE STATE HISTORICAL SOCIETY OF WISCONSIN. Madison: State Historical Society of Wisconsin, 1978. 3935923. 016.912775.

Moak, Jefferson M., comp. ATLASES OF PENNSYLVANIA: A PRELIMINARY CHECKLIST OF COUNTY, CITY AND SUBJECT ATLASES OF PENNSYLVANIA. Philadelphia: Moak, 1976. 2066245. 016.912.

The subject headings relative to plat books, county atlases, and land ownership maps are as follows:

> LC   REAL PROPERTY--LINN COUNTY, IOWA--MAPS
>
> Sears   IOWA--MAPS
>
> GD   IOWA, LINN - LAND AND PROPERTY - MAPS

COURT RECORDS

Some genealogists can find interesting historical material about their ancestors by checking civil and criminal court records. Genealogists could, by correspondence, ask a court clerk to check indexes for one or two ancestors at a time. However, in most cases they would have to visit the appropriate county court house or hire someone to do the research for them. A useful, brief explanation of court records is available in Chapter 18, pages 334-44, 352-57, "Court Records," of Greenwood's RESEARCHER'S GUIDE TO AMERICAN GENEALOGY (p. 218). THE HANDY BOOK FOR GENEALOGISTS (p. 50) also reports the availability of civil and criminal court records for some counties.

The subject headings relative to civil and criminal court records are as follows:

> LC   COURT RECORDS--LINN COUNTY, IOWA
>
> Sears   (None)
>
> GD   IOWA, LINN - CIVIL RECORDS
>   IOWA, LINN - COURT RECORDS

TAX LISTS

Tax lists have been used by genealogists as a substitute for other lost or destroyed records. Many tax lists predate the 1790 census and provide a means of identifying the county in which a head of household and/or land or property owner lived at the time a tax was collected. Tax lists are not very informative but are better than nothing.

Many tax lists are listed in Filby's AMERICAN & BRITISH GENEALOGY & HERALDRY. However, there are many more, unpublished, available at court houses. Very few lists have been microfilmed, and many have been discarded.

The subject headings relative to tax lists are as follows:

> LC   TAXATION--LINN COUNTY, IOWA--LISTS

> Sears   TAXATION--LINN COUNTY, IOWA
>
> GD   IOWA, LINN - TAXATION

POLL LISTS

The poll tax list and lists of registered voters are other sources of limited value for genealogists but are better than nothing. Again, they usually only give the name of the person and the county of residence. They are available at court houses. Few have been microfilmed, and many discarded; however, many have been published as official lists for use at polling places. Those that are published are not usually available in libraries, and therefore no bibliographic control is available for them.

The subject headings relative to poll tax lists and lists of registered voters are as follows:

Poll Tax Lists

> LC   POLL--TAX--LINN COUNTY, IOWA
>
> Sears   TAXATION--LINN COUNTY, IOWA
>
> GD   IOWA, LINN, ELY - ELECTORATE

Voter Lists

> LC   VOTING REGISTERS
> LINN COUNTY, IOWA--VOTING REGISTERS
> ELY, IOWA--VOTING REGISTERS
>
> Sears   (None)
>
> GD   IOWA - ELECTORATE

SCHOOL RECORDS

In some cases school records may be helpful. A few public school records are retained by county court houses. Most colleges maintain good records of their students and graduates, and many publish lists of the graduated alumni. Again, these records have limited value but are better than nothing.

The subject headings relative to school records for genealogical research are as follows:

> LC   SCHOOLS--RECORDS AND CORRESPONDENCE--LINN
> COUNTY, IOWA
>
> Sears   SCHOOL REPORTS--LINN COUNTY, IOWA
>
> GD   IOWA, LINN - SCHOOLS

COLLECTION DEVELOPMENT

The following free publications of the National Archives should be in all libraries:

MILITARY SERVICE RECORDS IN THE NATIONAL ARCHIVES OF THE UNITED STATES.

REVOLUTIONARY WAR PENSION AND BOUNTY-LAND WARRANT APPLICA-TION FILES.

The Colket-Bridgers GUIDE TO GENEALOGICAL RECORDS IN THE NATIONAL ARCHIVES should also be in every library.

If any library decides to acquire the 1790 census schedules and indexes, the cheapest way is to order the three reel microfilm edition of them available from the National Archives. There are several reprints available that are more expensive; all editions contain indexes.

SUMMARY

The records that list individuals are not as useful as those that list family groups; but they must be used, particularly if family grouped records are not available and also to gather some family history information. Librarians should try to remember that the most useful military record is the widow's pension application.

Chapter 16
UNIQUE RESEARCH SERVICES

There are a few unique free and fee research services that should be known to librarians. Genealogists should be encouraged to use these free services. Eventually, library services should be improved to the point where rental libraries and fee services will no longer be offered because of their lack of use.

FREE SERVICES

GENEALOGICAL HELPER includes a Good Samaritan column, "Genealogy Miscellany," of genealogists who are grateful for help given them and are willing to share their time and resources helping others by doing many of the things free that are advertised for a fee in the same periodical. Many of these people are very talented, skilled researchers that love to help others and enjoy corresponding.

Another service of the GENEALOGICAL HELPER is a fee advertisement program that permits genealogists to plead for help in finding their ancestors. Some distant cousins have found each other by reading such ads. Also, many enterprising genealogists, after having struck up a friendly correspondence program with other genealogists, have cultivated free researchers for themselves throughout the country. A number of genealogists have been very successful with such endeavors and have found satisfaction in reciprocating such services in their local court houses and cemeteries.

RENTAL SERVICES

The following are a few rental services that offer genealogists access to materials that may not be available because of inadequate public library services. The fact that such services have been successful in their development is a disgrace to the library profession. Any reference to a rental service should be made only as a last resort.

Unique Research Services

Ancestree House
708 South Maple
Ellensburg, Wash.   98926

>Rental fees include postage, a deposit of the purchase price of the material, and, the two-week rental fee is 25 percent of the book's price. The following is the newsletter that includes all new books and microfilm available for rent and/or sale: AN-CESTREE HOUSE RESEARCH LIBRARY NEWSLETTER. Issues 1 and 2 list the majority of the collection's five hundred items.

The Bookmark
P.O. Box 74
Knightstown, Ind. 46148

>Catalog of about 1,824 items is available for a fee; postage, and a deposit of the cost of the materials is required. The two-week rental fee is 20 percent of book's price for bound books and 25 percent for unbound.

Hoenstine Rental Library
414 Montgomery Street
P.O. Box 208
Hollidaysburg, Pa.   16648

>The renter has to purchase or have access to a twenty-six-hundred-item collection catalog and two hundred thousand reference cumulative index of Pennsylvania genealogy and history, entitled, GUIDE TO GENEALOGICAL & HISTORICAL RESEARCH IN PENNSYLVANIA, by Floyd G. Hoenstine, 4th ed. Rev. and enl. Hollidaysburg, Pa.: The author, 1978. A deposit is required for each book, and the rental fee is 25 percent of the deposit. The deposit fee is noted in the guide. Use is for thirty days.

National Genealogical Society
1921 Sunderland Place, N.W.
Washington, D.C.   20036

>Members may use the library by mail for a one-time registration fee and a small service charge per two-week loan. A seventy-nine-page list and supplements are furnished free. The main book list is as follows: National Genealogical Society. Library. BOOK LIST OF THE NATIONAL GENEALOGICAL SOCIETY LIBRARY. Prepared for users of the library loan service by Janis H. Miller under the direction of Virginia D. Westhaeffer. Washington, D.C., National Genealogical Society, 1965. 2185960. 016.9291.

New England Historic Genealogical Society
101 Newbury Street
Boston, Mass. 02116

> Members may purchase a two-volume family history catalog
> and/or one-volume local history catalog of New England and
> New York materials. A small service fee is charged for each
> loan. No institutional memberships are accepted. The catalog
> is as follows: New England Historic Genealogical Society. THE
> CATALOG TO THE CIRCULATING COLLECTION OF THE NEW
> ENGLAND HISTORIC GENEALOGICAL SOCIETY. 2d ed. 3
> vols. Boston: 1977. 3444620. 77-373861. 016.929/373.
> Z5305.U5N38 1977. Volume 1. GENEALOGIES, A-J. Volume
> 2. GENEALOGIES, K-Z. Oversize books. Biographies. Volume
> 3. LOCAL HISTORIES: NEW ENGLAND AND NEW YORK.

Rasmussen Books
Lucy Rasmussen
Gillett, Wis. 54124

> A deposit of the price of the book to be rented is required.
> A catalog is provided free. The latest includes 226 titles for
> seventeen eastern, southern and midwestern states. The renter
> pays return postage. A small fee per week is charged.

FEE SERVICES

There are a host of other smaller fee services offered through advertisements in
the GENEALOGICAL HELPER and other genealogical magazines. Genealogists,
for a fee, will check specific titles, either in their own libraries or in undis-
closed libraries near their homes. Indexes may be checked; census schedules
read; vital records offices visited; cemetery and sexton records searched; and
a number of other helpful services done.

GENEALOGICAL RESEARCH SURVEYS

The Genealogical Department of the Church of Jesus Christ of Latter-day Saints,
for a moderate fee, will conduct a short survey of some of their indexes and
records and make suggestions of where genealogists may pursue additional research. Librarians should be aware of this service and recommend it to the
seriously confused genealogist who is having difficulty getting started. There
are also professional researchers who will provide similar services, and many
research firms advertise survey services in some of the genealogical periodicals.

Genealogists should be encouraged to do their own research as long as it is
possible. Genealogy is like any other skill, hobby, pastime, or research en-
deavor: there is a lot of satisfaction in doing it yourself.

Unique Research Services

COMPUTER SEARCHES

A few data bases of machine- or computer-readable names and the vital statistics related to them are being developed. The data therein represent genealogical resources that may be unique to that data base and may well be worth the investment by a genealogist. Many advertisements are included in genealogical periodicals for these various computer services.

ANCESTRAL SURNAME INDEXES

Another popular method of getting related genealogists together in order to share findings, research, and family histories, traditions and tales is through surname indexes. These indexes usually are created by a genealogical society, and they index the names that are being researched by its members. There are many of these surname indexes published. The following are just a few that appear readily in bibliographic collections:

Chicago Genealogical Society. SURNAME INDEX, 1970-73. Chicago: 1970-74.

Christian, Margaret, comp. SURNAME INDEX. Richmond: British Columbia Genealogical Society, 1973. 5137878. 79-306476. 929.3/717. CS88.B74 C47.

Cunning, Robert A., comp. SURNAME INDEX. Mansfield: Ohio Genealogical Society, 1968. 3150527. 72-64032. 929.12.

Fargo Genealogical Society. SURNAME INDEX. Fargo, N.D.: 1973. 2530044. 929.1.

Genealogical Society of Riverside. SURNAME INDEX. Riverside, Calif.: 1972/73-- . Irregular. 1791691. 74-641036. 929/.1/0973. CS42.G48317.

High Plains Genealogical Society. Canyon, Texas. SURNAME INDEX. Canyon, Tex.: 1978. 4149121. F385.H6.

Hodges, Florence S., and Shaw, Mrs. Aurora C., eds. A SURNAME INDEX OF ALL ISSUES, EACH ISSUE INDEXED INDIVIDUALLY, 1957-1974, ISSUES NOS. 1-72, OF THE SOUTHERN GENEALOGIST'S EXCHANGE QUARTERLY. Tampa, Fla.: Hodges, 1975. 5139966. GD 1,036,948.

Iowa Genealogical Society. IOWA GENEALOGICAL SURNAME INDEX. Irregular. DesMoines: 1972--. 1786079. 73-642660. 929/.1/09777. CS44.158a.

Volume 1 contains 21,000; volume 2, 25,000; and volume 3,

50,000. All names are cross-indexed, and additions or corrections are made to earlier entries.

Mid-Michigan Genealogical Society. SURNAME INDEX: OF ANCESTORS AND COLLATORAL RELATIVES OF THE MID-MICHIGAN GENEALOGICAL SOCIETY. Lansing, Mich.: n.d. 4186811. F565.M54. GD 1,001,892, A-Rus; 1,001,893, Rut-Z.

North Oakland Genealogical Society. Lake Orion, Michigan. SURNAME INDEX: INCLUDING KEYS AND CLUES TO KITH, KIN AND COUSINS. Lake Orion, Mich.: 1978. 4238723. 929.3774

Oklahoma Genealogical Society. Projects Committee. SURNAME INDEX. Special Publication, no. 1. Edited by Jo Ann Garrison. Oklahoma City: 1969. 1727818. 976.6.

St. Cloud Area Genealogists. SURNAME INDEX. St. Cloud, Minn.: 1978. 3875495. 929.

Seattle Genealogical Society. SURNAME EXCHANGE. Seattle: 1970. 120646. 72-253731. 929.2. CS44.S4.

Sioux Valley Genealogical Society. Sioux Fall, South Dakota. SURNAME INDEX. Sioux Falls: 1976. 4131022. F650.S56 1976.

SURNAME INDEX. Wichita, Kans.: Midwest Genealogical Society, n.d. 1787473. 73-644577. 929/.3/781. CS42.S94.

SURNAME SEARCHER. Glendale: Southern California Genealogical Society, 1967-- . Irregular. 4481678. 929.1.

Another related form of the surname index is the regular column in GENE-ALOGICAL HELPER, "Bureau of Missing Ancestors." This column provides a means, for a fee, by which genealogists can advertise their needs. The HELPER prepares a surname index for each issue, creating a useful way genealogists can help each other.

MISSING PERSONS

Some genealogists may discover that in order to continue their research they need to locate a living but lost cousin, uncle, or aunt, grandparent, parent, brother or sister, or even a grown son or daughter. Some adult adoptees desire to find their real parents; and, in a few cases, a parent who may have had to give children up for adoption may want to find them as adults.

GENEALOGICAL HELPER has a column in each of its issues entitled, "Missing Folk Finder." The column is devoted to assisting genealogists to find persons presumed to be living.

Many detective agencies take on such cases, and many are successful in locating lost relatives. Telephone directory yellow pages list detective agencies under the subject heading "Investigators." A very successful national investigative service that specializes in lost persons is Tracers Company of America, Edw. H. Goldfader, president, 509 Madison Avenue, New York, New York 10022.

Adoptees have special research problems because the records concerning their adoptions are closed. There are two good explanations of how adult adoptees can proceed with some success:

Carroll, Susan. "Genealogy for Adult Adopted Persons--Not an Insoluble Problem." GENEALOGICAL HELPER 32 (November-December 1978): 8-12.

"Adoptees in Search of Their Natural Parents." In HOW TO FIND YOUR FAMILY ROOTS, by Timothy Field Beard and Denise Demong, pages 157-66. New York: McGraw-Hill, 1977.

The following are a few groups that assist adult adoptees who are desirous of finding their natural parents and/or natural parents desirous of finding their adult children:

ALMA (Adoptees' Liberty Movement Association)
P.O. Box 154, Washington Bridge Station,
New York, N.Y. 10033

> ALMA publishes a newsletter, ALMA SEARCHLIGHT, 1974-- .
> 3 per year.

Concerned United Birthparents
P.O. Box 573
Milford, Mass. 01757

> Publishes a newsletter, CUB COMMUNICATOR. Monthly.

Orphan Voyage
Cedaredge, Colo. 81413

> Publishes a periodical, ADOPTION CIRCLE, 1980-- . Quarterly.

SOUNDEX
c/o Emma May Vilardi
P.O. Box 2312
Carson City, Nev. 89701

This is a reunion file or matching file for uniting adult adoptees and natural parents. Enclose self-addressed stamped envelope with inquiry.

The following books relate the experiences of adult adoptees' searches for their natural parents:

Fisher, Florence. THE SEARCH FOR ANNA FISHER. New York: A. Fields Books, 1973. 654419. 72-94676. 301.43/7. HV881.F53.

Hulse, Jerry. JODY. New York: McGraw-Hill, 1976. 2213389. 76-16826. 973. HV875.H77.

Lifton, Betty Jean. TWICE BORN: MEMOIRS OF AN ADOPTED DAUGHTER. New York: McGraw-Hill, 1975. 1288446. 75-9855. 362.7/34/01/9. HV875.L46.

GENEALOGICAL LIBRARY FOR THE BLIND AND PHYSICALLY HANDICAPPED

Mrs. Diane Dieterle has established a genealogical library to serve the blind, deaf, or those who have motor difficulties (arthritis, cerebral palsy, and so on). Librarians need to be aware of this nonprofit corporation for referral of patrons with special needs. The address is:

> Genealogical Library for the Blind and Physically Handicapped
> 4176 English Oak Drive
> Doraville, Ga. 30340
> (404) 449-1533

COLLECTION DEVELOPMENT

GENEALOGICAL HELPER is an essential periodical subscription to assist genealogists to find distant cousins, free offers of assistance, and fee services, as well, that may be helpful and economical.

SUMMARY

Genealogists should be informed that rental libraries are available, and that fee and free services are advertised and columnarized in the GENEALOGICAL HELPER. Genealogists should not be encouraged to spend money on them, many genealogists find those offering free services to be excellent researchers.

Chapter 17
PERSONAL NAMES

Many genealogists will inquire as to the origin of their surname and also some given names. They are normally only interested in these origins for background information or for a proposed family history. However, often surname literature books will include the geographical area of a county where the name is prevalent. Thus, some genealogists may find information helpful for locating the roots of a family overseas.

GIVEN NAMES

The following is an excellent book about given names:

Stewart, George Rippey. AMERICAN GIVEN NAMES: THEIR ORIGIN AND HISTORY IN THE CONTEXT OF THE ENGLISH LANGUAGE. New York: Oxford University Press, 1979. 3966080. 78-17603. 929.4/03. CS2375.U6 S74.

SURNAMES

The following is a selected list of surname literature arranged alphabetically by country, race, and/or nationality:

Madubuike, Ihechukwu. A HANDBOOK OF AFRICAN NAMES. Washington, D.C.: Three Continents Press, 1976. 1582816. 75-25943. 929.4/096. CS2375.A33M3.

Puckett, Newbell Niles. BLACK NAMES IN AMERICA: ORIGINS AND USAGE. Collected by Newbell Niles Puckett. Edited by Murray Heller. Boston: G.K. Hall, 1975. 980389. 74-13553. 929.4/0973. E185.89.N3P82.

Barber, Henry. BRITISH FAMILY NAMES: THEIR ORIGIN AND MEANING, WITH LISTS OF SCANDINAVIAN, FRISIAN, ANGLO-SAXON, AND NORMAN

NAMES. 2d ed., enl. London: E. Stock, 1903. Reprint. Baltimore: Genealogical Publishing Co., 1968. 3994955. 2340. 03-30482. 68-54867. 929.4/0942. CS2501.B3.

Contains an estimated 10,200 surnames.

Cottle, Basil. THE PENGUIN DICTIONARY OF SURNAMES. 2d ed. London: Allen Lane, 1978. 4683688. CS2505.C67 1978.

Contains about twelve thousand British surnames.

Ewen, Cecil Henry L'Estrange. A HISTORY OF SURNAMES OF THE BRITISH ISLES: A CONCISE ACCOUNT OF THEIR ORIGIN, EVOLUTION, ETYMOLOGY, AND LEGAL STATUS. London: Paul, Trench, Trubner, 1931. Reprint. Baltimore: Genealogical Publishing Co., 1968. Detroit: Gale Research Co., 1968. 2290. 395653. 68-54687. 68-30597. 929.4/0947. CS2505.E8.

Chronological and subject arrangement with an index of nearly ten thousand surnames and name elements.

Bardsley, Charles Wareing Endell. A DICTIONARY OF ENGLISH AND WELSH SURNAMES, WITH SPECIAL AMERICAN INSTANCES. Rev. ed. New York: H. Frowde, 1901. Reprint. Baltimore: Genealogical Publishing Co., 1967. 1684013. 67-25404. 929.4/0942. CS2505.B3 1967.

Shanta. HANDBOOK OF HINDU NAMES. Calcutta: ARNICA International, 1969. 123270. 75-907083/SA. 929.4/0954. CS3030.S5.

Contains about 5,610 Indian given names.

MacLysaght, Edward. A GUIDE TO IRISH SURNAMES. Baltimore: Genealogical Book Co., 1964. 1626447. 64-22688. 929.4. CS415.M23.

Brief coverage of 2,500 surnames which are detailed in the author's three earlier works: IRISH FAMILIES (1957), MORE IRISH FAMILIES (1960), and SUPPLEMENT TO IRISH FAMILIES (1964).

Matheson, Robert Edwin. SPECIAL REPORT ON SURNAMES IN IRELAND. TOGETHER WITH VARIETIES AND SYNONYMES OF SURNAMES AND CHRISTIAN NAMES IN IRELAND. Dublin: H.M. Stationery Office, 1901, 1909. Reprint. Baltimore: Genealogical Publishing Co., 1968. 343618. 68-54684. 929.4/09415. CS2415.M32 1968.

Pages 37-75 list counties in which names are principally found.

Fucilla, Joseph Guerin. OUR ITALIAN SURNAMES. Evanston, Ill.: Chandler's, 1949. 1626351. 49-6230. 929.4. CS2715.F8.

The index contains about 7,260 surnames.

Rottenberg, Dan. FINDING OUR FATHERS: A GUIDEBOOK TO JEWISH GENEALOGY. New York: Random House, 1977. 2614220. 76-53493. 929/.1/028. CS21.R58.

    Contains more than 6,450 Jewish surnames.

Nitecki, Andrbe. PERSONAL NAMES AND PLACE NAMES OF NIGERIA. Ibadan: University of Ibadan, Institute of Librarianship, 1966. 4478596. Z695.95.N58.

Unbegaun, Boris Ottokar. RUSSIAN SURNAMES. Oxford: Clarendon Press, 1972. 548389. 72-171243. 929.4/0947. PG2576.U5.

    Arranged by morphologic and semantic aspects, with an index of over 10,400 surnames.

Black, George Fraser. SURNAMES OF SCOTLAND: THEIR ORIGIN, MEANING, AND HISTORY. New York: New York Public Library, 1974. 3911741. CS2435.B55 1974.

    Reprinted from the BULLETIN OF THE NEW YORK PUBLIC LIBRARY, August 1943-September 1946.

Rosenthal, Eric. SOUTH AFRICAN SURNAMES. Cape Town: H. Timmins, 1965. 66-48470. 929.40968. CS3080.S6R6.

    Contains about 2,349 surnames.

Maduell, Charles R. THE ROMANCE OF SPANISH SURNAMES. New Orleans, La.: The Author, 1967. 3657972. 929.4.

    Contains over fourteen hundred surnames.

Woods, Richard Donovon, and Alvarez-Altman, Grace. SPANISH SURNAMES IN THE SOUTHWESTERN UNITED STATES: A DICTIONARY. Boston: G.K. Hall, 1978. 3748640. 78-4127. 929.4. CS2745.W66.

SWAHILI NAME BOOK. Newark: Jihad Productions, 1971. 475099. CS3080.S9.

Smith, Elsdon Coles. NEW DICTIONARY OF AMERICAN FAMILY NAMES. New York: Harper and Row, 1972. 561491. 72-79693. 929/.4/0973. CS2481.S55 1973.

    Contains over ten thousand surnames. The best single source to have in all collections.

Foreign-language surname literature has been excluded from the above list because of their limited availability, as well as the incapability of the average genealogist to read in a foreign language. An excellent eight-page selected bibliography that contains many foreign language surname books is:

U.S. Library of Congress. General Reading Rooms Division. SURNAMES: A SELECTED LIST OF REFERENCES. Reference Guides, no. 8. Washington, D.C.: 1977.

The most comprehensive bibliography of surname literature is the following:

Smith, Elsdon Coles. PERSONAL NAMES: A BIBLIOGRAPHY. New York: New York Public Library, 1952. Reprint. Detroit: Gale Research Co., 1965. 556387. 173455. 52-12991. 66-31855. 016.9294. Z6824.S55 1965.

The above is supplemented by:

Smith, Elsdon C. "Literature on Personal Names in English, 1952." NAMES 1 (September 1953): 219-22.

_____. "Literature on Personal Names in English, 1953." NAMES 2 (June 1954): 144-47.

_____. "Literature on Personal Names in English, 1954." NAMES 3 (June 1955): 117-22.

_____. "Literature on Personal Names in English, 1955." NAMES 4 (June 1956): 122-26.

_____. "Literature on Personal Names in English, 1956." NAMES 5 (June 1957): 89-93.

_____. "Literature on Personal Names in English, 1957." NAMES 6 (December 1958): 234-40.

_____. "Literature on Personal Names in English, 1958." NAMES 7 (September 1959): 182-87.

_____. "Literature on Personal Names in English, 1959." NAMES 8 (September 1960): 172-79.

_____. "Literature on Personal Names in English, 1960." NAMES 9 (September 1961): 175-80.

_____. "Literature on Personal Names in English, 1961." NAMES 10 (December 1962): 285-89.

_____. "Bibliography of Personal Names, 1962." NAMES 11 (June 1963): 128-33.

_____. "Bibliography of Personal Names, 1963." NAMES 12 (September 1964): 220-25.

_____. "Bibliography of Personal Names, 1964." NAMES 13 (December 1965): 263-67.

_____. "Bibliography of Personal Names, 1965." NAMES 14 (December 1966): 215-20.

_____. "Bibliography of Personal Names, 1966." NAMES 15 (June 1967): 142-49.

_____. "Bibliography of Personal Names, 1967." NAMES 16 (January 1968): 141-45.

_____. "Bibliography of Personal Names, 1968." NAMES 17 (September 1970): 223-28.

_____. "Bibliography of Personal Names, 1969." NAMES 18 (December 1970): 304-310.

_____. "Bibliography of Personal Names, 1970." NAMES 20 (September 1972): 200-206.

_____. "Bibliography of Personal Names, 1971." NAMES 21 (December 1973): 236-40.

_____. "Bibliography of Personal Names, 1972." NAMES 22 (December 1974): 165-70.

_____. "Bibliography of Personal Names, 1973." NAMES 23 (December 1975): 290-95.

_____. "Bibliography of Personal Names, 1975." NAMES 24 (December 1976): 248-52.

The subject headings relative to given and personal names are as follows:

      LC   NAMES, PERSONAL--U.S.

      Sears   NAMES, PERSONAL--U.S.

      GD   U.S. - NAMES, PERSONAL

COLLECTION DEVELOPMENT

Only larger libraries need to purchase many surname literature books or Smith's bibliography (p. 240). However, some smaller libraries may desire to purchase titles of particular interest to ethnic and national groups in their communities. Almost all libraries might consider acquiring Elsdon Coles Smith's NEW DICTIONARY OF AMERICAN FAMILY NAMES and Stewart's AMERICAN GIVEN NAMES.

SUMMARY

Surname literature can be of assistance to genealogists in some cases by identifying parts of countries where a name is or was prevalent. Librarians should encourage genealogists to check surname literature some time during their research. Given name literature is of interest to a minority of genealogists and is not necessary or useful in genealogical research.

Chapter 18

WRITING FAMILY HISTORIES

Librarians are occasionally asked for a book dealing with how to write a family history. The best single article on the subject is the following:

Colket, Meredith B. "Creating a Worthwhile Family Genealogy." NATIONAL GENEALOGICAL SOCIETY QUARTERLY 56 (December 1968): 243-62.

> Colket explains how family histories should be organized, prepared, presented, indexed, and titled.

A SELECTED BIBLIOGRAPHY OF RECOMMENDED EXAMPLES OF FAMILY HISTORIES

A review of the following list of books found most of them to be good examples of well prepared family histories with sources mentioned, notes, illustration, full name indexes, and family numbering systems. Many of the books reviewed were authored by Fellows of the American Society of Genealogists, who are considered to be our foremost genealogists. Most of the information concerning the Fellows of the American Society of Genealogists was obtained from the unpaged end of volume 2 of GENEALOGICAL RESEARCH, METHODS AND SOURCES.

Adams, Arthur, and Risley, Sarah A. A GENEALOGY OF THE LAKE FAMILY OF GREAT EGG HARBOUR IN OLD GLOUCESTER COUNTY IN NEW JERSEY, DESCENDED FROM JOHN LAKE OF GRAVESEND, LONG ISLAND; WITH NOTES ON THE GRAVESEND AND STATEN ISLAND BRANCHES OF THE FAMILY. Hartford: Privately printed, 1915. 2625756. 15-21639. 929.2. CS71.L19 1915.

> Arthur Adams was a founding fellow of the American Society of Genealogists (ASG).

Adams, Enid Eleanor Smith, comp. ANCESTORS AND DESCENDANTS OF JEREMIAH ADAMS, 1794-1883, OF SALISBURY, CONNECTICUT, SULLIVAN COUNTY, NEW YORK, HARBOR CREEK, PENNSYLVANIA, AND VERMILION, OHIO, INCLUDING KNOWN DESCENDANTS OF HIS BROTHERS AND SISTERS, MOST OF WHOM WENT TO MICHIGAN: SEVENTH IN DESCENT FROM

HENRY ADAMS OF BRAINTREE, MASSACHUSETTS. Victor, Idaho: Ancestor Hunters, 1974. 2709535. 73-92391. 929/.2/0973. CS71.A2 1974.

> This work was a 1977 ASB Jacobus Award winner. Mrs. Adams was named an ASG fellow in 1978. The history is poorly printed.

_____. OUR BATEMAN ANCESTRY. Compiled for Robert Edwin Bateman by Enid Eleanor Adams. Victor, Idaho: Privately printed by Ancestor Hunters, 1971. 138089. 72-23680. 929.2/0973. CS71.B3675 1971. GD 897,467 Item 3.

> Poorly printed.

Arnold, Elisha Stephen. THE ARNOLD MEMORIAL: WILLIAM ARNOLD OF PROVIDENCE AND PAWTUXET, 1587-1675, AND A GENEALOGY OF HIS DESCENDANTS. Rutland, Vt.: Tuttle Publishing Co., 1935. 35-18561. CS71.A75 1935. GD 1,015,828 Item 7.

> Recommended by Meredith B. Colket, Jr.

Brainard, Homer Worthington; Gilbert, Harold Simeon; and Torrey, Clarence Almon. THE GILBERT FAMILY, DESCENDANTS OF THOMAS GILBERT, 1582-1659, OF MT. WOLLASTON (BRAINTREE), WINDSOR, AND WETHERSFIELD. Edited with a foreword by Donald Lines Jacobus. New Haven, Conn.: n.p., 1953. 4256669. 54-1734. 929.2.

> Recommended by Meredith B. Colket, Jr.

Colket, Meredith B., Jr. THE ENGLISH ANCESTRY OF ANNE MARBURY HUTCHINSON AND KATHERINE MARBURY SCOTT, INCLUDING THEIR DESCENT AND THAT OF JOHN DRYDEN, POET-LAUREATE, FROM MAGNA CHARTA SURETIES WITH NOTES ON THE ENGLISH CONNECTIONS OF THE SETTLERS WILLIAM WENTWORTH AND CHRISTOPHER LAWSON OF NEW HAMPSHIRE AND FRANCIS MARBURY OF MARYLAND. By Meredith B. Colket, Jr.; with the collaboration of Edward N. Dunlap. Philadelphia: Magee Press, 1936. 2528744. 36-36470. 929.2. CS71.M3 1936.

> Colket was a founding fellow of the ASG.

Cope, Gilbert. GENEALOGY OF THE SMEDLEY FAMILY, DESCENDED FROM GEORGE AND SARAH SMEDLEY, SETTLERS IN CHESTER COUNTY, PENNSYLVANIA WITH BRIEF NOTICES OF OTHER FAMILIES OF THE NAME, AND ABSTRACTS OF EARLY ENGLISH WILLS. PUBLISHED PURSUANT TO THE WILL OF SAMUEL LIGHTFOOT SMEDLEY, OF PHILADELPHIA, PA. Lancaster, Pa.: Wickersham Printing Co., 1901. Microfilm. Madison: State Historical Society of Wisconsin, 1978. 2501400. 3943905. CS71.S58 1901.

> Recommended by Meredith B. Colket, Jr.

Davis, Walter Goodwin. THE ANCESTRY OF MARY ISAAC, 1549-1613; WIFE OF THOMAS APPLETON OF LITTLE WALDINGFIELD, CO. SUFFOLK AND MOTHER OF SAMUEL APPLETON OF IPSWICH, MASSACHUSETTS. Portland, Maine: n.p., 1955. 3102349. 58-26417. CS439.I53 1955.

> Davis was a fellow and president of ASG. Recommended by Milton Rubincam in GENEALOGICAL RESEARCH, METHODS AND SOURCES (1966, vol. 1, p. 92): ". . . models of painstaking genealogical research and careful compilation."

Delafield, John Ross. DELAFIELD, THE FAMILY HISTORY. 2 vols. New York: Privately printed, 1945. 3505094. 46-4593. 929.2. CS71.D334 1945.

> This excellent history was limited to two hundred copies. Brigadier General Delafield was an ASG fellow.

Dorman, John Frederick. THE FARISH FAMILY OF VIRGINIA AND ITS FORE-BEARS. Richmond: Privately printed by B.R. Miller and A.G. Robertson, 1967. 2345009. 67-21049. CS71.F228 1967.

> The author is an ASG fellow. The history was limited to 250 copies.

_____. THE ROBERTSON FAMILY OF CULPEPER COUNTY, VIRGINIA. Richmond: n.p., 1964. 3493205. 64-66216. CS71.R645 1964.

> This history was limited to 250 copies.

Durand, Hortense Funsten, and Randolph, Howard S. THE ANCESTORS AND DESCENDANTS OF COLONEL DAVID FUNSTEN AND HIS WIFE SUSAN EVERARD MEADE. New York: Knickerbocker Press, 1926. 4366192. 27-20352. 929.273. CS71.F983 1926.

Engel, Beth Bland. THE MIDDLETON FAMILY (INCLUDING MYDDELTON AND MYDDLETON); RECORDS FROM WALES, ENGLAND, BARBADOS, AND THE SOUTHERN UNITED STATES. Jesup, Ga.: Press of the Jesup Sentinel, 1972. 663123. 73-161627. 929/.2/0973. CS71.M632 1972.

> A 1974 ASG Jacobus Award Winner.

Ferris, Mary Walton. DAWES-GATES ANCESTRAL LINES. A MEMORIAL VOLUME. 2 vols. Milwaukee: Privately printed by Wisconsin Cuneo Press, 1931-43. 1065631. 32-9942rev. CS71.D269 1931.

> Recommended by Milton Rubincam.

French, Howard Barclay, comp. GENEALOGY OF THE DESCENDANTS OF THOMAS FRENCH WHO CAME TO AMERICA FROM NETHER HEYFORD, NORTH-AMPTONSHIRE, ENGLAND, AND SETTLED IN BERLINGTON (BURLINGTON)

IN THE PROVINCE AND COUNTRY OF WEST NEW JERSEY, OF WHICH HE WAS ONE OF THE ORIGINAL PROPRIETORS, TOGETHER WITH WILLIAM PENN, EDWARD BYLLYNGE, THOMAS OLLIVE, GAUEN LAURIE AND OTHERS, WITH SOME ACCOUNT OF COLONIAL MANNERS AND DOINGS . . . TOGETHER WITH ONE HUNDRED AND FIFTY PICTURE PRINTS. Compiled and published by Howard Barclay French. 2 vols. Philadelphia: Privately printed, 1909-13. 9-11521 rev. CS71.F876 1909.

Recommended by Milton Rubincam.

Gerberich, Albert Horwell. THE BRENNEMAN HISTORY. Scottdale, Pa.: Printed by Mennonite Publishing House, 1938. 2042869. 38-14745. CS71. B835 1938.

Gerberich was a fellow of the ASG.

Greenwood, Isaac John. THE GREENWOOD FAMILY OF NORWICH, ENGLAND, IN AMERICA. Edited by H. Minot Pitman and Mary M. Greenwood. Concord, N.H.: Privately printed by Rumford Press, 1934. 3512248. 35-849. 929.2. CS71.G817 1934.

Harter, Mary E. McCollam. HARTER HISTORY. Doylestown, Ohio: 1964. 1145967. 65-6762. CS71.H328 1964. GD 525,283 & 1,017,408 Item 7.

Harter was a fellow of the ASG.

Hatfield, Abraham, comp. THE DESCENDANTS OF MATTHIAS HATFIELD. New York: New York Genealogical and Biographical Society, 1954. 4367120. 929.2. GD 1,036,700 Item 6.

Recommended by Meredith B. Colket, Jr.

Hawes, Frank Mortimer, comp. RICHARD HAWES OF DORCHESTER, MASSACHUSETTS, AND SOME OF HIS DESCENDANTS. Hartford, Conn.: Case, Lockwood and Brainard Co., 1932. 3390890. 32-30546. CS71.H39 1932. GD 928,077 Item 6.

Recommended by Meredith B. Colket, Jr.

Hazen, Tracy Elliot. THE HAZEN FAMILY IN AMERICA, A GENEALOGY. Edited for publication by Donald Lines Jacobus. Thomaston, Conn.: R. Hazen, 1947. 1333215. 47-24704. 929.2. CS71.H43 1947.

Holman, Alfred Lyman, comp. BLACKMAN AND ALLIED FAMILIES. Compiled for Nathan Lincoln Blackman. Chicago: n.p., 1928. 4244788. 28-16864.

Recommended by Meredith B. Colket, Jr.

Holman, Winifred Lovering, comp. DESCENDANTS OF ANDREW EVEREST OF YORK, MAINE. Concord, N.H.: n.p., 1955. 56-3150. CS71.E934 1955.

Recommended by Meredith B. Colket, Jr. Limited to 250 copies. Holman was a fellow of the ASG.

_____. DESCENDANTS OF SAMUEL HILLS. Concord, N.H.: Rumford Press, 1957. 929.273.

Recommended by Milton Rubincam.

Jacobus, Donald Lines. THE BULKELEY GENEALOGY: REV. PETER BULKELEY, BEING AN ACCOUNT OF HIS CAREER, HIS ANCESTRY, THE ANCESTRY OF HIS TWO WIVES, AND HIS RELATIVES IN ENGLAND AND NEW ENGLAND, TOGETHER WITH A GENEALOGY OF HIS DESCENDANTS THROUGH THE SEVENTH AMERICAN GENERATION. New Haven, Conn.: Tuttle, 1933. 3626722. 929.2.

Jacobus is considered by many as the dean of genealogists. He was a fellow of the ASG.

_____. THE GENEALOGY OF THE BOOTH FAMILY: BOOTH FAMILIES OF CONNECTICUT FOR SIX OR MORE GENERATIONS. Deland, Fla.: Eden C. Booth, 1952. 1727286. 929.2. GD 896,872 Item 4.

_____. THE GENEALOGY OF THE KIMBERLY FAMILY. Menasha, Wis.: George Banta Publishing Co., 1950. 3626733. 929.2.

_____, comp. AN AMERICAN FAMILY, BOTSFORD-MARBLE ANCESTRAL LINES. Compiled for Otis Marble Botsford. New Haven, Conn.: n.p., 1933. 4358910. 34-23196. 419.2. CS71.B751 1933.

_____. THE GRANBERRY FAMILY AND ALLIED FAMILIES, INCLUDING THE ANCESTRY OF HELEN (WOODWARD) GRANBERRY. Based on data collected by and for Edgar Francis Waterman and compiled by Donald Lines Jacobus. Hartford, Conn.: E.F. Waterman, 1945. 5149394. 45-5014. CS71.G76 1945.

_____. THE WATERMAN FAMILY. 3 vols. New Haven, Conn.: E.R. Waterman, 1939-1954. 2023265. 929.2.

_____, ed. THE PARDEE GENEALOGY. New Haven: Printed for the New Haven Colony Historical Society, 1927. 1671179. 27-18004. 929.2.

Jacobus, Donald Lines, and Waterman, Edgar Francis. HALE, HOUSE, AND RELATED FAMILIES: MAINLY ON THE CONNECTICUT RIVER VALLEY. Hartford: Connecticut Historical Society, 1952. Reprint. Baltimore: Genealogical Publishing Co., 1978. 4251997. 78-55590. 929/.2/0973. CS71. H163 1978.

Recommended by Milton Rubincam.

Long, Daniel Reid. JOHN LEWIS, "THE LOST PIONEER"; HIS ANCESTORS AND DESCENDANTS, 1670-1970. Baltimore: n.p., 1971. 240004. 70-182130. 929.2/0973. CS71.L675 1971.

A 1974 ASG Jacobus Award winner.

Moon, Robert Charles. THE MORRIS FAMILY OF PHILADELPHIA; DESCENDANTS OF ANTHONY MORRIS, BORN 1654-1721 DIED. 5 vols. Philadelphia: R.C. Moon, 1898-1909. 5173791. 98-1344. 929.2. CS71.M876. GD 1,036,503 & 1,036,504.

Recommended by Milton Rubincam.

Newman, Harry Wright. A BRANCH OF THE DOUGLAS FAMILY, WITH ITS MARYLAND & VIRGINIA CONNECTIONS. Garden City, N.Y.: Doubleday, 1973. 943976. 74-170864. 929/.2/0973. CS71.D734 1973.

Newman was an ASG fellow. This history was limited to two hundred copies.

_____. MAREEN DUVALL OF MIDDLE PLANTATION: A GENEALOGICAL HISTORY OF MAREEN DUVALL, GENT., OF THE PROVINCE OF MARYLAND AND HIS DESCENDANTS, WITH HISTORIES OF THE ALLIED FAMILIES OF TYLER, CLARKE, POOLE, HALL, AND MERRIKEN. Washington, D.C.: n.p., 1952. 219513. 74-110. CS71.D985 1952. GD 896,885 Item 1.

O'Gorman, Ella Foy, comp. DESCENDANTS OF VIRGINIA CALVERTS. Los Angeles: 1947. 4262743. 929.2. GD 897,096 Item 1.

Penrose, Maryly Barton. BAUMANN/BOWMAN FAMILY OF THE MOHAWK, SUSQUEHANNA & NIAGARA RIVERS. Franklin Park, N.J.: Liberty Bell Associates, 1977. 2929363. 77-6452. 929/.2/0973. CS71.B788 1977.

A 1978 ASG Jacobus Award winner. It is well documented but poorly printed and includes no illustrations.

Pitman, Harold Minot. THE FAHNESTOCK GENEALOGY, ANCESTORS AND DESCENDANTS OF JOHANN DIEDRICH FAHNESTOCK. Concord, N.H.: Privately printed by Rumford Press, 1945. 45-8168. CS71.F15 1945. GD 250,253.

Recommended by Meredith B. Colket, Jr.

Prindle, Paul Wesley, comp. ANCESTRY OF ELIZABETH BARRETT GILLESPIE: (MRS. WILLIAM SPERRY BEINECKE). New Orleans, La.: Polyanthos, 1976. 2716804. 76-15134. 929.2.

Prindle was an ASG fellow. The history was limited to 350 copies.

_____. ANCESTRY OF WILLIAM SPERRY BEINECKE. Summit, N.J.: Beinecke, 1974. 1733222. 74-83343. 929/.2/0973. CS71.B4442 1974.

Limited to 450 copies.

_____. DESCENDANTS OF JOHN AND MARY JANE (CUNNINGHAM) GILLESPIE. North Haven, Conn.: Printed by Van Dyck Printing Co., 1973. 994769. 73-85068. 929/.2/0973. CS71.G4748 1973.

Limited to four hundred copies.

Riggs, John Beverly. THE RIGGS FAMILY OF MARYLAND: A GENEALOGICAL AND HISTORICAL RECORD, INCLUDING A STUDY OF THE SEVERAL FAMILIES IN ENGLAND. Baltimore, Md.: Lord Baltimore Press, 1939. 39-82212. CS71.R57 1960. GD 1,036,564 Item 4.

Recommended by Meredith B. Colket, Jr.

Schempp, George C., comp. MY GENEALOGY. Edited by Charles W. Farnham. Ithaca, N.Y.: Seneca Printing, 1974. 2100746. 75-1752. 929.2. GD 1,036,168 Item 6.

Farnham is an ASG fellow.

Scott, Stanley Richmond, and Montgomery, Robert H., comps. FAMILY HISTORY OF WHITBURN, SCOTLAND, ROBERT HAMILTON BISHOP OF OXFORD, OHIO, EBENEZER BISHOP OF MCDONOUGH COUNTY, ILLINOIS, JOHN SCOTT OF IRELAND. WITH SOME ACCOUNT OF RELATED FAMILIES, SOME OF WHOM ARE NAMED IN THE GUIDE TO THE CONTENTS, ALL IN THE INDEX OF NAMES. Ann Arbor, Mich.: Lithoprinting by Edwards Brothers, 1951. 421490. 52-35976. 914.2. GD 896,872 Item 6.

Montgomery was a fellow of the ASG.

Sellers, Edwin Jaquett. GENEALOGY OF THE JAQUETT FAMILY. Philadelphia: 1896. 3810534. 929.2.

This work cannot be recommended because it doesn't have an index. It is, however, recommended by Meredith B. Colket, Jr. Sellers was an ASG fellow.

Smith, Frederick Kinsman. THE FAMILY OF RICHARD SMITH OF SMITHTOWN, LONG ISLAND: TEN GENERATIONS. Smithtown, N.Y.: Smithtown Historical Society, 1967. 4924134. F129.S69S58.

Recommended by Meredith B. Colket, Jr.

Stevenson, Noel C., and Walker, Rodney W., comps. ANCESTRY AND DESCENDANTS OF JOHN WALKER (1794-1869): OF VERMONT AND UTAH, DESCENDANT OF ROBERT WALKER, AN EMIGRANT OF 1632 FROM ENGLAND

TO BOSTON, MASS. N.p.: John Walker Family Organization, 1953.
4011146. 920.

Stevenson is an ASG fellow.

Thompson, Alice Smith. THE DRAKE FAMILY OF NEW HAMPSHIRE: ROBERT
OF HAMPTON AND SOME OF HIS DESCENDANTS, A GENEALOGY. With
an historical introd. on the family background in England by Sir Anthony Richard
Wagner. Designed by Ray Nash. Concord: New Hampshire Historical Society,
1962. 604582. CS71.D76 1962.

This excellent book was limited to 550 copies. Recommended
by Meredith B. Colket, Jr.

Van Rensselaer, Florence, and Randolph, Ethel L. Fitz. THE VAN RENSSE-
LAERS IN HOLLAND AND IN AMERICA. New York: n.p., 1956. 56-1675.
CS71.V274 1956.

Recommended by Meredith B. Colket, Jr.

Willoughby, Raymond Royce, and Willoughby, Miranda Goodrie. A NORWE-
GIAN HERITAGE: THE AUTHENTIC FAMILY HISTORY OF BIRGIT BOTTEN.
Riverside, R.I.: N.p., distributed by Farwill Publishing Co., 1970. 111904.
79-19768. 929.2. CS71.B75116 1970. GD 896,880 Item 6.

This work cannot be recommended as it has no index. However,
it was a 1974 ASG Jacobus Award winner.

Zabriskie, George Olin. THE ZABRISKIE FAMILY: A THREE HUNDRED AND
ONE YEAR HISTORY OF THE DESCENDANTS OF ALBRECHT ZABOROWSKIJ
(1638-1711) OF BERGEN COUNTY, NEW JERSEY. 2 vols. Salt Lake City:
n.p., 1963. 2907872. 63-21602. CS71.Z12 1963.

Zabriskie is a fellow of the ASG.

PRINTERS

Family historians may ask where they can get their family histories published.
Such histories normally have to be published at the expense of the author.
Vanity presses that are in the business of printing family histories advertise in
some of the genealogical magazines. There are usually two or three such press
advertisements in each issue of the GENEALOGICAL HELPER. Authors should
inquire of several and ask for bids.

GIFT COPIES TO LIBRARIES

Authors of family histories should be encouraged to donate copies of their work
to the Library of Congress, Washington, D.C. 20540 and the Genealogical

Society, 50 East North Temple Street, Salt Lake City, Utah 84150. Authors desirous of securing a copyright for their work must send two copies to the Library of Congress with the necessary copyright fee and application. Many family history authors do not copyright their work, but they should still send a gift copy to the Library of Congress in order for the work to receive complete bibliographic coverage and exposure through the Library of Congress catalogs. A letter of clearance should be sent with gift histories to the Genealogical Department, permitting them to microfilm the work in order for it to be made available for worldwide circulation. Of course other libraries with large genealogical collections usually welcome gifts, but letters of inquiry may be well advised.

COLLECTION DEVELOPMENT AND SUMMARY

Librarians should acquire a copy of Meredith B. Colket, Jr.'s article, "Creating a Worthwhile Family Genealogy." They should review the family histories in their collection to identify a few outstanding, well-indexed histories that could be used by genealogists as examples of good family histories.

Chapter 19

DIRECTORIES

Genealogists will inquire about the addresses of various libraries, archives, and genealogical and historical societies. The following directories are essential for that information:

AMERICAN LIBRARY DIRECTORY. 32d ed. New York: Bowker, 1979. 5770387. 021/.0025/73. Z731.A512 1979.

Ash, Lee; Calvert, Stephen J.; Miller, William, comps. SUBJECT COLLEC-TIONS: A GUIDE TO SPECIAL BOOK COLLECTIONS AND SUBJECT EM-PHASES AS REPORTED BY UNIVERSITY, COLLEGE, PUBLIC, AND SPECIAL LIBRARIES AND MUSEUMS IN THE UNITED STATES AND CANADA. 5th ed. New York: Bowker, 1978. 4493518. 78-26399. 026.00025/7. Z731.A78.

   Includes genealogical collections.

"Directory of Genealogical Societies, Libraries & Professionals." GENEA-LOGICAL HELPER, July-August issue. Annually.

DIRECTORY OF HISTORICAL SOCIETIES AND AGENCIES IN THE UNITED STATES AND CANADA. Madison, Wis.: American Association for State and Local History, 1956--. Biennial. 932245. 56-4164rev.59. 970.62. E172.A538.

GUIDE TO AMERICAN DIRECTORIES. Rye, N.Y.: B. Klein Publications, 1956-- . Irregular. 1644317. 5 4-4206rev.653. 016.380102573. Z5771.G8.

HEREDITARY REGISTER OF THE UNITED STATES OF AMERICA. Phoenix, Ariz.: Hereditary Register Publications, 1972-- . Irregular. 3469885. 76-184658. 369/.1. E172.7H47.

   A directory of patriotic societies.

Meyer, Mary Keysor, ed. DIRECTORY OF GENEALOGICAL SOCIETIES IN THE U.S.A. AND CANADA: WITH AN APPENDED LIST OF INDEPENDENT

GENEALOGICAL PERIODICALS. 2d ed. Pasadena, Md.: By the Author, 1978. 3964096. 78-56943. 929/.1/06273. CS44.M45 1978.

NATIONAL DIRECTORY OF MORTICIANS. Youngstown, Ohio: 1953-- . Annual. 5740345. 53-31440/L. RA622.A7N37.

NATIONAL DIRECTORY OF STATE AGENCIES. Washington, D.C.: Information Resources Press, 1974-- . Biennial. 1790831. 74-18864. 353.9/025. JK2443.N37.

     Includes lists of state archives and libraries.

OFFICIAL MUSEUM DIRECTORY. New York: American Association of Museums and National Register Publishing Co., 1971--. Annual. 1264511. 79-144808. 069/.025/7. AM10.A204.

     Some museums have genealogical materials in their libraries.

U.S. National Historical Publication and Records Commission. DIRECTORY OF ARCHIVES AND MANUSCRIPT REPOSITORIES. Washington, D.C.: 1978. 4493072. 78-23870. 016.091/025/73. CD3020.U54.

COLLECTION DEVELOPMENT

Smaller libraries will need to rely on larger libraries for reference service to many of the above directories. Larger libraries of a geographical area may wish to share the expense of acquiring these necessary sources.

Chapter 20

HISTORY, FOLKLORE, AND MIGRATION BACKGROUND

Many genealogical instructors and authors of how-to-do-it books advocate that one of the first things a beginning genealogist should do is read a history of the state or country and of its migration routes and patterns. This procedure may be useful at some point and of interest to the genealogists, but it is not absolutely necessary in order to begin.

HISTORICAL ATLASES

For those genealogists that are comfortable with maps and, perhaps, for all beginners that ask for state histories or histories of immigration, migration, or westward expansion, a referral to the following historical atlas may be the best solution to their problems:

> Jackson, Kenneth T., ed. ATLAS OF AMERICAN HISTORY.
> Rev. ed. New York: Scribner, 1978. 3585676. 77-76851/
> MAP. 911/.73. G1201.S1J3 1978.

The genealogists who find atlases perfectly acceptable to assist them in their understanding of history may also find the following state atlases useful:

Dodd, Donald B. HISTORICAL ATLAS OF ALABAMA. University: University of Alabama Press, 1974. 2696263. 73-36/MAP. 911/.761. G1340.D6 1974.

Walker, Henry Pickering, and Bufkin, Don. HISTORICAL ATLAS OF ARIZONA. Norman: University of Oklahoma Press, 1979. 4492419. 78-58086/MAP. 911/.791. G1510.W3 1979.

Beck, Warren A., and Haase, Ynez D. HISTORICAL ATLAS OF CALIFORNIA. Norman: University of Oklahoma Press, 1974. 947893. 74-5952/MAP. 911/.794. G1526.S1B4 1974.

Bonner, James Calvin. ATLAS FOR GEORGIA HISTORY. Milledgeville, Ga.:

Manufactured by the Georgia Duplicating Department, 1969. Fort Worth, Tex.: Miran Publishers, 1975. 121884. 1388822. 79-631523. 911/.758. F286. B63.

Morrison, Olin Dee. INDIANA, HOOSIER STATE: NEW HISTORICAL ATLAS, ECONOMIC, SOCIAL, POLITICAL, FOR SCHOOLS AND LIBRARIES, BUSINESS AND INDUSTRY. His Indiana Series, vol. 2. Athens, Ohio: E.M. Morrison, 1958. 3491772. Map59-264. G1401.S1M6 1958.

Socolofsky, Homer Edward, and Self, Huber. HISTORICAL ATLAS OF KANSAS. Norman: University of Oklahoma Press, 1972. 314217. 72-862/MAP. 911. 781. G1456.S1S6 1972.

Rone, Wendell Holmes, comp. AN HISTORICAL ATLAS OF KENTUCKY AND HER COUNTIES. N.p.: Mayfield Printing Co., 1965. 1163263. 976.9. F451.5.R6.

Raymong, Parish, Pine and Plavnick. THE STATE OF MARYLAND HISTORICAL ATLAS: A REVIEW OF EVENTS AND FORCES THAT HAVE INFLUENCED THE DEVELOPMENT OF THE STATE. Annapolis: State of Maryland, Department of Economic and Community Development, 1973. 2750975. 73-620104/MAP. 911/.752. G1271.S1R3 1973.

Beck, Warren A., and Haase, Ynez D. HISTORICAL ATLAS OF NEW MEXICO. Norman: University of Oklahoma Press, 1969. 7862. 73-653153/MAP. 911/.789. G1506.S1B4 1969.

Morrison, Olin Dee. HISTORICAL ATLAS OF OHIO. Athens, Ohio: E.M. Morrison, 1960. 2312544. F491.M67 v.3, 1960.

Morris, John Wesley; Goins, Charles R.; and McReynolds, Edwin C. HISTORICAL ATLAS OF OKLAHOMA. 2d ed., rev. and enl. Norman: University of Oklahoma Press, 1976. 1733756. 75-33129/MAP. 911/.766. G1366.S1M6 1976.

Pool, William C. A HISTORICAL ATLAS OF TEXAS. Austin: Encion Press, 1975. 1423612. 76-375887/MAP. 911/.764. G1371.S1P6 1975.

Miller, David E., comp. UTAH HISTORY ATLAS. Salt Lake City: Miller, 1977. 5095555. G1516.S1M5 1977.

The subject headings relative to historical atlases are as follows:

LC	IOWA--HISTORICAL GEOGRAPHY--MAPS
Sears	ATLASES, HISTORICAL--IOWA
GD	IOWA - ATLASES

HISTORIES

For those genealogists that are not satisfied with historical atlases, then let them find the historical background in the how-to-do-it books, the history books and the historical sections of description and travel books already in the library's collection. Those interested in immigration history may find the Immigrant Heritage of America Series useful. It is a well-documented series.

Perhaps some genealogists would find their introduction to United States history of emigration more palatable if librarians would refer them to the readable volumes in the American Trail Series, the American River Series, or the American Folklore Series. Many genealogists' ancestors traversed these trails. Some traveled the rivers, either on them or along them, and others settled by or near them. Some even lived in "them thar hills." The books in these series are listed below. Librarians might suggest to some genealogists that they enrich their understanding and appreciation of the life and times of their ancestors by reading these usually well written histories and folklore.

THE IMMIGRANT HERITAGE OF AMERICA SERIES

The following books are listed in alphabetical order by the name of the ethnic or national group:

Curran, Thomas J. XENOPHOBIA AND IMMIGRATION, 1820-1930. Boston: Twayne Publishers, 1975. 940693. 74-10865/AC. 325.73. JV6507.C87.

    General.

Miller, Sally M. THE RADICAL IMMIGRANT. New York: Twayne Publishers, 1974. 704915. 73-15847. 322.4/4. HN90.R3M5.

    General.

Neidle, Cecyle S. THE NEW AMERICANS. New York: Twayne Publishers, 1967. 518838. 67-25187. E184.A1N36.

    General.

_____. GREAT IMMIGRANTS. New York: Twayne Publishers, 1973. 623249. 72-3234. 920/.073. CT215.N45.

    General--Men.

_____. AMERICA'S IMMIGRANT WOMEN. Boston: Twayne Publishers, 1975. 1582550. 75-12738. 920.72. HQ1412.N44.

    General--Women.

Melendy, Howard Brett. ASIANS IN AMERICA: FILIPINOS, KOREANS, AND EAST INDIANS. Boston: Twayne Publishers, 1977. 3017046. 77-9268. 301.45/19/5073. E184.F4M44.

Coombs, Norman. THE BLACK EXPERIENCE IN AMERICA. New York: Twayne Publishers, 1972. New York: Hippocrene Books, 1972. Paperback. 517091. 548405. 73-186717. 72-172073. 301.45/19/6073. E185.C82.

Chinese Americans. See ORIENTAL AMERICANS.

De Jong, Gerald Francis. THE DUTCH IN AMERICA, 1609-1974. Boston: Twayne Publishers, 1974. 984159. 74-13738/AC. 917.3/06/3931. E184. D9D44.

East Indian Americans. See ASIANS IN AMERICA.

Filipino Americans. See ASIANS IN AMERICA.

Parsons, William T. THE PENNSYLVANIA DUTCH: A PERSISTENT MINORITY. Boston: Twayne Publishers, 1976. 1529490. 75-22044. 974.8/004/31. F160.G3P36.

Rippley, LaVern. THE GERMAN-AMERICANS. Boston: Twayne Publishers, 1976. 1602257. 75-26917. 973/.04/31. E184.G3R48.

O'Grady, Joseph P. HOW THE IRISH BECAME AMERICANS. New York: Twayne Publishers, 1973. 698376. 72-1501. 301.45/19/162073. E184.16044.

Japanese Americans. See ORIENTAL AMERICANS.

Iorizzo, Luciano J., and Mondello, Salvatore. THE ITALIAN-AMERICANS. New York: Twayne Publishers, 1971. 145362. 79-147187. 917.3/06/51. E184.I8I55.

Feingold, Henry L. ZION IN AMERICA: THE JEWISH EXPERIENCE FROM COLONIAL TIMES TO THE PRESENT. New York: Twayne Publishers, 1974. New York: Hippocrene Books, 1974. Paperback. 835220. 1188794. 74-3239. 74-15743. 917.3/06/924. E184.J5F377.

Korean Americans. See ASIANS IN AMERICA.

Lebanese Americans. See THE SYRIAN-LEBANESE IN AMERICA.

Coppa, Frank J., and Curran, Thomas J., eds. THE IMMIGRANT EXPERIENCE IN AMERICA. Boston: Twayne Publishers, 1976. 2121439. 76-8439. 973/. 04. E184.A1 I43.

Minorities.

Andersen, Arlow William. THE NORWEGIAN-AMERICANS. Boston: Twayne Publishers, 1975. 1008124. 74-14651. 917.3/06/3982.

Melendy, Howard Brett. THE ORIENTAL AMERICANS. New York: Twayne Publishers, 1972. New York: Hippocrene Books, 1972. Paperback. 530799. 515834. 73-187154. 301.45/19/51. E184.06M35 1972.

Hauberg, Clifford A. PUERTO RICO AND THE PUERTO RICANS. New York: Twayne Publishers, 1975. 914824. 74-8812. 917.295/03/53. F1971.H38 1975.

Prpic, George J. SOUTH SLAVIC IMMIGRATION IN AMERICA. Boston: Twayne Publishers, 1978. 3447580. 77-17041. 973/.04/918. E184.S6P73.

Kayal, Philip M., and Kayal, Joseph M. THE SYRIAN-LEBANESE IN AMERICA: A STUDY IN RELIGION AND ASSIMILATION. New York: Twayne Publishers, 1975. 1046125. 74-18424. 973/.04/9275691. E184.S98K33.

THE AMERICAN TRAILS SERIES

The following books are listed in alphabetical order by the name of the trail.

Holbrook, Stewart Hall. THE OLD POST ROAD: THE STORY OF THE BOSTON POST ROAD. New York: McGraw-Hill, 1962. 1393937. 62-9989. 388.1 F5.H6.

Stewart, George Rippey. THE CALIFORNIA TRAIL: AN EPIC WITH MANY HEROES. New York: McGraw-Hill, 1962. 479007. 62-18977. F591.S83.

Riesenberg, Felix. THE GOLDEN ROAD: THE STORY OF CALIFORNIA'S SPANISH MISSION TRAIL. New York: McGraw-Hill, 1962. 905222. 62-17374. F861.R54 1962.

Egan, Ferol. THE EL DORADO TRAIL: THE STORY OF THE GOLD RUSH ROUTES ACROSS MEXICO. New York: McGraw-Hill, 1970. 58908. 75-95799. 917.2/04. F593.E37.

Mexico to California.

Cushman, Dan. THE GREAT NORTH TRAIL: AMERICA'S ROUTE OF THE AGES. New York: McGraw-Hill, 1966. 703997. 65-19083. 978. F591.C89.

The Canadian Northwest.

Rouse, Parke. THE GREAT WAGON ROAD: FROM PHILADELPHIA TO THE SOUTH. New York: McGraw-Hill, 1973. 446080. 72-8673. 973.2. E188.R85.

Stegner, Wallace Earle. THE GATHERING OF ZION: THE STORY OF THE MORMON TRAIL. New York: McGraw-Hill, 1964. New York: McGraw-Hill, 1971. Paperback. 711219. 3811278. 64-19216. 978. F593.S85.

Daniels, Jonathan. THE DEVIL'S BACKBONE: THE STORY OF THE NATCHEZ TRACE. New York: McGraw-Hill, 1962. 499827. 61-18131/L. 976.2. F341.D24.

Lavender, David Sievert. WESTWARD VISION: THE STORY OF THE OREGON TRAIL. New York: McGraw-Hill, 1963. New York: McGraw-Hill, 1971. Paperback. 710917. 222406. 63-16467. 79-31324. 978. F880.L39.

Dillon, Richard H. SISKIYOU TRAIL: THE HUDSON'S BAY COMPANY ROUTE TO CALIFORNIA. New York: McGraw-Hill, 1975. 1091748. 74-23553. 917.95/03/3. F880.D57.

Carter, Hodding. DOOMED ROAD OF EMPIRE: THE SPANISH TRAIL OF CONQUEST. New York: McGraw-Hill, 1963. 478925. 63-20189. F389. C25.

Louisiana, Texas, Mexico.

Lavender, David Sievert. WINNER TAKE ALL: THE TRANS-CANADA CANOE TRAIL. New York: McGraw-Hill, 1977. 2911069. 77-4864. 971.01/1. F1030.L44.

THE AMERICAN RIVER SERIES

The following books are listed in alphabetical order by the name of the river.

Dietz, Lew. THE ALLAGASH. New York: Holt, Rinehart and Winston, 1968. 437021. 68-12043. 974.1/1. F27.A4D5.

Way, Frederick. THE ALLEGHENY. New York: Farrar and Rinehart, 1942. 967816. F157.A5W357.

Sanborn, Margaret. THE AMERICAN: RIVER OF EL DORADO. New York:

Holt, Rinehart and Winston, 1974. 707273. 73-15160. 917.94/41. F864.S22.

Davis, Clyde Brion. THE ARKANSAS. New York: Farrar and Rinehart, 1940. 968944. F417.A7D261.

Canby, Henry Seidel. THE BRANDYWINE. New York: Farrar and Rinehart, 1941. Reprint. Exton, Pa.: Schiffer, 1969. 1383661. 4376949. 41-5328. 974.813. F157.C4C23.

Ross, Malcolm Harrison. THE CAPE FEAR. New York: Holt, Rinehart and Winston, 1965. 1384026. 65-22461. 975.62. F262.C2R6.

Minter, John Easter. THE CHAGRES, RIVER OF WESTWARD PASSAGE. New York: Rinehart, 1948. 1321961. 48-7786rev. 986. F1569.C4M5.

Tourtellot, Arthur Bernon. THE CHARLES. New York: Rinehart, 1941. 488094. F72.C46T7.

Hansen, Harry. THE CHICAGO. New York: Rinehart, 1942. 484458. 42-25855. F547.C45H3.

Waters, Frank. THE COLORADO. New York: Holt, Rinehart and Winston, 1974. 899446. 73-10984. 917.91/3/03. F788.W3 1974.

Holbrook, Stewart Hall. THE COLUMBIA. New York: Rinehart, 1956. 1657899. 55-10527. 979.73. F853.H6.

Hard, Walter R. THE CONNECTICUT. New York: Rinehart, 1947. 409191. 47-3553. 974. F12.C7H3.

McCague, James. THE CUMBERLAND. New York: Holt, Rinehart and Winston, 1973. 623459. 72-91579. 917.68/5/03. F442.2.M3.

Ellis, William Donohue. THE CUYAHOGA. New York: Holt, Rinehart and Winston, 1966. Reprint. Dayton, Ohio: Landfall Press, 1975. 2771002. 3264069. 66-13558. F497.C95E55.

Wildes, Harry Emerson. THE DELAWARE. New York: Farrar and Rinehart, 1940. 967775. F106.W673D3.

Douglas, Marjory Stoneman. THE EVERGLADES: RIVER OF GRASS. New York: Rinehart, 1947. 1544388. 47-11064. 975.95. F317.E9D6.

Hutchison, Bruce. THE FRASER. New York: Rinehart, 1950. 1415165. 50-10549. 971.1. F1089.F7H8.

Dykeman, William. THE FRENCH BROAD. New York: Holt, Rinehart and Winston, 1974. 2200100. 73-10987. 917.68/895. F443.F8D9 1974.

Clune, Henry W. THE GENESEE. New York: Holt, Rinehart and Winston, 1963. 1330865. 63-12079. 917.4788. F127.G2C5.

Corle, Edwin. THE GILA, RIVER OF THE SOUTHWEST. New York: Rinehart, 1951. 1320321. 51-6152. 978.9. F817.G52C6.

Smith, Chard Powers. THE HOUSATONIC, PURITAN RIVER. New York: Rinehart, 1946. 911481. F102.H7S659.

Carmer, Carl Lamson. THE HUDSON. New York: Holt, Rinehart and Winston, 1974. 2200124. 73-10985. 917.47/3/03. F127.H8C3 1974.

Morgan, Dale Lowell. THE HUMBOLDT, HIGHROAD OF THE WEST. New York: Farrar and Rinehart, 1943. Reprint. Freeport, N.Y.: Books for Libraries Press, 1970. 1597801. 127303. 43-7564rev. 70-146867. 979.3/16. F847.H85M6.

Gray, James. THE ILLINOIS. New York: Rinehart, 1940. 484461. F547. I2G7.

Niles, Mrs. Blair. THE JAMES FROM IRON GATE TO THE SEA. New York: Farrar and Rinehart, 1945. 1864492. 45-3637. 975.5. F232.J2N5 1945.

Streeter, Floyd Benjamin. THE KAW. New York: Rinehart, 1941. Reprint. New York: Arno Press, 1975. 485515. 2180188. 75-124. F687.K3S77.

Coffin, Robert Peter Tristram. KENNEBEC, CRADLE OF AMERICANS. New York: Farrar and Rinehart, 1937. 512239. 37-27396. F27.K32C6.

Clark, Thomas Dionysius. THE KENTUCKY. New York: Farrar and Rinehart, 1942. 769007. 42-36052. 976.9. F456.K306.

Roberts, Leslie. THE MACKENZIE. New York: Rinehart, 1949. Reprint. Westport, Conn.: Greenwood Press, 1974. 800640. 73-20906. 917.193. F1100.M3R62.

Footner, Hulbert. RIVERS OF THE EASTERN SHORE: SEVENTEEN MARYLAND RIVERS. New York: Farrar and Rinehart, 1944. 566096. 44-8257. F187.E2F6.

Howe, Henry Forbush. SALT RIVERS OF THE MASSACHUSETTS SHORE. New York: Rinehart, 1951. 411133. 51-14004. 974.4. F64.H76.

Holden, Raymond Peckham. THE MERRIMACK. New York: Rinehart, 1958. 1216445. 58-10701. 974.27. F72.M6H6.

Jones, Evan. THE MINNESOTA: FORGOTTEN RIVER. New York: Holt, Rinehart and Winston, 1962. 484812. 62-8340. F612.M4J6.

Carter, Hodding. LOWER MISSISSIPPI. New York: Farrar and Rinehart, 1942. 484453. 42-23785. F396.C3.

Havighurst, Walter. UPPER MISSISSIPPI: A WILDERNESS SAGA. New York: Farrar and Rinehart, 1937. 485787. 37-37568. F597.H35.

Vestal, Stanley. THE MISSOURI. New York: Farrar and Rinehart, 1945. Reprint. Lincoln: University of Nebraska Press, 1964. 720624. 2094902. F598.V47.

Hislop, Codman. THE MOHAWK. New York: Rinehart, 1948. 943691. F127.M55H673.

Bissell, Richard Pike. THE MONONGAHELA. New York: Rinehart, 1952. 485803. 52-5562. F157.M58B5.

Braider, Donald. THE NIAGARA. New York: Holt, Rinehart and Winston, 1972. 309387. 76-155505. 917.47/98. F127.N6B7.

Banta, Richard Elwell. THE OHIO. New York: Rinehart, 1949. 342463. 49-11115. 977. F516.B18.

Passaic. See RARITAN.

Gutheim, Frederick Albert. THE POTOMAC. New York: Rinehart, 1949. 485515. 49-11856. F187.P8G8.

Burt, Maxwell Struthers. POWDER RIVER: LET 'ER BUCK. New York: Farrar and Rinehart, 1948. Reprint. St. Clair Shores, Mich.: Scholarly Press, 1971. 3657201. 215471. 73-144923. F767.P6B8.

Wildes, Harry Emerson. TWIN RIVERS, THE RARITAN AND THE PASSAIC. New York: Farrar and Rinehart, 1943. 943714. F142.R2W673.

Horgan, Paul. GREAT RIVER: THE RIO GRANDE IN NORTH AMERICAN HISTORY. New York: Holt, Rinehart and Winston, 1954. 478979. 60-14369/L. 976.44. F392.R5H65 1954a.

Dana, Julian. THE SACRAMENTO, RIVER OF GOLD. New York: Farrar and Rinehart, 1939. Reprint. St. Clair Shores, Mich.: Scholarly Press, 1971. 488086. 240353. 39-27898. 72-144963. 979.4/5. F868.S13D27.

Dunn, James Taylor. THE ST. CROIX: MIDWEST BORDER RIVER. New York: Holt, Rinehart and Winston, 1965. Reprint. St. Paul: Minnesota Historical Society Press, 1979. 951519. 5294195. 65-14452. 79-52970. F612.S2D78.

Cabell, James Branch, and Hanna, A.J. THE ST. JOHNS: A PARADE OF DIVERSITIES. New York: Farrar and Rinehart, 1943. 1447872. F317.S2C3.

Beston, Henry. THE ST. LAWRENCE. New York: Farrar and Rinehart, 1942. 1383595. 42-24091. 971.4. F1050.B47.

Fisher, Anne Benson. THE SALINAS, UPSIDE-DOWN RIVER. New York: Farrar and Rinehart, 1945. 1015915. F868.S133F533.

Masters, Edgar Lee. THE SANGAMON. New York: Farrar and Rinehart, 1942. 484463. 42-15541. F547.S3M3.

Savage, Henry. RIVER OF THE CAROLINAS: THE SANTEE. New York: Rinehart, 1956. Reprint. Chapel Hill: University of North Carolina Press, 1968. 1221704. 439125. 56-6469. 68-15799. 975.7/8. F277.S28S3.

Campbell, Marjorie Elliott Wilkins. THE SASKATCHEWAN. New York: Rinehart, 1950. 1015400. F1076.C189S2.

Davis, Julia. THE SHENANDOAH. New York: Farrar and Rinehart, 1945. 1613112. 45-8434. 975.59. F232.S5D3.

Stokes, Thomas Lunsford. THE SAVANNAH. New York: Rinehart, 1951. Reprint. Dunwoody, Ga.: N.S. Berg, 1969. 485516. 8460. 51-9387. 76-3631. 975.8/1. F277.S3S8.

Carmer, Carl Lamson. THE SUSQUEHANNA. New York: Rinehart, 1955. Reprint. New York: D. McKay, 1967. 1251528. 1832480. 53-8227. 67-27801. 974.8. F157.S8C3.

Matschat, Cecile Hulse. SUWANEE RIVER. New York: Farrar and Rinehart, 1938. 484454. 38-19573. F317.S8M3.

Jahoda, Gloria. RIVER OF THE GOLDEN IBIS. New York: Holt, Rinehart and Winston, 1973. 609268. 72-78126. 917.59/65. F317.H6J33.

Tampa Bay.

Davidson, Donald. THE TENNESSEE. 2 vols. New York: Rinehart, 1946-48. Reprint. Knoxville: University of Tennessee Press, 1978. 360571. 4135317. 46-11901. 78-15103. 976.8. F217.T3D3.

Wilson, William Edward. THE WABASH. New York: Farrar and Rinehart, 1940. 607664. F532.W2W6.

Hill, Ralph Nading. THE WINOOSKI, HEARTWAY OF VERMONT. New York: Rinehart, 1949. 1548949. 49-8844. 974.3. F57.W63H55.

Derleth, August William. THE WISCONSIN. New York: Farrar and Rinehart, 1942. 484456. 42-23237. F587.W8D4.

Smith, Frank Ellis. THE YAZOO RIVER. New York: Rinehart, 1954. 484455. 53-9242. F347.Y3S6 1954.

Mathews, Richard K. THE YUKON. New York: Holt, Rinehart and Winston, 1968. 1187. 68-21745rev.71. 979.8/6. F912.Y9M3.

THE AMERICAN FOLKLORE SERIES

The following books are listed in alphabetical order by locale.

White, William Chapman. ADIRONDACK COUNTRY. New York: Duell, Sloan and Pearce, 1954. 1525152. 52-12652. 974.753. F127.A2W5 1954.

Kennedy, Stetson. PALMETTO COUNTRY. New York: Duell, Sloan and Pearce, 1942. Reprint. Detroit: Gale Research Co., 1974. 1008075. 74-13851. 917.59/04/6. F316.K38 1974.

Alabama, Florida, and Georgia.

Williamson, Thames Ross. FAR NORTH COUNTRY. New York: Duell, Sloan and Pearce, 1944. 1335886. 44-4105. 979.8. F904.W68.

Alaska.

Nixon, Herman Clarence. LOWER PIEDMONT COUNTRY. New York: Duell, Sloan and Pearce, 1946. Reprint. Freeport, N.Y.: Books for Libraries Press, 1971. 488067. 133633. 46-8330. 78-142685. 917.5/03. F210.N5.

Atherton, Gertrude Franklin Horn. GOLDEN GATE COUNTRY. New York:

Duell, Sloan and Pearce, 1945. 1333782. 45-2766. 979.4.

San Francisco, California.

Powers, Alfred. REDWOOD COUNTRY: THE LAVA REGION AND THE RED-WOODS. New York: Duell, Sloan and Pearce, 1949. 1352368. 49-5224. 979.4. F861.P69.

Putnam, George Palmer. DEATH VALLEY AND ITS COUNTRY. New York: Duell, Sloan and Pearce, 1946. 4483253. 46-8329. 979.487. F868.D2P8.

Florida. See Alabama.

Georgia. See Alabama.

Corle, Edwin. LISTEN, BRIGHT ANGEL. New York: Duell, Sloan and Pearce, 1946. 1525741. 46-6417. 979.1. F788.C77.

Grand Canyon.

Bracke, William B. WHEAT COUNTRY. New York: Duell, Sloan and Pearce, 1950. 1335798. 50-6934. 978.1. F591.B78.

Great Plains.

Campbell, Walter Stanley. SHORT GRASS COUNTRY. By Stanley Vestal. New York: Duell, Sloan and Pearce, 1941. Reprint. Westport, Conn.: Greenwood Press, 1970. 1260882. 68454. 41-52003. 78-100185. 917.8. F591.V48.

Great Plains.

Callahan, North. SMOKY MOUNTAIN COUNTRY. New York: Duell, Sloan and Pearce, 1952. 608813. F443.G7C3.

Carter, Hodding, and Ragusin, Anthony. GULF COAST COUNTRY. New York: Duell, Sloan and Pearce, 1951. 1335319. 51-10125. 917.6. F296.C3.

Brownell, Baker. THE OTHER ILLINOIS. New York: Duell, Sloan and Pearce, 1958. 1517717. 58-6766. 917.73. F541.B88.

McMeekin, Clark, pseud. OLD KENTUCKY COUNTRY. New York: Duell, Sloan and Pearce, 1957. 1260295. 57-7574. 917.69. F451.M18.

Kane, Harnett Thomas. DEEP DELTA COUNTRY. New York: Duell, Sloan and Pearce, 1944. 305430. 917.63 K16.

Louisiana.

Le Sueur, Meridel. NORTH STAR COUNTRY. New York: Duell, Sloan and Pearce, 1945. 2397739. 45-37888. 977.4. F606.L56.

Minnesota and Wisconsin.

Webster, Clarence Mertoun. TOWN MEETING COUNTRY. New York: Duell, Sloan and Pearce, 1945. Reprint. Westport, Conn.: Greenwood Press, 1970. 67348. 79-100188. 917.4. F4W4.

New England.

Corle, Edwin. DESERT COUNTRY. New York: Duell, Sloan and Pearce, 1941. 877415. 41-51799. F786.C8 1941.

The new Southwest.

Long, Haniel. PINON COUNTRY. New York: Duell, Sloan and Pearce, 1941. Reprint. Santa Fe, N.Mex.: Sunstone Press, 1975. 919296. 2093152. 76-357679. 979. F786.L8.

The new Southwest.

Graham, Lloyd. NIAGARA COUNTRY. New York: Duell, Sloan and Pearce, 1949. 1525249. 49-9928. 971.4. F127.N6G7.

Henry, Ralph Chester. HIGH BORDER COUNTRY. By Eric Thane (Pseud.). Rev. ed. New York: Duell, Sloan and Pearce, 1942. 877407. 42-36241. F597.H4.

Northwestern states.

Oregon. See California. Powers, Alfred. REDWOOD COUNTRY.

Rayburn, Otto Ernest. OZARK COUNTRY. New York: Duell, Sloan and Pearce, 1941. 363122. 41-52073. 917.78. F417.09R3.

Swetnam, George. PITTSYLVANIA COUNTRY. New York: Duell, Sloan and Pearce, 1951. 1415523. 51-9280. 974.88. F159.P6S85.

Williams, Albert Nathaniel. ROCKY MOUNTAIN COUNTRY. New York: Duell, Sloan and Pearce, 1950. 1434509. 50-6038. 978. F721.W68.

Lewis, Oscar. HIGH SIERRA COUNTRY. New York: Duell, Sloan and Pearce, 1955. Reprint. Westport, Conn.: Greenwood Press, 1977. 1648903. 2798631. 55-9834. 77-883. 917.94. F868.S5L64.

McWilliams, Carey. SOUTHERN CALIFORNIA: AN ISLAND ON THE LAND.

New York: Duell, Sloan and Pearce, 1946. Reprint. Santa Barbara, Calif.: Peregrine Smith, 1973. 754614. 73-77787. 917.94/9/035. F867.M25 1973.

> Published in 1946 under title: SOUTHERN CALIFORNIA COUNTRY, AN ISLAND ON THE LAND.

Thomas, Jeannette Bell. BLUE RIDGE COUNTRY. New York: Duell, Sloan and Pearce, 1942. 1338102. 917.6.

Day, Donald. BIG COUNTRY: TEXAS. New York: Duell, Sloan and Pearce, 1947. 1514892. 47-4831. 917.64. F386.D3.

Stegner, Wallace. MORMON COUNTRY. New York: Duell, Sloan and Pearce, 1942. Reprint. New York: Hawthorn Books, 1975. 490452. 2606765. 42-22811. 75-24681. 979.2. F826.S75.

Croy, Homer. CORN COUNTRY. New York: Duell, Sloan and Pearce, 1947. 1306077. 47-3772. 917.7 F595.C963.

> The West.

Wisconsin. See Minnesota. LeSueur, Meridel. NORTH STAR COUNTRY.

COLLECTION DEVELOPMENT

All libraries should have the ATLAS OF AMERICAN HISTORY and, of course, the historical atlas of their state, if one has been published. Many general state historical questions can be answered by state histories and/or the history sections of description and travel books that may already be in a library's collection.

SUMMARY

At some point in a genealogist's research the use of a national or state historical atlas or the reading of a state history may be desirable. An attempt should be made to give the genealogist a more interesting history than the standard state history book. The best single national historical atlas is the ATLAS OF AMERICAN HISTORY. All genealogists researching American lines should be encouraged to use it.

Chapter 21

THE FAMILY COAT OF ARMS

The most important thing that librarians must provide to genealogists seeking a family coat of arms is the following statement of the Board for Certification of Genealogists concerning heraldry for United States citizens:

Heraldry for United States Citizens

Heraldry in the United States has no legal standing unless it has been registered as a trade mark or copyrighted under United States law. Any United States citizen may adopt and use any arms, devices, or badges of his or her own creation as long as they do not infringe on such insignia covered by such registration or copyright. [It should be noted, however, that should the citizen adopt arms, devices or badges acknowledged by the Heraldic Offices of a foreign nation as belonging to the descendant of any of their nationals, the person that uses those arms, etc., outside the limits of the United States law may find himself guilty of violation of the laws of another country, and subject to penalties.]

Arms do NOT belong to a "family name." They belong to an individual who is acknowledged as their owner, or who receives a grant for them [from a foreign government] or makes them up for himself. Under the laws of most countries, other than ours, the unbroken male line descendants* of any person who has a legally recognized right to bear heraldic arms, may use their progenitor's arms, inheriting them in the same manner that they inherit anything else. If this male line descendant changes his name, as for instance from Smith to Jones, he still may bear his father's arms, even though he now uses a different surname. He does NOT bear different arms associated in someone's mind with another person of his new surname. This is clear evidence that there is no such thing as "arms of your family name."

If your uninterrupted male line immigrant ancestor from England was entitled to use a coat of arms, then you have the right under English law to use this same coat of arms. If he had no such right, then neither do you [unless you buy a grant of arms for yourself from the College of Arms]. Thus, to establish the right under English (or German, French, Swiss, etc.) law to a coat-of-arms, it is necessary to prove your uninterrupted male line descent from someone who was legally entitled to use this coat armour. No "heraldry institute" or "heraldic artist" can look up a surname and provide the correct arms for <u>you</u> without first proving your descent. If they say that they can do so, then they are guilty of fraud.

There are several organizations in the United States that are seeking to register and to codify the use of arms. All such organizations are operating on a voluntary basis, and excellent as their intentions may be, they have no legal standing and are unable to enforce the registration or the uniform of coat of arms.

---

* In addition, daughters have the right to use their father's coat armour as long as they remain unmarried, or combined (by "impaling" or "escutcheon of pretense") with the arms of their husbands after marriage. If their husbands have no arms, they may continue for life to use their father's arms, but this right is not inherited by their children and expires with their deaths. If an "armiger" (one who has the right to bear [heraldic] arms) has no sons but only daughters, then under British law the daughters are heraldic heiresses and their children may "quarter" the arms of their mother with those of their father. If their father has no arms, the right is lost unless the arms are re-granted to them as heirs of their maternal grandfather.

For those genealogists who insist that they wish to find a coat of arms, the work that includes more examples than any other is the following black and white illustrated work:

Rolland, Victor. ARMOIRIES DES FAMILLES. V. & H.V. ROLLAND'S ILLUS-TRATIONS TO THE ARMORIAL GÉNÉRAL, by J.B. Rietstap. 6 vols. in 3. Paris: Institut Héraldique Universal, 1903-26. Reprint. Baltimore: Heraldic Book Co., 1967. 2595468. 66-29998/r68. CR1179.R653 1967.

Librarians that feel they must provide their patrons with additional books on heraldry will find adequate bibliographical coverage on the subject in P. William Filby's AMERICAN & BRITISH GENEALOGY & HERALDRY. 2d ed. Chicago: American Library Association, 1975.

INDEXES

Two extensive indexes to coats of arms in books on heraldry are available and may be useful for libraries that already have large collections of heraldry:

New Jersey. State Library, Trenton. INDEX TO COATS OF ARMS IN PRINTED BOOKS IN THE NEW JERSEY STATE LIBRARY. 3 reels. Baltimore: Magna Carta Book Co., 1970. 4819880. 78-32516. 929.8.

> Contains about seventeen thousand entries to over one thousand American and British books.

St. Louis Public Library. HERALDRY INDEX OF THE ST. LOUIS PUBLIC LIBRARY. 4 vols. St. Louis: 1980.

> Contains an estimated 81,270 cards. Indexes 860 books and periodicals and 100,000 coats of arms.

COLLECTION DEVELOPMENT AND SUMMARY

Larger libraries, may want to acquire ROLLAND'S ILLUSTRATIONS TO THE ARMORIAL GENERAL. Filby's AMERICAN & BRITISH GENEALOGY & HERALDRY has been recommended in other chapters for purchase by most libraries. Remember, "Arms do NOT belong to a 'family name.'"

Some libraries may want an official copy of "Heraldry for United States Citizens," which is printed on letterhead stationery. It may be obtained free by writing the Board for Certification of Genealogists, 1307 New Hampshire Avenue, N. W., Washington, D.C. 20036. Please enclose a self-addressed stamped envelope with the request.

Chapter 22
SUBJECT HEADINGS

Librarians should be aware that the MICROFILM CARD CATALOG at the branch libraries of the Genealogical Department is an indirect subject catalog only. The department has not microfilmed its card catalog entries for authors, titles, and direct subject headings. However, the library will provide any information needed from these parts of the catalog or updated data through the use of the reference questionnaire form available at branch libraries.

Librarians are familiar with direct subject headings, such as "ELY, IOWA--HISTORY." An indirect subject heading for the same book is "IOWA, LINN, ELY--HISTORY." The use of indirect subject headings, as practiced by the department, facilitates research for genealogists, as it groups catalog entries for all materials together by geographical areas. City histories will appear in the catalog near its county's histories, military, vital, probate, court, and land records.

The following table was prepared to illustrate the differences in subject headings for genealogical materials as used by the Genealogical Department and its branches, libraries using SEAR'S LIST OF SUBJECT HEADINGS, and libraries using SUBJECT HEADINGS USED IN THE DICTIONARY CATALOGS OF THE LIBRARY OF CONGRESS.

Archive Collections

LC	ARCHIVES--IOWA
Sears	ARCHIVES--IOWA
GD	IOWA - ARCHIVES

Atlases

LC	IOWA--MAPS
Sears	IOWA--MAPS
GD	IOWA - ATLASES
	IOWA, LINN - ATLASES

Bible Records

> LC   FAMILY RECORDS
>
> Sears   (None)
>
> GD   IOWA, LINN - VITAL RECORDS
>   IOWA, LINN, ELY - VITAL RECORDS

Bibliographies

> LC   IOWA--BIBLIOGRAPHY
>
> Sears   IOWA--BIBLIOGRAPHY
>
> GD   IOWA - BIBLIOGRAPHY

Biography

> LC   IOWA--BIOGRAPHY--DICTIONARIES
>   LINN COUNTY, IOWA--BIOGRAPHY
>
> Sears   IOWA--BIOGRAPHY--DICTIONARIES
>   LINN COUNTY, IOWA--BIOGRAPHY
>
> GD   IOWA - BIOGRAPHY
>   IOWA, LINN - BIOGRAPHY
>   IOWA, LINN - BIOGRAPHY - INDEXES

Birth Records. See Vital Records.

Boundaries

> LC   IOWA--BOUNDARIES
>   IOWA--HISTORY, LOCAL
>
> Sears   IOWA--BOUNDARIES
>
> GD   IOWA - COUNTIES - BOUNDARIES

Cemeteries

> LC   CEMETERIES--IOWA--LINN COUNTY
>   ELY, IOWA--CEMETERIES
>
> Sears   CEMETERIES--IOWA--LINN COUNTY
>   ELY, IOWA--CEMETERIES
>
> GD   IOWA, LINN - VITAL RECORDS
>   IOWA, LINN, ELY - VITAL RECORDS

Census Schedule Indexes

> LC   IOWA--CENSUS (year)
>
> Sears   IOWA--CENSUS

GD   IOWA - CENSUS - INDEXES
           IOWA, LINN - CENSUS - INDEXES

Census Schedules

     LC   IOWA--CENSUS (year)

     Sears   IOWA--CENSUS

     GD   IOWA - CENSUS
            IOWA, LINN - CENSUS

Church History

     LC   IOWA--CHURCH HISTORY
            LINN COUNTY, IOWA--CHURCH HISTORY
            ELY, IOWA--CHURCH HISTORY

     Sears   IOWA--CHURCH HISTORY

     GD   IOWA--CHURCH HISTORY

Church Memberships and Minutes

     LC   CHURCH RECORDS AND REGISTERS

     Sears   (By name of church)

     GD   IOWA - CHURCH RECORDS

City Directories

     LC   ELY, IOWA--DIRECTORIES

     Sears   ELY, IOWA--DIRECTORIES

     GD   IOWA, LINN, ELY - DIRECTORIES

City Histories

     LC   ELY, IOWA--HISTORY

     Sears   ELY, IOWA--HISTORY

     GD   IOWA, LINN, ELY - HISTORY

Civil Records

     LC   COURT RECORDS-- LINN COUNTY, IOWA

     Sears   (None)

     GD   IOWA, LINN - CIVIL RECORDS

County Atlases. See Plat Books.

County Histories

      LC   LINN COUNTY, IOWA--HISTORY

      Sears   LINN COUNTY, IOWA--HISTORY

      GD   IOWA, LINN - HISTORY

Criminal Court Records

      LC   COURT RECORDS--LINN COUNTY, IOWA

      Sears   (None)

      GD   IOWA, LINN - COURT RECORDS

Death Records. See Vital Records.

Emigration Records. See Ship Passenger Lists.

Family Histories

      LC   Surname of Family (e.g., JONES FAMILY)

      Sears   Surname of Family (e.g., JONES FAMILY)

      GD   Surname of Family (e.g., JONES FAMILY)

Gazetteers

      LC   IOWA--GAZETTEERS

      Sears   IOWA--GAZETTEERS

      GD   IOWA - GAZETTEERS

Genealogical Materials

      LC   ELY, IOWA--GENEALOGY
                 LINN COUNTY, IOWA--GENEALOGY
                 IOWA--GENEALOGY

      Sears   GENEALOGY

      GD   IOWA - GENEALOGY
                 IOWA - GENEALOGY - INDEXES
                 IOWA, LINN - GENEALOGY
                 IOWA, LINN, ELY - GENEALOGY

Geographical Names

      LC   NAMES, GEOGRAPHICAL--IOWA

      Sears   NAMES, GEOGRAPHICAL--IOWA

      GD   IOWA - NAMES, GEOGRAPHICAL

Ghost Towns

    LC   CITIES AND TOWNS, RUINED, EXTINCT, ETC.--IOWA

    Sears   CITIES AND TOWNS, RUINED, EXTINCT, ETC.--IOWA

    GD   IOWA - GEOGRAPHY
            IOWA - HISTORY

Historical Atlases

    LC   IOWA--HISTORICAL GEOGRAPHY--MAPS

    Sears   ATLASES, HISTORICAL--IOWA

    GD   IOWA - ATLASES

Historical Bibliographies

    LC   IOWA--HISTORY--BIBLIOGRAPHY

    Sears   IOWA--HISTORY--BIBLIOGRAPHY

    GD   IOWA - HISTORY - BIBLIOGRAPHY

Historical Societies

    LC   IOWA--HISTORY--SOCIETIES

    Sears   IOWA--HISTORY--SOCIETIES

    GD   IOWA - SOCIETIES

History

    LC   IOWA--HISTORY
            LINN COUNTY, IOWA--HISTORY
            ELY, IOWA--HISTORY

    Sears   IOWA--HISTORY
            LINN COUNTY, IOWA--HISTORY
            ELY, IOWA--HISTORY

    GD   IOWA - HISTORY
            IOWA, LINN - HISTORY
            IOWA, LINN, ELY - HISTORY

How-to-do-it Guides

    LC   IOWA--GENEALOGY

    Sears   GENEALOGY

    GD   IOWA - GENEALOGY

Immigration Records. See Ship Passenger Lists.

Land Ownership Maps. See Plat Books.

Land Records

     LC   DEEDS--LINN COUNTY, IOWA
                LAND TITLES--LINN COUNTY, IOWA--INDEXES

     Sears   REAL ESTATE--LINN COUNTY, IOWA

     GD   IOWA, LINN - LAND AND PROPERTY

Maps

     LC   IOWA--MAPS
                LINN COUNTY, IOWA--MAPS
                ELY, IOWA--MAPS

     Sears   IOWA--MAPS
                LINN COUNTY, IOWA--MAPS
                ELY, IOWA--MAPS

     GD   IOWA - MAPS
                IOWA, LINN - MAPS
                IOWA, LINN, ELY - MAPS

Marriage Records

     LC   MARRIAGE LICENSES--LINN COUNTY, IOWA

     Sears   REGISTERS OF BIRTHS, ETC.--LINN COUNTY, IOWA

     GD   IOWA, LINN - VITAL RECORDS

Military History

     LC   ELY, IOWA--HISTORY, MILITARY
                EUROPEAN WAR, 1914-1918--REGIMENTAL HISTORIES--
                    UNITED STATES
                U.S.--HISTORY--FRENCH AND INDIAN WAR, 1755-1763--
                    REGIMENTAL HISTORIES
                U.S.--HISTORY--REVOLUTION--REGIMENTAL HISTORIES
                U.S.--HISTORY--WAR WITH MEXICO, 1845-1848--
                    REGIMENTAL HISTORIES
                U.S.--HISTORY--WAR WITH MEXICO, 1845-1848--
                    REGISTERS, LISTS, ETC.
                U.S.--HISTORY--WAR WITH MEXICO, 1845-1848--
                    REGISTERS OF DEAD
                U.S.--HISTORY--CIVIL WAR, 1861-1865--REGIMENTAL
                    HISTORIES
                U.S.--HISTORY--WAR OF 1898--REGIMENTAL HISTORIES
                WORLD WAR, 1939-1945--REGIMENTAL HISTORIES--
                    UNITED STATES

Sears   WORLD WAR, 1939-1945--REGIMENTAL HISTORIES

GD   IOWA - MILITARY RECORDS - CIVIL WAR - REGIMENTAL
     HISTORIES

Military Records

LC   EUROPEAN WAR, 1914-1918--REGISTERS OF DEAD
    IOWA--MILITIA
    KOREAN WAR, 1950-1953--REGISTERS OF DEAD
    PENSIONS, MILITARY--IOWA
    PENSIONS, MILITARY--UNITED STATES
    PENSIONS--(by war)
    U.S.--ARMED FORCES--REGISTERS OF DEAD
    U.S. ARMY--REGISTERS OF DEAD
    U.S.--HISTORY--FRENCH AND INDIAN WAR, 1755-1763--
      REGISTERS, LISTS, ETC.
    U.S.--HISTORY--FRENCH AND INDIAN WAR, 1755-1763--
      REGISTERS OF DEAD
    U.S.--HISTORY--REVOLUTION--REGISTERS, LISTS, ETC.
    U.S.--HISTORY--WAR OF 1812--REGISTERS, LISTS, ETC.
    U.S.--HISTORY--WAR OF 1812--REGISTERS OF DEAD
    U.S.--HISTORY--WAR WITH MEXICO, 1845-1848--
      REGISTERS, LISTS, ETC.
    U.S.--HISTORY--WAR WITH MEXICO, 1845-1848--
      REGISTERS OF DEAD
    U.S.--HISTORY--CIVIL WAR, 1861-1865--REGISTERS,
      LISTS, ETC.
    U.S.--HISTORY--CIVIL WAR, 1861-1865--REGISTERS
      OF DEAD
    U.S.--HISTORY--WAR OF 1898--REGISTERS, LISTS, ETC.
    U.S.--HISTORY--WAR OF 1898--REGISTERS OF DEAD
    U.S. NAVY--REGISTERS OF DEAD
    WORLD WAR, 1939-1945--REGISTERS OF DEAD--U.S.

Sears   IOWA--MILITIA
    PENSIONS, MILITARY--IOWA

GD   IOWA - MILITARY RECORDS - REVOLUTION
    IOWA - MILITARY RECORDS - WAR OF 1812
    IOWA - MILITARY RECORDS - WAR WITH MEXICO,
      1845-1848
    IOWA - MILITARY RECORDS - CIVIL WAR
    IOWA - MILITARY RECORDS - CIVIL WAR - INDEXES
    IOWA - MILITARY RECORDS - EUROPEAN WAR, 1914-1918

Minorities

LC   (Name of ethnic groups, minorities, etc.)

Sears   MINORITIES

GD   IOWA - MINORITIES
    IOWA, LINN - MINORITIES

Subject Headings

Mortality Schedules

      LC   IOWA--GENEALOGY--SOURCES
                IOWA--CENSUS, (year)
                MORTALITY

      Sears MORTALITY

      GD   IOWA - VITAL RECORDS

Mortuary Records

      LC   MORTALITY--LINN COUNTY, IOWA

      Sears MORTALITY--LINN COUNTY, IOWA

      GD   IOWA, LINN - VITAL RECORDS
                IOWA, LINN, ELY - VITAL RECORDS

Naturalization

      LC   NATURALIZATION RECORDS

      Sears NATURALIZATION

      GD   U.S. - EMIGRATION AND IMMIGRATION

Newspapers

      LC   IOWA--NEWSPAPERS

      Sears NEWSPAPERS--IOWA

      GD   IOWA - NEWSPAPERS
                IOWA - NEWSPAPERS - INDEXES
                IOWA, LINN, ELY - NEWSPAPERS
                IOWA, LINN, ELY - NEWSPAPERS - INDEXES

Oral History

      LC   ORAL HISTORY

      Sears ORAL HISTORY

      GD   (None)

Patriotic Societies

      LC   PATRIOTIC SOCIETIES--DIRECTORIES

      Sears U.S.--SOCIETIES

      GD   U.S. - SOCIETIES

Periodicals

      LC   IOWA--GENEALOGY--PERIODICALS
                IOWA--HISTORY--PERIODICALS

Sears   GENEALOGY--PERIODICALS

GD   IOWA - PERIODICALS

Place Names. See Geographical Names.

Plat Books

LC   REAL PROPERTY--LINN COUNTY, IOWA--MAPS

Sears   IOWA--MAPS

GD   IOWA, LINN - LAND AND PROPERTY - MAPS

Poll Tax Lists

LC   POLL--TAX--LINN COUNTY, IOWA

Sears   TAXATION--LINN COUNTY, IOWA

GD   IOWA, LINN, ELY - ELECTORATE

Post Offices

LC   POSTAL SERVICE--IOWA--HISTORY

Sears   POSTAL SERVICE--IOWA--HISTORY

GD   IOWA - POSTAL GUIDES

Probates

LC   PROBATE RECORDS--LINN COUNTY, IOWA
         WILLS--LINN COUNTY, IOWA

Sears   WILLS--LINN COUNTY, IOWA

GD   IOWA, LINN - PROBATE RECORDS
         IOWA, LINN - PROBATE RECORDS - INDEXES

Public Land

LC   IOWA--PUBLIC LANDS

Sears   IOWA--PUBLIC LANDS

GD   IOWA - LAND AND PROPERTY

School Records

LC   SCHOOLS--RECORDS AND CORRESPONDENCE--
         LINN COUNTY, IOWA

Sears   SCHOOL REPORTS--LINN COUNTY, IOWA

GD   IOWA, LINN - SCHOOLS

Ship Passenger Lists

    LC   U.S.--EMIGRATION AND IMMIGRATION (names of
             national groups, e.g., MEXICANS IN THE U.S.)

    Sears   U.S.--IMMIGRATION AND EMIGRATION (names of
             nationality groups)

    GD   U.S. - EMIGRATION AND IMMIGRATION
             U.S. - EMIGRATION AND IMMIGRATION - INDEXES

Surnames

    LC   NAMES, PERSONAL--U.S.

    Sears   NAMES, PERSONAL--U.S.

    GD   U.S. - NAMES, PERSONAL

Tax Records

    LC   TAXATION--LINN COUNTY, IOWA--LISTS

    Sears   TAXATION--LINN COUNTY, IOWA

    GD   IOWA, LINN - TAXATION

Vital Records

    LC   REGISTERS OF BIRTH, ETC.--LINN COUNTY, IOWA

    Sears   REGISTERS OF BIRTH, ETC.--LINN COUNTY, IOWA

    GD   IOWA, LINN - VITAL RECORDS
             IOWA, LINN, ELY - VITAL RECORDS

Voter Lists

    LC   VOTING REGISTERS
             LINN COUNTY, IOWA--VOTING REGISTERS
             ELY, IOWA--VOTING REGISTERS

    Sears   (None)

    GD   IOWA - ELECTORATE

Wills. See Probates.

Chapter 23

CASE STUDIES

The pedigree chart and its related family group sheets in this chapter were prepared as a hypothetical sample case study. It is assumed that the patron has already consulted all home sources and relatives.

It is essential that the unknown dates of birth and marriage be estimated. The following guidelines are recommended:

Average age of father at birth of first child:	26
Average age of mother at birth of first child:	22
Average age of father at birth of only known child:	32
Average age of mother at birth of only known child:	28
Average number of years between birth of siblings:	2
Average number of years between marriage and birth of first child:	1

Try to estimate the unknown birth and marriage dates on the following charts and note them on a piece of scratch paper. After the dates are estimated, turn to the page following family group sheet number 14 and read the instructions for analyzing the pedigree and family group sheets which follow.

Case Studies

PEDIGREE CHART

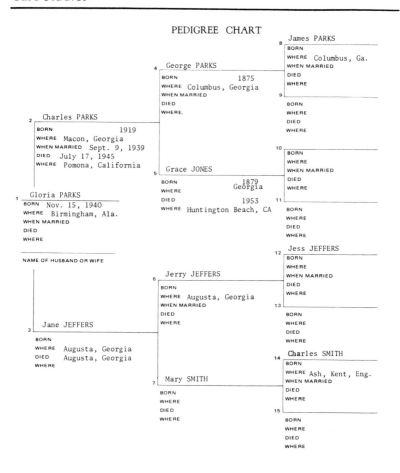

8 James PARKS
BORN
WHERE Columbus, Ga.
WHEN MARRIED
DIED
WHERE

4 George PARKS
BORN 1875
WHERE Columbus, Georgia
WHEN MARRIED
DIED
WHERE.

9
BORN
WHERE
DIED
WHERE

2 Charles PARKS
BORN 1919
WHERE Macon, Georgia
WHEN MARRIED Sept. 9, 1939
DIED July 17, 1945
WHERE Pomona, California

10
BORN
WHERE
WHEN MARRIED
DIED
WHERE

5 Grace JONES
BORN 1879
WHERE Georgia
DIED 1953
WHERE Huntington Beach, CA

11
BORN
WHERE
DIED
WHERE

1 Gloria PARKS
BORN Nov. 15, 1940
WHERE Birmingham, Ala.
WHEN MARRIED
DIED
WHERE

NAME OF HUSBAND OR WIFE

12 Jess JEFFERS
BORN
WHERE
WHEN MARRIED
DIED
WHERE

6 Jerry JEFFERS
BORN
WHERE Augusta, Georgia
WHEN MARRIED
DIED
WHERE

13
BORN
WHERE
DIED
WHERE

3 Jane JEFFERS
BORN
WHERE Augusta, Georgia
DIED Augusta, Georgia
WHERE

14 Charles SMITH
BORN
WHERE Ash, Kent, Eng.
WHEN MARRIED
DIED
WHERE

7 Mary SMITH
BORN
WHERE
DIED
WHERE

15
BORN
WHERE
DIED
WHERE

284

HUSBAND __2__   Charles PARKS

Born _____ 1919 _____ Place _____ Macon, Georgia

Chr. _____ Place _____

Mar _____ September 9, 1939 _____ Place _____ Atlanta, Georgia

Died _____ July 17, 1945 _____ Place _____ Pomona, California

Bur. _____ Place _____

HUSBAND'S FATHER   George PARKS   HUSBAND'S MOTHER   Grace JONES

HUSBAND'S OTHER WIVES

WIFE _____ Jane JEFFERS

Born _____ Place _____ Augusta, Georgia

Chr. _____ Place _____ Augusta, Georgia

Died _____ Place _____

Bur. _____ Place _____

WIFE'S FATHER   Jerry JEFFERS   WIFE'S MOTHER   Mary SMITH

WIFE'S OTHER HUSBANDS _____

SEX M/F	CHILDREN List each child (whether living or dead) in order of birth. Given Names	SURNAME	WHEN BORN DAY	MONTH	YEAR	WHERE BORN TOWN	COUNTY	STATE OR COUNTRY
1 F	Gloria	PARKS	15	Nov	1940	Birmingham		Ala.
2 M	Charles	PARKS						
3 F	Grace	PARKS						
4 M	Jerry	PARKS						
5 M	George	PARKS						
6								
7								
8								
9								
10								
11								

SOURCES OF INFORMATION   OTHER MARRIAGES

Case Studies

HUSBAND	4	George PARKS		
Born		1875	Place	Columbus, Georgia
Chr.			Place	
Mar			Place	
Died			Place	
Bur.			Place	

HUSBAND'S FATHER   James PARKS   HUSBAND'S MOTHER

HUSBAND'S OTHER WIVES

WIFE		Grace JONES		
Born		1879	Place	Georgia
Chr.			Place	
Died		1953	Place	Huntington Beach, California
Bur.			Place	

WIFE'S FATHER   WIFE'S MOTHER

WIFE'S OTHER HUSBANDS

SEX M/F	CHILDREN List each child (whether living or dead) in order of birth. Given Names / SURNAME		WHEN BORN			WHERE BORN		
			DAY	MONTH	YEAR	TOWN	COUNTY	STATE OR COUNTRY
1 M	George	PARKS			1900			
2 F	Elizabeth	PARKS			1902			
3 F	Sarah	PARKS			1904			
4 M	Edward	PARKS			1907			
5 F	Martha	PARKS			1912			
6 M	Charles	PARKS			1919	Macon		Ga.
7								
8								
9								
10								
11								

SOURCES OF INFORMATION

OTHER MARRIAGES

HUSBAND 6   Jerry JEFFERS
Born_____ Place ____ Augusta, Georgia _____
Chr._____ Place _____
Mar _____ Place _____
Died_____ Place _____
Bur._____ Place _____
HUSBAND'S FATHER   Jess JEFFERS   HUSBAND'S MOTHER _____
HUSBAND'S OTHER WIVES

WIFE _____ Mary SMITH _____
Born_____ Place _____
Chr._____ Place _____
Died_____ Place _____
Bur._____ Place _____
WIFE'S FATHER   Charles SMITH   WIFE'S MOTHER _____
WIFE'S OTHER HUSBANDS

SEX M/F	CHILDREN Given Names SURNAME	DAY	MONTH	YEAR	TOWN	COUNTY	STATE OR COUNTRY
1 M	Jess JEFFERS						
2 M	Austin JEFFERS						
3 F	Mary JEFFERS				Augusta		Ga.
4 M	William JEFFERS						
5 F	Jane JEFFERS				Augusta		Ga.
6							
7							
8							
9							
10							
11							

SOURCES OF INFORMATION   OTHER MARRIAGES

Case Studies

HUSBAND ___8___ James PARKS _____

Born_____ Place ___Columbus, Georgia_____

Chr._____ Place _____

Mar _____ Place _____

Died_____ Place _____

Bur._____ Place _____

HUSBAND'S FATHER _____ HUSBAND'S MOTHER _____

HUSBAND'S OTHER WIVES

WIFE_____

Born_____ Place _____

Chr._____ Place _____

Died_____ Place _____

Bur._____ Place _____

WIFE'S FATHER _____ WIFE'S MOTHER _____

WIFE'S OTHER HUSBANDS

SEX M/F	CHILDREN List each child (whether living or dead) in order of birth. Given Names / SURNAME		WHEN BORN			WHERE BORN		
			DAY	MONTH	YEAR	TOWN	COUNTY	STATE OR COUNTRY
1 M	James	PARKS			1866			
2 M	Edward	PARKS			1868			
3 M	Charles	PARKS			1870			
4 F	Margaret	PARKS			1873			
5 M	George	PARKS			1875	Columbus		Ga.
6 F	Mary	PARKS			1878			
7								
8								
9								
10								
11								

SOURCES OF INFORMATION

OTHER MARRIAGES

HUSBAND __12__ Jess JEFFERS _____

Born_____ Place _____
Chr._____ Place _____
Mar _____ Place _____
Died_____ Place _____
Bur._____ Place _____
HUSBAND'S FATHER _____ HUSBAND'S MOTHER _____
HUSBAND'S OTHER WIVES _____

WIFE_____

Born_____ Place _____
Chr._____ Place _____
Died_____ Place _____
Bur._____ Place _____
WIFE'S FATHER _____ WIFE'S MOTHER _____
WIFE'S OTHER HUSBANDS _____

SEX M F	CHILDREN — List each child (whether living or dead) in order of birth. Given Names	SURNAME	WHEN BORN — DAY	MONTH	YEAR	WHERE BORN — TOWN	COUNTY	STATE OR COUNTRY
1 M	Jess	JEFFERS						
2 M	Jerry	JEFFERS				Augusta		Ga.
3 F	Jane	JEFFERS						
4 M	James	JEFFERS						
5								
6								
7								
8								
9								
10								
11								

SOURCES OF INFORMATION

OTHER MARRIAGES

Case Studies

HUSBAND _14_   Charles SMITH _____
Born _____	Place	Ash, Kent, England
Chr. _____	Place	
Mar _____	Place	
Died _____	Place	
Bur. _____	Place	

HUSBAND'S FATHER _____ HUSBAND'S MOTHER _____
HUSBAND'S OTHER WIVES _____

WIFE _____
Born _____	Place	
Chr. _____	Place	
Died _____	Place	
Bur. _____	Place	

WIFE'S FATHER _____ WIFE'S MOTHER _____
WIFE'S OTHER HUSBANDS _____

SEX M F	CHILDREN List each child (whether living or dead) in order of birth. Given Names SURNAME	WHEN BORN			WHERE BORN			
		DAY	MONTH	YEAR	TOWN	COUNTY	STATE OR COUNTRY	
1								
F	Mary SMITH							
2								
3								
4								
5								
6								
7								
8								
9								
10								
11								

SOURCES OF INFORMATION

OTHER MARRIAGES

Try to analyze the pedigree chart and family group sheets and note the types
of sources that may help the hypothetical patron, Gloria Parks. Make notes
on scratch paper for each individual on the pedigree and for each family group
represented by the family group sheets. The answers following the next set of
pedigree and group sheets are arranged by these numbers. A duplicate set of
the pedigree and the family group sheets with estimated dates is provided following the "Checklist of Sources and Resources used for Genealogical Research."
The checklist will help determine what materials may be useful to the patron.

CHECKLIST OF SOURCES AND RESOURCES USED
FOR GENEALOGICAL RESEARCH

Atlases
Biographical Directories
Cemetery Records
Census Schedule Indexes
Census Schedules
Church Minutes and Memberships
City Directories
Civil Court Records
COMPUTER FILE INDEX
County and City Histories
Criminal Records
Divorce Records
Family History
Gazetteers
Genealogical Department Branch Library's
    MICROFILM CARD CATALOG
Genealogical Periodicals
Ghost Town Books
Land Records
Military Records
Mortality Schedules
Naturalization Application Records
Newspapers
Obituaries
Place Name Literature
Plat Books
Poll Lists
Post Office Lists
Probates
Ship Passenger Lists
Soundexes
Statewide Census Schedule Indexes
Statewide Indexes
Tax Lists
Temple Records Index Bureau
Vital Records (birth, marriage, divorce, and death)
Voter Lists
Wills

Case Studies

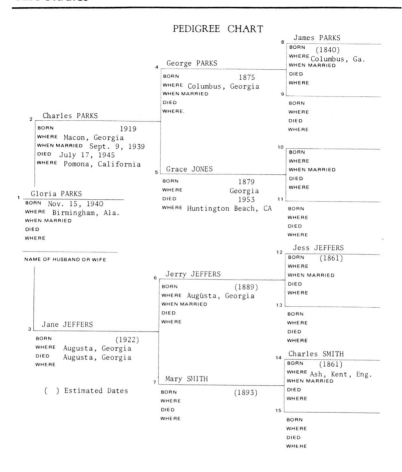

PEDIGREE CHART

8 James PARKS
BORN (1840)
WHERE Columbus, Ga.
WHEN MARRIED
DIED
WHERE

4 George PARKS
BORN 1875
WHERE Columbus, Georgia
WHEN MARRIED
DIED
WHERE.

9
BORN
WHERE
DIED
WHERE

2 Charles PARKS
BORN 1919
WHERE Macon, Georgia
WHEN MARRIED Sept. 9, 1939
DIED July 17, 1945
WHERE Pomona, California

10
BORN
WHERE
WHEN MARRIED
DIED
WHERE

5 Grace JONES
BORN 1879
WHERE Georgia
DIED 1953
WHERE Huntington Beach, CA

11
BORN
WHERE
DIED
WHERE

1 Gloria PARKS
BORN Nov. 15, 1940
WHERE Birmingham, Ala.
WHEN MARRIED
DIED
WHERE

NAME OF HUSBAND OR WIFE

12 Jess JEFFERS
BORN (1861)
WHERE
WHEN MARRIED
DIED
WHERE

6 Jerry JEFFERS
BORN (1889)
WHERE Augusta, Georgia
WHEN MARRIED
DIED
WHERE

13
BORN
WHERE
DIED
WHERE

3 Jane JEFFERS
BORN (1922)
WHERE Augusta, Georgia
DIED Augusta, Georgia
WHERE

14 Charles SMITH
BORN (1861)
WHERE Ash, Kent, Eng.
WHEN MARRIED
DIED
WHERE

( ) Estimated Dates

7 Mary SMITH
BORN (1893)
WHERE
DIED
WHERE

15
BORN
WHERE
DIED
WHERE

HUSBAND ___2___ Charles PARKS
Born_____1919__ Place ___Macon, Georgia_____
Chr._____ Place _____
Mar _September 9, 1939_____ Place ___Atlanta, Georgia_____
Died _July 17, 1945_____ Place ___Pomona, California_____
Bur._____ Place _____
HUSBAND'S FATHER ___George PARKS_____ HUSBAND'S MOTHER ___Grace JONES___
HUSBAND'S OTHER WIVES

WIFE_____ Jane JEFFERS
Born_____(1922)_ Place ___Augusta, Georgia_____
Chr._____ Place ___Augusta, Georgia_____
Died _____ Place _____
Bur._____ Place _____
WIFE'S FATHER ___Jerry JEFFERS_____ WIFE'S MOTHER ___Mary SMITH___
WIFE'S OTHER HUSBANDS

SEX M/F	CHILDREN List each child (whether living or dead) in order of birth. Given Names / SURNAME	WHEN BORN DAY	MONTH	YEAR	WHERE BORN TOWN	COUNTY	STATE OR COUNTRY
1 F	Gloria PARKS	15	Nov	1940	Birmingham		Ala.
2 M	Charles PARKS						
3 F	Grace PARKS						
4 M	Jerry PARKS						
5 M	George PARKS						
6							
7							
8							
9							
10							
11							

SOURCES OF INFORMATION

( ) Estimated Dates

OTHER MARRIAGES

Case Studies

HUSBAND __4__   George PARKS

Born	1875	Place	Columbus, Georgia
Chr.		Place	
Mar	(1899)	Place	
Died		Place	
Bur.		Place	

HUSBAND'S FATHER   James PARKS   HUSBAND'S MOTHER

HUSBAND'S OTHER WIVES

WIFE _____ Grace JONES

Born	1879	Place	Georgia
Chr.		Place	
Died	1953	Place	Huntington Beach, California
Bur.		Place	

WIFE'S FATHER   WIFE'S MOTHER

WIFE'S OTHER HUSBANDS

SEX M F	CHILDREN List each child (whether living or dead) in order of birth. Given Names SURNAME	WHEN BORN DAY	MONTH	YEAR	WHERE BORN TOWN	COUNTY	STATE OR COUNTRY
1 M	George PARKS			1900			
2 F	Elizabeth PARKS			1902			
3 F	Sarah PARKS			1904			
4 M	Edward PARKS			1907			
5 F	Martha PARKS			1912			
6 M	Charles PARKS			1919	Macon		Ga.
7							
8							
9							
10							
11							

SOURCES OF INFORMATION

OTHER MARRIAGES

( ) Estimated Dates

294

HUSBAND	6	Jerry JEFFERS			
Born		(1889)	Place	Augusta, Georgia	
Chr.			Place		
Mar		(1914)	Place		
Died			Place		
Bur.			Place		
HUSBAND'S FATHER		Jess JEFFERS		HUSBAND'S MOTHER	
HUSBAND'S OTHER WIVES					

WIFE		Mary SMITH			
Born		(1893)	Place		
Chr.			Place		
Died			Place		
Bur.			Place		
WIFE'S FATHER		Charles SMITH		WIFE'S MOTHER	
WIFE'S OTHER HUSBANDS					

SEX M F	CHILDREN — List each child (whether living or dead) in order of birth. Given Names / SURNAME		WHEN BORN DAY MONTH YEAR	WHERE BORN TOWN	COUNTY	STATE OR COUNTRY
1 M	Jess	JEFFERS	(1915)			
2 M	Austin	JEFFERS	(1917)			
3 F	Mary	JEFFERS	(1919)	Augusta		Ga.
4 M	William	JEFFERS	(1921)			
5 F	Jane	JEFFERS	(1922)	Augusta		Ga.
6						
7						
8						
9						
10						
11						

SOURCES OF INFORMATION

OTHER MARRIAGES

( ) Estimated Dates

Case Studies

HUSBAND　8　James PARKS

Born	(1840)	Place	Columbus, Georgia
Chr.		Place	
Mar	(1865)	Place	
Died		Place	
Bur.		Place	

HUSBAND'S FATHER _____ HUSBAND'S MOTHER _____

HUSBAND'S OTHER WIVES _____

WIFE _____

Born	(1844)	Place	
Chr.		Place	
Died		Place	
Bur.		Place	

WIFE'S FATHER _____ WIFE'S MOTHER _____

WIFE'S OTHER HUSBANDS _____

SEX M/F	CHILDREN List each child (whether living or dead) in order of birth. Given Names / SURNAME	WHEN BORN DAY MONTH YEAR	WHERE BORN TOWN	COUNTY	STATE OR COUNTRY
1					
M	James　PARKS	1866			
2					
M	Edward　PARKS	1868			
3					
M	Charles　PARKS	1870			
4					
F	Margaret　PARKS	1873			
5					
M	George　PARKS	1875	Columbus		Ga.
6					
F	Mary　PARKS	1878			
7					
8					
9					
10					
11					

SOURCES OF INFORMATION

( ) Estimated Dates

OTHER MARRIAGES

HUSBAND 12   Jess JEFFERS _____

Born _____ (1861) Place _____

Chr. _____ Place _____

Mar _____ (1886) Place _____

Died _____ Place _____

Bur. _____ Place _____

HUSBAND'S FATHER _____ HUSBAND'S MOTHER _____

HUSBAND'S OTHER WIVES _____

WIFE _____

Born _____ (1865) Place _____

Chr. _____ Place _____

Died _____ Place _____

Bur. _____ Place _____

WIFE'S FATHER _____ WIFE'S MOTHER _____

WIFE'S OTHER HUSBANDS _____

SEX M F	CHILDREN List each child (whether living or dead) in order of birth. Given Names / SURNAME		WHEN BORN DAY / MONTH / YEAR			WHERE BORN TOWN	COUNTY	STATE OR COUNTRY
1 M	Jess	JEFFERS			(1887)			
2 M	Jerry	JEFFERS			(1889)	Augusta		Ga.
3 F	Jane	JEFFERS			(1891)			
4 M	James	JEFFERS			(1893)			
5								
6								
7								
8								
9								
10								
11								

SOURCES OF INFORMATION   OTHER MARRIAGES

( ) Estimated Dates

Case Studies

HUSBAND _14_   Charles SMITH
Born _____ (1861) Place _____ Ash, Kent, England
Chr. _____ Place _____
Mar _____ (1892) Place _____
Died _____ Place _____
Bur. _____ Place _____
HUSBAND'S FATHER _____ HUSBAND'S MOTHER _____
HUSBAND'S OTHER WIVES

WIFE _____
Born _____ (1865) Place _____
Chr. _____ Place _____
Died _____ Place _____
Bur. _____ Place _____
WIFE'S FATHER _____ WIFE'S MOTHER _____
WIFE'S OTHER HUSBANDS

SEX M F	CHILDREN List each child (whether living or dead) in order of birth Given Names SURNAME	WHEN BORN DAY MONTH YEAR	WHERE BORN TOWN	COUNTY	STATE OR COUNTRY	
1						
F	Mary SMITH	(1893)				
2						
3						
4						
5						
6						
7						
8						
9						
10						
11						

SOURCES OF INFORMATION   OTHER MARRIAGES

(   ) Estimated Dates

DETAILS OF CASE STUDY ANSWERS

(Listed in order of importance, based on a logical, economical search strategy.)

1. Gloria PARKS

NEEDS	PRINCIPAL SOURCES
County of Birmingham, Ala.	Rand, McNally and Co. COMMERCIAL ATLAS AND MARKETING GUIDE.
Parks family histories	GENEALOGIES IN THE LIBRARY OF CONGRESS: A BIBLIOGRAPHY. New York (City) Public Library. DICTIONARY CATALOG OF THE LOCAL HISTORY AND GENEALOGY DIVISION.
	Genealogical Department. MICRO-FILM CARD CATALOG: FAMILY HISTORY.

2. Charles PARKS

NEEDS	PRINCIPAL SOURCES
County of Macon, Ga.	Rand, McNally and Co. COMMERCIAL ATLAS AND MARKETING GUIDE.
Birth record	COMPUTER FILE INDEX WHERE TO WRITE FOR BIRTH AND DEATH RECORDS. Temple Records Index Bureau.
Parks family histories	GENEALOGIES IN THE LIBRARY OF CONGRESS: A BIBLIOGRAPHY, and others.
Family histories and/or abstracts of vital records	Genealogical periodical indexes.
County histories that include Macon, Ga.	CONSOLIDATED BIBLIOGRAPHY OF COUNTY HISTORIES IN FIFTY STATES IN 1961, CONSOLIDATED 1935-1961.

3. Jane JEFFERS

Case Studies

NEEDS PRINCIPAL SOURCES

County that includes Rand, McNally and Co.
Augusta, Ga. COMMERICAL ATLAS AND MARKETING
GUIDE.

Birth record COMPUTER FILE INDEX
WHERE TO WRITE FOR BIRTH AND
DEATH RECORDS.
Temple Records Index Bureau.

Jeffers family histories GENEALOGIES IN THE LIBRARY OF
CONGRESS: A BIBLIOGRAPHY, and
others.

Family histories and/or Genealogical periodical indexes.
abstracts of vital records

County histories that include CONSOLIDATED BIBLIOGRAPHY OF
Augusta, Ga. COUNTY HISTORIES IN FIFTY STATES
IN 1961, CONSOLIDATED 1935-1961.

4. George PARKS

NEEDS PRINCIPAL SOURCES

County that includes Rand, McNally and Co.
Columbus, Ga. COMMERCIAL ATLAS AND MARKETING
GUIDE.

Birth and marriage records COMPUTER FILE INDEX
Temple Records Index Bureau

Parks family histories GENEALOGIES IN THE LIBRARY OF
CONGRESS: A BIBLIOGRAPHY, and
others.

Birth records from county Genealogical Department.
court house MICROFILM CARD CATALOG.
"VITAL RECORDS"
HANDY BOOK FOR GENEALOGISTS

Census records 1880 Soundex
1900 Soundex

Family histories and/or Genealogical periodical indexes
abstracts of vital records

County histories that include CONSOLIDATED BIBLIOGRAPHY OF
Columbus, Ga. COUNTY HISTORIES IN FIFTY STATES
IN 1961, CONSOLIDATED 1935-1961.

5. Grace JONES

NEEDS PRINCIPAL SOURCES

County name for Huntington Beach, Calif.	Rand, McNally and Co. COMMERCIAL ATLAS AND MARKETING GUIDE.
Birth and marriage records	COMPUTER FILE INDEX Temple Records Index Bureau
Jones family histories	GENEALOGIES IN THE LIBRARY OF CONGRESS: A BIBLIOGRAPHY, and others.
Census records of Georgia	1880 Soundex
Death records	WHERE TO WRITE FOR BIRTH AND DEATH RECORDS. Newspapers
Family histories and/or abstracts of vital records	Genealogical periodical indexes.

6. Jerry JEFFERS

NEEDS	PRINCIPAL SOURCES
County name for Augusta, Ga.	Rand, McNally and Co. COMMERCIAL ATLAS AND MARKETING GUIDE.
Birth and marriage records	COMPUTER FILE INDEX Temple Records Index Bureau
Jeffers family histories	GENEALOGIES IN THE LIBRARY OF CONGRESS: A BIBLIOGRAPHY, and others.
Birth record from county court house	Genealogical Department. MICROFILM CARD CATALOG. "VITAL RECORDS" HANDY BOOK FOR GENEALOGISTS.
Census records that include Augusta, Ga.	1900 Soundex. Census Schedules, 1900.
Land and Wills, etc.	GD MICROFILM CARD CATALOG: "LAND AND PROPERTY" "PROBATE RECORDS"
Family histories and/or abstracts of vital records	Genealogical periodical indexes
County histories that include Augusta, Ga.	CONSOLIDATED BIBLIOGRAPHY OF COUNTY HISTORIES IN FIFTY STATES IN 1961, CONSOLIDATED 1935-1961.

7. Mary SMITH

NEEDS	PRINCIPAL SOURCES

Birth and marriage records	COMPUTER FILE INDEX Temple Records Index Bureau

8. James PARKS

NEEDS	PRINCIPAL SOURCES
County name for Columbus, Ga.	Rand, McNally and Co. COMMER-CIAL ATLAS AND MARKETING GUIDE.
Birth and marriage records	COMPUTER FILE INDEX Temple Records Index Bureau
Parks family histories	GENEALOGIES IN THE LIBRARY OF OF CONGRESS: A BIBLIOGRAPHY, and others.
Census records that include Columbus, Ga.	1880 Soundex Census schedules, 1850, 1870, and 1880.
Family histories and/or abstracts of vital records	Genealogical periodical indexes
County histories that include Columbus, Ga.	CONSOLIDATED BIBLIOGRAPHY OF COUNTY HISTORIES IN FIFTY STATES IN 1961, CONSOLIDATED 1935-1961.

12. Jess JEFFERS

NEEDS	PRINCIPAL SOURCES AND ACTION
County of birth	Statewide indexes Valentine's LOCALITY FINDING AIDS FOR U.S. SURNAMES. Genealogical Department. MICRO-FILM CARD CATALOG. "GENEALOGY" "CENSUS - INDEXES"
Census records that include Augusta, Ga.	1900 Soundex Census schedules, 1900
County histories that include Augusta, Ga.	CONSOLIDATED BIBLIOGRAPHY OF COUNTY HISTORIES IN FIFTY STATES IN 1961, CONSOLIDATED 1935-1961.
Land and Wills	Genealogical Department. MICROFILM CARD CATALOG. "LAND AND PROPERTY" "PROBATE RECORDS"

14. Charles SMITH

NEEDS	PRINCIPAL SOURCES AND ACTION

Birth and marriage records	COMPUTER FILE INDEX Temple Records Index Bureau Naturalization Application Records
Smith family histories	GENEALOGIES IN THE LIBRARY OF CONGRESS: A BIBLIOGRAPHY, and others.
Birth records from the Registrar of England	Registrar General St. Catherine's House 10 Kingsway London WC2B-6JP England
Census records of Deane, Lancaster, England	Census schedules, 1871 and/or 1861
Family histories and/or abstracts of vital records	Genealogical periodical indexes

CASE STUDY, SUMMARY OF ANSWERS

Individuals' Numbers	Sources Useful for the Case Study (Listed in order of importance, based on a logical, economical search strategy.)
1-6, 8	Rand, McNally and Co. COMMERCIAL ATLAS AND MARKETING GUIDE.
2-8, 14	COMPUTER FILE INDEX.
1-6, 8, 14	Family Histories. GENEALOGIES IN THE LIBRARY OF CONGRESS: A BIBLIOGRAPHY.
	New York (City) Public Library. DICTIONARY CATALOG OF THE LOCAL HISTORY AND GE-NEALOGY DIVISION.
	Genealogical Department. MICROFILM CARD CATALOG: FAMILY HISTORY.
4, 6	Genealogical Department. MICROFILM CARD CATALOG. "VITAL RECORDS."
2,3	Birth records from state office of vital statistics: U.S. Public Health Service. WHERE TO WRITE FOR BIRTH AND DEATH RECORDS.
14	Immigration application records
4, 6	Birth records from county clerks. HANDY BOOK FOR GENEALOGISTS.
5	U.S. Public Health Service. WHERE TO WRITE FOR BIRTH AND DEATH RECORDS.

NEWSPAPERS

2-8, 14	Temple Records Index Bureau
14	Birth records from the Registrar of England, St. Catherine's House.
4-6, 8, 12	Soundex
6, 8, 12	Census schedules
14	English Census Schedules (1841, 1851, 1861, and 1871 are available from the Genealogical Department).
2-6, 8, 14	Genealogical periodical indexes for geographical places and family surnames.
6, 8, 12	County histories. CONSOLIDATED BIBLIOGRAPHY OF COUNTY HISTORIES IN FIFTY STATES IN 1961, CONSOLIDATED 1935-1961.
12	Statewide indexes. Vallentine's LOCALITY FINDING AIDS FOR U.S. SURNAMES, and the Genealogical Department. MICROFILM CARD CATALOG. "GENEALOGY" and "CENSUS - INDEXES."
6	Genealogical Department. MICROFILM CARD CATALOG. "LAND AND PROPERTY" and "PROBATE RECORDS."

Chapter 24

TYPICAL GENEALOGICAL RESEARCH PROBLEMS
AND REFERENCE QUESTIONS

There are many varying problems that lead to questions which genealogists ask librarians. The following are a few questions that may be asked the most often or be the most common problems. The answers are arranged in order of usefulness.

BIRTHDATE AND/OR PLACE NEEDED:

1. COMPUTER FILE INDEX

2. Birth records or abstracts of birth records in books or periodicals, and/or collected birth records on microfilm such as some available at the Genealogical Department Library or its branch libraries listed in the MICROFILM CARD CATALOG under the geographical location subdivided by "VITAL RECORDS"

3. Birth certificates, WHERE TO WRITE FOR BIRTH AND DEATH RECORDS

4. Newspapers

5. Naturalization applications, Neagles' LOCATING YOUR IMMIGRANT ANCESTOR: A GUIDE TO NATURALIZATION RECORDS

CITY UNKNOWN, BUT COUNTY, STATE, AND NAME OF ANCESTOR KNOWN:

I. County histories, CONSOLIDATED BIBLIOGRAPHY OF COUNTY HISTORIES IN FIFTY STATES IN 1961, CONSOLIDATED 1935-1961

2. County indexes, Genealogical Department's MICROFILM CARD CATALOG and GENEALOGICAL AND LOCAL HISTORY BOOKS IN PRINT

3. Statewide indexes, LOCALITY FINDING AIDS FOR U.S. SURNAMES

COUNTY UNKNOWN, BUT CITY, STATE, AND NAME OF ANCESTOR KNOWN:

1. Rand, McNally and Co. COMMERCIAL ATLAS AND MARKETING GUIDE

2. Gazetteers

3. Place name literature

4. Postal directories or histories

5. Ghost town books

Research Problems & Reference Questions

COUNTY UNKNOWN, BUT STATE AND NAME OF ANCESTOR KNOWN:
1. COMPUTER FILE INDEX
2. Statewide census schedule indexes
3. Statewide indexes, LOCALITY FINDING AIDS FOR U.S. SURNAMES

COUNTY UNKNOWN, BUT TOWNSHIP, STATE AND NAME OF ANCESTOR KNOWN: TOWNSHIP ATLAS OF THE UNITED STATES: NAMED TOWN-SHIPS

DEATH DATE AND/OR PLACE NEEDED:
1. Death records or abstracts of death records in books or periodicals, and/or collected death records on microfilm such as some available at the Genealogical Department Library or its branch libraries, listed in the MICROFILM CARD CATALOG under the geographical location, subdivided by "VITAL RECORDS"
2. Death certificate, WHERE TO WRITE FOR BIRTH AND DEATH RECORDS
3. Probate records
4. Sexton records
5. Cemetery records
6. Church death records (including burial records)
7. Newspaper obituaries
8. Mortician records
9. Mortality schedules

DIVORCE DATE AND/OR PLACE NEEDED:
1. Divorce records, WHERE TO WRITE FOR DIVORCE RECORDS
2. Newspapers

FAMILY BACKGROUND:
1. Family histories, GENEALOGIES IN THE LIBRARY OF CONGRESS: A BIBLIOGRAPHY, and others
2. Census schedules
3. County histories, CONSOLIDATED BIBLIOGRAPHY OF COUNTY HISTORIES IN FIFTY STATES IN 1961, CONSOLIDATED1935-1961
4. Wills and probates
5. Land and property records
6. Military records

MARRIAGE DATE AND/OR PLACE NEEDED:
1. Marriage records or abstracts of birth records in books or periodicals, and/or

306

collected marriage records on microfilm such as some available at the Genealogical Department Library or its branch libraries, listed in the MICROFILM
CARD CATALOG under the geographical location subdivided by "VITAL RECORDS"

2. Marriage certificates, WHERE TO WRITE FOR MARRIAGE RECORDS

3. Widow's military pension application

4. Newspapers

NAME NEEDED FOR THE FATHER OF AN ANCESTOR:

1. Birth record or abstracts of birth records in books or periodicals and/or
collected birth records on microfilm such as some available at the Genealogical
Department Library or its branch libraries, listed in the MICROFILM CARD
CATALOG under the geographical location, subdivided by "VITAL RECORDS"

2. Birth certificate, WHERE TO WRITE FOR BIRTH RECORDS

3. Family histories, GENEALOGIES IN THE LIBRARY OF CONGRESS: A
BIBLIOGRAPHY, and others

4. Census schedule, 1850-1880, 1900

5. County history, CONSOLIDATED BIBLIOGRAPHY OF COUNTY HISTORIES
IN FIFTY STATES IN 1961, CONSOLIDATED 1935-1961

6. Ship passenger lists, 1820-- .

NAME NEEDED FOR THE HUSBAND OF AN ANCESTOR: Marriage Certificate,
    WHERE TO WRITE FOR MARRIAGE RECORDS

NAME NEEDED FOR THE MOTHER OF AN ANCESTOR:

1. Birth records or abstracts of birth records in books and periodicals, and/or
collected birth records on microfilm such as some available at the Genealogical
Department Library or its branch libraries, listed in the MICROFILM CARD
CATALOG under the geographical location, subdivided by "VITAL RECORDS"

2. Birth certificate, WHERE TO WRITE FOR BIRTH RECORDS

3. Family histories, GENEALOGIES IN THE LIBRARY OF CONGRESS: A
BIBLIOGRAPHY, and others

4. Census schedules, 1850-1880, 1900

5. County histories, CONSOLIDATED BIBLIOGRAPHY OF COUNTY HISTORIES
IN FIFTY STATES IN 1961, CONSOLIDATED 1935-1961

6. Ship passenger lists, 1820-- .

NAME OF A RESEARCHER AT AN ARCHIVES: Write the archives, the Genea-
    logical Department, or the Board of Certification of Genealogists

NAME OF A RESEARCHER IN SALT LAKE CITY: Write the Genealogical De-
    partment or the Board of Certification of Genealogists

Research Problems & Reference Questions

NAMES NEEDED FOR THE CHILDREN OF AN ANCESTOR:

1. Birth records or abstracts of birth records in books or periodicals, and/or collected birth records on microfilm such as some available at the Genealogical Department Library or its branch libraries, listed in the MICROFILM CARD CATALOG under the geographical location, subdivided by "VITAL RECORDS"

2. Census schedules, 1850-1880, 1900

3. County histories, CONSOLIDATED BIBLIOGRAPHY OF COUNTY HISTORIES IN FIFTY STATES IN 1961, CONSOLIDATED 1935-1961

4. Will or probate

NAMES NEEDED FOR THE PARENTS OF AN ANCESTOR:

1. Birth record or abstracts of birth records in books or periodicals, and/or collected birth records on microfilm such as some available at the Genealogical Department Library or its branch libraries, listed in the MICROFILM CARD CATALOG under the geographical location subdivided by "VITAL RECORDS"

2. Birth certificate, WHERE TO WRITE FOR BIRTH RECORDS

3. Family histories, GENEALOGIES IN THE LIBRARY OF CONGRESS: A BIBLIOGRAPHY, and others

4. Census schedules, 1850-1880, 1900

5. Biographical sketch of prominent person, BIO-BASE

6. County histories, CONSOLIDATED BIBLIOGRAPHY OF COUNTY HISTORIES IN FIFTY STATES IN 1961, CONSOLIDATED 1935-1961

7. Ship passenger lists, 1820-- .

NAMES NEEDED FOR THE SIBLINGS OF AN ANCESTOR:

1. Birth records or abstracts of birth records in books or periodicals, and/or collected birth records on microfilm such as some available at the Genealogical Department Library or its branch libraries, listed in the MICROFILM CARD CATALOG under the geographical location, subdivided by "VITAL RECORDS"

2. Family histories, GENEALOGIES IN THE LIBRARY OF CONGRESS: A BIBLIOGRAPHY, and others

3. Census schedules, 1850-1880, 1900

4. County histories, CONSOLIDATED BIBLIOGRAPHY OF COUNTY HISTORIES IN FIFTY STATES IN 1961, CONSOLIDATED 1935-1961

5. Will or probate

6. Ship passenger lists, 1820-- .

NAME NEEDED FOR THE WIFE OF AN ANCESTOR:

1. Marriage records or abstracts of marriage records in books or periodicals, and/or collected marriage records on microfilm such as some available at the

Genealogical Department Library or its branch libraries, listed in the MICRO-FILM CARD CATALOG under the geographical location, subdivided by "VITAL RECORDS"

2. Marriage certificate, WHERE TO WRITE FOR MARRIAGE RECORDS

3. Family histories, GENEALOGIES IN THE LIBRARY OF CONGRESS: A BIBLIOGRAPHY, and others

4. Census schedules, 1850-1880, 1900

5. Biographical sketch of prominent person, BIO-BASE

6. County histories, CONSOLIDATED BIBLIOGRAPHY OF COUNTY HISTORIES IN FIFTY STATES IN 1961, CONSOLIDATED 1935-1961

7. Widow's military pension application

8. Ship passenger lists, 1820-- .

9. Wills and probates

10. Land and property records

STREET ADDRESS NEEDED: City directories

WHAT RESEARCH HAS ALREADY BEEN DONE?

1. COMPUTER FILE INDEX

2. Family histories, GENEALOGIES IN THE LIBRARY OF CONGRESS: A BIBLIOGRAPHY, and others

3. Temple Records Index Bureau

4. County and city histories, CONSOLIDATED BIBLIOGRAPHY OF COUNTY HISTORIES IN FIFTY STATES IN 1961, CONSOLIDATED 1935-1961, and others

5. Genealogical indexes

6. Periodical indexes

WHERE WERE THEY FROM?

1. Family histories, GENEALOGIES IN THE LIBRARY OF CONGRESS: A BIBLIOGRAPHY, and others

2. Statewide census schedule indexes

3. Census schedules, 1850-1880, 1900

4. County histories, CONSOLIDATED BIBLIOGRAPHY OF COUNTY HISTORIES IN FIFTY STATES IN 1961, CONSOLIDATED 1935-1961

5. Statewide indexes, LOCALITY FINDING AIDS FOR U.S. SURNAMES

6. Ship passenger lists, 1820-- .

SUMMARY

The problems, questions and answers listed above should help most librarians handle the average genealogical questions. There are, of course, any number of more difficult questions. GENEALOGICAL HELPER provides a regular column called, "Question and Answer Box." The regular reading of this column should help librarians to understand some of the problems of genealogical research and their answers. Some of the answers in this column are not as thorough as they should be; nevertheless, most would be helpful to read.

INDEX

This index serves as an author, title, and subject index. In some cases, titles have been shortened. Underlined page numbers refer to main areas of emphasis. Alphabetization is letter by letter. Census schedule dates are filed alphabetically by the century, but subdivided in chronological order for the decade and/or year. Abbreviations are filed at the beginning of each letter of the alphabet.

Index

how-to-do-it guide 51
mortality census schedules 83
postal history 29
ALABAMA: AN INDEX TO THE 1830
UNITED STATES CENSUS 148
ALABAMA CENSUS RETURNS, 1820
148
Alabama Department of Archives and
History 83
ALABAMA 1830 CENSUS INDEX 148
ALABAMA 1840 CENSUS INDEX 148
ALABAMA 1850 CENSUS INDEX 148
ALABAMA POSTAL HISTORY 29
Alabama State Department of Archives
and History 148
Alaska
bibliography 194
census schedule indexes 149
folklore 265
gazetteer 29
ghost towns 29
newspapers 208
place name literature 29
postal history 29
Alaska Historical Commission 194
ALASKAN CENSUS RECORDS, 1870-
1907 149
ALASKA PLACE NAMES 29
Alden, Timothy 81
ALLAGASH, THE 260
ALLEGHENY, THE 260
Allen, Morse S. 31
Allsopp, Frederick William 30
Alvarez-Altman, Grace 239
Amateur Treasure Hunters Association
37
AMERICAN: RIVER OF EL DORADO,
THE 260-61
AMERICAN & BRITISH GENEALOGY
& HERALDRY 5, 8, 11, 101,
123, 220, 225, 270
AMERICAN AND ENGLISH GENEAL-
OGIES IN THE LIBRARY OF
CONGRESS 105
American Antiquarian Society 123
Americana Unlimited 203-4, 223
AMERICAN DIARIES 111
AMERICAN DIARIES IN MANU-
SCRIPT 110
AMERICAN FAMILY, BOTSFORD-

MARBLE ANCESTRAL LINES,
AN 247
American Folklore Series, The 265-68
AMERICAN GENEALOGICAL INDEX,
THE 120
AMERICAN GENEALOGICAL-BIO-
GRAPHICAL INDEX TO
AMERICAN GENEALOGICAL,
THE 120
AMERICAN GENEALOGICAL
PERIODICALS 128
AMERICAN GENEALOGIST 108,
117, 120
AMERICAN GENEALOGIST (Periodi-
cal) 12, 129
American Geographical Society 26
AMERICAN GIVEN NAMES 237,
242
AMERICAN INDIAN GENEALOGI-
CAL RESEARCH 58
American Jewish Periodical Center
212
American Library Association 201,
213. See also ALA
AMERICAN LIBRARY DIRECTORY 8,
202, 253
AMERICAN NEWSPAPERS, 1821-1936
208
American Revolution. See Military
records
American River Series, The 260-65
American Society of Genealogists
xiv
Fellows 243
Jacobus Award. See Jacobus
Award
AMERICAN STATE PAPERS 121
American Trails Series, The 259-60
AMERICA'S IMMIGRANT WOMEN
257
ANCESTORS AND DESCENDANTS
OF COLONEL DAVID FUNS-
TEN, THE 245
ANCESTORS AND DESCENDANTS
OF JEREMIAH ADAMS 243-44
Ancestors as individuals 227
ANCESTOR'S INDEX 121
Ancestral surname indexes 232-33
ANCESTREE HOUSE RESEARCH
LIBRARY NEWSLETTER 230

mortality census schedules 85
newspapers 209
place name literature 31
postal history 31
COLORADO: A SELECTED BIBLIOG-
RAPHY 195
COLORADO, THE 261
COLORADO AREA KEY 52
COLORADO 1880 CENSUS INDEX
151
Colorado Historical Society Library
151
COLORADO PLACE NAMES 31
COLORADO PORTRAIT AND BIOG-
RAPHY INDEX 200
Colorado State Archives 85
COLUMBIA, THE 261
COLUMBIA LIPPINCOTT GAZETTEER
OF THE WORLD, THE 26
COMIC EPITAPHS FROM THE VERY
BEST OLD GRAVEYARDS 81
COMMERCIAL ATLAS AND MARKET-
ING GUIDE 9, 22, 25, 47-
48
Committee for a New England Bibliog-
raphy 196-97
COMPUTER FILE INDEX 22, 24, 75,
104, 122-23, 124
Computer searches 232
Concerned United Birthparents 234
CONFEDERATE SOLDIERS SERVICE
RECORD REGISTER 219
Confederate States of America 218
Connecticut
bibliography 195
census schedule indexes 151-53
gazetteer 31
how-to-do-it book 52
mortality census schedules 85
newspapers 209
place name literature 31
postal history 31
CONNECTICUT, THE 261
CONNECTICUT 1800 CENSUS INDEX
152
CONNECTICUT 1810 CENSUS INDEX
152
CONNECTICUT 1820 CENSUS INDEX
152
CONNECTICUT 1830 CENSUS INDEX
152

CONNECTICUT 1840 CENSUS INDEX
152
CONNECTICUT 1850 CENSUS INDEX
152
Connecticut Historical Society 31
Connecticut League of Historical
Societies 195
CONNECTICUT PLACE NAMES 31
CONNECTICUT RESEARCHER'S HAND-
BOOK 52, 195
CONNECTICUT 1670 CENSUS 151
CONNECTICUT SOURCES FOR
FAMILY HISTORIANS AND
GENEALOGISTS 52
Connecticut State Library 85, 152-53
Conrad, Agnes C. 52
CONSOLIDATED BIBLIOGRAPHY OF
COUNTY HISTORIES 8, 191,
204-5
CONSOLIDATED INDEX TO THIRTY-
TWO HISTORIES OF INDIA-
NAPOLIS AND INDIANA, A
200
Consumer Guide 6, 50
Coombs, Norman 258
Cooperation of libraries 2, 5-6, 10
Cope, Gilbert 244
Coppa, Frank J. 259
Corbitt, David Leroy 41
Corker, Mrs. U.W. 98-99
Corle, Edwin 262, 266-67
CORN COUNTRY 268
Correspondence 114
foreign-language 102-3
libraries 213
Cottle, Basil 238
Cottler, Susan Muriel 76
Coulter, John Wesley 33
COUNTIES OF ILLINOIS 33
COUNTIES OF MARYLAND AND
BALTIMORE CITY, THE 36
COUNTIES OF TENNESSEE 44
County atlases 224-25
subject headings. See Plat books,
subject headings
COUNTY BOUNDARIES OF NEW
MEXICO, THE 40
COUNTY BY COUNTY IN OHIO
GENEALOGY 198
County clerks 17

Index

SCOTLAND, ROBERT HAMIL-
TON BISHOP OF OXFORD,
OHIO, EBENEZER BISHOP OF
McDONOUGH COUNTY,
ILLINOIS, JOHN SCOTT OF
IRELAND 249
FAMILY OF RICHARD SMITH OF
SMITHTOWN, LONG ISLAND,
THE 249
Family records 121, 124
Family relationships 131–38
Family research, periodicals 125
Fargo Genealogical Society 232
FARISH FAMILY OF VIRGINIA,
THE 245
Farley, Alan W. 196
Farnham, Charles W. 56, 249
FAR NORTH COUNTRY 265
Faxon, Frederick Winthrop 126
Federal census schedules. See Census
schedules
FEDERAL DEATH RECORDS OF
NEVADA, JUNE 1, 1869 TO
JUNE 1, 1870 93
Federal Information Processing
Standards 9
Federal Information Standards Publi-
cation 25
Federal Land Series 220
Federal Mortality Census Schedules
82-101
FEDERAL MORTALITY CENSUS
SCHEDULES, 1860, 1870, 1880:
ABSTRACT AND INDEX,
KENTUCKY 89
FEDERAL POPULATION AND
MORTALITY CENSUS SCHED-
ULES, 1790-1890, IN THE
NATIONAL ARCHIVES AND
THE STATES 83
FEDERAL POPULATION CENSUS:
1820 MICHIGAN 167
FEDERAL POPULATION CENSUSES
1790-1890 7, 140
FEDERAL POPULATION SCHEDULES
ARKANSAS CENSUS 1840 150
Fee services 231
Feingold, Henry L. 258
Felldin, Jeanne Robey 187
Fellows, Jo-Ann 59

Fellows of the American Society of
Genealogists. See American
Society of Genealogists, Fellows
of
Ferris, Mary Walton 245
Field, Thomas Parry 35
Filby, P. William 5, 8, 11, 134,
138
heraldry 271
military records 220
state archive guides 101
statewide indexes 123
tax lists 225
Filipinos, immigration 258
FINDING AIDS TO THE MICRO-
FILMED MANUSCRIPT COLLEC-
TION OF THE GENEALOGICAL
SOCIETY OF UTAH 76-77
FINDING OUR FATHERS: A GUIDE-
BOOK TO JEWISH GENEAL-
OGY 59, 239
Finland 63, 103
Finnell, Arthur Louis 92
FINNISH GENEALOGICAL RESEARCH—
METHODS AND PROCEDURES
63
FIRST CENSUS OF KENTUCKY,
1790 161
FIRST FAMILIES OF UTAH, 1850
185
FIRST SYMPOSIUM ON GENEALOGI-
CAL AND HISTORICAL RE-
SEARCH TECHNIQUES, THE
SEATTLE GENEALOGICAL
SOCIETY, PROCEEDINGS 70
Fisher, Anne Benson 264
Fisher, Carleton Edward 53, 127
Fisher, Florence 235
Fisher, Richard Swainson 36
Fitzgerald, Daniel 35
Fitzpatrick, Lilian Linder 38
FIVE HUNDRED UTAH PLACE
NAMES 44
Flavell, Carol Willsey 56
Florida
bibliography 195
census schedule indexes 155-56
folklore 265
gazetteer 32
ghost towns 32

mortality census schedules 86
place name literature 32
postal history 32
FLORIDA 1830 CENSUS INDEX 155
FLORIDA 1840 CENSUS INDEX 155
FLORIDA 1850 CENSUS INDEX 155
Florida Federation of Stamp Clubs 32
FLORIDA GAZETTEER, THE 32
FLORIDA HISTORY: A BIBLIOG-
RAPHY 195
FLORIDA PLACE NAMES 32
Florida State University Library 86
FLORIDA U.S. CENSUS, 1840 155
Folkes, John Gregg 210
Folklore background 255, 265-68
FOLKLORE OF ROMANTIC
ARKANSAS 30
Footner, Hulbert 262
Forbes, Harriette Merrifield 81
Foreign census schedules 146-47
Foreign city histories. See City
histories, foreign
Foreign countries 47
Foreign county histories. See County
histories, foreign
Foreign family histories. See Family
histories, foreign
Foreign how-to-do-it books 60-71
Foreign-language correspondence.
See Correspondence, foreign
language
Foreign vital records 102
FORMATION OF THE NORTH
CAROLINA COUNTIES, 1663-
1943, THE 41
Forms 1, 21
Foster, Austin Powers 44
Fothergill, Augusta Bridgland 186
Fox, Michael J. 224
France
correspondence 103
family histories 105
how-to-do-it guides 63
Franklin, Helen H. 88-89
Franklin, W. Neil 82-83
FRASER, THE 262
Free services 229
French, Howard Barclay 245-46
French, John Homer 40
FRENCH BROAD, THE 262

FRENCH REFORMED CHURCH 66
Friesland, Netherlands 67
Fry, Ron 57
Fucilla, Joseph Guerin 238
Fullerton, Ralph O. 44
Funeral programs 21

G

Gallagher, John S. 37, 41, 45
Gambull, Georgia 109
Gandrud, Pauline Myra 148
Gannett, Henry 31, 34, 42, 44-46
Gard, Robert Edward 46
Gardner, David E. 63, 70, 77
Garrison, Jo Ann 233
GATHERING OF ZION, THE 260
GAZETTEER OF COLORADO, A 31
GAZETTEER OF DELAWARE, A 32
GAZETTEER OF GEORGIA, A 32
GAZETTEER OF ILLINOIS, A 33
GAZETTEER OF INDIAN TERRITORY,
A 42
GAZETTEER OF KANSAS, A 34
GAZETTEER OF NEW HAMPSHIRE,
A 39
GAZETTEER OF TEXAS, A 44
GAZETTEER OF THE STATE OF
MAINE 36
GAZETTEER OF THE STATE OF
MARYLAND 36
GAZETTEER OF THE STATE OF
MASSACHUSETTS, A 36
GAZETTEER OF THE STATE OF
MICHIGAN 37
GAZETTEER OF THE STATE OF
NEW JERSEY 39
GAZETTEER OF THE STATE OF
NEW YORK 40
GAZETTEER OF THE STATE OF
PENNSYLVANIA, A 43
GAZETTEER OF THE STATES OF
CONNECTICUT AND RHODE
ISLAND, A 31, 43
GAZETTEER OF THE TERRITORY OF
HAWAII, A 33
GAZETTEER OF UTAH, A 44-45
GAZETTEER OF VERMONT, A 45
GAZETTEER OF WEST VIRGINIA,
THE 46

GENEALOGICAL RESEARCH SOURCES
IN PORTUGAL 69
GENEALOGICAL RESEARCH SOURCES
IN THE FRENCH SPEAKING
PARTS OF BELGIUM 61
Genealogical Societies 12-13, 18
Genealogical Society 60-71, 219-20
gifts 250-51
See also Genealogical Department
Genealogical Society of Riverside
232
Genealogical Society of Weld
County, Colorado 151
GENEALOGICAL SOCIETY'S COMPU-
TER FILE INDEX, THE 123
GENEALOGIES AND FAMILY HIS-
TORIES ·113
GENEALOGIES AND FAMILY HIS-
TORIES: A CATALOG OF
OUT-OF-PRINT TITLES 9
GENEALOGIES IN THE LIBRARY OF
CONGRESS: A BIBLIOGRAPHY
9, 105-7, 116-17
Genealogists, professional. See Pro-
fessional genealogists
Genealogy 51
GENEALOGY IN AMERICA: MASSA-
CHUSETTS, CONNECTICUT,
AND MAINE 54
Genealogy, instruction 17
GENEALOGY: NEWSPAPER
COLUMNS 214
GENEALOGY OF THE BOOTH
FAMILY, THE 247
GENEALOGY OF THE DESCEN-
DANTS OF THOMAS FRENCH
245-46
GENEALOGY OF THE JAQUETT
FAMILY 249
GENEALOGY OF THE KIMBERLY
FAMILY, THE 247
GENEALOGY OF THE LAKE FAMILY,
A 243
GENEALOGY OF THE SMEDLEY
FAMILY 244
GENEALOGY RESEARCH SOURCES
IN TENNESSEE 56, 199
GENESEE, THE 262
Geographical names, subject headings
276

GEOGRAPHIC DICTIONARY OF
ALASKA 29
GEOGRAPHIC DICTIONARY OF
WASHINGTON, A 46
Geological Survey 80
Georgia
bibliography 195-96
boundaries 32
census schedule indexes 156-57
county history indexes 200
folklore 265
gazetteer 32
historical atlas 255-56
how-to-do-it book 52
mortality census schedules 86
place name literature 32
GEORGIA COUNTIES: THEIR
CHANGING BOUNDARIES 32
GEORGIA 1820 CENSUS INDEX 156
GEORGIA 1830 CENSUS INDEX 156
GEORGIA 1840 CENSUS INDEX 156
GEORGIA 1850 CENSUS INDEX 157
GEORGIA GENEALOGICAL BIBLIOG-
RAPHY 195
Georgia Historical Society 156
GEORGIA PLACE-NAMES 32
Gerberich, Albert Howell 246
GERMAN BOUNDARY AND LOCAL-
ITY NAME CHANGES 64
GERMAN-AMERICAN NEWSPAPERS
AND PERIODICALS, 1732-1955
212
GERMAN-AMERICANS, THE 258
Germans, immigration 258
Germany
correspondence 103
family histories 105
how-to-do-it guides 64
GHOSTS OF THE ADOBE WALLS 30
Ghost towns 29-47
subject headings 277
GHOST TOWNS AND LIVE ONES;
A CHRONOLOGY OF THE
POSTOFFICE DEPT. IN IDAHO,
1861-1973 33
GHOST TOWNS AND MINING
CAMPS OF CALIFORNIA 30
GHOST TOWNS AND MINING
CAMPS OF NEW MEXICO 40
GHOST TOWNS & SIDE ROADS OF
FLORIDA 32

Index

GHOST TOWNS OF ALASKA 29
GHOST TOWNS OF IDAHO 33
GHOST TOWNS OF KANSAS 35
GHOST TOWNS OF OKLAHOMA 42
GHOST TOWNS OF WASHINGTON
    AND OREGON 42, 46
GHOST TOWNS OF WYOMING 47
Gifts 12-13
GILA, RIVER OF THE SOUTHWEST, THE
    262
Gilbert, Harold Simeon 244
GILBERT FAMILY, THE 244
Gill, Helen Gertrude 35
Gill, James V. 158, 171
Gill, Maryan R. 158, 171
Gillis, Irene S. 92, 168-69
Gillis, Norman E. 168-69
Given names 237
Glazner, Capitola Hensley 84, 169
Gleason, Margaret 199
Glenn, Thomas Allen 109, 117
Godfrey Memorial Library 120
Goins, Charles R. 256
GOLDEN GATE COUNTRY 265-66
GOLDEN ROAD, THE 259
Goldfader, Edw. H. 234
Goldmann, Judy 95
"GONE TO TEXAS": SOURCES FOR
    GENEALOGICAL RESEARCH
    IN THE LONE STAR STATE
    56-57
Goodspeeds Bookshop 11, 114
Gordon, Thomas Francis 39, 43
Graham, Lloyd 267
GRANBERRY FAMILY, THE 247
Grand Canyon, folklore 266
Granger, Byrd H. 30
Grantee indexes 136
Grantor indexes 136
GRASSROOTS OF AMERICA 121
Gratz, Delbert 59
GRAVE HUMOR, A COLLECTION
    OF HUMOROUS EPITAPHS 81
GRAVESTONES OF EARLY NEW
    ENGLAND 81
Gray, James 262
Great Britain, family histories 105
GREAT IMMIGRANTS 257
GREAT NORTH TRAIL, THE 260
Great plains, folklore 266

GREAT RIVER: THE RIO GRANDE
    IN NORTH AMERICAN HISTORY
    264
GREAT WAGON ROAD, THE 260
Greene, Janet 82
GREENLAW INDEX OF THE NEW
    ENGLAND HISTORIC GENE-
    ALOGICAL SOCIETY, THE 127
Greenwood, Isaac John 246
Greenwood, Mary M. 246
Greenwood, Val D. 6, 50, 71
    abstracting 20, 131
    cemetery records 79
    census schedules 139
    church records 78
    court records 225
    divorce records 135
    land records 136
    military records 218, 220
    mortality census schedules 83
    probate records 131
    ship passenger lists 133
    vital records 74
GREENWOOD FAMILY, THE 246
Gregory, Winifred 208
Groningen, Netherlands 67
Grove, Pearce S. 210
Guatemala 64
Gubler, Greg 65
Gudde, Erwin Gustav 30
"Guidelines for Establishing Local
    History Collections" 19
GUIDE TO ALASKA'S NEWSPAPER,
    A 208
GUIDE TO AMERICAN DIRECTORIES
    253
GUIDE TO ANCESTRAL TRAILS IN
    MICHIGAN, A 167
GUIDE TO ARCHIVES AND MANU-
    SCRIPTS IN THE UNITED
    STATES, A 102, 110
GUIDE TO CHURCH RECORDS IN
    LOUISIANA, A 79
GUIDE TO COLORADO NEWSPAPERS,
    1859-1963 209
GUIDE TO FEDERAL ARCHIVES RE-
    LATING TO THE CIVIL WAR
    218
GUIDE TO GENEALOGICAL &
    HISTORICAL RESEARCH IN
    PENNSYLVANIA 230

Index

Index

Index

Index

Index

Index